The Justice Crisis

LAW AND SOCIETY SERIES
W. Wesley Pue, Founding Editor

We pay tribute to the late Wes Pue, under whose broad vision, extraordinary leadership, and unwavering commitment to socio-legal studies our Law and Society Series was established and rose to prominence.

The Law and Society Series explores law as a socially embedded phenomenon. It is premised on the understanding that the conventional division of law from society creates false dichotomies in thinking, scholarship, educational practice, and social life. Books in the series treat law and society as mutually constitutive and seek to bridge scholarship emerging from interdisciplinary engagement of law with disciplines such as politics, social theory, history, political economy, and gender studies.

Recent books in the series:

Amanda Nelund, *A Better Justice? Community Programs for Criminalized Women* (2020)

Jamie Baxter, *Inalienable Properties: The Political Economy of Indigenous Land Reform* (2020)

Jeremy Patrick, *Faith or Fraud: Fortune-Telling, Spirituality, and the Law* (2020)

Obiora Chinedu Okafor, *Refugee Law after 9/11: Sanctuary and Security in Canada and the United States* (2020)

Anna Jane Samis Lund, *Trustees at Work: Financial Pressures, Emotional Labour, and Canadian Bankruptcy Law* (2019)

Shauna Labman, *Crossing Law's Border: Canada's Refugee Resettlement Program* (2019)

Peter McCormick and Marc D. Zanoni, *By the Court: Anonymous Judgments at the Supreme Court of Canada* (2019)

Kate Puddister, *Seeking the Court's Advice: The Politics of the Canadian Reference Power* (2019)

Taryn Sirove, *Ruling Out Art: Media Art Meets Law in Ontario's Censor Wars* (2019)

Jennifer Tunnicliffe, *Resisting Rights: Canada and the International Bill of Rights, 1947–76* (2019)

Randy K. Lippert, *Condo Conquest: Urban Governance, Law, and Condoization in New York City and Toronto* (2019)

For a complete list of the titles in the series, see the UBC Press website, www.ubcpress.ca.

The Justice Crisis
The Cost and Value of Accessing Law

Edited by Trevor C.W. Farrow
and Lesley A. Jacobs

UBCPress · Vancouver · Toronto

29 28 27 26 25 24 23 22 21 20   5 4 3 2 1

Printed in Canada on FSC-certified ancient-forest-free paper
(100% post-consumer recycled) that is processed chlorine- and acid-free.

Library and Archives Canada Cataloguing in Publication

Title: The justice crisis : the cost and value of accessing law / edited by
    Trevor C.W. Farrow and Lesley A. Jacobs.
Names: Farrow, Trevor C. W., editor. | Jacobs, Lesley A., editor.
Series: Law and society series (Vancouver, B.C.)
Description: Series statement: Law & society | Includes bibliographical
    references and index.
Identifiers: Canadiana (print) 20200288083 | Canadiana (ebook) 20200288288 |
    ISBN 9780774863575 (hardcover) | ISBN 9780774863582 (softcover) |
    ISBN 9780774863599 (PDF) | ISBN 9780774863605 (EPUB) |
    ISBN 9780774863612 (Kindle)
Subjects: LCSH: Costs (Law) – Canada. | LCSH: Legal aid – Canada. |
    LCSH: Justice, Administration of – Canada.
Classification: LCC KE8517 .J87 2021 | LCC KF336 .J87 2020 kfmod |
    DDC 347/.71077—dc23

Canadä

UBC Press gratefully acknowledges the financial support for our publishing
program of the Government of Canada (through the Canada Book Fund), the
Canada Council for the Arts, and the British Columbia Arts Council.

Printed and bound in Canada by Friesens
Set in Helvetica Condensed and Minion by Artegraphica Design Co. Ltd.
Copy editor: Francis Chow
Proofreader: Kristy Hankewitz
Indexer: Margaret de Boer
Cover designer: Gerilee McBride
Cover image: Sydney Faith Photography/Creative Market

UBC Press
The University of British Columbia
2029 West Mall
Vancouver, BC V6T 1Z2
www.ubcpress.ca

To Mary, Morley, and Joseph –
  for your inspiration and support (TCWF)

To Brenda –
  for your support and confidence on this journey
  with me and so many others (LAJ)

Contents

Figures and Tables

Figures

Tables

Foreword
Giving Civil Justice Its Due

The Honourable Thomas A. Cromwell, CC

MY THESIS IS A simple one: we in the justice system – and also in society generally – undervalue civil justice both by what we do and by what we fail to do. This is not, I underline, an indictment for past offences. Indeed, as many contributors to this book have argued, many practical reforms have been made and many promising initiatives are under way. Rather, my objective is to suggest that we are not doing enough or doing it quickly enough, and as a result we are not giving civil justice its due.

Civil justice, in an admittedly quite narrow definition of the term, consists of a practical and fair outcome for civil legal problems. Access to civil justice means simply that people have access to the means – the resources, knowledge, skills, and institutions – needed for achieving those practical and fair outcomes. As Professors Trevor Farrow and Lesley Jacobs put it in their introduction to this book, meaningful access should be understood to include a long continuum of issues and options that begins with the identification of a justiciable problem. It should not focus just on the ultimate step of adjudication. Viewing the system as a continuum and committing to addressing needs earlier could have tremendous implications for reduced costs. And let us not forget that the system needs to be not only accessible but efficient and effective.

The value of civil justice, like the concept of value itself, is harder to define briefly, but it must include both qualitative and quantitative elements. The qualitative elements are concerned with the things that we generally do not value in monetary terms, even though, as Professor Michael Trebilcock notes in Chapter 1, efforts have been made to do so. The quantitative elements focus on the economic benefits of civil justice – in the sense of both value received and loss avoided.

On the qualitative side, we know that a strong civil justice system is an important part of the foundation of civil society. As Professor Gillian Hadfield has put it, a strong civil justice system is a platform on which we build everything else.[1] Without it, there can be no stability or certainty in transactions, no protection of intellectual property, and no peaceful resolution of disputes. As the British Columbia Chamber of Commerce noted in a 2014 resolution, "The ability to access the justice system to resolve issues in a timely and cost-effective manner is a foundation upon which our society is based."[2]

On the quantitative side, we know how uncertainty, cost, and delay in civil justice impose transaction costs on parties. And – thanks to, among others, the Cost of Justice project of the Canadian Forum on Civil Justice (CFCJ) – we are beginning to learn about the apparently enormous social costs we are incurring because we do *not* have a sufficiently effective civil justice system (many of which are documented in various chapters in this book). Perhaps a useful slogan might be, "If you think having an effective civil justice system is expensive, try not having one."

With those brief comments on the meaning of "civil justice" and "value," let me turn to five different ways in which we are undervaluing civil justice and provide some suggestions about how we can better value it.

1 *We undervalue civil justice by failing to keep our civil justice system in tune with contemporary legal needs.*

I suspect that many of us have an old trophy or two on our shelves – a souvenir of some significant past achievement. From time to time, the trophy becomes tarnished. And so we take it down from the shelf, give it a good polish, and put it back on the shelf, where it sits once again as a shining reminder of past glories. But whether newly polished or tarnished, it remains a reminder of a past achievement, not a witness to current realities.

Too often, I fear that we act as if the civil justice system were an old trophy. Our civil justice system, like a trophy, is the result of important achievements in the past. Society's capacity to resolve disputes by independent judges, the ability of parties to be represented by skilled and independent lawyers, and the institution of fair and predictable procedures are all important inheritances that we should celebrate and work hard to preserve.

Our civil justice system is not and cannot be static, however, and our reverence for the past must not blind us to current shortcomings. As the Action Committee on Access to Justice in Civil and Family Matters' *Roadmap for Change* put it in 2013:

> The civil and family justice system is too complex, too slow and too expensive. It is too often incapable of producing just outcomes that are proportional to the problems brought to it or reflective of the needs of the people it is meant to

serve. While there are many dedicated people trying hard to make it work and there have been many reform efforts, the system continues to lack coherent leadership, institutional structures that can design and implement change, and appropriate coordination to ensure consistent and cost-effective reform. Major change is needed.[3]

In other words, our civil justice system, for all of its virtues, has not kept pace with contemporary needs. And while giving it a good polish as though it were an old trophy may make it look better for a while, is not enough to get our system in tune with the needs of those it is meant to serve. Thus, while we do and ought to value the past achievements that put the pillars of a sound civil justice system in place, we undervalue civil justice by not recognizing how our current system falls far short of addressing the needs of those it is meant to serve.

The research from the CFCJ's Cost of Justice Project presented in several chapters in this book shows that the public does not necessarily agree that those of us working in the justice system are even very good at the things we think we are good at. For example, the system is not overwhelmingly perceived as even being fair.[4] And the gap between the technology that we have available in the system and the current state of technology in society is a further example of our system not keeping pace. The key point is that we value civil justice when we keep it responsive to current needs. We undervalue it when we simply rest on the achievements of the past.

2 *We undervalue civil justice by failing to act urgently to address the large and growing gap between our ideal of access to civil justice and the access that currently exists.*

We want to have a civil justice system that provides the necessary institutions, knowledge, resources, and services to avoid, manage, and resolve civil problems. As we all know, however, there is a large gap between that ideal and what we have. Of course, this gap has many elements, but one of the most important is the gap between peoples' need for legal services and their ability to obtain them. I wholeheartedly endorse Professor Trebilcock's main observation that we must address the cost structures of the system – particularly the cost of legal services.[5] This is not about forcing lawyers to charge less. It is about finding ways to encourage the delivery of legal services in ways that make sense economically for both lawyers and clients while protecting the public interest through high-quality and ethical legal services.

We are not doing nearly enough to close the legal services gap. Broadening accessibility to legal information, advice, and representation should be the number one priority for the legal profession in Canada. While legal aid and *pro bono* services are of course part of the solution, I agree completely with Professors Trebilcock[6] and Hadfield[7] that these are not and never will be complete solutions. It is not that nothing is being done: there are many promising signs of improvement. Nor is it that the legal profession is unique in not responding as vigorously as it should to the access to justice challenge. The same claim could be made about all sectors within the justice system. The point is simply that the profession as a whole needs to redouble its efforts to improve access to legal services, and to do so with a much greater sense of urgency than shown to date.

This is particularly true of the governing bodies of the profession. The problem of inadequate access to legal services is not fundamentally one of poverty, or insufficient commitment by lawyers to *pro bono* work, or even insufficient government funding. Professor Hadfield maintains that, at its root, the problem is one of regulation.[8] It follows that regulatory bodies must reconsider their regulatory work and the goals driving it. In particular, this transformation will require making access to legal services one of the key goals and priorities of regulation and a driver of regulatory change. The regulators may well need legislative change to pursue this agenda. But the expansion of legal services for the public should be a primary objective and a central outcome of legal services regulatory reform.

We need a lot more action on the relationship between regulatory activity and access to justice. Some governing bodies are reluctant to recognize the relationship between professional regulation and access to professional services. Others grasp this relationship but need to develop its implications with a much greater sense of urgency and priority. It is past time, however, for us to have started giving this issue the priority it deserves. I am not sure that my optimism has yet risen to the level of "cautious," but I am at least hopeful.

3 We undervalue civil justice by not having a coherent reform strategy.

The challenges of effecting change in the legal system have been noted in the international development literature concerning efforts to improve adherence to rule of law principles. Kirsti Samuels in her study of rule of law reform in post-conflict countries notes:

> Rule of law reform has suffered from a notable lack of strategy. Given the systemic nature of the changes that are sought to be brought about in rule of law reform

and the inherently interconnected nature of elements of a legal system, it is difficult to achieve sustainable change if the elements are not approached in a coherent fashion.[9]

The need for an overall strategy applies not only to the measures to be proposed but also to the ways by which the people who can implement them will be convinced to do so. The general point is that when we fail to think strategically, we undervalue civil justice.

The challenges of devising a coherent civil justice reform strategy are many in Canada. Let me mention three. The first is that the problems we face are intricate systemic problems. These problems cannot be tackled by measures that are narrowly conceived or that fail to take account of their overall – and often unintended – impact on other aspects of the system. Systems thinking does not come easily to most of us in the justice system, but that is what is needed. Second, leadership of the civil justice system is diffuse, which is a polite way of saying that no one is really in charge. Important elements of that system have a large measure of independence from the other elements: the judges are independent decision makers; the lawyers are independent advocates for their clients; and the government has unique responsibilities for the expenditure of public funds. Finally, the system itself is fragmented. As the Action Committee put it, "it is hard to say that there is a system – as opposed to many systems and parts of systems."[10]

There are some signs that a more strategic approach is being embraced. Following the recommendations of the Action Committee in its 2013 *Roadmap* report,[11] most jurisdictions have established broadly based access to justice groups. The hope is that these groups will permit a more cooperative and collaborative approach to civil justice reform and ensure that proposed solutions make sense in the overall scheme of things. I also hope that the nine Justice Development Goals set out by the Action Committee[12] will contribute to a more strategic approach to civil justice reform by serving as rallying points and unifying themes in civil justice reform from coast to coast to coast. The goals, I hope, provide some broad overall strategic direction and help all the actors see how their work – even work in very different areas – relates to the work of others.

4 We undervalue civil justice by failing to devote adequate resources to innovation in our civil justice system.

I am not persuaded that all of our problems in the civil justice system would be solved by an influx of funds. But I am persuaded that we are undervaluing civil justice by failing to fund it at appropriate levels and, in particular, to devote the resources and time to encourage innovation. We do not have the luxury of closing down our civil justice system while we build something better. All of our strategizing and innovation has to take place under the daily pressure of the ongoing work of the system. This makes bringing about change very challenging.

Although it is unrealistic to expect vast additions to justice system budgets, we should not give up on getting additional resources. Governments have a way of finding resources for the things that they think are important. At the very least, we need resources targeted at innovation – an investment that recognizes that fundamental change is not possible without additional resources to permit the sort of transformations that will end up making the system more efficient.

5 We undervalue civil justice by failing to engage the public with this issue.

The final point arises out of concern that the need for systemic change in our civil justice system is not an issue of great public concern. One of the fundamental questions we asked ourselves in the Action Committee was why we have such a large gap between ideas and action. We referred to this as the "implementation gap" – the gap between the many good ideas in volumes of reports about civil justice reform and our ability to implement them. We identified a number of factors that contribute to this gap and proposed some strategies to address them. I am increasingly persuaded, however, that an important factor contributing to this implementation gap is a lack of public interest and support.

Nearly everyone now accepts the need to involve non–justice system stakeholders in the process of civil justice reform. We recognize that we cannot put the public first unless we know what needs and expectations the public has, and without involving members of the public in the design and implementation of reforms. But while involving members of the public in designing and implementing reforms is one aspect of public engagement – and an important one – I am speaking here about a much broader form of public engagement. I am speaking of the need to have broad public support for fundamental, systemic reform of the civil justice system. If there is to be the political will to bring about these changes and the resources to make it possible to do so, civil justice reform needs to have a lot more public support than it currently does.

There has been some interesting academic work on how justice reformers might learn from the social science studies of social movements.[13] In particular, it has been argued that social science can help us understand why some pushes for reform succeed while others fail. And if there is any validity to this thesis, there is reason to think that at least some of the conditions for success are either present or within reach.

I would like to highlight three conditions. First, there is, I suggest, already an atmosphere ripe for change. And there is good reason to believe that we can make the case for change strongly and persuasively, although we need to do so to a much wider audience than we usually consider. Some of the research that Professors Farrow and Jacobs discuss in their introductory chapter suggests that this issue is important to a lot of people.

Second, social movements "are built on a foundation of organizers, movement organizations, and networks of communication."[14] There already exist broad and deep networks of people committed to civil justice reform. They are not sufficiently connected or ready or able to act in coordinated ways. But the potential for considerable mobilization is there from coast to coast to coast. Just think of the intersecting networks involved in the work of the Action Committee. By proxy, thousands of people committed to civil justice reform are engaged in this work. It is in reality a network of networks. We should not underestimate the potential of the many intersecting networks of people committed to reform. Social movement scholarship suggests that people need a means by which they can engage in collective action. While we are not generally providing those means now, there is great potential in the broad and wide networks of people committed to civil justice throughout Canada.

Third, it is important to frame the problems in a compelling way, which will help to develop a sense of collective identity among citizens from diverse communities who want change. As one writer put it, "[O]rganized action comes about when private grievances are redefined as a community's shared social problem."[15] While I suspect that we are not doing a good job of this, we have great potential to show how the "private grievances" of those who do not have adequate access to civil justice are in fact a community's shared problem. We can surely bring to light "tangible, ground-level instances of injustice," which will help transform those instances into "a collective call for systemic change."[16]

Conclusion

Let me conclude with this thought. We need more than a nudge on civil justice reform. We need a civil justice movement. And while I am not suggesting that we camp out in parks or picket, I am suggesting that we need to engage the public with both the need for and the possibility of fundamental civil justice reform. This book – a collection of chapters focused on the cost and value of access to justice – provides important research and thinking that will help to inform much-needed reform efforts. It also acts as a model for future collaborative and interdisciplinary access to justice research efforts.

Ultimately, we need leadership on this issue – and those of us working within the justice system and leading social movements are the ones who ought to be providing it. We undervalue civil justice if we don't.

Notes

1   Gillian Hadfield, *Rules for a Flat World: Why Humans Invented Law and How to Reinvent It for a Complex Global Economy* (New York: Oxford University Press, 2016).

2   BC Chamber of Commerce, "Providing Certainty for Business through the Timely Administration of Justice" (2014), online: <http://www.bcchamber.org/policies/providing -certainty-business-through-timely-administration-justice-2014>.

3   Action Committee on Access to Justice in Civil and Family Matters, *Access to Civil and Family Justice: A Roadmap for Change* (Ottawa: Action Committee on Access to Justice in Civil and Family Matters 2013) at 1, online: Canadian Forum on Civil Justice <http://www. cfcj- fcjc.org/sites/default/files/docs/2013/AC_Report_English_Final.pdf> [*Roadmap*].

4   For comments from the public regarding perceived systemic unfairness, see, e.g., Trevor C.W. Farrow, "What Is Access to Justice?" (2014) 51 Osgoode Hall LJ 957 at 972–74.

5   For further comments, see Chapter 1 of this book.

6   *Ibid.*

7   See further Hadfield, *supra* note 1.

8   Gillian Hadfield, "The Cost of Law: Promoting Access to Justice through the (Un)corporate Practice of Law" (2014) 38 Int'l Rev L & Econ 43 at 43.

9   Kirsti Samuels, "Rule of Law Reform in Post-Conflict Countries: Operational Initiatives and Lessons Learnt" (October 2006) World Bank Social Development Papers – Conflict Prevention and Reconstruction Paper No 37 at 16.

10   Action Committee on Access to Justice in Civil and Family Matters, *Roadmap, supra* note 3 at 7.

11   *Ibid* at 20–21.

12   *Ibid,* pt 3. See also Action Committee on Access to Justice in Civil and Family Matters, "Canada's Justice Development Goals," online: <http://www.justicedevelopmentgoals.ca/>.

13   See, e.g., Fran Quigley, "Growing Political Will from the Grassroots: How Social Movement Principles Can Reverse the Dismal Legacy of Rule of Law Interventions" (2009) 41 Colum HRL Rev 13.

14   *Ibid* at 52.

15   *Ibid* at 59, citing Donald C. Reitzes & Dietrich C. Reitzes, "Alinsky in the 1980s: Two Contemporary Chicago Community Organizations" (1986) 28 Sociological Quarterly 265.

16   *Ibid.*

Acknowledgments

IT TAKES A VILLAGE to produce any book, especially a diverse collection of essays by highly respected researchers from across Canada and the United States. We are grateful for the engaged participation by the entire author team throughout the writing and editing process.

In the preparation of this book, Lisa Moore (Canadian Forum on Civil Justice) provided significant strategic support in addition to her co-authored chapter. Rifa Lalani (Osgoode Hall Law School) tirelessly managed manuscript drafts.

The people at UBC Press – and in particular Randy Schmidt (Senior Editor), Ann Macklem (Production Editor), and their colleagues – have been excellent to work with on this book. We also benefited from constructive reports by two anonymous peer reviewers.

We are grateful for support from Osgoode Hall Law School, including its Research Intensification Fund, York University, the York Research Chair Program, and the Canadian Forum on Civil Justice.

Several chapters in this book first appeared as presentations at the Fall 2016 annual conference of the Canadian Institute for the Administration of Justice (CIAJ), "Civil Justice and Economics: A Matter of Value."

This book is a culminating project of the Canadian Forum on Civil Justice's seven-year Social Sciences and Humanities Research Council (SSHRC) Community-University Research Alliance (CURA) Cost of Justice project.

Abbreviations

ADR	alternative dispute resolution
AJA	*Access to Justice Act*
ATE	after-the-event
CBA	Canadian Bar Association
CFA	conditional-fee arrangements
CFCJ	Canadian Forum on Civil Justice
CLNP	Civil Legal Needs Project
COJP	Cost of Justice project
DBA	damages-based agreement
EJSRP	Evolving Justice Services Research Project
HiiL	Hague Institute for the Internationalization of Law
LAO	Legal Aid Ontario
LHC	Legal Health Check-up
LIZ	Legal Innovation Zone
LTB	Landlord and Tenant Board (Ontario)
MIP	Mandatory Information Program
MLP	medical-legal partnership
NSRLP	National Self-Represented Litigants Project
OECD	Organisation for Economic Co-operation and Development
PLEI	public legal education and information
SRL	self-represented litigant
TRC	Truth and Reconciliation Commission
TRP	temporary resident permit

The Justice Crisis

Introduction
Taking Meaningful Access to Justice in Canada Seriously

Trevor C.W. Farrow and Lesley A. Jacobs

ACCESS TO JUSTICE HAS long been recognized as among the most basic rights of democratic citizenship, but is also one of the least well understood in terms of its realization. This right is ordinarily framed in terms of individuals' ability to enforce their rights by going to court or accessing an alternative dispute resolution body, and to get a remedy where their rights are violated. Traditionally, the measure of access to justice was viewed principally as a matter of access to lawyers and adjudicated decisions in a timely and affordable manner. Since the early 1980s, there has been an increasingly expansive understanding of access to justice and an embrace in particular of the idea that access to civil and family justice is principally about having paths available for citizens to prevent, address, and resolve the legal challenges and problems they face in their everyday lives.

The general recognition of access to justice as a basic right of a citizenship is a reflection of the importance of law in modern democratic societies.[1] Law is everywhere in Canada, and everyone needs it. From consumer complaints, family breakdown, neighbour issues, and lost employment, most Canadians will experience a significant legal problem in the course of their lifetime.[2] Further, these problems can have major impacts – financial, physical, mental, and so-cial.[3] The justice system exists to address legal problems. Yet despite the pervasive nature, impact, and importance of legal problems, many Canadians are unable to navigate or afford the justice system.[4] Indeed, only a small percentage of those who experience everyday legal problems actually use the justice system.[5]

According to former Chief Justice of Canada Beverley McLachlin, there is a "lack of adequate access to justice in Canada."[6] Access to justice, in her view, "is the most important issue facing the legal system."[7] For many other current and former Canadian judges, the system is "sinking"[8] and in "crisis."[9] In 2008, in response to increasing and widespread civil and family justice challenges, McLachlin, under the leadership of the Honourable Justice Thomas Cromwell, convened the national Action Committee on Access to Justice in Civil and Family Matters, a collaborative organization made up of leading voices from all justice sectors across Canada. In its review of the justice system, the Action Committee concluded in 2013 that there is a "serious access to justice problem in Canada."[10] At the same time, former Supreme Court Justice Frank Iacobucci – in the report of his independent review of First Nations representation on juries in Ontario – stated that "the justice system generally as applied to First Nations peoples ... is quite frankly in a crisis."[11] The Canadian Bar Association (CBA), in its national justice review, claimed that the state of access to justice in Canada was "abysmal" and further, that inaccessible justice "costs us all."[12] In 2016, the Senate Standing Committee on Legal and Constitutional Affairs reached a similar conclusion regarding court delays affecting access to the criminal justice system.[13]

Canada is not alone in its difficulties in realizing access to justice as a basic right of citizenship. Similar claims are being made regularly around the world in developed and developing countries. For example, the justice system in the United Kingdom is in "crisis," according to the Bach Commission on Access to Justice.[14] Likewise, the American Bar Association (ABA) recognizes "the justice gap" and the need to "make meaningful access to justice a reality for all."[15] The Hague Institute for the Internationalization of Law (HiiL) has done a careful detailed inventory of access to justice challenges over the past decade in many developing countries, including Bangladesh, Kenya, Uganda, Lebanon, Tunisia, and Yemen.[16] Most recently, the Task Force on Justice found that "5.1 billion people – two-thirds of the world's population – lack meaningful access to justice."[17] With this shared international challenge, member states through the United Nations (UN) have agreed upon an obligation for all countries to improve access to justice as part of its Sustainable Development Goals.[18] In support of the UN's development initiative, the Organisation for Economic Co-operation and Development (OECD) has also committed to making the improvement of access to justice an important part of its development initiatives.[19] Each of these international initiatives involves important developments for access to justice. Taken together, they provide a stark recognition of the current global access to justice problem and a promising path for future reform.

Although the access to justice crisis is now well recognized among stakeholders in the Canadian justice system, a knowledge gap continues to exist regarding the degree of inadequacy in access to justice in Canada: the nature and level of unmet legal needs in Canada and elsewhere are neither well understood nor comprehensively researched. Compared with other areas of social services, such as medicine or education, we have comparatively little empirical data about justice issues, their social or financial impacts, or how to avoid or best deal with them.[20] Satisfactory answers based on comprehensive empirical data are available for few if any of these questions.[21] This is true in all areas of law, and it is particularly true in civil and family law, which are by far the most prevalent in daily life.[22] Unfortunately, these observations about a knowledge gap regarding access to justice are not new in Canada. For example, one of the main goals of the CBA's 1996 *Systems of Civil Justice Task Force Report* was to encourage collaboration and research-based policy reform within and across the civil justice system.[23] A decade later, the Canadian Forum on Civil Justice (CFCJ) released its *Civil Justice System and the Public* report, which was specifically designed to draw the public into civil and family justice reform efforts through collaborative, publicly engaged, and evidence-based policy-oriented research.[24]

A similar knowledge gap also exists in other countries. Rebecca Sandefur has observed, in an American context, that "[w]e have no idea of the actual volume of legal need and no idea of the actual volume of unmet legal need."[25] Further, Elizabeth Chambliss, Renee Knake, and Robert Nelson note:

> Ongoing, systematic research on civil legal needs and services is an essential component of improving the quality and availability of such services. Currently, however, we know little about the legal resource landscape – especially services for "ordinary Americans" – and our research infrastructure is underdeveloped compared to professions such as medicine.[26]

In a similar vein, the United Kingdom's Legal Education Foundation notes in its 2017 annual report:

> Research is vital to help us understand where legal need is greatest, and prioritise resources ... historically, the legal services and legal education sectors have placed little emphasis on the importance of evidence-led approaches to the design and delivery of services. Court and other data which is vital for methodological research is not collected or made available.[27]

The Australian government's Productivity Commission in its 2014 report, *Access to Justice Arrangements*, also reached this conclusion, noting the absence of empirical research while emphasizing that such research is essential to improving access to justice in Australia.[28] Fortunately, in all of these countries, including Canada, there have been significant strides in the past five years to narrow this knowledge gap through new data collection and analysis. The chapters in this book represent some of the most recent and exciting examples of such research.

The broad purpose of this book is to report on some of the innovative empirical research on access to civil and family justice undertaken in Canada over the past five years. Most contributors are members of the Cost of Justice research project, a major access to civil and family justice collaborative research initiative housed at the Canadian Forum on Civil Justice.[29] This project, funded by the Social Sciences and Humanities Research Council of Canada for seven years beginning in 2011, brought together leading researchers and policy makers from Canada and around the world to examine various aspects of the current access to justice crisis in civil and family law, focusing in particular on cost and affordability.[30] The project has focused primarily on undertaking empirical research to address two main research questions: (1) what does it cost to deliver an effective civil justice system? and (2) what does it cost – economically and socially – if we fail to do so?[31] Chief Justice McLachlin has commented: "This research ... will be essential in helping us understand the true extent of the problem of cost and how it impacts on the justice system. I believe that it will prove to be of great assistance to ... identify[ing] concrete solutions to the problem of access to justice."[32] Although much of the research reported here has a Canadian focus, the findings are significant for other countries, including Australia, the United Kingdom, and the United States, which are struggling to advance meaningful access to civil and family justice.

What Is Meaningful Access to Justice?

What precisely is access to justice? Scholarship has gone through numerous waves of conceptualizing access to justice and thinking about access to civil and family justice within a broader societal context than just the formal justice system and service provision by lawyers.[33] This is reflected, for example, in greater interest during the 1990s in alternative dispute resolution mechanisms such as mediation, negotiation, and arbitration; by procedural rule reform in the 2000s; and more recently by the trend towards the professionalization of paralegals and the organization of trusted legal intermediaries. Parallel to these developments have been shifting views about the ailments and crises within the civil justice system. At one time, issues of delay in Canadian courts were seen as the principal barrier to access to justice.[34] Today, it is reasonable to say that the preoccupation is often with self-represented litigants, the costs for individuals and the public of civil justice, and social inclusion. These current preoccupations have resulted in significant re-engagement with access to justice as a site for innovative empirical research and policy development, especially by socio-legal scholars in Canada and elsewhere.[35]

Here we contrast two approaches to framing access to civil justice. The more familiar approach focuses on timely access to formal legal institutions such as the courts in order to secure redress for some wrongs.[36] An alternative approach, which we call meaningful access to justice, is centred instead on the idea that access to civil justice is principally concerned with people's ability to access a diverse range of information, institutions, and organizations – not just formal legal institutions such as the courts – in order to understand, prevent, meet, and resolve their legal challenges and legal problems when those problems concern civil or family justice issues. Meaningful access to justice measures access for a person not necessarily in terms of access to lawyers and adjudicated decisions but rather by how helpful the path is for addressing and resolving that person's legal problem or complaint.

In contrast, the measure of access to justice in the first approach is understood principally in terms of access to lawyers and adjudicated decisions. In the United States, this was exemplified by the *Gideon v Wainwright* case, decided by the United States Supreme Court in 1963.[37] In this case, the unanimous opinion of the Supreme Court was that defendants facing criminal charges have a constitutional right to be provided with a lawyer by the state if they are unable to afford one.[38] Indeed, arguably, even today in the United States, the idea that access to justice means access to a lawyer is the prevailing view among many legal professionals, as is evident from the resurgence of interest in establishing, for example, a right to civil counsel among the so-called Civil Gideon Movement.[39] In Canada, this approach is reflected in the fact that state funding for lawyers secured initially in the 1960s for programs like Legal Aid Ontario remain the highest-profile commitment by governments to supporting access to justice. Research based on this first approach to access to justice typically focuses narrowly on what happens in the courts and, to some extent, with lawyer representation.

Although the legal profession and the judiciary traditionally subscribed to the first approach, in recent years there has been widespread embrace of the second approach. Meaningful access to justice is now a term used by both the ABA and the CBA. The ABA explains its view of access to justice as follows:

Our expansive view of access to justice includes not only one's ability to access the courts and legal representation, but also one's ability to engage effectively with law enforcement officials and to make use of informal, non-state justice mechanisms. Civil society can provide important support for individuals and communities and offer an effective counterbalance to the powers of the state and of the private sector.[40]

The CBA has embraced a similar view:

> We live in a society regulated by law. Everyone's lives are shaped by the law and everyone is likely to experience a legal problem at some point. This is not to say that everyone will engage with the formal justice system: many problems can and should be resolved in more informal ways. Still, we should know for certain that we – and those we care about – will have meaningful access to justice if and when we need it.[41]

The embrace of meaningful access to justice by these organizations constitutes an important milestone in public policy development and research on access to justice.[42]

The fundamental and distinctive feature of meaningful access to civil and family justice is that affordable and timely paths to justice are available to individuals and are well calibrated to their particular needs and situation. Much of the most important recent empirical research on access to justice, including the studies included in this book, have been undertaken through the lens of meaningful access to justice. This alternative research framework for access to justice has important pillars for framing, on the one hand, how to understand and measure access to justice and, on the other hand, how to advance access to justice.[43]

Four pillars are especially important for understanding and measuring meaningful access to justice. The first is that it is problem-focused in the sense that access to justice should be oriented towards addressing legal problems that arise in people's everyday lives, as opposed to, for example, the familiar resource-centred idea that access to justice is principally about affordable access to courts and lawyers.[44] At its core, meaningful access to justice is about assisting people with their legal problems and difficulties. We elaborate more on the nature of legal problems in the everyday lives of Canadians below.

The second pillar is that it is person-centred, as opposed to service provider- or system-centred.[45] The point is that legal services that promote meaningful access to justice are designed to serve the person in need, not the service provider or the legal profession.[46] The third pillar is that how these actors understand and make sense of legal rights – their legal consciousness – is of fundamental importance to their legal mobilization.[47] The important idea underlying this pillar is that legal consciousness affects when and whether people recognize their problems as legal and the decisions they make about how to address those problems. The fourth pillar is an acknowledgment that the barriers to meaningful access to justice are often systemic injustices – discrimination that is made visible by patterns of behaviour, policies, and practices that are part of the administrative structure or informal "culture" of an organization, institution, or sector that purposely or inadvertently create or perpetuate disadvantage and social exclusion based on grounds such as race, gender, immigration status, or disability.[48]

Three other complementary pillars are especially important for advancing meaningful access to justice. One is that few everyday legal problems are resolved within the formal court-based domestic justice system.[49] The point is that often the most important legal services that advance meaningful access to justice are community-based ones that operate within civil society. Another complementary pillar is that the emphasis should be on trying to get upstream on everyday legal problems (consumer, debt, employment, family) and in effect be proactive and take preventative measures. This is already a prevalent policy strategy in consumer protection and employment standards.[50] A further pillar is that within a problem-centred approach to access to justice, what matters for fair outcomes and fair processes are the paths to justice or legal journeys people take, and not so much (or only) the robustness of the legal services available to them. This pillar readily relates to important empirical work by Tom Tyler and others on fairness in the justice system.[51] As the HiiL has long emphasized, innovating in civil and family justice is at its core about "developing new ways to bring fairness between people."[52] There are different ways in which access to justice might be meaningfully tied to the impact or outcome of someone's legal problem. It might help someone resolve or address the problem, provide possibilities for compensation, or potentially have an impact in terms of legislative, policy, or social change.[53]

The Everyday Legal Problems of Canadians

At the core of meaningful access to justice is the idea that people have everyday legal problems and that it is important for legal services to assist them in resolving those problems. This claim is a reflection of the fact that in modern democratic societies, the legal system plays a fundamental role in the ordering of many aspects of daily life.[54] Everyday legal problems are those that come up in people's daily lives. They are problems that typically have both a legal element and potentially a legal solution. Consumer complaints, family breakdown, domestic violence, divorce, credit issues, discrimination, wrongful termination, unfair eviction, and neighbour disputes are some of the most frequent such problems (see Figure o.1).[55] Everyday legal problems are "justiciable" in that they can be dealt with through formal legal processes, although they may in fact be dealt with – or not – through other means. In her seminal research on everyday legal problems in England and Wales, Hazel Genn describes a justiciable problem as "a matter experienced by a respondent which raised legal

Figure 0.1 **Percentage of people with one or more everyday legal problems**

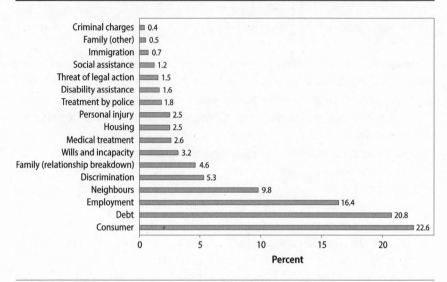

issues, whether or not it was recognized by the respondent as being 'legal' and whether or not any action taken by the respondent to deal with the event involved the use of any part of the civil justice system."[56] The central finding that Genn establishes is that almost everyone takes paths to address their justiciable problems – paths to justice – but often those paths do not involve the formal justice system. Meaningful access to justice in Canada requires taking seriously how the existence of many diverse paths to justice can assist Canadians to resolve (or prevent) their everyday legal problems and how those paths can be supported through innovative public policy.

Legal need studies are designed to help with that understanding. The World Justice Project has recently stated:

> The law provides a foundational framework of rights, responsibilities, and protections that impact virtually every aspect of modern life. This legal framework shapes how ordinary people navigate problems related to employment, housing, education, health, and family life, among many others. In addition to having a legal dimension, these everyday problems profoundly impact people's health, social stability, and ability to participate in the economy. For this reason, better understanding people's legal needs and experiences accessing justice provides vital insights for designing policies that foster economic development and inclusive growth.[57]

How do we better understand people's legal needs in a particular country? The prevalent research instrument are legal needs or legal problems general population surveys. These surveys enable researchers to construct a picture of the legal needs of citizens and the extent to which the justice system and other institutions are meeting those needs. Over the past twenty-five years, discrete comprehensive legal needs surveys have been undertaken in many different countries, including Canada, the United Kingdom, the Netherlands, and the United States.[58] In 2017, the World Justice Project completed a legal needs survey in forty-five countries.[59]

The 2016 national study of everyday legal problems – the Everyday Legal Problems and the Cost of Justice in Canada study – provides the most comprehensive, up-to-date picture of Canadians' legal needs and their experiences with legal problems.[60] The survey focused on the prevalence of everyday legal problems, the occurrence of multiple problems and problem clusters, what people do about legal problems, the extent to which people get the help they need and what happens when they do not, and the costs individuals incurred trying to get help. The findings were based on telephone interviews with 3,051 Canadians.[61]

In terms of the basics about everyday legal problems, we know that almost half of adult Canadians – 48.4 percent, or almost 12 million – will experience at least one legal problem over any given three-year period, amounting to essentially all of us over the course of our lifetime. Of the people surveyed for the study, 30 percent reported experiencing two or more legal problems, which – again over a three-year period – comes to over 35 million separate everyday legal problems. Put simply, these are huge numbers, showing that legal problems are pervasive in the everyday lives of Canadians.

The most common types of legal problems experienced by adult Canadians involve consumer, debt, and employment issues, followed by problems related to neighbours, discrimination, and family (relationship) issues. Other frequent problems reported include issues involving wills, medical treatment, housing, personal injury, disability, and social assistance. Criminal charges affect very few Canadians (see Figure 0.1). The range and frequency of everyday legal problems highlight why meaningful access to justice is important for and affects all Canadians.

How do adult Canadians deal with those problems? Approximately 95 percent report making some attempt to resolve their issue. However, we know from other research that approximately 65 percent of Canadians with legal problems are not certain about their rights, do not know how to manage legal problems, are afraid to access the legal system, or think nothing can be done.[62] Moreover,

Table 0.1 **Paths to justice for Canadians**

Path	Percentage of Canadians
Courts and tribunals	7
Legal advice (private lawyers, legal aid, clinics, etc.)	19
Non-legal assistance (union, advocacy group, etc.)	28
Internet	33
Other party (negotiation, etc.)	75
Friends and relatives	61

the survey found that less than 7 percent of people report going to courts and tribunals, and less than 20 percent report seeking legal advice. This finding is consistent with other research showing that a growing number of individuals attending court are representing themselves, with limited or no legal assistance. For example, Justice Annemarie Bonkalo in her 2016 review of Family Legal Services for Ontario's Ministry of the Attorney General reported that 57 percent of litigants in family court were unrepresented in 2014–15.[63] The vast majority of "paths to justice" for Canadians are outside the formal justice system, including non-legal assistance, the Internet, friends and family, and informal negotiations with the other disputing party (Table 0.1).

The Everyday Legal Problems and the Cost of Justice in Canada survey found that a relatively high percentage of people – 81 percent – who obtain legal advice find it to be helpful. Among those who do not or cannot access legal services, fewer find their service options as helpful: 68 percent of those who use both non-legal assistance and friends and relatives, 58 percent of those who use the Internet, and 49 percent of those who attempt to deal with the other party in a dispute.[64] We know that many cases that do enter the formal justice system end up being settled (or abandoned) before a final determination by a court.[65] Other studies have found that at least 90 percent of civil cases settle.[66]

What do we know about the 5 percent who do nothing about their legal problems? A recent independent study by Trevor Farrow found that cost, time, effort, and stress are among the factors identified as to why nothing is done. Participants in that study reported:

I have a family law situation that I can't afford to address. I have to just let it go.

I paid down on an apartment ... I didn't get it ... so I wanted my money back. I couldn't get my money back because the guy ... didn't give me back my cash and I didn't know how to go about it, I was new to the country ... I just checked at the tenant board ...

But it just looked like it was gonna be a lot stressful for me just to take that upon myself to try to figure that out. So, I was just like, whatever, leave that.

As far as I know, it's going to cost you ... So ... when I have issues, I just leave it.

I work three jobs. Am I gonna take off ... my full day to go pursue this? Probably not, so I'm just gonna let this slide.

Most people ... if it's not criminal ... won't pursue it. Like if it's a racial thing ... employ[ment] ... discrimination, I don't think they would pursue it.[67]

These statements reinforce concerns about meaningful access to justice for all Canadians.

Although almost everyone attempts to deal with their everyday legal problems, many problems go unresolved. The Everyday Legal Problems and the Cost of Justice in Canada study found that just over half – 55 percent – of adult Canadians report resolving their legal problems during a three-year period, leaving 30 percent with unresolved problems and 15 percent with mixed results (one problem resolved and others ongoing). As for the outcome of resolved problems, almost half – 46 percent – of people indicated that the outcome for one (or more) of their problems was unfair; further, 70 percent indicated that the outcome that they did obtain did not achieve all of what they had originally anticipated.

In a detailed analysis of the paths to justice for Canadians reporting consumer problems in the Everyday Legal Problems study, Lesley Jacobs and Matthew McManus discovered that people with consumer problems reported resolving their problems in 69 percent of the cases.[68] This compares with just less than 50 percent for all other reported problems combined. (When consumer problems are included in the entire dataset, 54 percent reported that their problem had been resolved.) This means that 20 percent more consumer problems were resolved than other everyday legal problems, which is a very significant difference. Canada's network of consumer protection mechanisms are designed to steer Canadians with consumer problems away from lawyers and adjudicated decisions and towards consumer organizations, consumer complaint processes, and other "softer" paths to justice. A reasonable inference, drawn by Jacobs and McManus, is that the consumer protection paths to justice available to Canadians are proving to be effective when Canadians experience consumer problems.

In terms of what individual adult Canadians spend on justice issues (excluding corporate, government, or other organizational or institutional expenditures), the study shows that, of those who experienced legal problems and who provided information on cost aspects of those problems, 43 percent indicated that they spent some money attempting to resolve their problems. Specifically, on average, adult Canadians spend approximately $6,100 when dealing with their problems. Collectively, this amounts to approximately $7.7 billion annually, which, if anything, is a conservative estimate.[69] Compared with what adult Canadians spend on average on other aspects of their life (based on annual spending figures for 2012), this amounts to almost 10 percent of annual spending on household expenditures ($75,443); over 10 percent of spending on goods and services ($56,279); almost half of spending on food ($7,739); almost three times the spending on out-of-pocket healthcare expenses ($2,285); and almost half of spending on shelter ($15,811). As for the types of individual expenses, 22 percent of those who spend money on legal problems report spending money on legal fees;[70] 16 percent on transportation; 13 percent on materials, copying, and printing; 11 percent on court fees; 10 percent on other advisers and mediators; 5 percent on telephone, fax, and so on; and 5 percent on child care and other related household expenses.

There are of course other costs associated with legal problems. For example, in addition to the specific financial costs discussed above (legal fees, court fees, transportation costs, and so on), people experiencing a legal problem often spend a lot of time trying to understand the problem, identifying potential solutions, and sorting out the rules and processes for various legal options. These costs, often referred to as "searching" or "temporal" costs, typically come in the form of hours and days of time spent and, as a result, lost opportunities.[71] Other important costs come in the form of lost employment, stress, physical and emotional costs,[72] costs related to gender-based violence,[73] cultural costs,[74] productivity costs, and potentially others.

While the impact of these costs on individuals is clearly enormous, the implications for public funds is also significant. In addition to paying for the infrastructure of the legal system (judges, courts, justice departments, and so on),[75] inadequate access to justice results in knock-on costs to other social services in society.[76] For example, the survey found that other annual costs to the state include approximately $248 million in additional social assistance payments, $450 million in additional employment insurance payments, and $101 million in additional healthcare costs. Besides these specific knock-on costs, the findings show that experiencing legal problems can lead to housing issues: 2.7 percent of adult Canadians (100,839) lose their housing each year as a direct result of experiencing a legal problem. Faced with homelessness, approximately 3.6 percent of those people (6,836) rely in turn on emergency shelters, many of them publicly funded. Thus, to the very real costs for individuals associated with losing their home or shelter must be added the resulting knock-on costs carried by the state.[77]

Each of these costs – economic and social, individual and collective – is significant. Taken together, they are cause for significant concern. To date, these costs and other related justice system costs and value-related considerations have been significantly understudied in the world-wide access to justice literature.[78] This lack of focus and understanding has created a major gap in the context of evidence-based policy thinking and reform. It is this gap that the contributions to this book explore.

Situating the Research Contributions in This Book

The chapters that follow, divided into four parts, are all focused on understanding why achieving timely and affordable meaningful access to civil and family justice is so challenging in Canada and elsewhere. Part 1, "Understanding the Access to Justice Crisis," situates Canadian public funding for the justice system within the broader public policy context. In Chapter 1, Michael Trebilcock stresses the importance and value of the rule of law and corresponding justice system institutions (courts, tribunals, legal aid, judges, lawyers, and public legal information), arguing that given fiscal constraints, cost and price choices need to be made regarding legal processes and services. In Chapter 2, Moktar Lamari, Pierre Noreau, and Marylène Leduc provide a detailed overview of the metrics of the publicly funded justice system in OECD countries, enabling a comparison of Canada's spending with those of other jurisdictions. In Chapter 3, Lisa Moore and Mitchell Perlmutter focus on the options for public spending on the justice system and the implications for access to civil and family justice.

Part 2, "Experiencing Everyday Legal Problems," shifts the focus to the lived experiences of Canadians. In Chapter 4, Ab Currie provides a careful review of the costs of inadequate access to justice and unresolved legal problems for ordinary Canadians. In Chapter 5, Matthew Dylag examines survey data to determine the paths to justice taken by people in Ontario with everyday legal problems, and in Chapter 6, Trevor Farrow examines the problematic legal experience and related costs for First Nations communities in the course of pursuing the resolution of residential schools claims and implications for truth and reconciliation. In Chapter 7, Jennifer Koshan, Janet Mosher, and Wanda Wiegers focus on costs for women in domestic violence cases.

Part 3, "Legal Services and Paths to Justice," examines specific developments and innovations in the justice system from the perspective of advancing access to justice. In Chapter 8, David Wiseman argues that the licensing of paralegals by the Law Society of Ontario has been effective at improving access to justice for landlords but has done little for tenants, who generally are unable to afford any fee-based legal assistance. In Chapter 9, Lesley Jacobs and Carolyn Carter focus on the Mandatory Information Program for applicants and respondents in the family courts in Ontario. They argue that, despite its promise, the program has significant shortcomings that need to be addressed before it can contribute to meaningful access to family justice. More optimistically, Catherine Piché shows in Chapter 10 that class actions in Quebec are proving to be quite effective in achieving significant outcomes for plaintiffs in most cases. Lorne Sossin and Devon Kapoor argue in Chapter 11 that, based on some preliminary case studies, social enterprise and social innovation are able to fill an important gap in the justice system with regard to paths to justice for some communities.

Part 4, "The Legal Profession and Meaningful Access to Justice," considers the role of the legal profession as both an impediment and a vehicle for change on the issue of meaningful access to justice in Canada. In Chapter 12, Jerry McHale – further to some of the themes raised in the Foreword by Justice Thomas Cromwell – provides a narrative about the legal profession in Canada and its role as an impediment to improving access to justice. Herbert Kritzer argues in Chapter 13 that although legal fees are a key cost consideration in access to justice debates, it is in practice, drawing on recent experiences in the United Kingdom, very difficult to reform the structure of a country's legal fees to make civil legal services more affordable. In Chapter 14, Michaela Keet and Heather Heavin draw on insights from behavioural economics to better understand recommendations lawyers make to their clients about paths to justice, especially regarding litigation. Chapter 15, by Noel Semple, concludes with a discussion of legal fees and their contribution to the existence of unmet legal needs in Canada.

Conclusion

Understanding access to justice has become a priority for justice researchers, policy makers, and practitioners in Canada and elsewhere. Everyday legal research studies have helped frame the access to justice crisis and further our collective understanding about how ordinary people around the world manage and address their everyday legal problems in similar ways. Groundbreaking national policy efforts – such as the Action Committee's *Roadmap for Change* report[79] and the CBA's *Reaching Equal Justice* report[80] – have moved the dial significantly in terms of awareness in Canada, especially within the legal profession. Notwithstanding these important strides, however, we continue to lack an adequately informed understanding of the access to justice crisis in Canada, lessons to be learned from the global access to justice crisis, practical ways to address this crisis, and the costs and benefits of different solutions. In essence, we have reached the limits of the current access to justice "1.0" moment and now need to move our thinking forward in terms of specific elements of and solutions to the access to justice crisis, in order to animate evidence-based reform initiatives in various parts of the justice system (e.g., housing, gender violence, justice for Indigenous communities, legal aid services, litigation analysis, social innovation, family justice, public spending, etc.). Put simply, we are entering an access to justice "2.0" moment, which requires building on – and contributing to – current international access to justice initiatives.[81]

We hope that this book provides readers with an entry point to the emerging access to justice 2.0 moment. The organization of the chapters into four themes promises new insights on the crisis, develops fresh empirical data and evidence about how people understand and experience justice (particularly in specific contexts), and points to evidence-based ideas for policy-based reform about how best to achieve meaningful access to justice, not only in Canada but also around the world.

Notes

1 T.H. Marshall, *Citizenship and Social Class and Other Essays* (Cambridge: Cambridge University Press, 1950).
2 Trevor C.W. Farrow et al, *Everyday Legal Problems and the Cost of Justice in Canada: Overview Report* (Toronto: Canadian Forum on Civil Justice, 2016), online: Canadian Forum on Civil Justice <http://www.cfcj-fcjc.org/sites/default/files//Everyday%20Legal%20Problems%20and%20the%20Cost%20of%20Justice%20in%20Canada%20-%20Overview%20Report.pdf> [*Everyday Legal Problems*]. See also Figure 0.1.
3 *Ibid.*
4 *Ibid* at 3; Trevor C.W. Farrow, "What Is Access to Justice?" (2014) 51:3 Osgoode Hall LJ 957 at 974 ["What Is Access to Justice?"].
5 Farrow et al, *Everyday Legal Problems, supra* note 2 at 9.
6 Rt. Hon. Beverley McLachlin, PC, "Foreword" in Michael Trebilcock, Anthony Duggan, & Lorne Sossin, eds, *Middle Income Access to Justice* (Toronto: University of Toronto Press, 2012) at ix.
7 Rt. Hon. Beverley McLachlin, PC, "The Challenges We Face," citing the former Chief Justice of Ontario (Remarks presented at Empire Club of Canada, Toronto, 8 March 2007), online: Supreme Court of Canada <https://www.scc-csc.ca/judges-juges/spe-dis/bm-2007-03-08-eng.aspx>.
8 See *York University v Markicevic,* 2013 ONSC 4311 at 8, 229 ACWS (3d) 888.
9 Hon. R. Roy McMurtry, "Remarks" (Address delivered at the Civil Justice Reform Conference, 7 December 2006) at 3–4, online: Canadian Forum on Civil Justice <http://cfcj-fcjc.org/docs/2006/mcmurtry-en.pdf>.
10 Action Committee on Access to Justice in Civil and Family Matters, *Access to Civil and Family Justice: A Roadmap for Change* (Ottawa: Action Committee on Access to Justice in Civil and Family Matters, October 2013) at 1, online: Canadian Forum on Civil Justice <http://www.cfcj-fcjc.org/sites/default/files/docs/2013/AC_Report_English_Final.pdf>.

11 Hon. Frank Iacobucci, *First Nations Representation on Ontario Juries: Report of the Independent Review* (February 2013) at para 4, online: Government of Ontario <http://www.attorneygeneral.jus.gov.on.ca/english/about/pubs/iacobucci/pdf/First_Nations_Representation_Ontario_Juries.pdf>. See also Chapter 6.

12 Canadian Bar Association Access to Justice Committee, *Reaching Equal Justice: An Invitation to Envision and Act* (Ottawa: Canadian Bar Association, 2013) at 6, online: Canadian Bar Association <http://www.cba.org/CBA-Equal-Justice/Equal-Justice-Initiative/Reports>.

13 Senate, Standing Committee on Legal and Constitutional Affairs, *Delaying Justice Is Denying Justice: An Urgent Need to Address Lengthy Court Delays in Canada* (Ottawa: Senate of Canada, August 2016).

14 See Bach Commission on Access to Justice, *The Crisis in the Justice System in England and Wales*, Interim Report (Fabian Society, November 2016), online: Fabian Society <http://www.fabians.org.uk/wp-content/uploads/2016/11/Access-to-Justice_final_web.pdf>.

15 William C. Hubbard & Juldy Perry Martinez, "Introduction: What We Know and Need to Know about the State of 'Access to Justice' Research" (Winter 2016) 67:2 SCL Rev 191 at 191–92.

16 See the various HiiL country reports, online: HiiL <http://www.hiil.org/publications/data-reports>.

17 Task Force on Justice, *Justice for All* (New York: Pathfinders for Peaceful, Just and Inclusive Societies, April 2019) at 12, online: <https://www.justice.sdg16.plus/report>.

18 United Nations, Sustainable Development Goals, "Transforming Our World: The 2030 Agenda for Sustainable Development," Goal 16: Peace, Justice and Strong Institutions ("Promote peaceful and inclusive societies for sustainable development, provide access to justice for all and build effective, accountable and inclusive institutions at all levels"), online: UN <https://sustainabledevelopment.un.org/?menu=1300>.

19 See, e.g., OECD, *Leveraging the SDGs for Inclusive Growth: Delivering Access to Justice for All* (Paris: OECD, 2016) as well as "Why Does Access to Justice Matter?" online: OECD <http://www.oecd.org/gov/access-to-justice.htm>.

20 See, e.g., Canadian Bar Association Access to Justice Committee, *supra* note 12 at 34.

21 For current discussions about justice data, see Chapters 2 and 5.

22 To the extent that significant justice data do exist, they more typically focus on criminal law. See, e.g., Benjamin Perrin and Richard Audas, *Report Card on the Criminal Justice System: Evaluating Canada's Justice Deficit* (Ottawa: Macdonald-Laurier Institute, September 2016), online: Macdonald-Laurier Institute <http://www.macdonaldlaurier.ca/files/pdf/JusticeReportCard_F4.pdf>. See more generally Statistics Canada, "Crime and Justice," online: Government of Canada <https://www.statcan.gc.ca/eng/subjects/crime_and_justice>.

23 Task Force on Systems of Civil Justice, *Systems of Civil Justice Task Force Report* (Ottawa: Canadian Bar Association, August 1996).

24 Barbara Billingsley, Diana Lowe, & Mary Stratton, *Civil Justice Systems and the Public: Learning from Experiences to Find Practices That Work* (Edmonton: Canadian Forum on Civil Justice, 2006), online: Canadian Forum on Civil Justice <http://www.cfcj-fcjc.org/sites/default/files/docs/2006/cjsp-learning-en.pdf>. See also other related initiatives discussed in the same report, at 25–29.

25 Rebecca L. Sandefur, "What We Know and Need to Know about the Legal Needs of the Public" (2016) 67 SCL Rev 443 at 453.

26 Elizabeth Chambliss, Renee Knake, & Robert Nelson, "Introduction: What We Know and Need to Know about the State of 'Access to Justice' Research" (2016) 67:2 SCL Rev 193 at 193.

27 Legal Education Foundation (UK), *Annual Review 2017* (London: Legal Education Foundation, 2017) at 34, online: <https://www.thelegaleducationfoundation.org/wp-content/uploads/2017/12/TLEF_AR17.pdf>.
28 Australian Government Productivity Commission, *Access to Justice Arrangements,* Inquiry Report No. 72 (Canberra: 5 September 2014), online: <https://www.pc.gov.au/inquiries/completed/access-justice/report/access-justice-volume1.pdf>.
29 See Canadian Forum on Civil Justice, "Cost of Justice," online: Canadian Forum on Civil Justice <http://www.cfcj-fcjc.org/cost-of-justice>.
30 *Ibid.*
31 See Trevor Farrow, Lesley Jacobs, & Diana Lowe, *The Cost of Justice: Weighing the Costs of Fair and Effective Resolution to Legal Problems* (Toronto: Canadian Forum on Civil Justice, 2012), online: Canadian Forum on Civil Justice <http://www.cfcj-fcjc.org/sites/default/files/docs/2012/CURA_background_doc.pdf>.
32 Farrow et al, *Everyday Legal Problems, supra* note 2 at 1.
33 Roderick MacDonald, "Access to Justice in Canada Today: Scope, Scale, Ambitions" in Julia Bass, W.A. Bogart, & Frederick H Zemans, eds, *Access to Justice for a New Century: The Way Forward* (Toronto: Law Society of Upper Canada, 2005), and "Access to Civil Justice" in Peter Cane & Herbert M. Kritzer, eds, *The Oxford Handbook of Empirical Legal Research* (Oxford: Oxford University Press, 2010) at 492. See also Trevor C.W. Farrow, "A New Wave of Access to Justice Reform in Canada" in Adam Dodek & Alice Woolley, eds, *In Search of the Ethical Lawyer: Stories from the Canadian Legal Profession* (Vancouver: UBC Press, 2016) 164.
34 See, however, Senate, Standing Committee on Legal and Constitutional Affairs, *supra* note 13.
35 See especially Catherine Albiston & Rebecca Sandefur, "Expanding the Empirical Study of Access to Justice (2013) 101 Wis L Rev 101–21; Cane & Kritzer, *supra* note 33; Chambliss, Knake, & Nelson, *supra* note 26; Ab Currie, *The Legal Problems of Everyday Life: The Nature, Extent and Consequences of Justiciable Problems Experienced by Canadians* (Ottawa: Department of Justice Canada, 2009); David Engel, *The Myth of the Litigious Society: Why We Don't Sue* (Chicago: University of Chicago Press, 2016); Farrow et al, *Everyday Legal Problems, supra* note 2; Hazel Genn, *Paths to Justice: What People Do and Think about Going to Law* (Oxford: Hart Publishing, 1999); James Greiner, Cassandra Wolos Pattanayak, & Jonathan Hennessy, "The Limits of Unbundled Legal Assistance: A Randomized Study in a Massachusetts District Court and Prospects for the Future" (2012) 126 Harv L Rev 901; Lesley Jacobs & Matthew McManus, "Meaningful Access to Justice for Everyday Legal Problems: New Research on Consumer Problems among Canadians" (Fall 2017) 6 J Civil Litigation & Practice 148; Lesley Jacobs, *Privacy Rights in the Global Digital Economy: Everyday Legal Problems and Canadian Paths to Justice* (Toronto: Irwin Law Books, 2014) [*Privacy Rights*]; Pascoe Pleasence, Nigel Balmer, & Alexy Buck, *Causes of Action: Civil Law and Social Justice,* 2d ed (Norwich, UK: Stationery Office, 2006); Pascoe Pleasence, Nigel Balmer, & Rebecca Sandefur, *Paths to Justice: A Past, Present and Future Road Map* (Oxford: Nuffield Foundation, 2013); Trebilcock, Duggan, & Sossin, *supra* note 6.
36 An influential early statement is Mauro Cappelletti & Bryan Gareth, "Access to Justice and the Welfare State: An Introduction" in Mauro Cappelletti, ed, *Access to Justice and the Welfare State* (Florence: European University Institute, 1981) at 1–2. A more recent statement comes in Michael Trebilcock, Anthony Duggan, & Lorne Sossin, "Introduction" in Trebilcock, Duggan, & Sossin, *supra* note 6 at 3.
37 372 US 335 (1963).

38 The classic account of this case is by Anthony Lewis: *Gideon's Trumpet* (New York: Torch Books, 1964).

39 See, e.g., Russell Engler, "Reflections on a Civil Right to Counsel and Drawing Lines: When Must Counsel Be Appointed, and When Might Access to Justice Mean Less Assistance?" (2011) 9 Seattle J Soc Just 97.

40 American Bar Association, "Human Rights and Access to Justice: Enhancing Access to Justice," online: American Bar Association <https://www.americanbar.org/advocacy/rule_of_law/what-we-do/human-rights-access-to-justice.html>.

41 Canadian Bar Association Access to Justice Committee, *supra* note 12 at 52.

42 See also Action Committee on Access to Justice in Civil and Family Matters, *supra* note 10 at 2.

43 This characterization of meaningful access to justice in terms of pillars draws on various other works by Lesley Jacobs: Brenda Jacobs & Lesley Jacobs, "Multidisciplinary Paths to Family Justice: Professional Challenges and Promising Practices" (Research paper prepared for the Law Commission of Ontario's family law reform project, Best Practices at Family Justice System Entry Points: Needs of Users and Response of Workers in the Justice System, June 2010), online: <http://www.lco-cdo.org/wp-content/uploads/2010/11/family-law-process-call-for-papers-jacobs.pdf>; Lesley Jacobs, "Investor-State Dispute Mechanisms in International Economic Law: The Shifting Ground for Meaningful Access to International Justice from Private Commercial Arbitration to Standing Tribunals and Sectoral Carve-Outs" in Daniel Drache & Lesley A. Jacobs, eds, *Grey Zones of International Economic Law and Global Governance* (Vancouver: UBC Press, 2018); Jacobs, *Privacy Rights, supra* note 35; Jacobs & McManus, *supra* note 35.

44 See, e.g., Genn, *supra* note 35; Farrow et al, *Everyday Legal Problems, supra* note 2.

45 Genn, *supra* note 35.

46 The Law Society of Upper Canada undertook a project oriented precisely to the importance of listening to the voices of users of the justice system in Ontario. Ontario Civil Legal Needs Project, *Listening to Ontarians* (Toronto: Ontario Civil Legal Needs Project Steering Committee, May 2010), online: <https://lawsocietyontario.azureedge.net/media/lso/media/legacy/pdf/m/may/may3110_oclnreport_final.pdf>. See also Farrow, "What Is Access to Justice?" *supra* note 4.

47 See Patricia Ewick & Susan Silbey, *The Common Place of Law* (Chicago: University of Chicago Press, 1998); Lesley Jacobs, "Rights and Quarantine during the SARS Global Health Crisis: Differentiated Legal Consciousness in Hong Kong, Shanghai, and Toronto" (2007) 41 Law & Soc'y Rev 511; Jacobs, *Privacy Rights, supra* note 35; Farrow, "What Is Access to Justice?" *supra* note 4.

48 Pleasence, Balmer, & Buck, *supra* note 35; Shaheen Azmi et al, eds, *Racial Profiling and Human Rights Policy in Canada: The New Legal Landscape* (Toronto: Irwin Law Books, 2018).

49 Farrow et al, *Everyday Legal Problems, supra* note 2.

50 Lesley Jacobs, David Kryszajtys, & Matthew McManus, *Paths to Justice and the Resolution of Consumer Problems* (Toronto: Canadian Forum on Civil Justice, April 2016); and Jacobs & McManus, *supra* note 35.

51 Tom Tyler, "Procedural Justice" in Austin Sarat, ed, *The Blackwell Companion to Law and Society* (Malden, MA: Blackwell, 2004) 435; Tom Tyler, *Why People Obey the Law: Procedural Justice, Legitimacy, and Compliance,* new ed (Princeton, NJ: Princeton University Press, 2006); N. Zimerman & Tom Tyler, "Between Access to Counsel and Access to Justice: A Psychological Perspective" (2010) 37 Fordham Urb LJ 473.

52 Sam Muller et al, *Innovating Justice: Developing New Ways to Bring Fairness between People* (The Hague: HiiL, 2013).

53 Lesley Jacobs, *Pursuing Equal Opportunities* (New York: Cambridge University Press, 2004), c 1.

54 See Trevor C.W. Farrow, *Civil Justice, Privatization, and Democracy* (Toronto: University of Toronto Press, 2014).

55 Farrow et al, *Everyday Legal Problems, supra* note 2.

56 Genn, *supra* note 35 at 12.

57 World Justice Project, *Global Insights on Access to Justice: Findings from the World Justice Project General Population Poll in 45 Countries* (Washington, DC: World Justice Project, 2018) at 2.

58 Pascoe Pleasence, "'Legal Need' and Legal Needs Surveys: A Background Paper" (London: Open Society Justice Initiative, 2016); Nicole Aylwin and Mandi Gray, *Selected Annotated Bibliography of National and Regional Legal Needs Surveys* (Toronto: Canadian Forum on Civil Justice, 2015), online: Canadian Forum on Civil Justice <http://www.cfcj-fcjc.org/ sites/default/files//CFCJ%20Cost%20of%20Justice%20Project%20-%20Selected%20 Annotated%20Bibliography.pdf>.

59 See World Justice Project, online: <https://worldjusticeproject.org/>.

60 All the findings reported here come from Farrow et al, *Everyday Legal Problems, supra* note 2. See also David Northrup et al, *Design and Conduct of the Cost of Justice Survey* (Toronto: Canadian Forum on Civil Justice, 2016), and Canadian Forum on Civil Justice, *Everyday Legal Problems and the Cost of Justice in Canada: Survey* (Toronto: Canadian Forum on Civil Justice, 2016) [*Survey*], both available online: Canadian Forum on Civil Justice <http://www.cfcj-fcjc.org/cost-of-justice>.

61 The random telephone survey included 3,051 adults with landlines and 212 adults using cellphones (for a total of 3,263 adult Canadians). The results reported here are based on the landline calls (3,051 people) between October 2013 and March 2014. For detailed discussions of the study's methodology and survey, see Northrup et al, *supra* note 60; Canadian Forum on Civil Justice, *Survey, supra* note 60.

62 See Currie, *supra* note 35 at 55–56, 55–67, 88; Farrow, "What Is Access to Justice?" *supra* note 4 at 964–65.

63 Justice Annemarie Bonkalo, *Family Legal Services Review* (Toronto: Ministry of the Attorney General, 2016), pt 1.2.a. See also Julie Macfarlane, "The National Self-Represented Litigants Project: Identifying and Meeting the Needs of Self-Represented Litigants, Final Report" (May 2013), online: <https://lawsocietyontario.azureedge.net/media/lso/media/legacy/ pdf/s/self-represented_project.pdf>.

64 See the more in-depth discussion of the Mandatory Information Program in the Ontario family courts in Chapter 9.

65 Focus Consultants, *Civil Non-Family Cases Filed in the Supreme Court of BC: Research Results and Lessons Learned* (Victoria, BC: Canadian Forum on Civil Justice, 2015), online: Canadian Forum on Civil Justice <http://www.cfcj-fcjc.org/sites/default/files//Attrition %20Study%20Final%20Report.pdf>.

66 See Farrow, *Civil Justice, Privatization, and Democracy, supra* note 54 at 117–20.

67 Farrow, "What Is Access to Justice?" *supra* note 4 at 980–81.

68 Jacobs & McManus, *supra* note 35.

69 For other findings on how people finance litigation, see British Columbia Law Institute, *Study Paper on Financing Litigation*, BCLI Study Paper No 9 (Vancouver: British Columbia Law Institute, October 2017), online: BCLI <https://www.bcli.org/wordpress/

wp-content/uploads/2017/10/2017-10-04-BCLI-Study-Paper-on-Financing-Litigation
-PUBLICATION-COPY-rev.pdf>.

70 For further discussions on legal fees, see Noel Semple, "The Cost of Seeking Civil Justice
in Canada" (2015) 93 Can Bar Rev 639. See also Chapters 13 and 15.

71 See, e.g., Semple, *supra* note 70 at 660–62.

72 See the detailed discussion in Chapter 4.

73 See Chapter 7.

74 See Chapter 6.

75 See the discussion of the price of a justice system and the rule of law in Chapter 1, as well
as the comparative OECD data discussed in Chapter 2.

76 See Chapter 3.

77 See also Task Force on Justice, *supra* note 17, c 2.

78 *Ibid.*

79 Action Committee on Access to Justice in Civil and Family Matters, *supra* note 10.

80 Canadian Bar Association Access to Justice Committee, *supra* note 12.

81 See, e.g., Task Force on Justice, *supra* note 17.

Part 1
Understanding the Access to Justice Crisis

1

Prices, Costs, and Access to Justice

Michael Trebilcock

THIS CHAPTER ADDRESSES some basic economic dimensions of the administration of justice, including access to justice. While I am often associated with
the founding of the law and economics school of scholarship in Canada, dating
back to the mid-1970s, and have until recently held the Chair in Law and Economics at the University of Toronto Faculty of Law, I do not approach my remit
here in a narrow or unidimensional way. Indeed, my engagement with issues
pertaining to the regulation of the provision of legal services and access to justice
has been multi-dimensional and interdisciplinary, dating back to my role as
research director of the Professional Organizations Committee, a task force set
up by the then Attorney General for Ontario, Roy McMurtry, in the mid-1970s,
to examine the regulation of several professions that reported to him, including
the legal profession.[1] This was followed by my role as research director of the
McCamus Task Force, set up in the mid-1990s to examine the future of legal
aid in Ontario,[2] followed, in turn, by my role as research director several years
later of the Houlden/Kaufman Task Force on Legal Aid Tariffs set up by Legal
Aid Ontario.[3] This was followed by my appointment by the Attorney General
of Ontario, Michael Bryant, in 2007, to undertake a one-person review (released
the following year) of the state of legal aid and access to justice in Ontario, almost
ten years after the reforms introduced following the report of the McCamus
Task Force.[4] Subsequently, I and colleagues at the University of Toronto Faculty
of Law organized an extensive consultation and colloquium on middle-income
access to justice, which led to the publication of a volume of papers by Canadian
and international experts related to this theme.[5]

A widely quoted quip from Oscar Wilde motivates my discussion. He said
that "a cynic is a person who knows the prices of everything and the value of
nothing." This quip has been widely amended subsequently as "an economist
is a person who knows the prices of everything and the value of nothing." Is it
true that an economic perspective on the administration of justice and access
to justice sees prices everywhere but cannot appreciate the value of dimensions

of the administration of justice that are not readily reducible to monetary terms? I begin this exploration with some brief comments on the centrality of the rule of law in our society in general and as a unifying lodestar of the legal profession in particular. I then move on to argue that prices of legal services simply cannot be ignored in any evaluation of strategies to improve access to justice in Canada. I then argue that, in turn, the prices of legal services and proposals to reduce these cannot be usefully analyzed without squarely addressing the underlying cost structures that drive these prices and the potential for organizational and technological innovations to reduce these costs over time. Finally, I offer some brief concluding thoughts on whether the self-regulatory model of professional regulation has the capacity to address potential innovations in the provision of legal services.

The Value of the Rule of Law

As a scholar who for many years has both taught and written extensively about the role of law and institutions in developing countries, I have come to appreciate that what distinguishes developing countries from developed countries most strikingly is in most cases the relative quality of their institutions: political, bureaucratic, and legal. Over the past twenty years or so, the mantra "institutions matter" or "governance matters" has moved to centre stage in much scholarly literature and policy thinking about development. Focusing on legal institutions and comparisons and contrasts between the quality of these institutions in developed and developing countries quickly leads to a focus on the role of the rule of law in development, and both its meaning and challenges to its effective implementation. Sometimes one is able to value what one has only by observing countries or societies that lack institutional analogues. Failed states, or even minimally functional but chronically impoverished states, typically or often exemplify a state of lawlessness, massive incompetence or corruption in political, bureaucratic, and legal institutions, high levels of political and policy instability, and minimal levels of transparency and accountability.

Since the institutional perspective on development moved to centre stage in the early 1990s, attempts have been made both to define and to measure the impact of the quality of the rule of law on development. Here, one should immediately acknowledge enormous ambiguity as to the meaning of the rule of law in both historical and contemporary discourse.[6] We have all been guilty, at one time or another, of casually throwing out the phrase as the lodestar of our profession (e.g., at law school orientation, convocation ceremonies, and the like) without bothering much to define what we mean by it. In fact, in the scholarly literature relating to the rule of law, all kinds of understandings are manifest. Some understandings stress the non-instrumental nature of the rule of law as a kind of intrinsic universal human right inherent in our basic humanity and basic notions of human dignity and autonomy. So-called thin conceptions of the rule of law emphasize essentially procedural values of due process or natural justice, while much "thicker" conceptions of the rule of law emphasize the importance of a substantively just legal system, which in turn quickly becomes largely elided with substantive notions of a just society. More instrumental conceptions of the rule of law (often espoused by economists) tend to emphasize features of the legal system that plausibly generate desirable economic and social consequences for a society. In this respect, economists' conceptions of the rule of law tend to emphasize the importance of legal pre-dictability and stability, along with strong legal protection of private property rights and enforcement of contracts, on the grounds that these are likely to increase levels of domestic and foreign investment and activity and hence eco-nomic growth.

Despite these ambiguities, the World Bank and other international bodies or agencies have attempted to measure the impact of the rule of law on develop-ment and have reached extremely striking findings. For example, the World Bank in one of its early governance studies found that an improvement in the rule of law by one standard deviation from the current levels in the Ukraine to those middling levels prevailing in South Africa at the time would lead to a fourfold increase in per capita income in the longer run.[7] For purposes of the World Bank governance studies, the rule of law has been defined as capturing perceptions of the extent to which citizens have confidence in and abide by the rules of society, and in particular the quality of contract enforcement, property rights, the police, and the courts, as well as the likelihood of crime and vio-lence. A more recent study by Dani Rodrik, Arvind Subramanian, and Francesco Trebbi estimate the respective contributions of institutions, geography, and international trade in determining income levels around the world. The au-thors use a number of measures of institutional quality that capture the pro-tection afforded to property rights as well as the strength of the rule of law (largely derived from World Bank data). The quality of institutions, they find, trumps everything else. For example, they conclude that an increase in institutional quality of one standard deviation, corresponding roughly to the difference between measured institutional quality in Bolivia and South Korea, produces a rise of 2 log-points in per capita incomes, or a 6.4-fold difference, which, not coincidentally, is also roughly the income difference between the two countries.[8]

The development of these and similar legal indicators has not gone without challenge on various methodological grounds, pertaining to both whether they are measuring the appropriate variables and, even if they are, whether their data derived from various investor and citizen surveys provide reliable measures of the variables in question.[9]

Relative to these earlier studies, the World Justice Project (a widely respected international NGO based in Washington, DC) now publishes annually much more detailed rule of law ratings for more than 100 countries, developed and developing, around the world. The World Justice Project adopts a somewhat more capacious definition of the rule of law than the World Bank, comprising nine factors: constraints on government power; absence of corruption; open government; fundamental rights; order and security; regulatory enforcement; civil justice; criminal justice; and informal justice (each of which is defined by several subindicators).

Canada rates well compared with all countries surveyed, but relative to European and North American countries and other high-income countries, it is somewhere in the middle of the pack, with relatively low ratings on delays in the civil justice system and the cost of accessing legal representation[10] – a point that former Chief Justice of Canada Beverley McLachlin made in the Foreword to our book *Middle Income Access to Justice* in commenting on similar earlier findings by the World Justice Project, thus providing a salutary caution against excessive complacency on our part.[11]

Even if one bridles at the notion of applying a general utilitarian or social welfare calculus to how the rule of law should be valued relative to other social goals (a perspective widely adopted by many economists on most resource allocation issues),[12] even a non-instrumental perspective on the rule of law must confront painful choices in the allocation of scarce social resources, and thus might be willing to join forces with economists in asking whether alternative arrangements to the status quo have the potential to stretch scarce resources further, both now and in the future, through facilitating and incentivizing innovations in the provision of legal services, and whether access to justice can be made more broadly available.

The Price of the Rule of Law

So far, I have discussed the meaning and value of the rule of law, narrowly or broadly construed, and viewed either non-instrumentally or instrumentally. Whether one thinks that the rule of law is intrinsically valuable or instrumentally valuable, in both cases we must confront an obvious, painful reality: no society, including Canada, assigns infinite resources to the administration of justice or access to justice. To take, by way of example, the province of Ontario, with which I am most familiar: the provincial government assigns annual budgets for the administration of justice, including the courts, police, prosecutorial services, correctional services, and legal aid, but resources assigned to each of these components of the administration of justice are, by definition, limited and compete with demands by citizens for public expenditures on other functions of importance to them, including healthcare, education, infrastructure, social safety nets, and so on. Politicians, like most of us, operate within a particular institutional incentive structure – in their case, to win election or re-election, which requires them to be responsive to the demands and concerns of their voters, who typically have a whole range of preoccupations that need to be addressed if their political representatives are to achieve electoral success and political survival. Thus, as I pointed out in my report of the Legal Aid Review (2008), it is almost certainly wishful thinking to assume that governments across the country are likely, in the foreseeable future, to allocate substantial additional resources, in the current fiscal environment, to any of these elements of the administration of justice. Legal aid is particularly vulnerable in this respect, given that, in public perceptions, it mostly caters to the poor and (inaccurately) mostly criminal defendants (given the substantial resources devoted to family law, refugee claimants, and the community legal services clinic system in Ontario). The middle class, who make up the bulk of voters and taxpayers, see themselves as having little stake in the legal aid system beyond their role as taxpayers, and certainly not as beneficiaries, in contrast to the stakes they widely perceive themselves as having in the public healthcare and educational systems.[13] In most jurisdictions, financial eligibility for legal aid is stringent, and legal aid is available for only a limited range of civil matters. While many of us may espouse "equality before the law" as a central element in our normative conception of the rule of law,[14] we are far from realizing this ideal.

There are other important institutional actors whose policies and conduct also significantly affect the price of justice. If access to civil justice is interpreted to mean primarily access to civil courts, then judges individually and collectively, in the procedures they adopt and apply to civil litigation, will significantly affect the price of justice. The more prolix and protracted civil proceedings are, the greater the monetary, temporal, and psychological costs experienced by many litigants, creating pressures on them to settle cases or to move disputes to less costly and more expeditious venues, such as private mediation or arbitration, or simply to "lump" their grievances, leading to the much-studied phenomenon of the "vanishing trial" in the United States (and, I suspect, in Canada, although there is less systematic Canadian evidence on this issue).[15] Under classical conceptions of the adversarial system, judges were largely passive umpires between legally well-armed adversaries who would be accorded substantial latitude in how they presented their case to courts, for example, in terms of number of witnesses, time for examination and cross-examination, scope of discovery, scheduling of hearings, adjournments, and so on – the "Full

Court Press," as I have called it.[16] While in recent years, there has been significant movement away from the classical adversarial model of judges as relatively
neutral umpires of proceedings largely controlled by the legal representatives
of litigants to more active forms of judicial case management, in partial recognition of the fact that perfect justice for the few is a denial of justice for the many,
controversy still persists as to what form case management should take, whether
it should be mandatory or voluntary, and at what stage of proceedings it is most
appropriate.[17] Proportionality-oriented civil justice reforms (recently endorsed
by the Supreme Court of Canada[18]) in the form of an expanded role for Small
Claims Courts and summary judgment procedures reflect further movement
away from the classical adversarial model. Pilot reform initiatives that are subject to rigorous evaluation and can be scaled up if successful may be a more
prudent strategy than across-the-board systemic reforms.

Another recent and controversial body of predominantly law and economics
scholarship seeks to explore the incentive structure and utility functions of
judges (both trial judges and appellate court judges), seeking to understand
what motivates them as they go about the discharge of their judicial duties (in
Richard Posner terms, what do judges maximize?).[19] This literature explores,
inter alia, how judges make the work-leisure trade-off that all or most of us face;
the role of ideology and political partisanship in judicial decision making; the
role of collegiality in motivating consensus in appellate courts; and so on. Most
of this literature is focused on the US judicial system, where federal judicial
appointments are subject to a formal political confirmation process and most
state court judges are popularly elected, so that findings from this literature
should be extrapolated with extreme caution to other legal systems (as Posner
himself readily acknowledges).[20] Notwithstanding this important caveat, it is
true that the factors that motivate judicial decision making in Canada (and probably elsewhere) remain something of a "black box," unlike much more developed
bodies of literature on what motivates politicians and bureaucrats.[21]

Courts, of course, are not the only institutions that perform adjudicative
functions in our society. A plethora of administrative tribunals, bodies, and
program administrators within government perform adjudicative or quasi-
adjudicative roles in resolving claims or disputes, and many of the same questions that one might pose of courts can, with appropriate adaptations, be applied
to these quasi-adjudicative bodies, as well as private adjudicative mechanisms
(such as arbitration).

Beyond courts and other adjudicative bodies, the policies adopted by
university-based law schools obviously influence the price of justice: the number of students they admit; the length and nature of course requirements; and
tuition fees (which in recent years have been increasing substantially, reflecting

in part reductions in real levels of government support for professional education and increasingly intense international competition for academic talent,
both faculty and student).[22] In contrast to the United States, where the number
of students taking the LSAT and applications and enrolments at many second-
tier law schools have sharply declined, there is little evidence to date of similar
trends in Canada, and indeed calls to the Ontario bar in recent years have been
increasing, in large part because of the significant number of foreign-trained
lawyers gaining Canadian certification.[23]

Provincial law societies as self-regulators of the legal profession also significantly influence the price of justice in terms of a wide range of policies that they
have adopted or might adopt with respect to entry requirements and post-entry
regulation of the conduct of lawyers and the permissible scope of activities of
paralegals and cognate professionals, and of non-lawyer relationships with
lawyers in the provision of legal services.

For many good reasons, courts, university law schools, and law societies
are all fiercely protective of their institutional autonomy. These contending
autonomies, however, along with the political decisions, both federal and
provincial, that bear on the administration of justice, carry the offsetting risk
of disarticulation of any coherent approach to enhancing access to justice
(including the development of any systematic database on the administration
of justice).[24]

Moving from the systemic or institutional perspective on the allocation of
resources to the administration of justice, it is useful to undertake a reality check
on the incentives facing lawyers in private practice and private citizens with
respect to their needs or concerns that could potentially benefit from legal assistance or representation. First, from the perspective of lawyers in private
practice, especially smaller practices, despite periodic proposals to mandate
some level of *pro bono* services, it seems to me unrealistic to expect them to
devote substantial proportions of their time to *pro bono* services or to dramatically reduce fees for large classes of cases to impecunious clients below those
they would normally charge for these services and hence the opportunity costs
of their time. These lawyers are presumably constrained by the need to maintain a business model that ensures the long-term viability of their practices.
Second, from a citizen's or client's perspective, whatever their personal resources,
it makes no economic sense to pursue a grievance where the costs of legal
representation exceed the expected returns from pursuing it – better to "lump"
it than litigate it in such cases. Even in cases where the expected returns from
pursuing a matter exceed the legal costs of representation, impecunious clients
will find it neither rational nor in many cases even possible to pay for retainers
or ongoing time-based legal fees before the matter is resolved, given many other

pressing and competing claims on their limited resources.[25] Contingency fees and class action procedures can alleviate some of these constraints, but in a limited range of cases.

In the case of all these actors – institutional and individual – an economic perspective on the administration of justice tends to focus on two recurrent issues: what is the *incentive structure* of the parties in question in motivating their behaviour; and what are the *opportunity costs* (both private and, importantly, social) of choosing one course of action or set of policies over another?

Hence, despite Oscar Wilde's quip, it turns out that at a systemic level, at the individual practitioner level, and at the individual citizen or client level, justice does indeed have a price, however disagreeable this brute reality may be. This reality then leads me to a critical cluster of issues – the relationship between prices and costs – where my central argument will be that the only way to substantially reduce the price of justice is to reduce its costs (recognizing that prevailing prices are largely a function of prevailing, underlying cost structures).

Prices and Costs

In most economic activities, economists assume that prices confronting consumers of the goods and services in question bear some, and typically a close, relationship to the costs of providing those goods or services. This is as true of legal services as of most other categories of goods and services. Thus, if we are concerned (as we should be) about the price of justice, and how the prevailing price of justice prevents many citizens from obtaining access to justice (for civil justice in particular, for the purposes of my comments), we cannot avoid focusing on the costs (fixed and variable) of providing legal and related services (including adjudicative services).

In this respect, a number of contemporary scholars argue that there is substantial potential for reducing the cost and hence the price of justice through two emerging and overlapping trends: liberalization of the rules governing the business structures through which legal services may be provided; and the role of information technology (IT) and artificial intelligence (AI) in reducing the costs of assembling, disseminating, and applying legally relevant information to the needs of individual citizens or firms.

A prominent proponent of this view is Richard Susskind, who has argued in a number of books that legal institutions and the legal profession are at a crossroads and are poised to change more radically over the next two decades than they have over the past two centuries. He argues that the bespoke specialist who handcrafts solutions for clients will be challenged by new working methods, characterized by lower labour costs, mass customization, recyclable legal knowledge, pervasive use of IT, and more. In his book *Tomorrow's Lawyers: An Introduction to Your Future,* Susskind argues that there will be three main drivers of change: the more-for-less challenge, liberalization, and information technology.[26]

The more-for-less challenge reflects the concern of many users or potential users of legal services over their costs, particularly in a low-growth economic environment. This concern applies across the spectrum, from large corporate clients and their in-house counsel to small businesses and individual citizens. The liberalization challenge refers to prevailing concerns about the absence of choice in modes of legal service delivery. In this respect, the United Kingdom has led the way with the enactment of the *Legal Services Act 2007,* following a review of the regulatory framework for legal services by Sir David Clementi in 2004. This act, *inter alia,* permits the setting up of new types of legal businesses, called "alternative business structures" (ABSs), so that non-lawyers can own and run legal businesses; permits external investment, such as private equity or venture capital, to be injected into legal businesses by outside investors; and allows non-lawyers to become partners or principals in law firms.[27] Since the enactment of the *Legal Services Act 2007,* new modalities for the delivery of legal services have emerged in the United Kingdom and also in some states of Australia where similar reforms have been adopted. Several law firms have issued public offerings to finance a large network of branch offices, while a major British building society has announced plans to provide legal services from its 330 bank branches in the United Kingdom, and a private equity–backed group of law firms – in effect, a franchise network – have obtained concessions in many of the stores of a major retail giant.

In the case of information technology, many new and emerging applications of IT and AI do not simply computerize and streamline pre-existing and ineffi- cient manual processes. Rather than automate, many systems innovate, which means they allow tasks to be performed that were previously not possible or even imaginable, including the use of big data collections of court or regulatory decisions or rulings and their application to the facts of particular clients' cir- cumstances. While Susskind may be a "techno optimist,"[28] it is difficult to gainsay his central claim that lawyers are in the information business through the as- sembly, dissemination, and application of information, and IT and AI innova- tions are as likely to disrupt traditional business models in law as they already have in the print and broadcast media, online shopping, taxi and ride-sharing services, hospitality services, and other sectors of society. It is equally difficult to gainsay the proposition that disruptive innovations often originate with upstarts outside an established industry, rather than incumbents who are more focused on sustaining innovations to existing business models.[29]

It is common to describe and often decry the legal profession as having a monopoly on the provision of legal services, but this is equally true of many other professions and skilled trades that impose entry requirements. However, this does not preclude competition within their licensed domain. In Ontario, there are about 24,000 lawyers with active practising certificates, and a preliminary study by Edward Iacobucci and me finds that most legal services markets in Ontario, by specialty and region, are structurally competitive.[30] Thus, the term "monopoly" is, economically speaking, misleading. But just as bricks-and-mortar retail stores vigorously competed against each other prior to online shopping, the advent of this new business model has profoundly affected competitive dynamics in many retail markets.

Susskind argues that the more-for-less challenge, liberalization, and information technology will drive immense and irreversible change in the way that lawyers work. He calls this a perfect storm in the making.[31] Frank Stephen similarly argues that a combination of more liberal rules on alternative business structures and a more expansive role for IT and AI has the potential for bringing about a technological revolution in lawyering by facilitating access to more sources of capital and managerial, marketing, and IT expertise, permitting the realization of greater economies of scale, scope, and specialization in more efficiently transforming a wider range of inputs into more highly valued outputs.[32] In the United States, the emergence and growth of legal service providers such as Legal Zoom and Rocket Law, which provide a combination of online interactive legal advice and assistance, supported by a referral network of fixed-fee lawyers, exemplifies a similar, albeit more muted, trend in North America. In short, the future of the legal profession is likely to be more entrepreneurial and more IT- and AI-intensive. While this may threaten existing business models in the profession, it does not necessarily imply less employment for lawyers.

Lawyers will practise in increasingly varied business structures with different roles and responsibilities that better respond to the demand for legal services by citizens who presently lack effective access to them. There may not be a fortune to be made at the bottom of the pyramid, but almost certainly professional incomes will be adequate.[33] Susskind also argues that the courts will not be immune from these trends and predicts a dramatic expansion of online dispute resolution and virtual trials, as well as a dramatic expansion of non-court-based online dispute resolution, citing by way of example the fact that eBay has resolved some 60 million complaints through informal online dispute resolution (e-adjudication). Private arbitration generally of commercial, family, consumer, and employment disputes is already expanding dramatically (although often raising legitimate concerns in the latter two cases of coerced consent through fine print, take-it-or-leave-it clauses in standard form contracts).[34] Courts are thus not the only game in town for resolving civil disputes (and progressively less so). However, if they price themselves out of the market for resolving civil disputes, this will come at a significant social cost in terms of forgoing the incremental development of the law through the accumulation of a body of authoritative judicial precedents and the public articulation of important social norms.[35] In the near future, legal education may in turn be exposed to various disruptive technologies, including online course offerings from a variety of sources.[36]

In terms of enhancing access to justice and realizing more fully our ideal of equality before the law, we really have only two basic choices: either to devote substantially more public resources to the administration of justice within the existing modalities and institutions, or to devise much more innovative, lower-cost, lower-priced modalities for ensuring that many more legal services are within the reach of our fellow citizens. Both choices present major political economy challenges. In my concluding comments, I mainly focus on the challenges posed by the latter choice.

Self-Regulation of the Legal Profession

In his insightful book *Legal Services Regulation at the Crossroads: Justitia's Legions,* Professor Noel Semple compares two models of legal services regulation: the professionalist-independent model that has largely prevailed in North America historically and continues to prevail today, and the competitive-consumerist paradigm that has increasingly come to predominate in much of Western Europe and Australasia.[37] Semple argues that regulators must make four key policy choices with respect to legal services regulation: (1) *occupational structure:* whether to institute occupational unity (a single occupation of lawyer) as opposed to occupational multiplicity; (2) *governance:* how much scope to allow for self-regulation as opposed to state or co-regulation; (3) *insulation:* whether to pursue regulatory insulation of legal service providers from business relationships with non-lawyers (through prohibition of non-lawyer investment in firms providing legal services), as opposed to regulatory openness to such relationships; and (4) *the unit of regulatory focus:* whether individual legal service providers should be the exclusive focus of regulatory efforts, as opposed to also regulating the firms and enterprises in which they work. Semple concludes that the competitive-consumerist paradigm has been more open to innovation with respect to all four of these issues than the traditional professionalist-independent model. He goes on to argue, however, that the latter has many virtues in terms of preserving the independence of the legal profession from the state, which is often adverse in interest to many citizens that lawyers represent, and that the legal profession as a self-regulatory institution is able to bring expertise and appreciation of the day-to-day realities of legal practice to the challenges of formulating, monitoring, and enforcing appropriate regulations.

However, many critics of the traditional professionalist-independent model of self-regulation of the legal profession argue that the model exhibits inherent professional protectionist biases that render it inimical to innovation in the provision of legal services and in disciplining incompetent or dishonest practitioners, and that the unity of the profession is something of a mirage, given the increasingly diverse demographic makeup of the profession, the increasing fragmentation of the profession into different areas of specialization, the increasing diversity of law firm size and orientation from solo and small practices to major national and international law firms, and a proliferating and diverse range of interactions between lawyers and members of cognate professions and other business actors.[38]

In *Tomorrow's Lawyers,* Susskind argues that in law there are two distinct camps (and a few in between): the benevolent custodians and the jealous guards. The benevolent custodians are those who regard it as their duty to nurture the law and make it affordable and accessible to members of society. In contrast, the jealous guards wish to fence in areas of legal practice and make them their exclusive preserve, whether or not the activity genuinely requires the experience of lawyers and with little regard to the impact of this quasi-protectionism on the affordability and viability of legal service. As Susskind puts it, "turkeys rarely vote for an early Christmas." He implores tomorrow's lawyers to take up the mantle of the benevolent custodian.

I take a position somewhere between the two extremes of unqualified self-regulation and extensive direct state regulation of the legal profession, and have argued for the preservation of a qualified form of self-regulation of the legal profession, for most of the same reasons for Semple's defence of this model, but most particularly the importance of preserving the independence of the legal profession from direct control by government.[39] My views here are influenced by my observation of the severely deleterious impacts of subjugation of the judiciary and the legal profession by often autocratic and repressive governments in many developing countries. Self-regulation cannot be unqualified and unaccountable, however. Hence, I argue for strengthening both the number and quality of lay representatives on the governing bodies of the legal profession, in particular, ensuring that lay members are genuinely representative of a range of demand-side interests, paralegals, and cognate professions; that rules of conduct promulgated by the governing bodies of legal professions should take the form of regulations that are subject to ministerial or Cabinet approval; and that consideration be given to appointing non-lawyer ombudspersons to oversee and publicly report on the efficacy of the disciplinary processes of the legal profession.

Whether the legal profession in Canada is open to the challenges of regulatory rejuvenation both in terms of its governance structures and in terms of the substantive policies that it chooses to adopt in future with respect to the four major policy choices that Semple identifies, at least in the absence of a credible threat of direct regulation by government, is an open question. I remain cautiously optimistic, although the stakes are so large in terms of enhancing access to justice that failure to rise to these challenges will progressively undermine the credibility of the organized legal profession and inevitably (as evident from recent experience in Western Europe and Australia with co-regulation) invite direct government intervention, for the simple reason that a broad range of the political constituents of government representatives will demand it.

In conclusion, to return to Oscar Wilde's quip, no sensible person would argue that everything of value in life has a price.[40] However, many dimensions of the justice system in the real world do have a price, and discounting the importance of rigorous analysis of the determinants of these prices is likely to continue compromising our collective commitments to access to justice and the rule of law, *especially* if we value these commitments highly.

Notes

I am greatly indebted to Justice Georgina Jackson of the Saskatchewan Court of Appeal, who is also president of the Canadian Institute for the Administration of Justice, for extremely helpful conversations on a number of the issues discussed in this presentation, and to Anita Anand, Ben Alarie, Julia Bass, David Dyzenhaus, Judith McCormack, Mariana Prado, Noel Semple, Albert Yoon, Trevor Farrow, Les Jacobs, and Ron Daniels for comments on earlier drafts.

1 Michael Trebilcock, Carolyn Tuohy, and Alan Wolfson, *Professional Regulation,* Staff Study (Toronto: Government of Ontario, 1979); *Report of the Professional Organizations Committee* (Toronto: Government of Ontario, 1980).

2 McCamus Task Force, *Report of the Ontario Legal Aid Review: A Blueprint for Publicly Funded Legal Services,* 3 vols (Toronto: Government of Ontario, 1997).

3 Holden-Kaufman Task Force, *Report on the Legal Aid Tariff* (Toronto: Legal Aid Ontario, 2000).

4 Michael Trebilcock, *Report of Legal Aid Review, 2008* (Toronto: Ontario Ministry of the Attorney General, 2008).

5 Michael Trebilcock, Anthony Duggan, & Lorne Sossin, eds, *Middle Income Access to Justice* (Toronto: University of Toronto Press, 2012).

6 See Michael Trebilcock and Mariana Prado, *Advanced Introduction to Law and Development* (London: Edward Elgar, 2014), c 4 and c 5; Michael Trebilcock, "Between Universalism and Relativism: Reflections on the Evolution of Law and Development Studies" (2016) 66 UTLJ 330.

7 Daniel Kaufman, *Governance Redux: The Empirical Challenge* (Washington, DC: Brookings Institution, 2004).

8 Dani Rodrik, Arvind Subramanian, & Francesco Trebbi, "Institutions Rule: The Primacy of Institutions over Geography and Integration in Economic Development" (2004) 9 J Economic Growth 131.

9 See Kevin Davis, "Legal Indicators: The Power of Quantitative Measures of Law" (2014) 10 Annual Rev L & Social Sciences 37.

10 World Justice Project, *World Justice Project Rule of Law Index 2015* (Washington, DC: World Justice Project, 2015).

11 Trebilcock, Duggan, & Sossin, *supra* note 5.

12 See, e.g., Louis Kaplow and Steven Shavell, *Fairness versus Welfare* (Cambridge, MA: Harvard University Press, 2002).

13 See Canadian Bar Association Access to Justice Committee, *Equal Justice: Balancing the Scales* (Ottawa: Canadian Bar Association, 2013) at 48, 49.

14 See David Dyzenhaus, "Normative Justifications for the Provision of Legal Aid" (Background study for the Ontario Legal Aid Task Force Report, 1999); Trebilcock, *supra* note 4 at 61–70.

15 See Marc Galanter, "The Vanishing Trial: An Examination of Trials and Related Matters in Federal and State Courts" (2004) 1 J Empirical Leg Studies 459; Gillian Hadfield, "Where Have All the Trials Gone?" (2004) 1 J Empirical Leg Studies 713.

16 Michael Trebilcock and Lisa Austin, "The Limits of the Full Court Press: Of Blood and Mergers" (1998) 48 UTLJ 1.

17 See Judge David Price, "A New Model for Civil Case Management: Efficacy through Intrinsic Engagement" (2015) 50 Court Rev 174.

18 *Hryniak v Mauldin*, 2014 SCC 7.

19 See Richard A. Posner, "What Do Judges Maximize? (The Same Thing Everybody Does)" (1993) 3 Sup Ct Econ Rev 1; Richard A. Posner, *How Judges Think* (Cambridge, MA: Harvard University Press, 2010), especially c 1 for an overview of various theories of judicial behaviour; Richard A. Posner, *Reflections on Judging* (Cambridge, MA: Harvard University Press, 2013); Lee Epstein, ed, *The Economics of Judicial Behavior* (London: Edward Elgar, 2013).

20 See Richard Posner, "Judicial Behavior and Performance: An Economic Approach" (2005) 32 Fla St UL Rev 1259.

21 But see Ben Alarie and Andrew Green, "Charter Decisions in the McLachlin Era: Consensus and Ideology at the Supreme Court of Canada" (2009) 47 Sup Ct L Rev 475.

22 For a 2018 survey of the impact of rising tuition fees on law students in Ontario, see Law Students' Society of Ontario, *Just or Bust?* (Toronto: January 2019).

23 See Noel Semple, "Personal Plight Legal Practice and Tomorrow's Lawyers" (2014) 39 J Leg Profession 25 at 27, 28.

24 See Action Committee on Access to Justice in Civil and Family Matters, *Access to Civil and Family Justice: A Roadmap for Change* (Ottawa: Action Committee on Access to Justice in Civil and Family Matters, 2013), online: Canadian Forum on Civil Justice <http://www.cfcj-fcjc.org/sites/default/files/docs/2013/AC_Report_English_Final.pdf>.

25 Noel Semple, "The Cost of Seeking Civil Justice in Canada" (2015) 93 Can Bar Rev 1; for a recent survey of the costs of civil justice in Canada, see Trevor Farrow et al, *Everyday Legal Problems and the Cost of Justice in Canada: Overview Report* (Toronto: Canadian Forum on Civil Justice, 2016).

26 Richard Susskind, *Tomorrow's Lawyers: An Introduction to Your Future* (Oxford: Oxford University Press, 2013); see also Richard Susskind, *Online Courts and the Future of Justice* (Oxford: Oxford University Press, 2019).

27 For a more detailed exploration of alternative business structures for the practice of law, drawing on economic theories of the firm and optimal capital structure, see Edward Iacobucci and Michael Trebilcock, "An Economic Analysis of Alternative Business Structures for the Practice of Law" (2013) 92 Can Bar Rev 57; for proposals for multiple licensing tracks for legal service providers with limited but specialized training and limited sphere of practice, see Alice Woolley and Trevor Farrow, "Addressing Access to Justice through New Legal Service Providers: Opportunities and Challenges" (2016) 13 Texas A & M L Rev 549.

28 See more generally, Erik Brynjolfsson and Andrew McAfee, *The Second Machine Age: Work, Progress and Prosperity in the Time of Brilliant Technologies* (New York: W.W. Norton, 2014); for a more pessimistic view of the impact of new technology, see Robert Gordon, *The Rise and Fall of American Growth: The US Standard of Living since the Civil War* (Princeton, NJ: Princeton University Press, 2016).

29 See Clayton Christensen, *The Innovators Dilemma: When New Technologies Cause Great Firms to Fail* (Cambridge, MA: Harvard Business School Press, 1997); Roy Worthy Campbell, "Rethinking Regulation and Innovation in the US Legal Services Market" (2012) 9 NYU J Law & Business 1.

30 See Edward Iacobucci and Michael Trebilcock, "Self-Regulation and Competition in Ontario's Legal Services Sector: An Evaluation of the Competition Bureau's Report on Competition and Self-Regulation in Canadian Professions" (Report to the Federation of Law Societies of Canada, November 2008).

31 For similar prognoses, see Frank H. Stephen, *Lawyers, Markets and Regulation* (London: Edward Elgar, 2013); Noel Semple, *Legal Services Regulation at the Crossroads: Justitia's Legions* (London: Edward Elgar, 2015) [*Legal Services Regulation*]; Gillian Hadfield and Deborah Rhode, "How to Regulate Legal Services to Promote Access, Innovation and the Quality of Lawyering" (2016) 67 Hastings LJ 1191; Gillian Hadfield, "Legal Barriers to Innovation: The Growing Economic Cost of Professional Control over Corporate Legal Markets" (2008) 60 Stan L Rev 102 ["Legal Barriers"]; Gillian Hadfield, "Higher Demand, Lower Supply? A Comparative Assessment of the Legal Resource Landscape for Ordinary Americans" (2010) 37 Fordham Urb LJ 129; Gillian Hadfield, *Rules for a Flat World: Why Humans Invented Law and How to Reinvent It for a Complex Global Economy* (New York: Oxford University Press, 2017); Deborah Rhode, *The Trouble with Lawyers* (New York: Oxford University Press, 2015); Benjamin Barton and Stephanos Bibos, *Rebooting Justice: More Technology, Fewer Lawyers* (New York: Encounter Books, 2017).

32 Stephen, *supra* note 31, c 8.

33 See C.K. Prahabad, *The Fortune at the Bottom of the Pyramid: Eradicating Poverty through Profits* (New York: Prentice Hall, 2010).

34 See Margaret Jane Radin, *Boilerplate: The Fine Print, Vanishing Rights, and the Rule of Law* (Princeton, NJ: Princeton University Press, 2012).

35 See Trevor Farrow, *Civil Justice, Privatization, and Democracy* (Toronto: University of Toronto Press, 2014), c 6.

36 See, e.g., Michele Pistone & Michael Horn, "Disrupting Law School: How Disruptive Innovation Will Revolutionize the Legal World" (Boston: Clayton Christenson Institute for Disruptive Innovation, March 2016).

37 Noel Semple, *Legal Services Regulation, supra* note 31.

38 Stephen, *supra* note 31; Gillian Hadfield, "Legal Barriers," *supra* note 31; Harry Arthurs, "Will the Law Society of Alberta Celebrate Its Bicentenary?" (2008) 45 Alta L Rev 15; Richard Devlin and Porter Heffernan, "The End(s) of Self-Regulation?" (2008) 45 Alta L Rev 169; Philip Slayton, *Lawyers Gone Bad: Money, Sex and Madness in Canada's Legal Profession* (Toronto: Viking Canada, 2007).

39 See Michael Trebilcock, "Regulating the Market for Legal Services" (2008) 45 Alta L Rev 215.

40 See, e.g., Michael Sandel, *What Money Can't Buy: The Moral Limits of Markets* (New York: Farrar, Straus and Giroux, 2012).

2

Measuring Justice System Performance in Quebec and Canada
Indicators for Benchmarking Systems and Highlighting Best Practices

Moktar Lamari, Pierre Noreau, and Marylène Leduc

BOTH THOSE INVOLVED IN conducting research on the justice system and those responsible for its administrative management have long complained that they lack statistical indicators required for monitoring and assessing justice performance. This problem arises at the levels of both Canada and Quebec. This issue is directly related to the principle of transparency, which should normally be part of the various forms of public action, of which the justice system is a part. This orientation is consistent with the principles of open governance. For proof that this is a requirement, we need only recall that the justice system is funded by the state (that is, by the people) and that it is a public service. Access to the data necessary for monitoring court performance and evaluating the use of resources invested in the justice system is, by extension, a specific form of access to law and justice.

The purpose of this chapter is to bring together a diverse set of research that measures the performance of national justice systems in member countries of the Organisation for Economic Co-operation and Development (OECD).[1] Our work is grounded in the databases that provide indicators that measure justice in the OECD. This chapter explores the justice performance of OECD countries by organizing these indicators into three categories: justice input indicators, justice output indicators, and justice impact indicators.

Concepts and Method

The OECD defines performance as "the degree to which a development intervention or a development partner operates according to specific criteria/standards/guidelines or achieves results in accordance with stated goals or plans."[2] Based on this definition, when and where can we say that a justice system performs well? Do contemporary justice systems, particularly those of so-called advanced democracies, perform well? These two questions concern both individual states and supranational organizations. The fact that the stakes to be measured are multi-dimensional cannot obscure the disparities in measurement and units of observation. This complicates, without biasing, international comparison of the performance of justice systems.

The European Union evaluates the performance of justice systems with respect to accessibility, resources mobilized, evaluation practices, and the use of appropriate standards likely to favour access to justice. Accessibility is also evaluated with respect to the integration of new information technologies at every stage along the way through the judicial system, access to legal aid, and voluntary use of extrajudicial dispute resolution methods.[3] The efficiency of justice is evaluated principally in terms of the speed of court decisions, which is based on comparison of the length of proceedings, the case clearance rate, and the number of pending cases in the different jurisdictions.

In its Just Development project, the World Bank discusses justice performance indicators with regard to the courts. Just Development identifies five performance attributes in justice: efficiency, quality, transparency and accountability, access, and independence.[4]

The OECD defines an indicator as a "quantitative or qualitative factor or variable that provides a simple and reliable means to measure achievement, to reflect the changes connected to an intervention, or to help assess the performance of a development actor."[5] A performance indicator makes possible "the verification of changes in the development intervention or shows results relative to what was planned."[6]

The OECD classifies justice systems according to their legal origin.[7] Table 2.1 situates the entities in terms of their legal tradition.

Table 2.1 Classification of justice systems according to legal tradition

Legal tradition/ political regime	Common law	Civil law
Presidential	Unitary: Ireland	Federal: Germany Unitary: France[1]
Parliamentary	Federal: United Kingdom,[2] Australia, Canada/Quebec (province)[3] Unitary: New Zealand	Federal: Belgium, Canada/Quebec (province) Unitary: Finland, Luxembourg, Sweden, Denmark, Netherlands

1 The political regime is semi-presidential. Executive powers are divided between the President and the Prime Minister.
2 The justice system of Scotland, which is part of the United Kingdom, is based on a combination of common law and civil law.
3 Canada's legal system is based on common law, except in Quebec, where a combination of common law and civil law is applied.
Source: Perspective monde, Université de Sherbrooke /Centre de recherche sur les systèmes juridiques, JuriGlobe.

Benchmarking refers to all of the operations that make it possible to identify, compare, and implement the practices that are most likely to improve access to justice and ensure that justice systems perform well. It provides useful measurements for identifying the strengths and weaknesses of such systems from a comparative perspective.[8] Awareness of performance gaps can be a major motivator when planning and carrying out reforms designed to improve institutions and public services.

Data and Analysis

For our study, we summarized each country's writings and ministerial reports available from the databases of the OECD Library as well as through university search engines and government sites. We answered the following question: How do the justice systems of most of the OECD member countries compare in terms of performance?

A number of OECD and European Union reports were used to identify numerous key determining factors in justice performance that could be compared across a sample of countries: France, Belgium, Germany, Denmark, Ireland, Luxembourg, the Netherlands, Finland, Sweden, New Zealand, and Australia. Government reports from the United Kingdom, New Zealand, Australia, Canada, and Quebec were also consulted to find annual performance indicators.

Next, using numbered quantifiable indicators, the various entities were benchmarked in order to identify the best practices in justice and establish how the countries compare with one another. Table 2.2 recapitulates the indicators used in the study.

Findings

This section presents the findings obtained for the key indicators used by multilateral organizations (OECD, European Commission for the Efficiency of Justice [Commission européenne pour l'efficacité de la justice, or CEPEJ], European Commission) and government bodies to evaluate the performance of their justice systems. In order to facilitate our performance analysis, the indicators are classified into three categories: input, output, and effect/impact indicators. Only indicators providing data on the majority of the countries in our sample, and for Quebec, are used in the comparison.

Inputs

The input indicators used here are the annual public budget for legal aid (per inhabitant), legal aid per recipient case, and access to affordable justice. They are a proxy for expenditure, useful for decision makers even if better additional information and caution are required before interpretation.

Table 2.2 **Indicators used in the study**

Quebec and OECD countries, excluding Canada	Canada and OECD countries
Financial resources	
1 Public budget for legal aid/inhabitant 2 Annual public budget for legal aid/recipient case	18 Access to affordable justice
Human resources	
3 Number of lawyers per 100,000 inhabitants 4 Number of judges per 100,000 inhabitants 5 Number of lawyers per judge 6 Number of prosecution system employees per 100,000 inhabitants 7 Judges' gross salary	
Material and information technology resources	
8 Total number of courts per 100,000 inhabitants	19 Public access to laws and legal data 20 Use of ICT (information and communications technology)
Length of proceedings	
9 Length of first-instance proceedings in number of days 10 Length of second-instance proceedings in number of days 11 Length of highest-court proceedings in number of days	21 Reasonable length of civil proceedings 22 Reasonable length of administrative proceedings 23 Accessibility, impartiality, and efficiency of dispute resolution mechanisms
Case clearance rate	
12 Rate of cases resolved at first instance 13 Number of cases receiving legal aid per 100,000 inhabitants	24 Efficiency of the criminal justice system 25 Efficiency of the civil justice system
14 Public level of confidence in the justice system 15 Public level of knowledge of legal aid services 16 Public perception of the independence of the justice system 17 Public perception of the fairness of judgments	26 World Justice Project Rule of Law Index 27 Non-discriminatory civil justice 28 Fair application of laws and respect for the rights of the accused 29 Impartiality of the criminal justice system 30 Perceived independence of the justice system 31 Reliability of police services

INPUT INDICATORS — OUTPUT INDICATORS — EFFECT/IMPACT INDICATORS

Financial Resources Indicators

The indicators concerning the public budget allocated to legal aid (per person and per recipient case) come from the *2016 EU Justice Scoreboard* and show the annual amount of the public budget earmarked for legal aid per inhabitant or recipient case.[9] The amounts do not include the administrative costs generated by the proceedings. They are useful for measuring individuals' access to justice and the financial means invested by the government to provide legal and justice services to individuals who do not have sufficient resources to gain access to such services otherwise.

In order to facilitate comparison, the amounts from the budgets of the various countries were converted into Canadian dollars in accordance with the exchange rate in effect on the date to which the data refer (Figures 2.1 and 2.2). The amounts were then divided by the population of the country or province (or the number of recipient cases) according to the official figures published by the organizations responsible for such statistics.

In the case of Australia, it was not indicated whether the data included administrative costs, and in that of New Zealand, the available data were limited to legal aid payments to professionals or accredited bodies. They did not include legal aid for criminal, family, or civil cases, or for cases before the Waitangi Tribunal. However, they did cover certain expenses that were not taken into account by other states.

In the cases of Australia, Canada, and the province of Quebec, there was a risk of double counting because these are federal states with several levels of government incurring justice expenditures. It is therefore important to exercise restraint when generalizing from these findings.

According to the estimate based on this indicator, Quebec dedicated approximately $18.50 per inhabitant per year to legal aid. This figure is similar to that for Canada, which was $19.30. The average of the sample countries was $18.70.

According to these findings, Canada and Quebec compared favourably with certain other countries (in particular, Germany, Belgium, France, and Luxembourg), but spent less than Sweden, the Netherlands, and Ireland.

Unfortunately, data on the budget allocated per "recipient case" were available for only four countries and Quebec. Quebec, at $661, was below the average, which was $830.

When these two indicators are used as the yardstick, great disparity is revealed. To gain a better picture of the situation in each country, other indicators are necessary. Indicator 18 in Table 2.2, which comes from the World Justice Project, assesses whether civil courts are accessible to and affordable for the public, whether the public is aware of the remedies available, and whether individuals have access to legal advice and representation. This indicator takes into account

Figure 2.1 **Public budget for legal aid, in dollars per inhabitant**

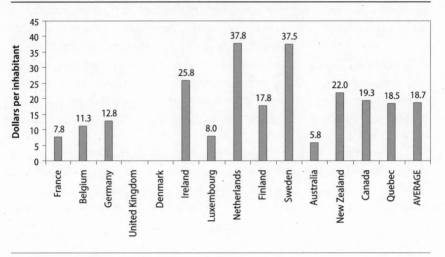

Source: Compilation by the authors.

Figure 2.2 **Public budget for legal aid, in dollars per case**

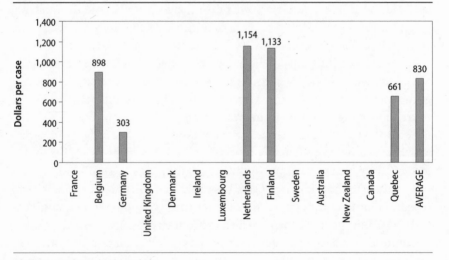

Source: Compilation by the authors.

the amount of general expenses incurred and any procedural obstacles (physical or linguistic barriers, etc.).[10] This indicator misses the issue of middle-class income access to justice.

According to the indicator, Canada was below average in relation to the countries covered by the study, close to Australia and Finland. Moreover, analysis

Figure 2.3 World Justice Project measurement of affordable justice

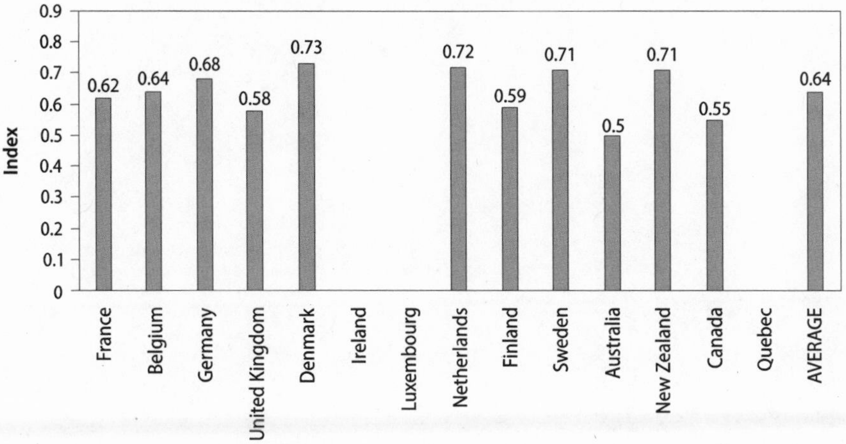

Source: Compilation by the authors.

of the data suggests that recourse to justice was relatively more costly for Canadians. It is interesting to see that Australia, a country with Anglo-Saxon roots like Canada, is at the same level, unlike civil law countries (Figure 2.3).

The main purpose of a survey done by the Canadian Forum on Civil Justice was to identify the direct and indirect legal costs incurred by individuals and by the state.[11] For example, our estimate is that Canadians spend on average $6,100 to deal with their civil legal problems.

Human Resources Indicators

The human resources indicators used in this study were related to the number of lawyers, judges, and prosecution system employees per 100,000 inhabitants; the number of lawyers per judge; and judges' gross salaries. These indicators provided information on resources (lawyers, judges, prosecution system employees) who are essential to the smooth functioning of justice systems and to ensuring that individuals have sufficient access to such public services. Figure 2.4 presents these indicators and proxy collected for our investigations.

The number of lawyers per 100,000 inhabitants is one measurement of the availability and accessibility of lawyers to inhabitants.[12] It must be handled with care and be accompanied by other indicators of financial inputs, such as the average costs to individuals and lawyers' average fees. Lawyers in different countries do not necessarily all have the same rights, and other stakeholders can play roles. The data must therefore be interpreted cautiously.

Figure 2.4 Human resources indicator – lawyers, judges, and other employees per 100,000 inhabitants

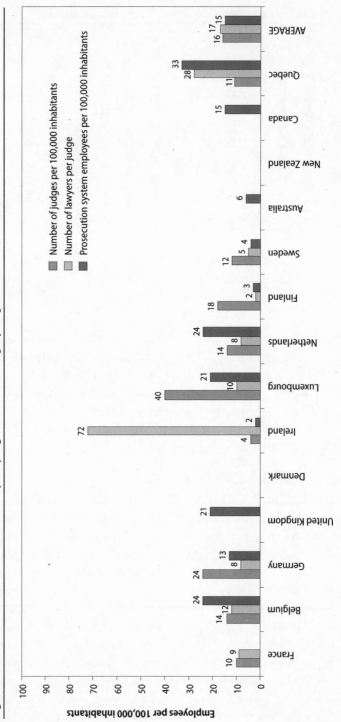

Source: Compilation by the authors.

Figure 2.5 **Human resources indicator – salaries in thousands of dollars**

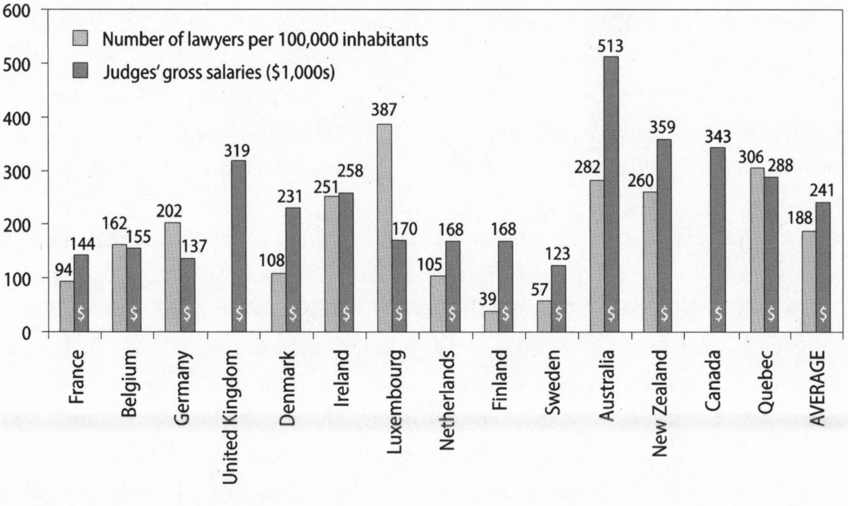

Source: Compilation by the authors.

The number of judges includes all the judges working in all of the courts, in both common law jurisdictions and specialized tribunals. According to the CEPEJ, prosecutors and their staff should be excluded from this indicator.[13] This indicator helps to measure individuals' access to judges, classified into three categories by the CEPEJ (full-time paid, part-time paid, and unpaid). In Quebec, for example, judges are classified as regular or supernumerary.

Figures 2.4 and 2.5 present different comparative statistics and indicators.

Quebec had approximately 11 judges per 100,000 inhabitants, which made it comparable to France, Sweden, Belgium, and the Netherlands, but below the average for the sample (which was slightly above 16 judges per 100,000 inhabitants) (Figure 2.4). However, Quebec does not have jurisdiction over all areas of justice, some of which fall under federal responsibility. The United Kingdom and Ireland, two common law countries, were also difficult to compare with the rest of the sample since 90 percent of their cases are handled by magistrates.

The number of lawyers per judge in Quebec was approximately 28, far more than the average of the countries in the sample, which was 17.

In accordance with the CEPEJ's methodology, the indicator measuring the number of prosecution system employees per 100,000 inhabitants included full-time prosecution system employees who were neither prosecutors nor judges' staff.[14] The ratios between the number of prosecutors and prosecution system employees vary widely between countries.[15]

Quebec was the jurisdiction with the largest number of prosecution system employees per 100,000 inhabitants (33). It was well above the average, and in this respect had similarities with Belgium and the Netherlands (Figure 2.4).

Regarding the indicator measuring judges' salaries (average gross full-time salary), the CEPEJ says that the data must be interpreted cautiously because salaries depend on many different factors. Exchange rate equivalencies do not necessarily take into account differences among countries in terms of the cost of living.

For a given reference period, judges of the highest court of Quebec received a gross salary that was 20 percent higher than the average salary of judges in other OECD countries, although the justices of Canada's highest court received an even higher salary. Indeed, Quebec offered a gross salary that was higher than that in a number of European countries, including France, Belgium, Germany, Denmark, Ireland, Luxembourg, the Netherlands, Finland, and Sweden. The Commonwealth countries, functioning with a parliamentary system and under the common law tradition, were those that offered the highest gross salaries. In contrast, the countries that used only civil law had the lowest gross salaries. Figure 2.5 illustrates these comparisons.

Material and Information Technology Resource Indicators

The following material and information technology resource indicators were used in this study: the number of courts per 100,000 inhabitants (information

Figure 2.6 **Number of courts per 100,000 inhabitants**

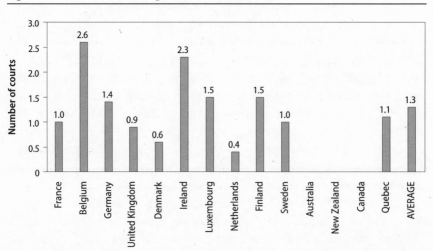

Source: Compilation by the authors.

available for Quebec but not for Canada), public access to laws and legal data, and use of information and communications technologies (ICTs). The number of courts can be a proxy measure of the geographical proximity of courts to the population, which facilitates assessment of the physical accessibility of law and justice (Figure 2.6). According to the CEPEJ's methodology, a court can be considered either as a legal entity or as a geographical site.[16] However, this indicator is not very relevant owing to the geographical, cultural, and historical differences specific to each country, which make comparison difficult.

Countries with very large territories, such as Canada and Australia, are extremely difficult to compare with small European countries, which have very different population densities. In Europe, there has been a trend towards reducing the number of courts, which has been particularly strong in France, Finland, and Sweden. This trend seems to be continuing, according to announced justice reforms. In contrast, physical access to the courts is subject to other constraints in a country like Canada, where remote regions can generate needs for additional courts despite a small population.

To gauge public access to laws and legal information, the World Justice Project measures the public availability of laws and legal information. This involves seeing whether such information is available in paper format or online, in language that is accessible to everyone, and in all of the official languages recognized in the country.[17]

Canada ranked well among the 113 countries in the World Justice Project sample with respect to the "open government" indicator, which assesses the level of publication of laws and government data (Figure 2.7). With an index of 0.69 (the maximum possible was 1.00), Canada was one of the top countries. Its performance was comparable with that of countries such as the United Kingdom, Denmark, Finland, France, and Belgium. New Zealand came first, with an index of 0.80.

The OECD has developed an indicator for measuring the use of ICTs in justice systems.[18] It evaluates the simple average of eight subindicators measuring courts' use of various electronic communications and information exchange technologies (electronic web forms, online case records [minutes], electronic records, etc.). As shown in Figure 2.8, a scale of 0 to 6 measures the level of implementation of ICTs. Greater use of technologies can be a way to improve public access to justice.[19]

Clearly, it seems that Quebec, and to a lesser degree Canada, performed at a level that is equal to or higher than the average of the countries in the sample for most of the input indicators. This means that both jurisdictions invested major resources in the justice system. In the next section, the output indicators will show the efficiency of those investments.

Figure 2.7 **Public access to laws and legal data (index)**

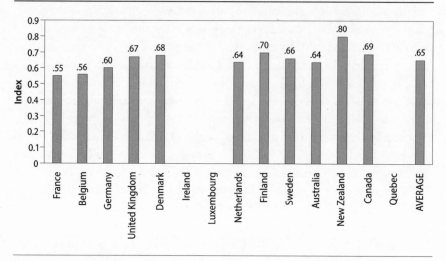

Source: Compilation by the authors.

Figure 2.8 **Use of information and communications technologies (index)**

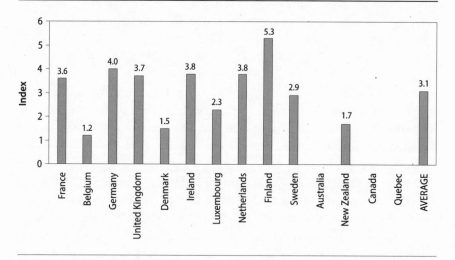

Source: Compilation by the authors.

Output Indicators

The output indicators essentially measure the length of justice proceedings, the accessibility of the justice system, and management of the caseload, that is, the cases that enter or could enter the justice system.

Length of Proceedings

Length of proceedings indicators are useful for measuring the efficiency of justice systems. The length of a proceeding is the time (expressed in days) necessary for a case to be resolved in court.[20] The indicators are the length of time taken to reach a decision at first instance and at second instance (in days); the length of time taken to reach a decision in the highest court (in days); the reasonable length of time for civil justice; and the reasonable length of time for administrative proceedings.

The OECD measures the length of civil proceedings using the following formula:[21]

$$Indicator = \frac{pending_{t-1} + pending_t}{incoming_t + resolved_t}$$

The length of proceedings is measured by the number of days that pass from the date proceedings are initiated to the date the case is resolved. In the cases of countries where there is no information available on the estimated or real length of time a case takes, the length was calculated using the value drawn from the estimated regression of the DB *(Doing Business)* length. The DB length is based on the hypothesis of a commercial dispute resolved at first instance (in days). It includes the length of time required to file and serve an action in justice, the length of time for the trial and to obtain a judgment, and the length of time for enforcement of the judgment.[22] Figure 2.9 illustrates these indicators.

A comparable measurement could not be obtained for Quebec because of the lack of precision of the data provided by the various courts. The OECD's definition concerning the measurement of this indicator does not make it possible to standardize data. Quebec's performance was lower than the average for the sample countries, taking longer to resolve civil cases at first instance. The province's performance was very similar to that of the United Kingdom.

Comparisons must be treated with circumspection, however. For Quebec, the data were less complete than for the OECD indicator because only litigated first-instance cases were taken into account, while the data for the OECD included all first-instance cases without any differentiation. Nonetheless, in civil cases in 2011–12, the length of time to resolve a case at second instance in Quebec was estimated at 304 days. The time required to resolve cases in the province was longer than the 261-day average found for the sample countries. Sweden (117 days), Denmark (127 days), and New Zealand (191 days) had the best performance, while Luxembourg, where it took 555 days, had the worst (Figure 2.10).

Figure 2.9 Length of proceedings by jurisdiction (number of days)

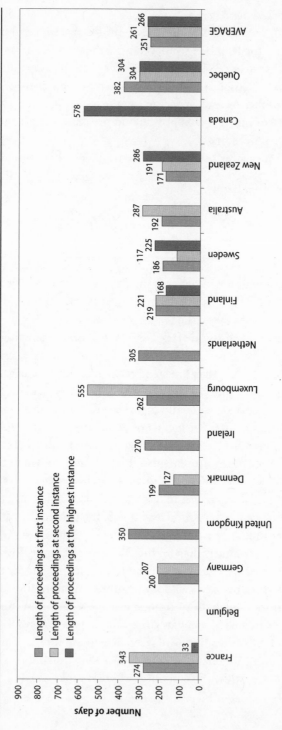

Source: Compilation by the authors.

Figure 2.10 **Reasonable length of time for civil justice and administrative proceedings**

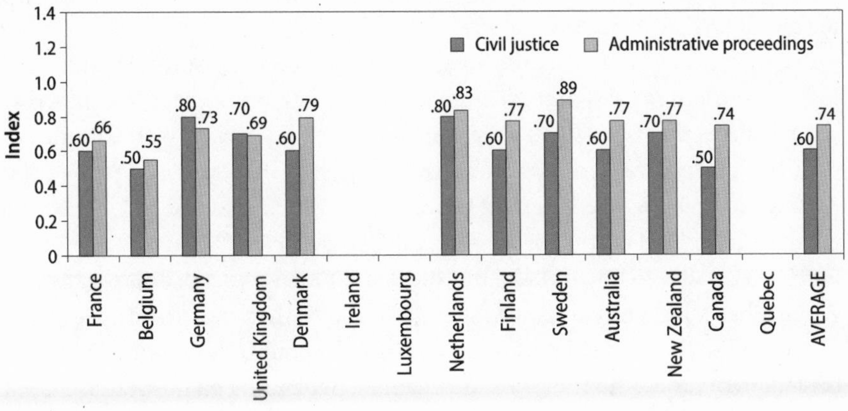

Source: Compilation by the authors.

The indicator, in terms of number of days, for the highest court was taken from the OECD's 2013 report on justice system performance. In Canada, the Supreme Court measures the average length of time in accordance with three periods: between the filing of and decision on the application for leave to appeal, between the date leave is granted and the hearing, and between the hearing of the appeal and the judgment.[23]

In 2011, the average length of time between the filing of and decision on the application was 125 days. The average time between the date leave was granted and the hearing was held was 265 days. The average time between the hearing and the judgment was 189 days. When the three periods are added together, the average time between the filing of the application for leave to appeal and the judgment was thus 19 months, that is, 578 days.

The Court of Appeal of Quebec is the highest court in Quebec. The data on Quebec were based on indicators 9 and 10, that is, on the length of time for a case to be resolved at second instance (304 days). Quebec's performance is fairly comparable with that of France and New Zealand but was slightly lower than the average, which was 315.7 days. Finland had the best result (168 days). However, time indicators must be treated with prudence because there is no guarantee that they are always based on the same kinds of measurements.

Finally, note that New Zealand uses an indicator that measures the average number of court events per case,[24] and the United Kingdom an indicator that measures the number of cases halted by the court, in addition to an indicator that measures hearing time and related court processes.[25] The Quebec Ministry of Justice's 2015/2020 strategic plan states the intention to improve the performance of the justice system by "developing and measuring key indicators of the performance of the justice system, in particular with respect to length of time for civil, penal and criminal case resolution."[26]

Regarding length of time, the World Justice Project measures whether civil justice proceedings and administrative proceedings are resolved within a reasonable time, that is, with no unreasonable delays.[27] Canada, with an index of 0.47, was in a relatively poor position. Those findings were consistent with earlier findings concerning the length of proceedings, which also placed Quebec at a relatively poor level in comparison with OECD countries. Canada's performance was fairly similar to that of Belgium (0.45) and Finland (0.57). This means that Canada has a long way to go to catch up to the Netherlands (0.76), Germany (0.75), and the United Kingdom (0.73). Since the countries do not all measure the length of proceedings in the same manner, depending on the points chosen as the beginning and end of justice proceedings, comparison is difficult.

Clearance Rate of Pending Cases

The rate of pending case resolution, generally known as the "clearance rate," is an indicator of whether a jurisdiction manages incoming and pending cases well. It also shows the speed with which jurisdictions manage to resolve cases. "When the clearance rate is about 100% or higher, it means the judicial system is able to resolve at least as many cases as come in. When the clearance rate is below 100%, it means that the courts are resolving fewer cases than the number of incoming cases." It is important to measure the rate each year because if a

Figure 2.11 **Clearance rate of pending cases (index)**

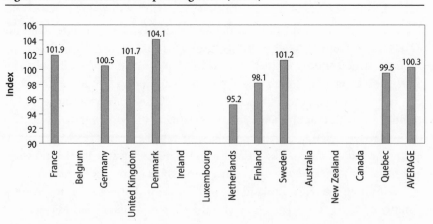

Source: Compilation by the authors.

jurisdiction has a rate lower than 100 percent over a number of consecutive years, it has management problems.[28]

The rate of criminal cases resolved at first instance in Quebec was 99.5 percent, which means that the province resolved fewer cases than the number of new cases filed each year (Figure 2.11).

Other Output Indicators

In addition to the indicators concerning the length and number of pending cases, this study looked at other output indicators: the number of cases in which legal aid was received per 100,000 inhabitants; the accessibility, impartiality, and efficiency of dispute resolution mechanisms; the efficiency of the criminal justice system; and the efficiency of civil justice.

The number of cases in which legal aid was received per 100,000 inhabitants is an indicator used by the CEPEJ.[29] When it is combined with an indicator measuring the amount allocated for legal aid, it makes it possible to calculate the average amount of legal aid provided per case. The CEPEJ makes a distinction between cases heard in court and those that do not go to court.[30] This distinction is also made respecting the budgets allocated because some states provide amounts to prevent disputes from ending up in court, and those amounts are not necessarily counted in the budget for legal aid.[31]

The data show that 2,776 cases per 100,000 inhabitants received legal aid in Quebec in 2012, that is, around 700 cases per 100,000 inhabitants, which was more than the average for the sample countries (2,091 cases per 100,000 inhabitants). However, data on this were available for only four countries (Belgium,

Figure 2.12 **Number of cases receiving legal aid, per 100,000 inhabitants**

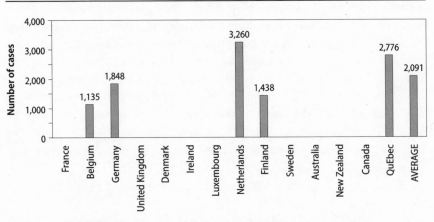

Source: Compilation by the authors.

Figure 2.13 **Accessibility, impartiality, and efficiency of dispute resolution mechanisms (index)**

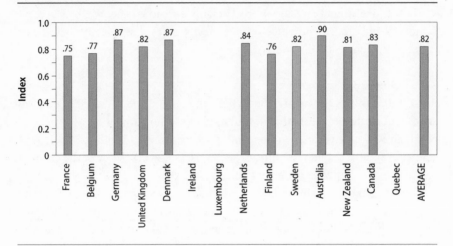

Source: Compilation by the authors.

Germany, the Netherlands, and Finland), which greatly limits its value as a means of comparison (Figure 2.12).

According to the survey by the Canadian Forum on Civil Justice, Canadians are inclined to use other avenues and tools to resolve disputes. Only 7 percent of respondents said they used the justice system. Similarly, while 33 percent of respondents said they had done research online, 58 percent of those reported that the information they had found had been useful. Among the 28 percent of respondents who had obtained help from an organization (union or rights advocacy group), 68 percent said that the advice had been useful. Of the 19 percent who had received legal advice from lawyers, 81 percent said that it had been useful. In contrast, 49 percent of respondents who had tried to resolve their problem through negotiation said that the attempt had not been successful.[32]

The indicator of the efficiency of the criminal justice system evaluates whether offenders are prosecuted and punished in accordance with the law and within a reasonable time.[33] Although Canada's score of 0.68 was close to the average, the World Justice Project noted that Canada did better in other categories. The efficiency and speed of Canada's criminal and penal justice system was comparable with that of Sweden (0.70), Germany (0.69), France (0.69), the Netherlands (0.65), and Belgium (0.65) (Figure 2.14). Finland stood out with a score of 0.80 (Figure 2.13).

The indicator for the efficiency of the civil justice system measures whether civil cases are dealt with efficiently, that is, whether they are resolved within a

Figure 2.14 Efficiency of the criminal justice system and civil justice (index)

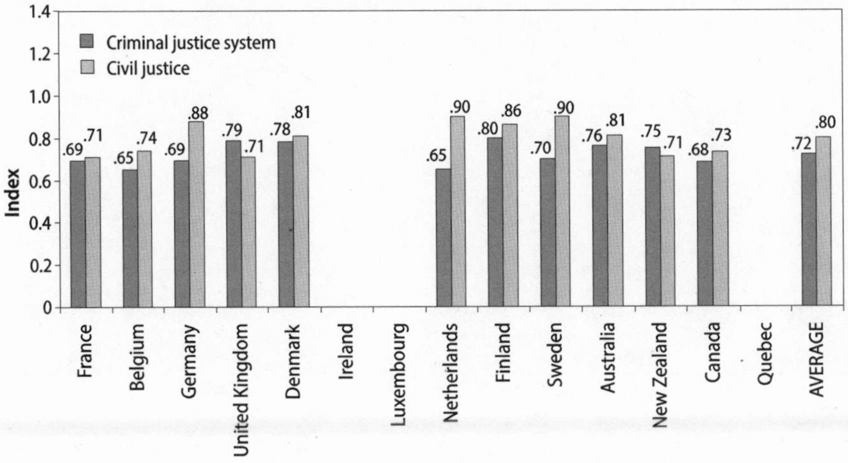

reasonable time.[34] The level of efficiency of civil justice in Canada (0.73) was comparable with that of New Zealand (0.75), France (0.69), the United Kingdom (0.79), and Belgium (0.74) (Figure 2.14). However, progress could be made to rise to the levels of the Netherlands (0.90), Sweden (0.90), Germany (0.88), Australia (0.81), and Denmark (0.81).

Indicators of Effect and Impact

An exact measurement of access to justice requires taking into consideration inhabitants' opinions about their justice system and the legal services offered by governments, with respect to civil, commercial, and administrative matters, and criminal and penal cases. The effect and impact indicators used in this study concern confidence, knowledge, perception, signs, access, enforcement, impartiality, and opinions about the justice system and its special features in relation to the general public.

The data on the level of public confidence in the justice system were taken from the United Nations *Human Development Report 2015*,[35] except for the data concerning Canada and Quebec. The data correspond to the percentage of people who answered yes to the Gallup World Poll question: "In this country, do you have confidence in the judicial system and courts?" Prudence is required when generalizing from these comparative findings because some of the data for Quebec were collected in 2016 while in the other cases they were collected in 2013.

Figure 2.15 **Public confidence in the justice system and knowledge of public legal aid (index)**

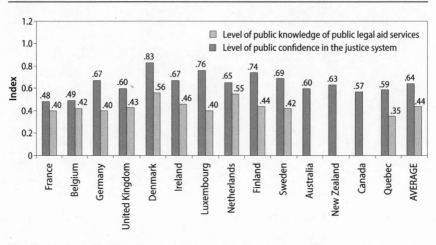

Source: Compilation by the authors.

The data for Quebec and Canada came from the findings of the General Social Survey on Social Identity.[36] The size of the sample (27,695 Canadians) was different from that of the Gallup World Poll, which was at least 1,000 respondents. Other data for Quebec were published in April 2016 in INFRAS Inc.'s *Enquête sur le sentiment d'accès et la perception de la justice au Québec.*[37] That survey found that in Quebec, the level of public confidence in the justice system was 59 percent (Figure 2.15). This was comparable with those of Canada, Australia, and the United Kingdom.

The data measuring public knowledge of public legal aid services came from two surveys. The questions asked in those two surveys were not the same, so it is important to remain cautious when using this comparison. The data for the European countries were gathered in the 2013 *Eurobarometer Report 385: Justice in the EU.*[38] In contrast, the data for Quebec were taken from the final report of the *Enquête sur le sentiment d'accès et la perception de la justice au Québec.*[39] The question asked was: "How would you rate your knowledge of the services offered by public legal aid?" (our translation). The respondents had to answer, "very good," "fairly good," "rather poor," or "none at all" (our translation).

Quebec ranked below average since only 35 percent of respondents said they had very good or fairly good knowledge of legal aid services (Figure 2.15). This percentage was comparable with the situation in France, Germany, and Luxembourg. In contrast, Denmark and the Netherlands were the two states whose citizens claimed to have the most knowledge about their country's public legal aid services. Quebec's poor performance is inconsistent with indicator 13 in Table 2.2, concerning the number of cases per 100,000 inhabitants in which legal aid was received, since the province's score was higher than average in that respect. However, it is important to take into consideration that in the European countries, the data refer to the percentage of the population that claimed to be informed about free legal aid services in their respective countries. This difference makes it difficult to perform a precise comparison with the data gathered for Quebec. That said, the data for the Netherlands showed once again that it seems to be a country where good legal aid services are offered, in terms of both quality and quantity.

The data on the public perception of the independence of the justice system (courts and judges) also came from two surveys of the public. The two surveys did not ask the same question, so it is important to use the comparison prudently. The data for the European countries were taken from the *Flash Eurobarometer Report 385*.[40] The same question was asked three times, with respect to three different jurisdictions: criminal and penal, administrative, and civil and commercial. The data combine the answers of people who answered, "very good" or "fairly good." In the end, the average of those three findings was used in this study, since the study done for Quebec made no distinctions concerning the type of jurisdiction.

For Quebec, we used the final report of the *Enquête sur le sentiment d'accès et la perception de la justice au Québec*.[41] The question that was asked concerned agreement with the statement "The justice system is independent from political powers" (our translation). The measurement used in this case was based on how many people said that they completely or partially agreed with the statement.

The finding was 51 percent, indicating that Quebec ranks far lower than the average for the sample jurisdictions, which was 70 percent (Figure 2.16). The difference was due in part to the fact that the question that was asked in the cases of the European countries was not the same, which means that generalizing from these findings must be done with care. Once again, the Netherlands stood out, with 81 percent. Finland and Denmark also had good scores (78 and 74 percent, respectively), while France and Ireland performed less well (63 and 67 percent, respectively).

The data on public perception of the fairness of the justice system came from the two above-mentioned surveys. As in the case of the independence of the justice system, the question was asked for each of three types of tribunal. In the case of Quebec, the question concerned agreement with the statement that judgments were fair. Respondents had to say how much they agreed with it. Once again, the measurement combined the percentages for the first two

Figure 2.16 **Public perception of the independence and the fairness of the justice system (index)**

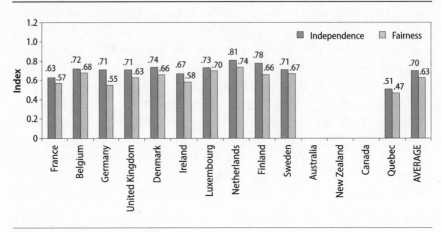

Source: Compilation by the authors.

options (partially or wholly in agreement). For the same reasons as before, prudence must again be employed when comparing the findings for this indicator. Quebec again ranked below average, with only 47 percent of respondents agreeing that judgments were fair (Figure 2.16).

The World Justice Project measures the strength of rule of law by taking into account the experiences and perceptions of the public and of legal experts around the world. Its report provides a view of the rule of law in each of the countries studied by ranking them in accordance with eight factors: constraints on government powers, absence of corruption, application of the principles of open government, respect for fundamental rights, order and security, regulatory enforcement, civil justice, and criminal justice. The findings come from surveys of over 100,000 people, including legal experts, in 102 different countries and jurisdictions. The ranking is from 0 to 1 (where 1 indicates the strongest rule of law). They are based on the answers of a representative sample of 1,000 people interviewed in the three largest cities of each country.

Canada ranked fourteenth out of the 102 countries analyzed by the World Justice Project (Figure 2.17).[42] Among the OECD countries included in the study, only France and Belgium ranked lower than Canada. This outcome was the product of the aggregation of all the subcategories taken into account. It must be noted, however, that the gap between the various countries was small.

The indicator of the perceived level of discrimination in the civil justice system is similar to the rule of law indicator but applies only to civil justice. Canada

Figure 2.17 **Rule of law and absence of discrimination in civil justice (index)**

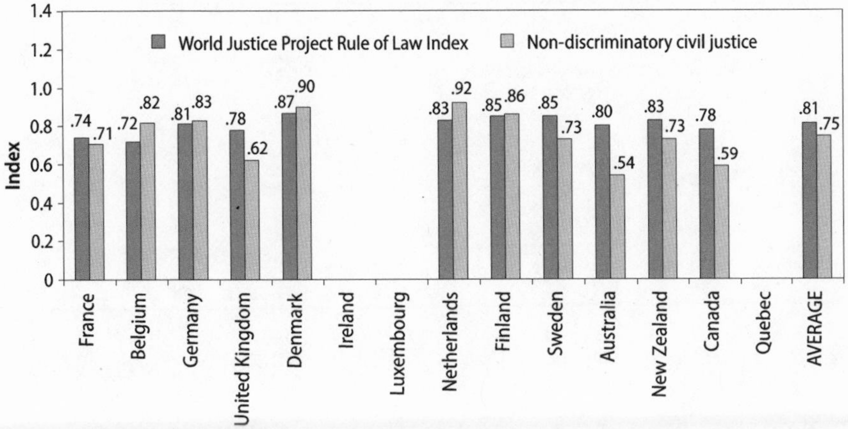

Source: Compilation by the authors.

(0.59) ranks lower than average with respect to equal treatment and absence of discrimination before civil courts. Australia (0.54) ranks below both Canada and the average for the sample. Denmark (0.90), the Netherlands (0.92), and Finland (0.92) stand out, with better scores than the other countries studied.

The indicator of the efficiency and quality of legal practices with respect to the fundamental rights of persons accused of an offence or crime measures respect for suspects and the absence of abusive treatment. Those rights refer to the presumption of innocence, the absence of arbitrary arrest, and the right to reasonable pretrial detention.[43] The compilations done in the framework of the World Justice Project rank Canada (0.74) below the average for the sample of countries (0.82) (Figure 2.18). The highest-ranking countries were Scandinavian: Finland (0.92), Sweden (0.90), and Denmark (0.89). France (0.73) was the only country in the sample whose performance was worse than Canada's, according to the World Justice Project data. Quebec's performance was similar to that of Canada.

Canada's criminal and penal system is not considered the most impartial (0.61) among the OECD countries. Perceptions regarding its impartiality are comparable with those of Australia (0.57), Belgium (0.58), and France (0.61) (Figure 2.18).

According to the European Commission, judicial independence "assures the fairness, predictability, certainty and stability of the legal system."[44] The indicator for evaluating public perceptions regarding the independence of the justice

Figure 2.18 **Fair application of laws and respect for the rights of the accused, and impartiality of the criminal justice system (index)**

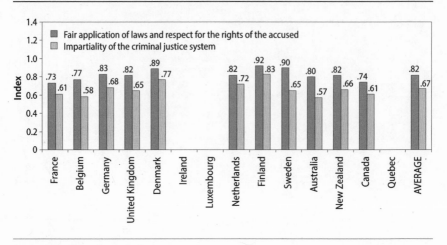

Source: Compilation by the authors.

system from influence by members of the government, individuals, and companies came from the World Economic Forum's *Global Competiveness Report.* A high score close to 7 corresponds to a positive perception, while a score near 1 indicates a critical view of such independence. The average score for the 144 countries studied was 3.9. The findings must be analyzed carefully because the sample used during the data gathering was mainly representative of companies active in certain traditional sectors of the economy, such as agriculture, manufacturing, non-manufacturing industries, and services.[45]

Canadians (6.2) perceive their justice system as independent from the influence of government, individuals, and companies; the score is the same as for the United Kingdom, Denmark, Sweden, and the Netherlands (Figure 2.19). The average for the countries in the sample was 5.9. New Zealand (6.7) and Finland (6.6) had the best scores. Quebec's score was different from that of Canada since it was below the average for indicator 16.

The indicator for measuring the reliability of police services also came from the World Economic Forum's *Global Competiveness Report.* The data were based on answers to the following question: "In your country, to what extent can police services be relied upon to enforce law and order?" A score close to 7 means that there is a positive perception of the reliability of police services, while values closer to 1 mean the perception is more negative. The average score for the 144 countries covered by the World Economic Forum survey was 4.3.[46]

Figure 2.19 **Perceived independence of the justice system and reliability of police services (index)**

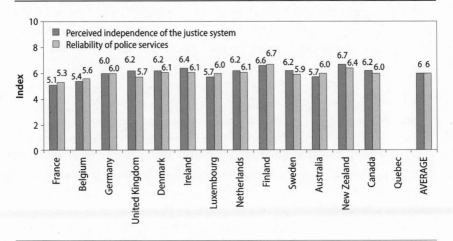

Source: Compilation by the authors.

With a score of 6.0, Canada ranked very slightly higher than the average for the OECD countries studied (5.99) (Figure 2.19). As with the preceding indicator, Finland and New Zealand were out in front, both with 6.7. France was at the back of the pack, with 5.3. Confidence in the reliability of the national police in Luxembourg, Australia, Germany, Denmark, Ireland, the Netherlands, and Sweden was comparable with that in Canada.[47]

In summary, it seems that the performance of Canada and Quebec is generally ranked lower than the average for the sample of countries in terms of both outcomes and effect and impact indicators. This finding is surprising in some respects since Quebec and Canada rank average, or even often above average, with respect to inputs.

Conclusion

Canada ranks around the middle of the sample countries regarding public access to laws and legal information (indicator 19), length of administrative proceedings (indicator 22), accessibility, impartiality and efficiency of dispute resolution mechanisms (indicator 23), perceived independence of the justice system (indicator 30), and reliability of police services (indicator 31). However, Canada scores lower than average with respect to affordable justice (indicator 18), efficiency of the criminal justice system (indicator 24), efficiency of the civil justice system (indicator 25), non-discriminatory civil justice (indicator 27), fair application of laws and respect for the rights of the accused (indicator 28), impartiality of the criminal justice system (indicator 29), and finally the effect and impact indicators of the World Justice Project Rule of Law Index (indicator 26). In addition, no reliable indicator or data could be found for Quebec or Canada on the use of information and communications technologies in justice systems.

It is crucial to develop indicators for measuring public confidence, satisfaction, knowledge, and perceptions. The theme of public confidence merits special attention owing to how Canada and Quebec scored in that respect. The governments of Canada and Quebec could take inspiration from the instruments developed by the European Commission, the Centre for Research in Public Law (Centre de recherche en droit public),[48] and the Canadian Forum on Civil Justice,[49] or through the *Enquête sur le sentiment d'accès et la perception de la justice au Québec.*[50]

It would be useful to develop and publish an annual compendium on the state and evolution of tracking indicators and benchmarks for access to justice. A comparative chronological approach should be given priority in order to measure and compare, over the years, the evolution of the performance of the Quebec and Canadian justice systems. It would also be useful to develop more detailed indicators for assessing how long it takes for justice proceedings to be completed. It takes more time in Quebec for court decisions to be rendered than it does in the sample OECD countries. These issues are directly related to the conclusions of the recent *Jordan* judgment.[51] More precise indicators are necessary to measure such times more accurately.

Notes

1 Giuliana Palumbo et al, "Judicial Performance and Its Determinants: A Cross-Country Perspective" (2013) OECD Economic Policy Papers No 5 ["Judicial Performance"]; European Commission, *Le tableau de bord 2014 de la justice dans l'Union européenne, COM(2014) 155 final, Communication de la Commission au Parlement européen, au Conseil, à la Banque centrale européenne, au Comité économique et social et au comité des régions* (Brussels: European Commission, 2014) [*2014 EU Justice Scoreboard*]; European Commission, *Le tableau de bord 2015 de la justice dans l'Union européenne, COM(2015) 116 final, Communication de la Commission au Parlement européen, au Conseil, à la Banque centrale européenne, au Comité économique et social européen et au comité des régions* (Brussels: European Commission, 2015) [*2015 EU Justice Scoreboard*]; European Commission, *Le tableau de bord 2016 de la justice dans l'Union européenne, COM(2016) 199 final, Communication de la Commission au Parlement européen, au Conseil, à la Banque centrale européenne, au Conseil économique et social européen et au comité des régions* (Brussels: European Commission, 2016) [*2016 EU Justice Scoreboard*]; Ingo Keilitz et al, "An Introduction to Selecting the Right Indicators to Improve Court Performance," *Just Development* (May 2014).

2 Organisation for Economic Co-operation and Development (OECD), *Glossary of Key Terms in Evaluation and Results Based Management* (Paris: OECD, 2002) at 29.
3 European Commission, *2016 EU Justice Scoreboard, supra* note 1 at 42–44.
4 Keilitz et al, *supra* note 1 at 1.
5 OECD, *supra* note 2.
6 *Ibid* at 29.
7 Palumbo et al, "Judicial Performance," *supra* note 1 at 37.
8 S. Helgason, "Benchmarking Experiences from OECD Countries" (Paper presented at the International Benchmarking Conference, Copenhagen, 20–21 February 1997) at 1.
9 European Commission, *2016 EU Justice Scoreboard, supra* note 1 at 21.
10 World Justice Project, *World Justice Project Rule of Law Index 2015* (Washington, DC: World Justice Project, 2015) at 164.
11 Trevor C.W. Farrow et al, *Everyday Legal Problems and the Cost of Justice in Canada: Overview Report* (Toronto: Canadian Forum on Civil Justice, 2016) at 11, 12–19, online: Canadian Forum on Civil Justice <http://www.cfcj-fcjc.org/sites/default/files//Everyday%20Legal%20Problems%20and%20the%20Cost%20of%20Justice%20in%20Canada%20-%20Overview%20Report.pdf>.
12 European Commission, *2016 EU Justice Scoreboard, supra* note 1 at 32.
13 European Commission, *2015 EU Justice Scoreboard, supra* note 1 at 39; CEPEJ (Commission européenne pour l'efficacité de la justice [European Commission for the Efficiency of Justice]), *Systèmes judiciaires européens – Édition 2014 (2012): efficacité et qualité de la justice* (Strasbourg: Conseil de l'Europe, 2014) at 9–10 [*Systèmes judiciaires européens*].
14 CEPEJ, *Systèmes judiciaires européens, supra* note 13 at 277; CEPEJ, *Note explicative à la grille pour l'évaluation des systèmes judiciaires – Cycle 2012–2014*, CEPEJ (2012) 13 Rev (Strasbourg: Conseil de l'Europe, 2013) at 14 [*Note explicative*].
15 CEPEJ, *Systèmes judiciaires européens, supra* note 13 at 282.
16 CEPEJ, *Systèmes judiciaires européens, supra* note 13.
17 World Justice Project, *supra* note 10 at 162.
18 Palumbo et al, "Judicial Performance," *supra* note 1 at 26.
19 Canadian Bar Association, *Justice pour tous: trouver l'équilibre* (Ottawa: Canadian Bar Association, 2013) at 10.
20 European Commission, *2015 EU Justice Scoreboard, supra* note 1 at 7–9.
21 Palumbo et al, "Judicial Performance," *supra* note 1 at 38.
22 *Ibid* at 50.
23 Supreme Court of Canada, "05 Average Time Lapses," SCC <https://www.scc-csc.ca/case-dossier/stat/cat5-eng.aspx>.
24 New Zealand, Ministry of Justice, *Statement of Intent 2013–2016* (Wellington, 2013).
25 United Kingdom, Ministry of Justice, *Business Plan 2012–2015* (London, 2012).
26 Quebec, Ministry of Justice, *Plan stratégique 2015/2020 du Ministère de la Justice du Québec* (Quebec City, 2016).
27 World Justice Project, *supra* note 10 at 164.
28 European Commission, *2015 EU Justice Scoreboard, supra* note 1 at 12.
29 CEPEJ, *Systemes judicaires européens, supra* note 13 at 76–81.
30 *Ibid*.
31 CEPEJ, *Note explicative, supra* note 14 at 8–9.
32 Farrow et al, *supra* note 11 at 9–10.
33 World Justice Project, *supra* note 10 at 164.
34 *Ibid*.

35 United Nations Development Programme, *Human Development Report 2015: Work for Human Development* (New York: United Nations, 2015) at 266.

36 Statistics Canada, "Table 1: Confidence in Institutions, by Province and Census Metropolitan Area, 2013," online: Statistics Canada <https://www150.statcan.gc.ca/n1/daily-quotidien/151207/t001a-eng.htm>.

37 INFRAS Inc., *Enquête sur le sentiment d'accès et la perception de la Justice au Québec, Rapport réalisé pour le Ministère de la Justice* (Lévis, QC, 15 April 2016).

38 European Commission, *Flash Eurobarometer 385: Justice in the EU* (Survey requested by the European Commission, Directorate-General for Justice, and coordinated by Directorate-General for Communication; November 2013) [*Eurobarometer 385*].

39 INFRAS Inc., *supra* note 37 at 20.

40 European Commission, *Eurobarometer 385, supra* note 38.

41 INFRAS Inc., *supra* note 37 at 13.

42 World Justice Project, *supra* note 10 at 6.

43 *Ibid* at 164.

44 European Commission, *2015 EU Justice Scoreboard, supra* note 1 at 45.

45 K. Schwab & X. Sala-i-Martin, *The Global Competitiveness Report 2013–2014* (Geneva: World Economic Forum, 2013).

46 *Ibid* at 425.

47 Schwab & Sala-i-Martin, *supra* note 45.

48 Pierre Noreau, "La scolarité, la socialisation et la conception du droit: un point de vue sociologique," (1997) 38 C de D 741; Pierre Noreau, "Accès à la justice et démocratie en panne: constats, analyses et projections" in Pierre Noreau, ed., *Révolutionner la justice* (Montreal: Thémis, 2010) at 13–43.

49 Farrow et al, *supra* note 11.

50 INFRAS Inc., *supra* note 37.

51 *R v Jordan*, [2016] 1 SCR 631.

3
Public Spending on Access to Justice
Where Do We Go from Here?

Lisa Moore and Mitchell Perlmutter

IN CANADA, AS IN other "law-thick" societies, the phrase "access to justice" is synonymous with the divide that we aim to bridge between the complex legal rules governing our societies and their ability to be indiscriminately and seamlessly accessed and applied.[1] That is, to improve access to the civil and family justice system, we must (as much as possible) remove the obstacles that prevent the law from doing what it was designed to do and from serving those it is meant to serve. For Canadians who try to resolve their civil and family justice problems either through the formal legal system or independent of it, the obstacles are numerous. They include challenges recognizing everyday legal problems, understanding law and legal processes, navigating courts, affording the cost of legal representation, and dealing with delays that inhibit timely resolution. Collectively, these obstacles have become the defining characteristics of Canada's current access to justice crisis in civil and family matters.

It is no secret that Canadians face significant challenges in achieving meaningful access to justice. The extent of Canada's access to justice crisis is a well-documented phenomenon that has been bemoaned by some of the highest members of our judiciary.[2] The Action Committee on Access to Justice in Civil and Family Matters (Action Committee), a national organization made up of leading voices from all justice sectors across Canada, described our civil and family justice system as "too complex, too slow and too expensive ... [and] too often incapable of producing just outcomes that are proportional to the problems brought to it or reflective of the needs of the people it is meant to serve."[3] This sentiment that our civil justice system is failing us is consistent with the mediocre rankings that it has received in recent years on international scales of efficiency and accessibility.[4]

Obstacles have long existed as a part of our legal framework, and the packaging of these obstacles as part of an access to justice problem is not new. The term "access to the courts of justice" originated in the 1840s,[5] and its successor, "access to justice," dates back to the 1970s.[6] While an open, fair, accessible legal system has endured as an ultimate goal of societies regulated by law, our understanding of what is meant by "access to justice" is very different. Once framed narrowly as access to formal court processes, the term has now broadened to incorporate a myriad of other considerations, including how legal problems trigger other problems, when and where people seek help for their problems, how the formal justice system facilitates problem resolution, and the costs (economic, temporal, social, and other) of experiencing legal problems. Furthermore, the body of research has expanded to include a variety of factors traditionally considered to be outside the scope of the law, such as poverty and residential location (i.e., rural or remote living).[7] With new ways of thinking about and understanding these challenges, our approach to addressing them must also evolve. A solution that may have been plausible yesterday may be less practical today.[8]

How do we know whether a proposed solution will result in impactful, comprehensive improvements? Les Jacobs posits that meaningful access to civil justice can be measured in terms of impacts or outcomes for people with legal problems: either it helps people resolve or address their problem, it can provide compensation or some other sort of remedy, or it can potentially have an impact or an effect in terms of legislation, policy, or social change.[9] It therefore stands to reason that at the root of our inability to solve the access to justice problem, there is a disconnect between our understanding of meaningful access to justice on the one hand and the ways that we work and spend to address this framing of our access to justice problem on the other. How we define the access to justice problem determines our approach to resolving it.

To better grasp why diverse and ongoing efforts have been unsuccessful in curbing our access to justice crisis, we must revisit some of the conclusions about the problem borne out through research and public discourse. In order to determine where we go from here, we must first discuss where we are, how we got here, and the extent of the problems that we are dealing with in order to inform a path forward. This chapter will begin by examining how the framing of Canada's access to justice problem has evolved, and its impact on public spending. It will then explore issues related to the cost of law and where individuals spend money on the resolution of legal problems in the context of our present-day understanding of access to justice. With respect to public and individual spending, this chapter will argue that our spending on justice fails to accord with our current definition of access to justice, and that our policies, spending, and efforts must also evolve to achieve meaningful access to civil justice. It will conclude by looking ahead to some investments that have the potential to reduce costs and achieve immediate and meaningful improvements in access to justice.

Evolution of Our Understanding of Access to Justice

> *Given one hour to save the world, I would spend 55 minutes defining the problem and 5 minutes finding the solution.*
>
> – ALBERT EINSTEIN

In describing the development and evolution of the access to justice movement, authors Mauro Cappelletti and Bryant Garth classically identified three "waves." The first wave was marked by the emergence of legal aid in the postwar period as a program focused on providing access to legal representation in the courts for the economically disadvantaged.[10] Focusing more on "diffuse interests," the second wave, by contrast, saw movement towards public interest litigation and class actions as part of a shift in focus from individual to collective rights.[11] Finally, beginning to emerge in the 1970s, the third wave saw the development of a more holistic and fully integrated approach to access to justice beyond case-centred advocacy.[12] Some proponents of the access to justice movement have argued that we are currently riding this "third wave"[13] – that is, our efforts in addressing access to justice reform define the problem in terms of substantive inequality rather than mere exclusion from legal institutions. Other proponents have argued that we are on the brink of a "fourth wave," to the extent that our efforts at reform are beginning to focus more on users of the system rather than those who administer it.[14]

Some two and a half decades after Cappelletti and Garth mapped the progression of access to justice through three waves, Roderick A. Macdonald proposed five waves spanning approximately ten years each, beginning in the 1960s and continuing into the 2000s.[15] He explains that in the first wave, cost, delay, and complexity in the legal system were seen as the primary impediments, thus driving a focus on investments in community clinics, certificates, and other measures aimed at facilitating formal legal representation. In the second wave, access to justice took on a more nuanced meaning and incorporated a shift in thinking towards institutional redesign and modification of rules and streamlining of processes to make them fairer.[16] In the third wave, developments such as alternative dispute resolution (ADR) and public legal education and information (PLEI) began sprouting.[17] In the fourth wave, access to justice came to be identified as a complex problem that required multiple points of entry to the legal system and a collective understanding of legal problems and the law. Finally, Macdonald's fifth wave contemplates access to justice as a culmination of preventative law, better public legal education, and "enhancing access to official and a myriad of unofficial institutions where law is made and administered."[18]

Increasingly, through discourse and research, we have been able to view the challenges of engaging and accessing legal services and information from a much broader vantage point – Cappelletti and Garth's fourth wave or Macdonald's fifth wave. We are beginning to recognize the ubiquitous nature of legal problems and the manner in which they intersect with the mundane transactions of everyday life. We are also beginning to understand the cumulative costs of legal problems in terms of emotional health and physical well-being. Findings from the Action Committee and the Canadian Forum on Civil Justice (CFCJ) helped bring these ancillary costs to the forefront of public consciousness.[19]

In addition to the financial, physical, and emotional costs associated with everyday legal problems, we also now know more about the associated temporal costs. A substantial number of respondents from a 2009 legal needs study reported that it took them more than three years to resolve their civil legal problem.[20] Furthermore, respondents from the 2013 National Self-Represented Litigants Project (NSRLP) study on self-represented litigants (SRLs) expressed similar frustration about the length of time that their civil legal problems dragged on.[21] Within the formal justice stream, users may also encounter setbacks owing to factors such as delays in court trials,[22] dated service delivery methods,[23] and exhausted funds for legal representation.[24] Adding to the complexity of this problem, language barriers, cultural factors, and location may also influence the associated temporal costs of resolving legal problems.[25]

Though we now understand that access to civil justice requires multi-faceted and holistic solutions, our current efforts to address the access to justice crisis seem to evidence an antiquated understanding of the problem. In 2017, the CFCJ produced the first *Canadian Access to Justice Initiatives: Justice Development Goals Status Report*.[26] The purpose of the *Status Report* was to present a snapshot of how organizations across Canada were responding to the nine goals envisioned in the Action Committee's *Roadmap for Change* report.[27] While some findings from the *Status Report*'s national survey are encouraging, they overwhelmingly suggest that much of today's work on the access to justice front conforms to older ways of understanding the problem. For example, while a majority of respondent organizations (60 percent) indicated that they offer some form of PLEI, only 31 percent said that they use new and innovative legal service delivery methods.[28] Furthermore, while we now understand that everyday legal problems are capable of affecting Canadians' physical and mental health, only 25 percent of respondents indicated that they collaborate with medical or healthcare organizations.[29]

The Disconnect between Spending Habits and Our Understanding of the Problem

Recognizing where we are today, how the framing of access to justice has evolved, and understanding the extent of the barriers that persist are prerequisites to charting a path forward. The fundamental problem is that our justice spending patterns as a collective and our present-day efforts to improve access to justice still adhere to traditional "old wave" understandings of the access to justice problem. This becomes apparent when we look at the manner in which the Canadian government expends resources on legal aid, court services, tribunal services, and public legal education and information.

Consider as an example the contributions that provincial governments have made to legal aid programs in recent years. In Ontario, the government increased the funding of Legal Aid Ontario (LAO) by $153 million from 2013 to 2017,[30] but then reduced it by $133 million in 2019.[31] While smaller in scale, the Alberta and British Columbia governments also committed additional legal aid funding for the 2018 fiscal year.[32] While government contributions to legal aid plans are important and should be commended, it is important to recognize that they still benefit only low-income individuals.[33] Thus, what critics have called for is a more comprehensive overhaul of the legal system, which would incorporate more technology and information sharing in the provision of legal services.[34] At the end of the day, provincial legal aid programs need to contemplate ways of effecting broad-scale systems-level change if they are to move beyond a first-wave approach to addressing a fifth-wave conception of access to justice.

In addition to legal aid spending, another major area of government expenditure that evidences a first-wave treatment of the access to justice problem is court services. The federal and provincial/territorial governments share responsibility for the administration of Canada's system of courts. A 2014 Fraser Institute report on court services expenditures in Canada estimated total spending to be $4.5 billion for the 2011/12 fiscal year.[35] This figure represents a marked rise from the $1.15 billion figure cited for the 2002/03 fiscal year in a 2008 Department of Justice report.[36] While the cost figures from both reports are inclusive of both criminal and civil court services spending, we know that civil cases comprise a majority of the overall cases processed within our court system. For example, Statistics Canada estimates that there were about 914,000 active civil cases in Canada in the 2017/18 fiscal year,[37] compared with 345,000 adult criminal court cases in the same year.[38]

Operating beneath the Canadian courts as agencies that perform specialized adjudicative, regulatory, and licensing functions, administrative tribunals are also a significant area of government expenditure within the justice sector. Inasmuch as there are thousands of administrative tribunals and agencies across the country, it would be difficult to tabulate their collective annual expenditures. In Ontario alone, there are over 500 agencies, boards, and commissions.[39] That said, one can be certain that expenditures on tribunal services represent a substantial proportion of overall justice services expenditures in Canada. For example, the Immigration and Refugee Board (IRB), Canada's largest tribunal, alone reported over $160 million in operating expenses in the 2017/18 fiscal year.[40] Similarly, the Social Justice Tribunals of Ontario, which comprises eight adjudicative tribunals, reported a total of $51 million in operating expenses in the same fiscal year.[41]

For all this justice sector spending on courts, tribunals, and administrative boards, how much access to justice bang are we getting for our public spending bucks? When thinking about access to justice, we need to ensure that public spending on justice contributes to improving efficiency and ease of problem resolution within the traditional system, and also improves pathways for problem resolution outside of the traditional legal system. In terms of Macdonald's fifth-wave framing of access to justice, this means enhancing access to both formal and informal legal structures and institutions. We continue to see, however, that our legal structures are operating in antiquated ways, resulting in greater costs for litigants. In 2020, a time when you can access a digital wallet, send digital information rapidly across the globe, and track the location of the International Space Station online in real time, many courts across Canada still accept documents only in hard copy format or via fax.[42] Furthermore, many, if not most, courts do not offer options for remote appearances.[43] All in all, this divide between the ways we connect and interact in today's "flattened world"[44] and the limitations to these exchanges within our legal system are striking. If the technological limitations in our court structures are not addressed, the resulting delays and inefficiencies will continue to have negative cost repercussions.[45]

With respect to our courts and tribunals, the *Roadmap for Change* report asserts that the problem is not with quality but with accessibility.[46] While Macdonald's second-wave conception of access to justice identifies a focus on institutional redesign, the Action Committee report goes beyond a top-down approach to encourage a shift towards developing and positioning courts and tribunals as accessible "multi-service centres" that are among the many avenues available for resolving legal disputes.[47] Courts, tribunals, and administrative boards are an important part of our legal framework and should therefore be funded in a way that allows them to be user-friendly and reflective of modern society. Additional public spending on justice would need to be based on those goals in order to align with the current wave of thinking about access to justice. Most people do not want to have to resolve their problems in court or with a lawyer.[48] Furthermore, based on our current understanding of legal problems, we know that most serious civil and family justice problems begin long before they make their way through the formal court system.[49] Thus, where possible, spending in access to justice should also target early resolution outside of the formal justice system, when costs are lowest.[50]

Beyond courts and tribunal services, spending on government-funded PLEI organizations also appears to be lagging behind our modern understanding of the access to justice crisis. Across Canada, there are at least twenty government-funded PLEI organizations that provide an array of programs, resources, and services to consumers.[51] From a costs perspective, it is difficult to provide an accurate picture of what these organizations' cumulative expenditures are. However, expenditures range on average from a few hundred thousand dollars to a few million dollars annually per organization. The variance in spending can be attributed to the size of the organization, the number of people it services, and the breadth of its service deliveries. For example, Legal Info Nova Scotia, a small PLEI organization, spent approximately $373,000 in the 2018/19 fiscal year.[52] By contrast, the Justice Education Society of British Columbia, a larger PLEI organization, spent approximately $3.1 million in the previous fiscal year.[53]

The overarching goal of all these organizations is to equip individuals with legal literacy skills that will enable them to effectively address their legal issues. The challenge in one respect lies in effecting a holistic approach that embodies a shift from Macdonald's third-wave investment in PLEI for the delivery of general legal information to a fifth-wave enhancement of information and tools for preventative law, building legal capability, and addressing the various legal and non-legal dimensions of justiciable problems. The second issue is that there is a lack of solid empirical evidence to corroborate the ability of PLEI services to sufficiently deliver on these objectives.[54] Once we know more about their effectiveness, we should tailor PLEI programs to align with our current understanding of the ways in which people access information, how they experience everyday legal problems, and the associated costs.

According to data from the CFCJ's *Status Report,* only 41 percent of respondent PLEI organizations provided public legal information or resources related to the non-legal aspects of legal problems.[55] If, in accordance with the fifth-wave understanding of access to justice, we acknowledge that legal problems are "wicked problems"[56] that do not exist in a vacuum and have non-legal financial, physical, and emotional dimensions, then there should be an increased focus on addressing their associated non-legal aspects. The *Status Report* also revealed that only 48 percent of respondent PLEI organizations provide information or resources on problem prevention. Given what we now know about the "trigger effect"[57] of legal problems, PLEI organizations should also consider placing greater emphasis on problem prevention.

All these justice sector expenditures highlight another important fact: law is expensive. As Gillian Hadfield explains, "[T]he cost of law is the product of the complexity of law and the amount of legal process required to get an outcome."[58] Maintaining our complex legal infrastructure requires public spending at various levels. Similarly, on an individual level, we know that engaging with the formal justice system can be costly. In addition, it seems that for some litigants, the more they spend and rely on lawyers for the resolution of legal problems, the less satisfied they are with outcomes. In the NSRLP Report, for example, there was a prevailing view among respondents that the legal services they paid for simply did not represent value for money.[59] This should perhaps come as little surprise, given the cost of legal representation in Canada. Data from the 2019 *Canadian Lawyer* Magazine Legal Fees Survey revealed that the national average hourly rate for lawyers ranged from $195 (1 year call) to about $450 (20+ year call).[60] Given what we now understand about access to justice and the complex dimensions of legal problems, in order to assist individuals who experience serious civil and family justice problems, our efforts must target ways to address problems that do not rely exclusively on lawyers.

Where the legal problem does not require the assistance of a lawyer, paralegal fees can also be a substantial monetary cost that litigants incur. As a means of combatting the access to justice crisis, provincial regulators have given paralegals more power in recent years to provide an array of legal services. In Ontario, for example, paralegals are now authorized to provide legal representation in Small Claims Court, for matters under the *Provincial Offences Act,* on summary conviction offences, and before administrative tribunals.[61] Furthermore, there were recommendations by the Ontario Ministry of the Attorney General in the Bonkalo Report for paralegals to be able to deliver certain family legal services.[62] Although engaging paralegals may be a less costly option for some, David Wiseman points out in "Paralegals and Access to Justice for Tenants" (Chapter 8 in this volume) that paralegals may still not be a viable alternative for some low- and middle-income earners. Nevertheless, given their lower fees and the general level of public satisfaction with their services, paralegals may offer some relief for litigants who can afford to use their services and whose legal problems fall within their ambit.[63]

In addition to paying legal professional fees, litigants wishing to access and enforce their legal rights should also expect to pay an assortment of court fees. Most courts and some administrative tribunals have fee tables that delineate the various costs associated with different court processes. For example, the commencement fee for filing a statement of claim in court may be as low as $100 or as high as $750, depending on the province and level of court.[64] Other common court fees pertain to things like filing applications, commencing motions, setting trials, conducting searches, requisitioning orders, and paying experts. Of the various court fees listed, perhaps the most costly are trial fees, which can cost litigants upwards of $500 per day of trial.[65] When tallied together, these administrative fees can impose a substantial cost burden on litigants.

A comprehensive assessment of justice system costs must also consider the time spent dealing with legal problems – temporal costs. Within the formal justice system, temporal costs are affected by factors such as delays in court trials,[66] antiquated service delivery methods,[67] and a lack of funds for legal representation.[68] Even without the challenges of navigating a complex justice landscape, resolving a justiciable problem can be time-consuming. The temporal costs of justice need to be considered when discussing ways to improve efficiency and make the most of different spending choices within the justice system. Adding to the complexity of this problem, legal consciousness and legal capability influence points of entry into the justice system,[69] while the ability to receive legal assistance or representation affects the length of time spent addressing a problem.[70] Language barriers, cultural factors, and location[71] may also influence the associated temporal costs of resolving legal problems. Ultimately, if the temporal costs of justice are to be reduced in a major way, administrators of the justice system must put into action strategies to reduce the time between problem recognition and resolution.[72]

All in all, as Trevor Farrow has noted, "the gap between what people need and what they can access and afford is significant and growing."[73] Nevertheless, a first-wave approach to spending that exclusively and drastically seeks to reduce the costs that individuals pay to access the formal justice system also presents problems. As Fabien Gélinas and colleagues explain, if litigation is too cheap or too accessible, the court system may be overburdened.[74] Further, research shows that the more people interact with the courts, the more likely they are to see them as unfair.[75] Finally, and perhaps most importantly, we now understand that legal problems do not exist in a vacuum and may also be seen as health problems, social welfare problems, and myriad other problems. As a stand-alone measure, freer access to the courts will fail to address the complex multi-dimensional realities of legal problems. According to Farrow, "to the extent that we try to solve all social issues with legal tools, or to the extent that we do not see social issues as having legal components, much is missed."[76]

The challenge in delivering an accessible justice system lies in striking a balance between a functioning, structured, fair legal framework and ensuring various paths to affordably and satisfactorily resolve legal (and related non-legal) problems.

Changing Policy and Spending Habits in Line with Our New Understanding of Access to Justice

Recognizing that a new paradigm for access to justice has emerged around the concept of "everyday justice,"[77] we are faced with the question of how to recalibrate our policies and spending habits to accord with our new understanding of the problem. As Jerry McHale argues in Chapter 12, the challenge in many respects lies in our resistance to doing away with status quo and embracing a new way of doing things. We are aware of the problems we face and much of what is needed to address them; what we have not done is bridge the divide between recommendations and implementation. In order to bridge this chasm and effectively address the implementation gap, we must reorient our policy and spending habits in a way that reflects a broadly defined view of the problem.

From the perspective of policy, the first step towards making positive change begins with the economics of justice. Put candidly, policy governing the provision of legal services must do a better job of adapting to the economic realities of our rapidly changing global marketplace. "Law and economics" academics like Gillian Hadfield have argued that our traditional approach of a closed legal profession no longer works, and that our legal infrastructure must do more to facilitate innovation and investment.[78] On a practical level, this would mean harnessing market incentives to invent more effective and cost-efficient rules and regulatory systems.[79] If the public is to have confidence in the administration of justice, the legal profession must proactively catch up to the expectations in the marketplace.

It was with this recognition that the Canadian Bar Association launched its Futures initiative in 2014, which sought to develop a framework for leveraging technology and new modes of business practice as a means of facilitating access to justice. One of the main recommendations stemming from the final report is to allow for the creation of alternative business structures (ABSs), which would permit non-lawyer investment in legal practice.[80] Upon registering as an ABS, the legal corporation would be permitted to share fees with non-lawyers within the confines of a regulated environment. From an access to justice perspective, the benefits of such an arrangement are promising. Non-lawyer investment in the provision of legal services will presumably drive down costs and allow for collaboration, innovation, and entrepreneurship in a rapidly globalizing legal marketplace. The experience of this type of regulatory liberalization in places like Australia and the United Kingdom has been generally positive, and has led to significant innovation and greater access to justice.[81] That said, some jurisdictions have been ambivalent about embracing an ABS model due to the regulatory concerns it poses, particularly where there is non-lawyer majority ownership.[82]

Independent of the economics, multidisciplinary programs and centres that offer avenues to address overlapping issues have also shown promise as worthwhile investments.[83] A complex family problem, for example, that involves a domestic violence issue that in turn results in child custody and employment problems could potentially be addressed by a multidisciplinary team operating in one location.

A similar "systems shift" in thinking has also caught hold in the healthcare sector. In 2009, the Canadian Institutes of Health Research (CIHR) released the first part of its five-year strategic plan focused on fostering innovative research to better the Canadian healthcare system.[84] One of the strategic directions adopted by the report involved partnering with private sector organizations to support innovation and commercialization breakthroughs.[85] The CIHR subsequently reaffirmed this market-based strategic goal in its 2015 report, recognizing that collaboration with the private sector is needed in order to "move health knowledge along the innovation pipeline."[86] Fortunately for us, the Canadian medical space has responded in kind to the CIHR's call for innovation, which has led to a boom in the Canadian medical start-up ecosystem.[87] The rise in Canadian-made healthcare innovations can be attributed in large part to a collaborative financing platform launched in September 2014 between the Funding Portal Inc. and the University Health Network. This financing platform was established as a means of improving access to capital and commercialization opportunities for innovators in the Canadian healthcare sector.[88]

In addition to focusing more on an economics-based view of legal service delivery, the government should also consider changing where it allocates resources towards the resolution of everyday legal problems. As the Action Committee points out, most justice sector funding is devoted to the resolution of legal problems at the back-end stage. The problem, however, is that only a small portion of legal problems (6.5 percent) actually reaches the formal justice system.[89] Thus, if the justice system is to reduce costs and maximize the effectiveness of its resources, it should adopt a front-end focus on problem prevention and early resolution.[90] A central component of this involves investing in PLEI resources and programs that will enable individuals to spot their legal problems and build legal capability to effectively address them early on. After all, the Ontario Civil Legal Needs Project's 2010 report revealed that the longer legal problems linger, the more they tend to cascade into greater problems over time for individuals and their families.[91]

On a practical level, what type of front-end legal service delivery model should the government consider investing in? Both the Connecting Ottawa project and the Legal Health Check-up (LHC) project offer exemplary models of inexpensive approaches that facilitate early-stage legal problem and non-legal problem resolution at a community level.[92] For example, the more recent LHC model adopted an integrated and holistic approach to legal service delivery by developing partnerships between legal aid clinics and trusted intermediaries.[93] It used a special intake form to identify individuals' legal and associated non-legal problems. In the event that non-legal problems were identified at intake, the legal clinic would then make a referral to one of its intermediary service agencies. During the initial six-month implementation period of the project, the twelve participating LHC clinics established 125 partnerships and facilitated the completion of over 1,700 LHC forms.[94] Further, from a user perspective, we know the LHC system worked because it was viewed favourably by participating clinics and intermediaries, and most LHC clients said they would definitely return to the clinic with a problem in the future.[95]

Medical-legal partnerships (MLPs) offer promise as another worthwhile front-end integrated service delivery model for government investment. The MLP model embraces the "new-wave" principles of innovation, integration, and collaboration by bringing legal services into healthcare settings to address the social determinants of health. Under the MLP model, "triage" lawyers provide services and referrals within healthcare settings, and "triage" healthcare professionals are trained to screen patients for potential legal problems.[96] Although there are only a handful of MLPs in Canada, the success of the model in the United States is well documented. A 2010 pilot study of MLPs in pediatrics, for example, found that they decreased barriers to healthcare and increased access to legal and social services.[97] Furthermore, a 2013 paper found that existing data point to MLP's as "a promising innovation ... [that] should be scaled up to improve care at the patient, institution, and policy level."[98] Finally, despite the paucity of data concerning Canadian MLPs, we know from the SickKids MLP that the model has seen a certain degree of success in Canada as well.[99]

Beyond the work of the LHC and SickKids MLP pilot projects, we are starting to see a new theory of change emerge in Canada with respect to developments such as the Reforming the Family Justice System (RFJS) initiative in Alberta. Stemming from a recognition that family justice issues are complex and multi-faceted, the RFJS initiative established itself with a mandate to effect systems-wide change in the Alberta family justice system.[100] It has partnered with various justice system stakeholders (e.g., courts, government, the legal community, and social and health organizations) to ensure that a wide array of resolution and post-resolution support services are available for users and their families. The theory behind the RFJS initiative is that lasting reform can be achieved only when legal and non-legal institutions work together as part of an integrated service delivery approach. At the end of the day, instead of simply feeding the legal aid machine to expand certificate services, provincial governments should consider devoting resources to projects such as the RFJS initiative, which actively embrace the new-wave approach in access to justice thinking.

While there is ample evidence of the success of alternative service delivery models such as LHC and MLPs, there is still a lot that is unknown within the access to justice landscape. In order to understand what works and what opportunities are available for innovation, it is important for governments, nonprofits, researchers, the bar, the judiciary, and other justice stakeholders to work together to promote research and information sharing. As it is, only about one-thirteenth of all law-related research funding in Canada goes to access to justice research.[101] The Action Committee's *Roadmap for Change* report, the Canadian Bar Association's *Reaching Equal Justice* report, and the work of the Canadian Forum on Civil Justice (CFCJ) and others highlight the importance of research, information sharing, and benchmarking on best practices to help advance access to justice.[102] The problem is that there is still a lack of coordinated data on the effectiveness of legal service delivery methods. According to the CFCJ *Status Report,* only 47 percent of respondent organizations reported having a standard set of metrics or benchmarks to evaluate the success of their activities.[103] Without knowing what works and why it works, it is difficult to gauge what adjustments are needed, how they will be received, and what impact they will have. Research and benchmarking are needed for substantive, evidentiary conclusions about ways to make services more efficient, effective, and inexpensive. Ultimately, justice stakeholders must do a better job of tracking what developments are working and disseminating that information as part of a coordinated research effort.

Conclusion

Thanks largely to the research of organizations like the Action Committee, the CBA, and the CFCJ, we are beginning to understand the access to justice problem in Canada from a new-wave perspective – that is, we now recognize the pervasiveness of legal problems and their far-reaching consequences. There is, however, as academics such as Jerry McHale have described, a fundamental gap between what we understand to be the case and what we are doing in practice. This implementation gap is apparent in individual and particularly government spending habits, which, as this chapter argues, largely conform to an "old-wave" understanding of the access to justice problem. At the government level, there is a need to channel efforts and spending in ways that support broad-scale projects that aim to effect systems-level change. From the perspective of the individual, litigants are made to rely too heavily on legal counsel to solve their problems in lieu of alternative (and less costly) holistic strategies that actually contextualize the problem.

As a means of bridging the implementation gap and reconciling this discrepancy between understanding and action, this chapter has argued that governments should reorient their policies and spending habits in a number of ways. First, from a broad policy perspective, they should consider following the examples of jurisdictions such as Australia and the United Kingdom in liberalizing the legal marketplace to allow for greater investment and innovation in the provision of legal services. Given the success of the alternative business structures model in other jurisdictions, it is also a worthwhile consideration for provincial regulators. Second, recognizing the trigger effect of legal problems, the government should adopt a front-end focus on prevention and early resolution, as called for by the Action Committee. This means investing in resources that enable individuals to spot problems early on and strategize accordingly. Third, from a service delivery perspective, governments should be open to investing in alternative models of legal services delivery, such as LHC, medical-legal partnerships, and the RFJS initiative, which actively embrace the new theory of access to justice thinking. Finally, in exploring the potential for innovation moving forward, governments must be open to promoting the sharing of research with other justice stakeholders as part of a collaborative effort.

Notes

The authors are grateful to Nicole Aylwin, Trevor C.W. Farrow, and Lesley Jacobs for their comments on an early draft of this chapter.

1   The concept of the "law-thick" world has been used by Gillian Hadfield to describe the prevalence and ubiquity of everyday legal problems. See Gillian Hadfield, "The Cost of Law: Promoting Access to Justice through the (Un)Corporate Practice of Law" (2014) 38 Intl Rev L & Econ 43 (USC Law Legal Studies Paper No. 13-16).

2   See, e.g., former Chief Justice Beverley McLachlin's foreword and Justice Thomas Cromwell's introduction in Action Committee on Access to Justice in Civil and Family Matters, *Access to Civil and Family Justice: A Roadmap for Change* (Ottawa: Action Committee on Access to Justice in Civil and Family Matters, 2013), online: Canadian Forum on Civil Justice <http://www.cfcj-fcjc.org/sites/default/files/docs/2013/AC_Report_English_Final.pdf> [*Roadmap*].

3   Action Committee on Access to Justice in Civil and Family Matters, *Roadmap, supra* note 2 at iii. For information about the Action Committee, see "Action Committee on Access to Justice in Civil and Family Matters," online: Canadian Forum on Civil Justice <http://www.cfcj-fcjc.org/action-committee>.

4   In its 2020 report, the World Justice Project found that civil justice was the weakest feature of the Canadian justice system. See World Justice Project, *World Justice Project Rule of*

Law Index 2020 (Washington, DC: World Justice Project, 2020) at 56, online: <https://worldjusticeproject.org/sites/default/files/documents/WJP-ROLI-2020-Online_0.pdf>.

5 See *Lessee of Pollard's Heirs v Kibbe*, 39 US 353 (1840) (WL), as quoted in Marc Galanter, "Access to Justice as a Moving Frontier" in Julia H. Bass, W.A. Bogart, & Frederick H. Zeamans, eds, *Access to Justice for a New Century: The Way Forward* (Toronto: Law Society of Upper Canada, 2005) at 147.

6 *Ibid.*

7 For more information on rural and remote access to justice, see Nicole Aylwin & Lisa Moore, *Rural and Remote Access to Justice: A Literature Review* (Toronto: Canadian Forum on Civil Justice, 2015), online: The Boldness Project <http://boldnessproject.ruralandremoteaccesstojustice.com/wp-content/uploads/2016/01/Rural-Remote-Lit-Review_newcoverpage.pdf>.

8 See Gillian K. Hadfield, *Rules for a Flat World: Why Humans Invented Law and How to Reinvent It for a Complex Global Economy* (New York: Oxford University Press, 2017) at 59. [*Rules for a Flat World*].

9 Lesley Jacobs & Matt McManus, "Meaningful Access to Justice for Everyday Legal Problems: New Research on Consumer Problems among Canadians" (2017) 6 J Civil Litigation & Practice 148 at 150.

10 M. Cappelletti and B. Garth, "Access to Justice: The Newest Wave in the Worldwide Movement to Make Rights Effective" (1978) 27 Buff L Rev 181 at 197.

11 *Ibid* at 209.

12 *Ibid* at 222.

13 See, e.g., Ab Currie, "Riding the Third Wave – Notes on the Future of Access to Justice" in *Expanding Horizons, Rethinking Access to Justice in Canada: Proceedings of a National Symposium* (Ottawa: Department of Justice Canada, 2000).

14 See, e.g., Trevor C.W. Farrow, "A New Wave of Access to Justice Reform in Canada" in Adam Dodek & Alice Woolley, eds, *In Search of the Ethical Lawyer: Stories from the Canadian Legal Profession* (Vancouver: UBC Press, 2016) [Farrow, "A New Wave"].

15 Roderick A. Macdonald, "Access to Justice in Canada Today: Scope, Scale and Ambitions" in Julia Bass, W.A. Bogart, & Frederick H. Zeamans, eds, *Access to Justice for a New Century – The Way Forward* (Toronto: Law Society of Upper Canada, 2005) at 20–23.

16 *Ibid.*

17 *Ibid.*

18 *Ibid.*

19 The Action Committee underscores the fact that legal problems often create and exacerbate other legal, social, and health-related problems: Action Committee on Access to Justice in Civil and Family Matters, *Roadmap, supra* note 2 at 3. The Canadian Forum on Civil Justice reports that Canadians experience increased stress, poor work performance, family problems, anxiety, and other health-related problems as a result of their legal problems: Trevor C.W. Farrow et al, *Everyday Legal Problems and the Cost of Justice in Canada: Overview Report* (Toronto: Canadian Forum on Civil Justice, 2016) at 16–19, online: Canadian Forum on Civil Justice <http://www.cfcj-fcjc.org/sites/default/files/Everyday%20Legal%20Problems%20and%20the%20Cost%20of%20Justice%20in%20Canada%20-%20Overview%20Report.pdf> [*Everyday Legal Problems*].

20 The proportion of respondents who had not yet resolved their legal problems within the three-year reference period ranged from 23 to 44 percent, depending on the problem type. See Ontario Civil Legal Needs Project, *Civil Legal Needs of Lower and Middle-Income Ontarians: Quantitative Research* (Toronto: Ontario Civil Legal Needs Project, October 2009) at 46.

21 Julie Macfarlane, "The National Self-Represented Litigants Project: Identifying and Meeting the Needs of Self-Represented Litigants, Final Report" (May 2013) at 54, online: <https://lawsocietyontario.azureedge.net/media/lso/media/legacy/pdf/s/self-represented_project.pdf> ["NSRLP Report"].

22 Chief Justice Beverly McLachlin spoke out about this issue in the context of the *R v Jordan* decision. See Clare Hennig, "Chief Justice Beverly McLachlin Says Judges Should Speak Out about Delays," *CBC News* (31 May 2017), online: <http://www.cbc.ca/news/canada/british-columbia/chief-justice-beverley-mclachlin-speaks-out-about-delays-1.4139750>.

23 See, e.g., Olivia Stefanovich, "Courts Scramble to Modernize to Keep the System Working in a Pandemic," *CBC News* (31 March 2020), online: <https://www.cbc.ca/news/politics/stefanovich-covid19-exposes-court-shortcomings-1.5502077>.

24 In Professor Macfarlane's study, more than half (53 percent) of the SRL sample had exhausted their available resources for a lawyer. See Macfarlane, "NSRLP Report," *supra* note 21 at 42.

25 For more on the ways in which location influences the temporal costs of justice, see Aylwin and Moore, *supra* note 7.

26 See Action Committee on Access to Justice in Civil and Family Matters, *Canadian Access to Justice Initiatives: Justice Development Goals Status Report* (Ottawa: Action Committee on Access to Justice in Civil and Family Matters, 2017), online: Canadian Forum on Civil Justice <http://www.cfcj-fcjc.org/sites/default/files/docs/Canadian%20Access%20to%20Justice%20Initiatives%20-Justice%20Development%20Goals%20Status%20Report.pdf> [*Status Report*].

27 For a fulsome definition of what the term "organizations" collectively refers to, see *ibid* at 3.

28 *Ibid* at 20.

29 *Ibid* at 76. For more on the pervasiveness of everyday legal problems, see Farrow et al, *Everyday Legal Problems, supra* note 19 at 16–21; see also Chapter 4 in this volume, by Ab Currie.

30 Ontario, Ministry of the Attorney General, News Release, "Ontario Providing Improved Access to Legal Aid Services: Province to Increase Legal Aid Eligibility Threshold on April 1, 2017" (27 March 2017), online: <https://news.ontario.ca/mag/en/2017/03/ontario-providing-improved-access-to-legal-services.html>.

31 Fatima Syed, "Doug Ford Cut Support for Affordable Justice. Legal Aid Ontario Explains What Happens Next," *Canada's National Observer* (25 July 25 2019), online: <https://www.nationalobserver.com/2019/07/25/news/doug-ford-cut-support-affordable-justice-legal-aid-ontario-explains-what-happens>.

32 In Alberta, an additional $3.5 million in legal aid funding was committed: CBC News, "Legal Aid Wins Funding Boost in Alberta Budget," *CBC News* (20 March 2017), online: <http://www.cbc.ca/news/canada/edmonton/legal-aid-wins-funding-boost-in-alberta-budget-1.4032884>. Similarly, in British Columbia, the government announced that it would be investing an additional $16 million to support a series of legal aid initiatives: British Columbia, Ministry of Justice, News Release, "Provincial Investments in Justice Keep Families Together, Assist with Everyday Legal Issues" (27 March 2017), online: <https://news.gov.bc.ca/releases/2017JAG0008-000860>.

33 For LAO financial eligibility guidelines, see Legal Aid Ontario, "Details on Legal Aid Ontario's Financial Eligibility Increase for 2019" (10 March 2019), online: <http://www.legalaid.on.ca/en/news/newsarchive/2019-03-20_financial-eligibility-increase.asp>.

34 See, e.g., Omar Ha-Redeye, "Better Alternatives to Legal Aid Increases" (19 March 2017), *CanLII Connects* (blog), online: <http://canliiconnects.org/en/commentaries/45089>.

35 Stephen Easton, Hilary Furness, & Paul Brantingham, *The Cost of Crime in Canada: 2014 Report* (Vancouver: Fraser Institute, October 2014) at 96, online: <https://www.fraser institute.org/sites/default/files/cost-of-crime-in-canada.pdf>.

36 Canada, Department of Justice, "Costs of Crime in Canada, 2008," Table 2, online: <http://www.justice.gc.ca/eng/rp-pr/csj-sjc/crime/rr10_5/a.html>.

37 Statistics Canada, "Civil Court Cases, by Level of Court and Type of Case, Canada and Selected Provinces and Territories," Table 35-10-0112-01, online: <https://www150.statcan.gc.ca/t1/tbl1/en/tv.action?pid=3510011201>.

38 Statistics Canada, "Adult Criminal Courts, Number of Cases and Charges by Type of Decision," Table 35-10-0027-01, online: <https://www150.statcan.gc.ca/t1/tbl1/en/tv.action?pid=3510002701>.

39 For a list of the agencies in Ontario, see Government of Ontario, "Agencies and Current Appointees," online: <https://www.pas.gov.on.ca/Home/Agencies-list>.

40 Immigration and Refugee Board of Canada, "Future-Oriented Statement of Operations – Years Ending March 31, 2018 and 2019," online: <https://irb-cisr.gc.ca/en/reports-publications/finance/pages/etafinstafut1819.aspx>.

41 Social Justice Tribunals of Ontario, *Social Justice Tribunals Ontario 2017–2018 Annual Report,* online: <http://www.sjto.gov.on.ca/documents/sjto/2017-18%20Annual%20Report.html>.

42 Brooke MacKenzie, "Speaker's Corner: Time for Courts to Go Paperless," *Law Times* (24 April 2017), online: <https://www.lawtimesnews.com/archive/speakers-corner-time-for-courts-to-go-paperless/262518>.

43 Kathryn Marshall, "Opinion: Maybe COVID-19 Is What It Will Take to Modernize Canada's Antiquated Courts," *National Post* (8 April 2020), online: <https://nationalpost.com/opinion/opinion-maybe-covid-19-is-what-it-will-take-to-modernize-canadas-antiquated-courts>.

44 The term "flat world" was first used by Thomas L. Friedman as a metaphor for understanding the world as a level playing field for competitors within a free-market system. Gillian Hadfield applied this metaphor in a law and economics context, arguing that our legal infrastructure must develop a new system of rule making in order to remain relevant in the free market. See Thomas L. Friedman, *The World Is Flat: A Brief History of the Twenty-First Century* (New York: Farrar, Straus and Giroux, 2005); Hadfield, *Rules for a Flat World, supra* note 8.

45 Amanda Jerome, "Access to Justice Week Speakers Urge Profession to Embrace Innovation," *Lawyer's Daily* (24 October 2017), online: <https://www.thelawyersdaily.ca/articles/4981>.

46 Action Committee on Access to Justice in Civil and Family Matters, *Roadmap, supra* note 2 at 15.

47 *Ibid.*

48 Kent Roach & Lorne Sossin, "Access to Justice and Beyond" (2010) 60 Osgoode Hall LJ 373 at 378, referencing Michael J. Trebilcock, "Rethinking Consumer Protection Policy" in Charles E.F. Rickett & Thomas G.W. Telfer, eds, *International Perspectives on Consumer Access to Justice* (Cambridge: Cambridge University Press, 2003) at 68.

49 This is what civil legal needs researchers like Ab Currie argue when they contend that justiciable problems exist in the "shadow of the law." See Ab Currie, *The Legal Problems of Everyday Life: The Nature, Extent and Consequences of Justiciable Problems Experienced by Canadians* (Ottawa: Department of Justice Canada, 2009) at 85, online: Department of Justice Canada <http://www.justice.gc.ca/eng/rp-pr/csj-sjc/jsp-sjp/rr07_la1-rr07_aj1/rr07_la1.pdf> [*Legal Problems of Everyday Life*].

50 Action Committee on Access to Justice in Civil and Family Matters, *Roadmap, supra* note 2 at 12.

51 A list of the major PLEI organizations in Canada (on both federal and provincial/territorial levels) can be found on LawCentral Alberta's website. See LawCentral Alberta, "Public Legal Education – Canada," online: <http://www.lawcentralalberta.ca/en/help/public-legal -education-canada>.

52 Legal Information Society of Nova Scotia, *Annual Report 2018–19* at 6, online: <https:// www.legalinfo.org/index.php?option=com_docman&view=download&alias=404-2018 -2019-annual-report&category_slug=annual-reports&Itemid=1359>.

53 Justice Education Society of British Columbia, *Annual Report 2017–2018* (Vancouver: Justice Education Society, n.d.) at 10, online: <https://www.justiceeducation.ca/sites/default/files/ JES-2018-AR-103018.pdf>.

54 Macdonald explains in his characterization of the third wave of access to justice that PLEI was embraced as a tool to "demystify" law. To date, however, empirical data on the effectiveness of PLEI in preventing legal problems or assisting people with problems remains a research vacuum. Data from the "Evolving Legal Services" research project, a longitudinal study led by Community Legal Education Ontario in partnership with the Institute for Social Research at York University, seeks to gather much-needed empirical evidence on the effectiveness of PLEI in two jurisdictions in Canada. See Community Legal Education Ontario, "Evolving Legal Services Research Project: Executive Summary," online: <https://cleoconnect.ca/wp-content/uploads/2019/06/ELSRP-Executive -Summary.pdf>.

55 Action Committee on Access to Justice in Civil and Family Matters, *Status Report, supra* note 26 at 16.

56 "Wicked problems" are socially complex problems that do not lend themselves to easily identifiable solutions. See H.W.J Rittel & M.M. Webber, "Dilemmas in a General Theory of Planning" (1973) 4:2 Policy Sciences 155.

57 The "trigger effect" refers to the potential for legal problems to trigger multiple other legal and non-legal problems. See Ab Currie, *Nudging the Paradigm Shift, Everyday Legal Problems in Canada* (Toronto: Canadian Forum on Civil Justice, 2016) at 10, online: <http:// cfcj-fcjc.org/sites/default/files//publications/reports/Nudging%20the%20Paradigm %20Shift%2C%20Everyday%20Legal%20Problems%20in%20Canada%20-%20Ab%20 Currie.pdf>.

58 Hadfield, *Rules for a Flat World, supra* note 8 at 180.

59 Macfarlane, "NSRLP Report," *supra* note 21 at 44.

60 See "Steady Optimism – 2019 Legal Fees Survey," *Canadian Lawyer* (April 2019) at 20, online: <https://www.canadianlawyermag.com/staticcontent/AttachedDocs/CL_Apr_19-survey. pdf>.

61 Law Society of Ontario, "By-Law 4: Licensing" (1 May 2007), s 6(2).

62 See Recommendations 4–6 in Justice Annemarie E. Bonkalo, *Family Legal Services Review* (Toronto: Ontario Ministry of the Attorney General, 2016), online: <https://www. attorneygeneral.jus.gov.on.ca/english/about/pubs/family_legal_services_review/#_ Toc469667412>.

63 Results from the paralegal performance survey of the Law Society of Ontario (formerly the Law Society of Upper Canada) indicated that 74 percent of clients were satisfied or very satisfied with the services they had received. See Law Society of Upper Canada, *Report to the Attorney General of Ontario Pursuant to Section 63.1 of the* Law Society Act (Toronto: Law Society of Upper Canada, June 2012) at 25, online: <http://lawsocietygazette.ca/wp -content/uploads/2012/07/Paralegal-5-year-Review.pdf>.

64 The fee for commencing action in New Brunswick's Court of Queen's Bench is $100: Government of New Brunswick, "Court Fees – Court of Queen's Bench," online: <http://www2.gnb.ca/content/gnb/en/services/services_renderer.629.Court_Fees_-_Court_of_Queen__s_Bench.html#serviceFees>. The fee for commencing an action in Saskatchewan's Court of Queen's Bench is generally $750: Government of Saskatchewan, "Tariff of Costs" at 7, online: <http://www.qp.gov.sk.ca/documents/English/QBRules/23Tariff.pdf>.

65 As of 1 August 2016, civil hearing fees in British Columbia were reinstituted. While there are no fees for the first three days of trial, for days 4–10 the fee is $500 per day, and for each day beyond day 10 the fee is $800 per day. See Government of British Columbia, News Release, "B.C. Reinstates Civil Hearing Day Fees" (22 July 2016), online: <https://news.gov.bc.ca/releases/2016JAG0023-001343>.

66 Chief Justice Beverly McLachlin spoke out about this issue in the context of the *R v Jordan* decision. See Hennig, *supra* note 22.

67 See Action Committee on Access to Justice in Civil and Family Matters, *Roadmap, supra* note 2 at 14.

68 In Professor Macfarlane's study, over half (53 percent) of the SRL sample had exhausted their available resources for a lawyer. See Macfarlane, "NSRLP Report," *supra* note 21 at 42.

69 For more on the role of legal capability and legal consciousness in problem resolution, see Chapter 4 in this volume.

70 Trevor C.W. Farrow et al, "Addressing the Needs of Self-Represented Litigants in the Canadian Justice System: A White Paper Prepared for the Association of Canadian Court Administrators" (2012) at 18–19, online: Canadian Forum on Civil Justice <http://www.cfcj-fcjc.org/sites/default/files/docs/2013/Addressing%20the%20Needs%20of%20SRLs%20ACCA%20White%20Paper%20March%202012%20Final%20Revised%20Version.pdf>.

71 Aylwin and Moore, *supra* note 7.

72 Ab Currie has noted that one of the contributing factors to the persistence of legal problems is that people fail to take action simply because they do not recognize that what they are experiencing is, in fact, a legal problem. See Currie, *Legal Problems of Everyday Life, supra* note 49 at 85.

73 Farrow, "A New Wave," *supra* note 14 at 177.

74 Fabien Gélinas et al, *Foundations of Civil Justice: Toward a Value-Based Framework for Reform* (Cham, Switzerland: Springer International Publishing, 2015).

75 See Laura Nader, "The Life of the Law – A Moving Study" (2002) 36:3 Val UL Rev 655 at 657–58.

76 Farrow, "A New Wave," *supra* note 14 at 167.

77 The concept of "everyday justice" connotes a wide-angle view of civil justice problems as problems that are one and the same with the problems of everyday life. See Currie, *Legal Problems of Everyday Life, supra* note 49 at 2.

78 Hadfield, *Rules for a Flat World, supra* note 8 at 4.

79 *Ibid.*

80 Canadian Bar Association Legal Futures Initiative, *Futures: Transforming the Delivery of Legal Services in Canada* (Ottawa: Canadian Bar Association, 2014) at 24, online: <http://www.cba.org/CBAMediaLibrary/cba_na/PDFs/CBA%20Legal%20Futures%20PDFS/Futures-Final-eng.pdf>.

81 Edward M. Iacobucci & Michael J. Trebilcock, "An Economic Analysis of Alternative Business Structures for the Practice of Law" (Paper commissioned by the Law Society of Upper Canada for the Alternative Business Structures symposium held on 4 October 2013) at 59–61, online: <https://lawsocietyontario.azureedge.net/media/lso/media/legacy/pdf/a/abs-report-iacobucci-trebilcock-september-2014.pdf>.

82   In Ontario, for example, the Law Society of Ontario's Working Group on Alternative Business Structures recommended against the implementation of a majority or controlling non-licensee ownership model. The Working Group felt that the regulatory risks outweighed the potential access to justice benefits. See Law Society of Upper Canada Professional Regulation Committee, "Report to Convocation, September 24, 2015" (2015) at 111, online: <https://lawsocietyontario.azureedge.net/media/lso/media/legacy/pdf/c/convocation-september-2015-prc.pdf>.

83   See, e.g., Brenda Jacobs & Lesley Jacobs, "Multidisciplinary Paths to Family Justice: Professional Challenges and Promising Practices" (Research paper prepared for the Law Commission of Ontario's family law reform project, Best Practices at Family Justice System Entry Points: Needs of Users and Response of Workers in the Justice System, June 2010), online: <http://www.lco-cdo.org/wp-content/uploads/2010/11/family-law-process-call-for-papers-jacobs.pdf>.

84   See Canadian Institutes of Health Research (CIHR), *Health Research Roadmap: Creating Innovative Research for Better Health and Health Care* (Ottawa: CIHR, 2009), online: <http://www.cihr-irsc.gc.ca/e/40490.html>.

85   *Ibid* at "Strategic Direction 3."

86   See Canadian Institute of Health Research, *Health Research Roadmap II: Capturing Innovation to Produce Better Health and Health Care for Canadians* (Ottawa: CIHR, 2015) at 24, online: <http://www.cihr-irsc.gc.ca/e/documents/CIHR-strat-plan-eng.pdf>.

87   See "Canadian Startup Ecosystem Keeping Our Medical Sector Innovations Alive," *Financial Post* (17 March 2017), online: <http://business.financialpost.com/entrepreneur/0320-biz-sw-health/wcm/06a05298-1380-4b8e-bf19-e759aaa61c7c>.

88   See "The Funding Portal and University Health Network Form Joint Venture in Canadian HealthTech Sector" (17 June 2014), online: TECHNA Institute for the Advancement of Technology for Health <http://technainstitute.com/the-funding-portal-and-university-health-network-form-joint-venture-in-canadian-healthtech-sector/>. For more on social enterprise vehicles as tools to improve access to justice, see Chapter 11 in this volume.

89   Action Committee on Access to Justice in Civil and Family Matters, *Roadmap, supra* note 2 at 11, quoting Ab Currie, "Self-Helpers Need Help Too" (2010) [unpublished] at 1, online: <http://lawforlife.org.uk/wp-content/uploads/2013/05/self-helpers-need-help-too-ab-currie-2010-283.pdf>.

90   This shift in focus from back-end to front-end service delivery is what the Action Committee called for as part of its first innovation goal.

91   *Listening to Ontarians: Report of the Ontario Civil Legal Needs Project* (Toronto: Ontario Civil Legal Needs Project, May 2010) at 3, online: <https://lawsocietyontario.azureedge.net/media/lso/media/legacy/pdf/m/may3110_oclnreport_final.pdf>.

92   See Connecting Ottawa, "About Us," online: <http://connectingottawa.com/about>; Legal Health Check-up, "Welcome," online: <https://www.legalhealthcheckup.ca/en/>.

93   Ab Currie, *Engaging the Power of Community to Expand Legal Services for Low-Income Ontarians* (Toronto: Canadian Forum on Civil Justice, April 2017) at 10, online: <http://www.cfcj-fcjc.org/sites/default/files//Engaging%20the%20Power%20of%20Community%20to%20Expand%20Legal%20Services.pdf>.

94   *Ibid* at 46.

95   *Ibid* at 47.

96   Robin Nobleman, "Addressing Access to Justice as a Social Determinant of Health" (2014) 21 Health LJ 49 at 69.

97   Dana Weintrab et al, "Pilot Study of Medical-Legal Partnerships to Address Social and Legal Needs of Patients" (2010) 21 J Health Care for the Poor and Underserved 157 at 165.

98 Tishra Beeson, Brittany Dawn McAllister, & Marsha Regenstein, *Making the Case for Medical-Legal Partnerships: A Review of the Evidence* (Washington, DC: National Center for Medical Legal Partnerships, 2013), online: <http://medical-legalpartnership.org/wp-content/uploads/2014/03/Medical-Legal-Partnership-Literature-Review-February-2013.pdf>.

99 The SickKids MLP was piloted in 2009 by the Hospital for Sick Children in collaboration with Pro Bono Law Ontario (PBLO) as Canada's first MLP. See Nobleman, *supra* note 96 at 70–72; Focus Consultants, *PBLO at Sick Kids: A Phase II Evaluation of the Medical-Legal Partnership between Pro Bono Law Ontario and Sick Kids Hospital* (Toronto: PBLO, 2012) at 61–62.

100 Michelle Jehn et al, "Reforming the Family Justice System Initiative: A Case Study in Systemic Design" (Paper presented at the Relating System Thinking and Design [RSD4] 2015 Symposium, Banff, Alberta, September 2015), online: <http://openresearch.ocadu.ca/id/eprint/2034/>.

101 Andrew Pillar, "The Cost of Justice (Research)," online: (20 April 2017) Slaw <http://www.slaw.ca/2017/04/20/the-cost-of-justice-research/>.

102 Action Committee on Access to Justice in Civil and Family Matters, *Roadmap, supra* note 2 at 23.

103 Action Committee on Access to Justice in Civil and Family Matters, *Status Report, supra* note 26 at 82.

Part 2
Experiencing Everyday Legal Problems

4

The Monetary Costs of Everyday Legal Problems and Expanding Access to Justice

Ab Currie

IT IS ALMOST AXIOMATIC that cost matters. Although cost is not always the most important factor in public policy decisions, cost-benefit analysis to determine whether the cost of implementing a policy outweighs the benefits has been a central element in public policy for decades, the logic being that if problems are costing people or public institutions a large amount of money, then something should be done to reduce the costs. Similarly, it is universally accepted that programs and services should be cost-effective, even if, from a certain point of view, some values should be held even above monetary costs.

In the area of legal problems and legal needs, it is also axiomatic that people should have access to the help they need to resolve the legal problems they experience. The research has mainly focused on the affordability of assistance, usually legal advice or representation, or somewhat more generally on cost as factor determining the extent to which people take action to resolve law-related problems. This is reflected in a review of legal problems studies compiled by Pascoe Pleasence and Nigel Balmer showing that all but one of the forty-two major studies they had reviewed, out of fifty major studies making up the entire body of research, includes some questions on the cost of dealing with legal problems.[1]

Three previous legal problems studies have been carried out in Canada by the author of this chapter.[2] These studies focused on intangible costs of experiencing everyday legal problems such as social and health-related problems but did not include monetary costs. The Canadian Forum on Civil Justice (CFCJ) survey of Everyday Legal Problems and the Cost of Justice was groundbreaking Canadian research, the first study to address monetary costs of everyday legal problems.[3] Within the broad spectrum of issues in the study of the cost of justice, this chapter examines the cost of justice to public institutions. These are costs that are borne by the state as individuals experiencing legal problems make use of publicly funded institutions, such as healthcare, as a direct consequence of experiencing legal problems. The underlying concern in an analysis of the cost of justice is the widely acknowledged need to expand access to justice. In Canada, access to justice programs have traditionally been funded by government.[4] Historically in the access to justice movement, having government accept primary responsibility for funding access to justice represents a great accomplishment, leaving aside the all-important question of the adequacy of funding. There are many public goods competing for available and limited public money. Governments have a responsibility to spend public money wisely. The proposition underlying this analysis is that if the costs to public institutions associated with the public's experiencing of legal problems become a substantial and significant component of expenditures in publicly funded institutions, government will be persuaded to invest money to address unmet legal need to achieve savings in those other parts of the social safety net. This analysis will ask two main questions about the cost to public institutions: (1) What is the cost of legal problems to three major publicly funded programs that in part make up the social safety net? (2) What proportions of overall program costs in these three areas are attributable to people's experiencing of legal problems?

The cost of legal problems to individuals is also a concern. The prevalence of everyday legal problems is high, and one might expect that the aggregate costs resulting from people's experiencing of everyday legal problems may be correspondingly high. Establishing the magnitude of the aggregate cost of everyday legal problems to individuals is therefore of interest.

Monetary Costs in the Legal Problems Literature

A number of legal problems studies have focused on monetary cost as a factor influencing whether or not people take action to resolve the problems they experience. Typically, studies have asked respondents about the importance of cost compared with other factors in their decision not to attempt to resolve the problem. From this point of view, the results have suggested that cost is a minor factor in decisions not to take some action to resolve legal problems, although the numbers vary. Results from the US Comprehensive Legal Needs study show that 16 percent of low- and moderate-income Americans cited cost as a concern in the decision to take action for a legal problem.[5] In Hazel Genn's Paths to Justice study, among the 13 percent of respondents who took no action to resolve their problem, the percentage of those saying that the fact they thought it would "cost too much" was the a major reason for taking no action ranged from 2 percent for employment problems to 16 percent for problems related to rented accommodation.[6]

Summarizing the American research, Rebecca Sandefur writes that "surveys of Americans who considered and decided not to use lawyers have found that the decision is motivated by cost in only a minority of instances."[7] This is confirmed in a recent study carried out by Sandefur in which 17 percent of respondents who took no action said cost was a major reason.[8] Sandefur provides a sociological perspective on why cost is a minor factor as a barrier to access to justice. Legality is socially constructed: "One important reason why people do not turn to law to deal with their legal problems is that they do not consider them as legal."[9] This explanation is supported by the reasons often reported more frequently than costs by respondents in legal problems surveys for not taking action to resolve legal problems; they did not think anything could be done, did not know their legal rights, or did not think advice would make any difference.[10] More recent research by Sandefur reveals some of the explanations of legal problems held by some people – just bad luck; it was part of God's plan.[11]

Taking the research in a new direction, the 2014 CFCJ study asked respondents about the extent to which they were forced to rely on publicly funded services as a consequence of experiencing an everyday legal problem, and how much money they received or the extent to which they used the service.

Everyday Legal Problems: Monetary Costs to Individuals

Respondents to the CFCJ survey were asked: "Did it cost you any money to deal with this problem?" This and subsequent questions related to cost were asked in this way to obtain a global cost to the public of experiencing everyday legal problems, similar to the now well-established findings on the prevalence of everyday legal problems. This very broad approach was taken as a starting point because the vast majority of people deal with problems outside of any formal problem-solving or dispute resolution process, and we know little about how much is spent and the items on which they spend money.

The survey revealed that just over a quarter, 26.4 percent, of respondents in the weighted sample said they spent money in dealing with the problem. A conservative estimate of the global cost to the Canadian public, including all aspects of experiencing everyday legal problems, was $7.76 billion annually.[12] A cost of approximately $7.8 billion annually related to everyday legal problems is on the surface a very large number. There does not appear to be a comparable figure from other research that might provide a benchmark or comparison with which to establish the reliability of this first estimate. It is a new element added to the now familiar narrative that has emerged from legal problems research over the past twenty years emphasizing the magnitude of everyday legal problems as a social issue. The $7.8 billion figure is plausible. Logically, a large number of people, even if many individuals spend relatively small amounts of money, can spend a large amount in the aggregate. Searching for a broad comparator from another social domain, the consulting firm Deloitte estimated that

Table 4.1 Quartile distribution of money spent dealing
with everyday legal problems

Quartile (%)	Amount spent per individual
25	$300
50	$1,400
75	$6,000
100	$82,000

Canadians would spend $8.7 billion on marijuana when it became legal in 2018, approximately the same amount as wine sales.[13]

The average amount spent was $6,010. The median was $1,400, meaning that 50 percent of all those spending money to deal with the problem spent that amount or more. Table 4.1 shows the quartile distribution. Each quartile represents an estimated 317,000 people on an annual basis.

At the higher end of the spending continuum, 10.0 percent of the weighted sample spent $17,000 or more dealing with the problem. This would comprise approximately 95,000 individuals annually.

These estimates could be very low because of the removal of twelve high-value observations from the data. This adjustment was made entirely on the basis of skepticism about the reliability of the very high values rather than on any knowledge of the actual circumstances related to the responses. As readers will be aware, however, a few large values in a sample can make an enormous difference in the weighted data. Even if those values had been left in the data, only the fourth quartile would have been affected. There would still have been a large number of people spending relatively small amounts and a smaller number spending large amounts. Dropping the high-value cases reduces the estimated (weighted) percentage of people spending money dealing with the problem from about 35 percent to 26 percent of the population.[14] With the high values, the estimated amount spent annually would then be about $26.1 billion rather than $7.8 billion. The uncertainty about the inclusion or elimination of the high values clearly suggests that more work should be carried out to obtain data that can be used with greater confidence.

Methodological Complexities in Examining Costs to Individuals

Expenditures need to be studied more carefully. In the 2014 CFCJ study, respondents were asked about the items on which they spent money. The question allowed six closed-end responses plus a residual category. The data for specific categories of expenditure are presented in Table 4.2.

Table 4.2 **Percentage of respondents indicating specific monetary expenditures to deal with problems**

Problem	Percentage of respondents
Lawyers' fees	18.2
Other advisers or mediators	8.6
Court fees	7.8
Purchasing material and photocopying	9.8
Long distance telephone and fax	4.0
Transportation	12.9

These expenditures are quite clearly related to resolving the problem. In addition to these expenditure categories, about 58 percent of respondents, well over half, who reported having spent money dealing with the problem said they had spent money on something else.[15] Examining these responses would be especially helpful in clarifying the uncertain aspects of what people do when "dealing with the problem" within the everyday legal problems framework.

This may be especially challenging within such a framework because of the complex patterns in describing the actions people take to deal with problems. Determining the cost of resolving problems is relatively straightforward with formal, structured dispute resolution or problem-solving processes.[16] Based on this sample, however, only approximately 6.7 percent of the population used the courts to resolve problems.[17] A further 1.8 percent said they used some form of mediation. Otherwise, the actions taken by the vast majority of people to deal with or resolve everyday legal problems take a great many forms.

Taken separately, 19.1 percent obtained legal advice, 28.5 percent obtained non-legal advice from an organization, 33.5 percent searched the Internet for advice, 75.6 percent attempted to negotiate with the other party, and 61.6 percent obtained advice from friends or relatives. Most people took multiple actions. More than half of respondents said they took three or more actions to deal with the problem (Table 4.3).

The order in which people took different actions varied (Table 4.4). The first action that most people took was talking to the other party. This was followed by taking advice from friends and relatives and searching for information on the Internet. Obtaining legal advice ranks fifth as a first action. Second actions occur in a different order, but legal advice remains low on the list. Legal advice is the action taken most frequently only as a third action. Whether or not the formal justice system is ultimately used, it is possible that obtaining legal advice early produces the best outcomes at lowest cost in both monetary and human terms, such as high levels of stress and stress-related physical health problems.

Table 4.3 **Percentage of respondents taking one or more separate actions to deal with a problem**

Number of actions	Percentage of respondents	Cumulative percentage
1	22.3	–
2	20.7	43.0
3	18.7	61.7
4	13.8	75.5
5	8.3	83.8
6 or more	16.2	100.0

Table 4.4 **Order in which actions were taken**

	First action		Second action		Third action	
	%	Order	%	Order	%	Order
Negotiate with the other party	38.5	1	16.0	4	12.1	6
Advice from friends or relatives	23.5	2	32.2	1	17.4	5
Search the Internet	21.0	3	16.7	2	14.4	3
Non-legal help from an organization	8.5	4	16.2	3	20.0	2
Legal advice	4.7	5	10.4	5	20.9	1
Something else	3.8	6	8.3	6	15.2	4

The complexity of the problem is also an important factor determining the complex relationships between cost, the actions people take, and outcomes. However, because the data in surveys of self-reported legal problems of this kind are basically subjective, determining the complexity of the problems is very difficult. Making an assessment of the legal complexity of everyday legal problems is probably not possible in a telephone survey. The everyday legal problems approach departs from the traditional definition of a legal problem, however, and much is therefore open to exploration. Large-scale legal problems surveys may use the degree to which the problem was disruptive to the person experiencing it as a measure of seriousness. This has some value with respect to the impact of the problem on the individual but is a poor proxy for legal seriousness. Case characteristics can be developed to measure the seriousness or complexity, but these probably would have to be applied to studies with more specifically defined problems, involving far fewer problem scenarios than are typically used in a legal problems survey. Measuring the complexity of everyday legal problems is a challenge in the type of legal problems research presented here because large proportions of respondents say that when the problem first occurred, they did not understand its seriousness or recognize its legal complications.

Costs to the State of Everyday Legal Problems

Although they have not been included directly in legal problems surveys, the "knock-on" costs of legal problems to public services has received some attention elsewhere. It was estimated that over the three and one-half periods covered by the English and Welsh civil and social justice survey, the cost of problems people experience to individuals, healthcare, and other public services was at least £13 billion.[18]

The 2014 CFCJ survey collected information about three areas in which there were costs to publicly funded programs that were, according to respondents, a direct consequence of a legal problem they had experienced. These were healthcare, employment insurance, and social services.[19] These three areas do not represent a comprehensive estimate of costs to the public purse, but they do serve to illustrate the magnitude of costs. The results illustrate one important point: while the estimated monetary impacts represent on the face of it large amounts of money, they are very small relative to the overall spending in each of these areas.

Additional Costs to Healthcare

Respondents were asked about the extent to which they made greater than normal use of the healthcare system as a direct consequence of the legal problem they experienced. They were not asked about the specific number of additional events in which they used the healthcare system. Due to the constraints imposed by a telephone interview format, no attempt was made to distinguish between visits to physician's offices and visits to the emergency departments of hospitals. Respondents were asked about increased use of the healthcare system for up to two problems. Weighted to the overall population, Canadians said they used the healthcare system an estimated 5,232,582 times over the three-year reference period as a consequence of an everyday legal problem.[20] Without any detail about the exact nature of the use of the healthcare system, the estimate assumes that each use was a visit to a physician's office. In 2012–13, the average cost of such a visit was $58.15 for the office visit and related services.[21] Using these figures, a rough estimate of the cost of additional use of the healthcare system directly attributable to legal problems would equal $304.3 million over the three-year period, or approximately $101 million on an annual basis.[22] Because the estimate assumes only one use of the healthcare system per problem, this may be a conservative estimate.

Expenditures on physicians in the Canadian healthcare system in 2013 amounted to $31.4 billion.[23] The cost to the healthcare system was based on a figure for the average cost of physician visits. Therefore, the proportion is

calculated on that component of overall healthcare costs. The $101 million es-
timate is 0.0032 percent of the total amount billed by physicians.

Loss of Employment
Respondents were asked whether they had lost employment as a direct consequence of the legal problem they had experienced. Weighted to the population
aged eighteen years and older, 8.4 percent of adult Canadians experiencing an
everyday legal problem lost employment as a direct consequence of the problem.[24] This represents 932,416 individuals over the three-year reference period.
Respondents were asked to recall the details of their period of unemployment.
Estimated for the population, people spent an average of 35.9 weeks on employment insurance and received an average of $384.03 weekly. The average amount
of time spent on employment insurance was 21.6 weeks. Using these figures,
the total estimated cost for the three-year period was $1.35 billion, for an esti-
mated annual cost of approximately $450 million.

Total expenditures on employment insurance for 2013 were $18.8 billion.[25]
The estimated cost to employment insurance as a direct consequence of legal
problems is 0.024 percent of total expenditures.

Social Assistance
An estimated 2.1 percent of respondents said they had to rely on social assistance as a direct consequence of experiencing a legal problem.[26] This equals an
estimated 238,102 people over the three-year reference period, receiving an
average amount of $285.86 weekly for an average of 34.2 weeks. Based on these
data, everyday legal problems cost the public coffers an estimated $745 million
for the three-year reference period, or about $248 million annually.

The most recent estimate available for the cost of social assistance in Canada
annually is $14.6 billion.[27] The estimated additional cost to social services at-
tributable to legal problems is approximately 0.017 percent of the total expenditure on social services in Canada. This includes provincial programs of last
resort rather than Old Age Security, Quebec or Canada pension benefits, or
other income maintenance programs.

The Cost of Everyday Legal Problems and Expanding Access to Justice

The knock-on cost of everyday legal problems to the three publicly funded
programs examined here arising as a direct consequence of those problems is,
in each case, a tiny fraction of overall payments under these programs. The very
small costs to these publicly funded programs relative to overall expenditures
suggest that costs to the state may not be a significant or persuasive argument

in favour of expanding access to justice. The absolute amounts are considerable on the face of it, but in relation to total expenditures, the impact on government programs is minimal.

A similar point of view relating to legal aid suggests that costs to publicly funded programs may not have been persuasive or decisive in protecting legal aid funding. Graham Cookson estimated that that the knock-on cost to government programs of the cuts to legal aid in the United Kingdom amounted to £139 million.[28] However, this very solid work apparently made no difference for the fate of legal aid. Professor Cookson's work entered the debate when the decision had already been made, a situation that would almost inevitably have limited its impact. Another general perspective on the importance of cost is that the decision was caught up in the political complexity of government-wide spending reductions. While couched by the government in the language of cost saving, the decision may have been largely political rather than economic, with many programs having their budgets reduced as a tsunami of austerity swept all before it.

From another perspective, there are econometric analyses, such as the Perryman Group study in Texas, indicating that every dollar invested in legal aid will yield many times that amount in savings to public programs and in financial benefits to the economy.[29] Although the results of studies like this create excitement among champions of legal aid, they do not seem to have had much impact on increasing funding to legal aid.

Whether government is a fool to cut funding or a fool for failing to invest in it, arguments about the impacts of spending on legal aid do not seem to have been very persuasive in either protecting or expanding funding for legal aid. The important issue may be political rather than economic. As David Luban has remarked, the compromise between the principle of universality and reality of rationing of access to justice has come about because of the high cost of legal services. Luban argues that "while equality before the law holds a privileged place in our system, and to deny equality before the law delegitimizes that system, access to equal legal services would, however, take more money than our society can be expected to provide for its poor."[30] Consistent with that view, J. Cooper observes that legal aid is not politically popular and will be vulnerable to cuts whenever costs become large enough to catch the attention of politicians.[31] This is especially likely to occur following recessionary periods, when governments are pressed to balance their budgets. Cooper refers to this as the "Cinderella effect," in which, after a time in the limelight at the ball, legal aid is dispatched towards its more customary place in the cellar.

If costs to publicly funded institutions fail to deliver the intended effect in support of expanded access to justice, a more detailed examination of the cost to individuals of everyday legal problems may be more strategic in making the case for expanding access to justice. The amount spent by individuals is an order of magnitude larger, from millions to billions, than the knock-on costs to publicly funded institutions; as noted above, the estimate that is currently being proposed on the basis of the CFCJ survey is almost certainly minimal. The $7.8 billion figure may be far too low because of uncertainties about the reliability of the results produced by the inclusion of several high-value responses, representing appropriate caution in dealing with the data but not confidence on substantive grounds. However, in order to examine how much money people spend, we need to know much more about what people spend money on and about the consequences of having to spend that money on the legal problem. In view of the much greater number and variety of paths to justice that exist within the everyday legal problems framework other than the formal justice system, this may make for interesting and challenging research.

It was remarked earlier that the paradigm shift in access to justice has occurred from the domain of socio-legal research to the realms of public policy and programs, creating a new narrative about how we think about the nature of legal problems and what assistance should appropriately be offered to people experiencing them. Apart from being adopted into the professional discourse of public policy and programs, the paradigm shift that is occurring in the area of legal problems might also find its way into the broader public discourse about legal problems and access to justice. At present, the public view of legal problems and access to justice is probably largely consistent with the traditional courts-and-lawyers narrative about the nature of a legal problem. Legal problems are viewed as the complex legal issues lawyers deal with, and access to justice means access to the formal justice system.

However, there are fundamental difficulties to be overcome in moving the everyday legal problems paradigm into public discourse. As Professor Sandefur has pointed out, people do not recognize the legal aspects of everyday problems; they do not act on them appropriately.[32] Importantly, they are therefore not likely to demand access to justice services they do not recognize as being appropriate and helpful to them. It is difficult to imagine a successful effort to raise public demand for expanded access to justice services against the background of this lack of legal consciousness.

On the other hand, research consistently shows that the vast majority of people do something to resolve the problems they experience. In the CFCJ study, 95 percent of respondents experiencing a legal problem said they took some action in an attempt to resolve it. A very substantial majority of people, 85 percent, said that it was important to resolve the problem. A majority, slightly over 50 percent, said that experiencing the problem made daily life more difficult. If legal consciousness were to shift in the direction of the everyday legal problems narrative rather than the court-centred narrative, people's everyday experience should provide the foundation for demanding greater access to justice on the basis of a broader understanding of legal problems, legal needs, and access to justice.[33] This is similar to the implication drawn out by a report by the Public Welfare Foundation and the Kresge Foundation relating to support for legal aid. The authors argued that people from the middle class would be more likely to support legal aid if they benefited from it, rather than viewing it as a program only for poor people.[34] In a similar way, the broader segment of the public that would benefit from access to justice programs reflecting the everyday legal problems narrative, compared with the poor and with people who use the formal justice system, might be more likely to demand access to justice services if they recognized their troubling problems as having legal aspects. This is supported by more recent research suggesting that broad public support for legal aid depends on the expectation that the broader public, and not only the poor, will get help when needed.[35]

Many people who spend money dealing with problems they do not consider legal, even though they are legal in nature, do not realize the potential seriousness of the problem at the outset, do not obtain much of what they had expected in the outcome, and do not feel the outcome is fair. If the money spent dealing with these problems carries some independent importance in people's lives, drawing an association between the money spent and the experience of dealing with the problem might encourage the development of a legal consciousness that many problems arising in everyday life involve legal issues and that some help in dealing with them ought to be available. The potential for public support is huge. In one way of looking at it, the challenge for expanding access to justice within the everyday legal problems paradigm is to dig down below the level of problems dealt with in the formal justice system.

A good metaphor for the landscape of legal problems represented by the everyday legal problems narrative is an iceberg. Using the CFCJ data, the relatively small part above water comprises the 6.7 percent of people who used the courts to resolve the problem, plus the 1.3 percent who said they used some form of mediation. The part below the water comprises the 92 percent of people experiencing self-reported problems with legal aspects, the majority of whom made some attempt to resolve the problem that did not involve an aspect of the formal justice system. This is the vast terrain of legal problems presented by the contemporary body of legal problems research. Assume, for heuristic purposes only, that the seriousness of problems can be approximately arrayed from the top of the iceberg to the bottom, from most to least serious. Assume further that there is a band of problems just below the waterline of unknown width representing people who should have greater access to the formal system. Further, envision successive bands of people with problems farther down the iceberg, each one possibly broader and deeper than the layer above. Are these people to be abandoned to their own devices in trying to resolve their law-related problems? Surly not, at least as a matter of principle, but there are impediments to building a broader access to justice system that reflects a continuum-of-service approach, providing proportional levels of assistance to the appropriate problems. Moving the agenda for access to justice from the domain of socio-legal research into the public discourse confronts a hurdle that can be framed in terms of sociologist C. Wright Mills's socio-logical imagination noted above. We know from the results of many legal problems surveys that everyday legal problems are ubiquitous in modern urbanized, bureaucratic societies. As much as they are ubiquitous, they are also hidden, hidden in plain sight, partly because they are integral aspects of everyday human adversity, and, second, because of the absence of legal consciousness and legal capability among the public that recognizes the legal aspects of these elements of daily life. As Mills might have framed the question in an expression of the sociological imagination, can the very high prevalence of these isolated personal troubles that we call everyday legal problems be usefully framed as a public issue about which something should be done?[36] To what extent is cost the linkage between private troubles and public issues?

What role might cost play in shaping this agenda? The money spent by the public to deal with everyday legal problems would probably not be the magic bullet to bring about an expansion of access to justice services. It would be just one more brick in the wall, a part of the shift in legal consciousness and legal capability. As an addition to the narrative on access to justice that is emerging from the everyday legal problems perspective, cost might contribute to nudging the paradigm shift forward, forming a part of a strategy to breathe life into the justice development goals proposed by the Canadian Forum on Civil Justice to expand access to justice to meet boundaries defined by the everyday legal problems approach.[37]

A culture shift in access to justice is occurring in Canada, defining a new agenda for expanding such access. The report of the Action Committee on Access to Justice in Civil and Family Matters concluded that "a new way of thinking – a culture shift – is required to move away from old patterns and approaches" and proposed six guiding principles for change, suggesting how this culture shift can be transformed into action.[38] The Canadian Bar Association (CBA) has proposed a bold approach towards achieving the goal of 100 percent access: "Full representation is not required in every case: meaningful access can be assured through a range of legal services and forms of assistance, depending on the circumstances. The key is to provide a seamless continuum of legal and non-legal services, and ensure that representation is available when needed to have meaningful access to justice."[39] More recently, the CBA has encouraged the development of a more inclusive system of public legal assistance services, involving a spectrum of services in which public legal service providers use "discrete and systemic strategies and work in collaboration with non-legal service providers to offer a broad range of services from outreach to aftercare, targeted and tailored to people's legal needs, circumstances and capabilities."[40] Innovative projects being developed across the country illustrate how the new thinking about access to justice expressed in the Action Committee and Canadian Bar Association reports are rolling out on the ground. How might these developments connect with the cost issue?

This chapter has focused on the monetary cost to individuals of experiencing everyday legal problems and has speculated on the extent to which costs borne by individuals and publicly funded institutions might be a factor in advancing the contemporary movement in access to justice. However, there are other perspectives on the importance of monetary costs in the evolution of the new access to justice movement. To borrow Professor Sandefur's phrase but turn it to a different purpose, perhaps "money isn't everything."[41] On the one hand, the ideals and principles of justice and access to justice may have a great deal of influence independent of cost. The work of the Action Committee and the Canadian Bar Association and the efforts of dedicated people working on the ground in organizations providing access to justice services may lead to considerable progress in the laborious process of "getting it done" over time, mainly fuelled by professional sweat equity. We may find that money isn't as important as one might think. Other resources are available to legal aid in expanding access to legal services. There are many service agencies and other non-governmental organizations already working in the community helping people resolve everyday problems. Following the logic of the everyday legal problems narrative, these everyday life problems have legal aspects and represent legal need. These community organizations have poverty reduction objectives in common with community legal services. Some project experience and research with community legal clinics in Ontario has demonstrated that by partnering with community agencies, community legal clinics can extend the reach of legal aid beyond their own traditional resources. Through collaborative partnerships that create new paths to justice for the people who initially approach community agencies for help, these initiatives engage the dedicated sense of purpose and the resources existing in the community to identify unmet legal need and to support organizations in more effectively helping their clients with problems having legal elements, problems that can be resolved at the community agency level with advice from legal professionals.[42] The cost of these approaches to expanding legal aid may be considerable, but the cost is not primarily money. The cost is found mainly in the efforts of the lawyers, paralegals, and community legal workers in legal clinics and legal aid staff offices to carry out community development approaches that make legal aid an integral part of the communities they serve, develop collaborative partnerships with community organizations, and make access to justice a significant dimension of the structure of local communities.

Notes

1   Pascoe Pleasence & Nigel Balmer, *Measuring Access to Justice and Legal Need through Legal Needs Surveys: Introduction, Guide and Resources* (Paris: Organisation for Economic Co-operation and Development [OECD]and the Open Society Initiative, 2017) at 76.

2   A. Currie, "A National Survey of the Civil Justice Problems of Low- and Moderate-Income Canadians: Incidence and Patterns" (2006) 13 Int'l J Legal Profession 217; A. Currie, "The Legal Problems of Everyday Life" in Rebecca L. Sandefur, ed, *The Sociology of Law, Crime and Deviance*, vol 12 (Bingley, UK: Emerald, 2009) at 1–42; A. Currie, "Lives of Trouble: Criminal Offending and the Problems of Everyday Life" (Paper presented at the International Legal Aid Group Conference, Wellington, New Zealand, April 2009).

3   Trevor C.W. Farrow et al, *Everyday Legal Problems and the Cost of Justice in Canada: Overview Report* (Toronto: Canadian Forum on Civil Justice, 2016).

4   For example, between 80 and 98 percent of the costs of provincial and territorial legal aid programs are funded by governments. See Statistics Canada, "Legal Aid in Canada: Resource and Caseload Statistics," online: Statistics Canada <https://www150.statcan.gc.ca/n1/en/catalogue/85F0015X>; most recent data available through CANSIM, tables 258-0001 to 258-0004.

5   American Bar Foundation, *Agenda for Access: The American People and Civil Justice. Final Report on the Implications of the Comprehensive Legal Needs Study* (Chicago: American Bar Foundation, 1996) at 10.

6   Hazel Genn, *Paths to Justice: What People Do and Think about Going to Law* (Oxford: Hart Publishing, 1999) at 41.

7   Rebecca L. Sandefur, "Money Isn't Everything: Understanding Moderate Income Households' Use of Lawyers' Services" in Anthony Duggan, Lorne Sossin, & Michael Trebilcock, eds, *Middle Income Access to Justice* (Toronto: University of Toronto Press, 2012) at 221 ["Money Isn't Everything"].

8   Rebecca L. Sandefur, *Accessing Justice in the Contemporary USA: Findings from the Community Needs and Services Study* (Chicago: American Bar Foundation, 2014) at 13 [*Accessing Justice*].

9   *Ibid* at 245.

10 Pascoe Pleasence, *Causes of Action: Civil Law and Social Justice,* 2d ed (London: Legal Services Commission, 2006) at 82.

11 Sandefur, *Accessing Justice, supra* note 8 at 14.

12 This estimate was calculated after removing twelve cases for which there were very high expenditures, ranging from $100,000 to over $1 million. These figures may have been outliers that would produce a misleading or inflated estimate. Leaving these observations

in the dataset would produce an estimate of $70.4 billion over the three-year period, or $22.6 billion annually.

13 "Legalized Marijuana in Canada Would Be Worth Up to $22.6 B per Year," *Huffington Post* (27 October 2016), online: <https://www.huffingtonpost.ca/2016/10/27/marijuana-legalization-market-size-canada_n_12676754.html>.

14 The 35 percent figure was derived by averaging the percentages of respondents indicating they had spent money dealing with the problem for problems one and two, calculated without removing high-value cases. See Table 4.2.

15 The 58 percent figure was derived by averaging the percentage of respondents indicating they had spent money on something other than the fixed responses shown in Table 4.2, 52.6 percent for problem one and 59.8 percent for problems two, using weighted data.

16 The Hague Institute for the Internationalization of Law (HiiL) has developed a framework for measuring the cost and quality of justice, taking into account the basic concepts of the everyday legal problems framework. It is fundamentally people-centred and takes into account both tangible and intangible costs experienced by people engaged in dispute resolution.

17 The courts referred to include small claims courts or administrative tribunals.

18 Pleasence, *supra* note 10 at i.

19 The survey asked about costs in a fourth area: costs due to loss of housing. Although, 2.7 percent of respondents experiencing problems said they had lost their housing as a direct consequence of experiencing a legal problem, there were no responses to the question about the subsidy received for alternative housing.

20 Based on the weighted sample data, Canadians used the healthcare system an estimated 1,306,024 times for physical health problems resulting from a legal problem (problem one), plus 621,538 times for problem two, for a total of 1,927,562 additional uses over the three-year reference period of the study. Similarly, Canadians used the healthcare system an estimated 2,188,143 times as a result of extreme stress or emotional problems directly attributable to an everyday legal problem (problem one), plus 1,116,877 times related to problem two, for a total of 3,305,020 additional uses. Together these total 5,232,582 visits. Questions were asked for up to two problems experienced by respondents.

21 *Physicians in Canada 2013: Summary Report* (Ottawa: Canadian Institute for Health Information, 2014).

22 This could be an overestimate because in some instances respondents used healthcare services that cost less than a visit to a physician's office. On the other hand, the estimate is based on only two problems for which detailed data were collected. An estimated 41.3 percent of respondents experiencing at least one everyday legal problem experienced three or more problems. Also, the estimate assumes only one additional visit for each problem for which a respondent said he or she used the healthcare system more than normal. For these reasons, the figure of $101 million annually could be an underestimate.

23 Total expenditures on healthcare for 2013 were $128.5 billion. This included $62.6 billion on hospitals, $34.5 billion on drugs, and $31.4 billion on physicians.

24 This is derived from 7.6 percent (*n* = 105) of the sample.

25 Office of the Chief Actuary, Office of the Superintendent of Financial Institutions Canada, *2015 Actuarial Report on the Employment Insurance Premium Rate* (Ottawa: Minister of Public Works and Government Services, 2014), online: <http://www.

osfi-bsif.gc.ca>; <https://www.canada.ca/content/dam/canada/employment-social
-development/migration/documents/Eng/Docs/EI2015.pdf>.

26 The sample percentage is 1.8 percent ($n = 25$).

27 Unpublished data provided by the Caledon Institute, Ottawa.

28 Graham Cookson, *Unintended Consequences: The Cost of the Government's Legal Aid Reforms: A Report for the Law Society of England and Wales* (London: King's College London, 2011), Executive Summary.

29 Perryman Group, *The Impact of Legal Aid Services on Economic Activity in Texas: An Analysis of Current Effects and Expansion Potential* (Waco, TX: Perryman Group, 2009).

30 David Luban, "The Right to Legal Services" in A.A. Paterson & T. Goriely, eds, *Resourcing Civil Justice* (Oxford: Oxford University Press, 1996) at 61.

31 J. Cooper, "Legal Aid Policy: A Time for Reflection" (1984) 2 Environment and Planning C: Government and Policy 432; or more recently, John Kilwein, "The Decline of the Legal Services Corporation: It's Ideological, Stupid!" in Francis Regan et al, eds, *The Transformation of Legal Aid: Comparative and Historical Studies* (Oxford: Oxford University Press, 1999) at 41–64.

32 Sandefur, *Money Isn't Everything, supra* note 7 at 222–45.

33 Trevor C.W. Farrow, "What Is Access to Justice?" (2014) 51 Osgoode Hall LJ 957 at 971. Based on interview data, Professor Farrow demonstrates that people are more likely to think in terms of broader rights and social justice than the specific legal problems they experience. For a further discussion of legal consciousness as an important part of understanding the access to justice landscape, see Chapter 5 in this volume.

34 Lake Research Partners and the Tarrance Group, *Expanding Civil Legal Aid: Strategies for Branding and Communications* (Washington, DC: Public Welfare Foundation and Kresge Foundation, 2013) at 13.

35 Celinda Lake, Anat Shenker Osario, Daniel Gotoff, & Corey Teter, *Building a Civil Justice System That Delivers Justice for All* (Washington, DC: Voices for Civil justice and Public Welfare Foundation, 2017); Richard Zorza, "A Broader Branding Perspective for Access to Justice" (9 September 2017) *Richard Zorza's Access to Justice Blog* (blog), online: <https://accesstojustice.net/2017/09/09/a-broader-branding-perspective-for-access-to-justice-service-and-change/>.

36 C. Wright Mills, *The Sociological Imagination* (New York: Grove Press, 1959) at 8.

37 Action Committee on Access to Justice in Civil and Family Matters, *Canadian Access to Justice Initiatives: Justice Development Goals Status Report* (Ottawa: Action Committee on Access to Justice in Civil and Family Matters, 2017) at 13, online: Canadian Forum on Civil Justice <http://www.cfcj-fcjc.org/sites/default/files/docs/Canadian%20Access%20to%20Justice%20Initiatives%20-Justice%20Development%20Goals%20Status%20Report.pdf>: Justice Development Goal One: Refocus the Justice System to Reflect and Address Everyday Legal Problems.

38 Action Committee on Access to Justice in Civil and Family Matters, *Access to Civil and Family Justice: A Roadmap for Change* (Ottawa: Action Committee on Access to Justice in Civil and Family Matters, 2013) at 4 and 5, online: Canadian Forum on Civil Justice <http://www.cfcj- fcjc.org/sites/default/files/docs/2013/AC_Report_English_Final.pdf>.

39 Canadian Bar Association Access to Justice Committee, *Reaching Equal Justice: An Invitation to Envision and Act* (Ottawa: Canadian Bar Association, 2013) at 16, online: <http://www.cba.org/CBA-Equal-Justice/Equal-Justice-Initiative/Reports>.

40 Melina Buckley, *A National Framework for Meeting Legal Needs: Proposed National Benchmarks for Public Legal Assistance Services* (Ottawa: Canadian Bar Association, 2016)

at 6 and 10, online: <https://www.cba.org/CBAMediaLibrary/cba_na/PDFs/LLR/A-National-Framework-for-Meeting-Legal-Needs_Proposed-National-Benchmarks.pdf>.

41 Sandefur, *Money Isn't Everything, supra* note 7 at 222–45.

42 Ab Currie, *Engaging the Power of Community to Expand Legal Services for Low-Income Ontarians* (Toronto: Canadian Forum on Civil Justice, 2016); Ab Currie, *Legal Secondary Consultation: How Legal Aid Can Support Communities and Expand Access to Justice* (Toronto: Canadian Forum on Civil Justice, 2017).

5

How Ontarians Experience the Law
An Examination of Incidence Rate, Responses, and Costs of Legal Problems

Matthew Dylag

IF MODERN ACCESS TO justice scholarship takes as a fundamental premise that legal reform must centre on the unmet legal needs of a population, then key to this discussion is an understanding of how that population interacts with the law.[1] In recent years, many jurisdictions have conducted civil legal needs surveys in an attempt to empirically assess how people utilize the law and to better understand the civil legal needs landscape of their own jurisdiction.[2] Following in this tradition of legal needs research, the Canadian Forum on Civil Justice recently completed a multi-year national survey as part of its Cost of Justice project examining the legal problems experienced in the everyday lives of Canadians.[3] In this context, legal problems were defined as any non-trivial issue with a legal remedy. As discussed in the Introduction to this volume, the survey was national in scope: 3,051 randomly selected adults from all ten provinces were interviewed between September 2013 and May 2014 and were asked about the nature and frequency of legal problems in their everyday lives.[4] While a national perspective of civil legal needs is important in developing a Canada-wide strategy to address access to justice issues, the reality is that most of the heavy lifting – at least in terms of legislated reform – will have to come from the provinces.

There are three fundamental reasons for this. The first reason has to do with the types of civil legal problems experienced by Canadians. The Cost of Justice project survey found that the most common problems experienced by Canadians are consumer, debt, and employment, which together account for approximately 60 percent of all civil legal problems.[5] The authority to legislate concerning these types of problems, as well as most other civil legal needs, falls under provincial governments' jurisdiction.[6] A second reason has to do with the administration of justice, including the administration of the courts and procedure in civil matters, which, constitutionally, is also a provincial mandate. Thus, if there are to be any changes made to the Rules of Civil Procedure or to the alternative dispute resolution regimes, these too have to come from the provinces. Closely connected to the administration of justice is the regulation of the provision of legal services. In Canada, the provincial law societies are granted the authority to regulate legal services by provincial legislation. Therefore, any changes to who can provide legal services necessarily comes, if not from the provinces themselves, then from the provincial law societies. A third reason why the provinces will have to bear the burden of addressing access to justice concerns has to do with the availability of public legal assistance, which again falls within the purview of the provinces. In Ontario, for example, Legal Aid Ontario (LAO) is the publicly funded independent corporation established by the province that is wholly responsible for providing all public legal assistance. It is provincial legislation that sets up LAO's mandate, structure, and program areas, so any amendments to existing public legal assistance must also come from the province. Since most legislated reforms will have to originate at the provincial level, province-specific data are necessary to inform policy decisions. This is especially true because each province has its own distinctive demographics, geography, laws, and legal services, and may therefore also have distinctive legal needs.

Besides a provincial perspective, a comprehensive understanding of the civil legal needs landscape also requires older survey data for comparison. There is no reason to assume that civil legal needs are static and do not change over time. As economies, demographics, and policies change, so too do legal needs. Comparators can provide insight into whether any gaps in accessing justice have been met or are widening. Moreover, these comparators may assist in confirming or rejecting conclusions that were based on a single dataset. In Ontario, there are two comparative legal needs surveys of note. The first was conducted in 2006 by Ab Currie for the Department of Justice Canada and was presented in a report titled *The Legal Problems of Everyday Life: The Nature, Extent and Consequences of Justiciable Problems Experienced by Canadians.*[7] This survey examined the degree to which Canadians experience legal problems and had a sample size of 6,665 adults from all ten provinces. The second important survey was conducted in June 2009 for the Ontario Civil Legal Needs Project (CLNP). It consisted of 2,000 telephone interviews with Ontarians who had a combined annual household income of less than $75,000.[8] The survey resulted in the report titled *Listening to Ontarians: Report of the Ontario Civil Legal Needs Project,* released in 2010.[9]

Like the Cost of Justice project (COJP) survey, these two earlier surveys examined civil legal needs and are therefore able to provide some basis for comparison. However, there are differences in methodology that make direct comparisons difficult. Although the methods and survey questions of the 2006 Justice Canada survey are very similar to those of the COJP survey – with Ab Currie taking a leading role in the design of both surveys – and although the

resulting report did provide some findings at the provincial level, it was fundamentally from a national perspective. Conversely, the 2009 CLNP survey focused
on Ontario; moreover, unlike the other two surveys, it interviewed only individuals with a household income of $75,000 or less. While this was a deliberate
choice by the authors in order to focus on the needs of lower-income individuals,
it does not provide a comprehensive picture since a large part of the population
was excluded. Moreover, the CLNP survey used a completely different methodology from that used by the Justice Canada and COJP surveys. Where the
latter two surveys asked respondents whether they experienced specific types
of legal problems (asking about eighty and eighty-five specific problems, respectively), the CLNP survey limited itself to a single open-ended question,
preferring that respondents define legal needs themselves. Nevertheless, while
these differences make a direct comparison difficult, as long as each survey is
placed in its methodological context, they do assist in providing a more comprehensive understanding of how Ontarians experience the law.

Using the three legal needs surveys discussed above, this chapter will examine three aspects of Ontario's legal needs landscape. It will look at the incident
rate of legal problems, examine how individuals respond to those problems,
and discuss the costs – financial and otherwise – associated with having a legal
problem. The particular findings of the COJP survey will be compared with
the results of the two earlier surveys. We shall see that Ontarians are more likely
to recognize a legal need as one that requires formal access to either courts or
a lawyer; that they may not conceptualize informal paths to resolution as a
legitimate means of resolving legal problems; and that, as a result, almost all
Ontarians who have experienced a legal problem will experience significant
financial, health, and social costs.

Incidence of Civil Legal Problems

Frequency, Type, and Number of Problems
In speaking of the incidence of civil legal problems experienced by Ontarians,
there are three important indicators, namely, the frequency, types, and number
of problems experienced. With regard to frequency, 52.9 percent of Ontarians
surveyed for the COJP experienced one or more justiciable problems during
the three-year reference period.[10] This number does not tell us whether these
individuals were able to resolve their problem or whether they were satisfied
with the resolution, but it does show that legal problems are pervasive in the
day-to-day lives of Ontarians.

In terms of types of problems experienced, the three most common can be
categorized as consumer (22.7 percent of all reported incidences), debt (22.1

Table 5.1 Types and number of legal problems reported

Type of legal problem	Number reported	Percentage reported
Consumer	464	22.7
Debt	451	22.1
Employment	314	15.4
Neighbours	177	8.7
Family	122	6.0
Discrimination	111	5.4
Wills and powers of attorney	79	3.9
Medical treatment	63	3.1
Police	56	2.7
Housing	53	2.6
Personal injury	38	1.9
Immigration	33	1.6
Obtaining social assistance	29	1.4
Threat of legal action	29	1.4
Obtaining disability assistance	20	1.0
Criminal	6	0.3
Total	2,045	100.2[a]

a Total percentage of problems experienced exceeds 100 percent due to rounding.

Table 5.2 Number of problems experienced

Number of problems	Percentage of Ontarians
1	36.7
2	21.1
3	12.1
4	7.1
5	7.3
6 or more	15.7

percent), or employment (15.4 percent). The most infrequent were criminal law problems (0.3 percent of all reported incidences), problems regarding disability assistance (1.0 percent), problems with obtaining social assistance (1.4 percent), and incidences of being threatened with a legal action or court proceedings (1.4 percent) (see Table 5.1).

Regarding the number of problems experienced by respondents over the three-year reference period, the majority (36.7 percent) experienced only one problem. Fewer individuals experienced two problems (21.1 percent), and even fewer, three problems (12.1 percent). The response rate plateaus at four and five problems (7.1 and 7.3 percent, respectively) but rises for those who have experienced six or more problems (15.7 percent) (see Table 5.2).

Comparison with Other Surveys

When comparing the COJP survey with previous surveys, the first observation of note is the rate of incidence of legal problems. As noted above, the COJP survey found that 52.9 percent of Ontarians experienced a legal problem during the three-year period. The Justice Canada survey conducted in 2006 found comparable numbers, noting that 44.6 percent of Canadians and 49.4 percent of Ontarians experienced one or more legal problem over a three-year reference period.[11] The CLNP survey conducted in 2009 found that only about 38 percent of Ontarians had a civil legal need over a three-year reference period.[12] More striking, however, are the substantial differences between the survey results regarding the *type* of legal problems experienced. Similar to the COJP survey, the Justice Canada survey found that employment, debt, and consumer problems were the three most common categories of legal problems reported by Canadians.[13] Yet the three most common types of problems reported through the CLNP were related to either family relationship (30 percent of all reported incidences), wills and powers of attorney (13 percent), or housing or land (10 percent).[14] All three of these categories were actually found to make up a fairly small percentage of the total problems reported in the other two surveys (see Figure 5.1). These striking differences warrant further exploration and will be discussed in the last section of this chapter.

Figure 5.1 **Comparison between three surveys regarding types of legal problems experienced by Ontarians and Canadians**

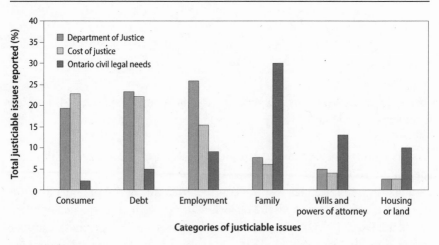

Response to Civil Legal Problems

Methods of Resolution

Inaction

Of the 630 Ontarians who experienced one or more legal problems during the three-year reference period, a strong majority took some type of action to resolve their issue. The COJP survey found that only 5.3 percent of Ontarians with legal problems failed to take any steps at all.[15] Figure 5.2 shows that the most common reason cited by Ontarians for not taking action was a belief that nothing could be done (cited by 48.1 percent of respondents who took no action). Other common reasons included the belief that resolution would be too stressful (29.6 percent), the concern that resolution would take too much time (22.2 percent), and the perception that the legal problem was not that serious (20.0 percent). Interestingly, the belief that resolution would cost too much was only the fifth most cited reason (18.5 percent) for inaction, which suggests that the high cost of legal services is not the main deterrent. These patterns generally hold true when compared with the national responses, with the exception that "not that serious" (30.9 percent nationally), "uncertain of my rights" (16.9 percent), and "help was too hard to reach" (13.3 percent) were all more commonly cited nationally than in Ontario alone.

Figure 5.2   **Reasons cited by COJP survey respondents who took no action to resolve their civil legal problems**

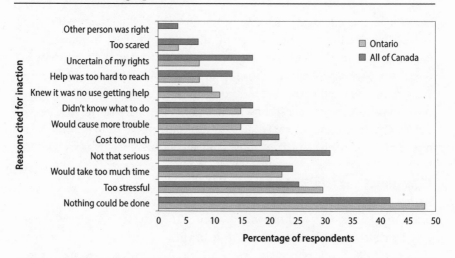

Figure 5.3 **Methods used by COJP survey respondents to resolve their civil legal problems**

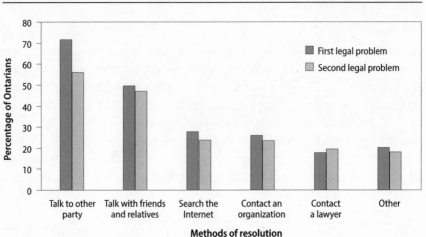

Informal Self-Help

More Ontarians will attempt to do something to resolve their legal problems than do nothing at all. The most common methods cited for resolution were talking to the other party directly (71.5 percent), seeking the advice of friends or relatives (49.6 percent), and/or searching for information on the Internet (27.8 percent). Taken together, these three methods can be classified as forms of self-help. It is interesting that even when Ontarians with legal needs seek assistance beyond their friends and family, they are more likely to contact an organization, such as the police, a union, or a professional association, for assistance or guidance (26.2 percent) than to contact a lawyer for advice (17.9 percent) at some point during their resolution process (see Figure 5.3). If we look at how the respondents resolved a second legal problem, we see that the numbers do not change significantly, except that fewer respondents talked to the other party directly (56.1 percent) and a few more contacted a lawyer (19.7 percent).[16]

Legal Advice and Formal Adjudication

As noted above, most people do not seek legal advice when resolving their problem. The majority of those who did contacted private legal representation (77.0 percent) (the survey made no distinction between whether or not a private lawyer was offering service on a pro bono basis). A few received help from a free legal clinic (7.0 percent), qualified for legal aid (4.0 percent), or called a telephone legal aid service (3.0 percent). There was no indication of whether these services were provided by Legal Aid Ontario or some other government or non-government agency (e.g., Office of the Worker Adviser). Finally, a not insignificant number of Ontarians who sought legal advice did not know where they received their legal advice from (8.0 percent). These numbers show that most people will obtain their legal advice – whether due to necessity or choice – from private legal representation rather than publicly funded services.

More dramatic, however, was the finding that few Ontarians with legal problems actually had their issue adjudicated by a formal court or tribunal. Only 5.9 percent attended a formal court or tribunal for their first legal problem. This figure rises slightly to 6.9 percent for those who had a second legal problem. Most of those who went to formal adjudication appeared before either the superior or provincial court (48.5 percent), many attended at a tribunal or other non-court body (36.4 percent), and only a few attended at small claims court (6.1 percent). Of the remainder, a significant proportion did not know what kind of forum they appeared before (9.1 percent). Almost half of Ontarians who appeared before a formal adjudicative body were self-represented (48.5 percent); only about a third were represented by a lawyer (36.4 percent). A few stated that they were represented by a trained advocate but not a lawyer, such as a paralegal (3.0 percent), or had a friend or relative represent them (3.0 percent). This high number of self-represented litigants may be problematic as such persons are commonly understood to be particularly vulnerable due to a lack of income, assets, and legal education.[17]

Comparison with Other Surveys

The COJP survey findings relating to responses to legal problems are difficult to compare with those of the two other surveys for reasons of methodology. In terms of the rate of inaction, the CLNP survey appears to confirm the findings of the COJP survey, as it found that 4.0 percent of respondents either gave up trying to solve their legal problem or did nothing about it in the first place,[18] a figure not that different from the 5.3 percent of Ontarians that the COJP survey found took no action to resolve their problem. Because of the design of the CLNP survey questionnaire, however, the results of the two surveys are not comparable. The CLNP survey included a screening question that precluded anyone who failed to seek legal advice from answering any follow-up questions regarding their method of resolution or their failure to resolve the problem. This means that the CLNP survey actually found that 4.0 percent *of those who sought legal advice* eventually gave up trying to resolve the problem or did nothing further to resolve it. It is impossible to know how this number would have changed had the CLNP survey encompassed all respondents with legal problems rather than just those who sought legal advice.

The 2006 Justice Canada survey is somewhat more comparable with the COJP survey in that it examined how all respondents resolved their justiciable issues – not just those who went to a lawyer. However, it found that 22.2 percent of respondents took no action to resolve their legal problems, a far greater figure than that reported by the COJP survey.[19] The inconsistent findings of these two surveys may be partly due to differences in the design of the questionnaires. The Justice Canada survey asked respondents how they resolved up to three of their problems. If a respondent had more than three problems, the survey randomly selected three of the problems and asked about those. The COJP survey, on the other hand, asked about only two of their problems.[20] If more than two were identified, then two were randomly selected for the questions regarding resolution. Further, respondents who reported more than six problems in the COJP survey skipped this part of the survey, whereas no such filter was applied to the Justice Canada survey. This is of some importance given that 15.7 percent of Ontarians who experienced justiciable issues reported experiencing six or more problems. These extra filters – one less problem and screening out those with six or more problems – may partially explain why the COJP survey showed a lower rate of inaction than the Justice Canada survey: intuitively, one may assume that the rate of inaction would increase with the number of problems experienced, due to growing frustration or fatigue. However, there may also be a more theoretical reason for the difference, which will be discussed in the last section of this chapter.

In terms of those who took action to resolve their problem, the CLNP survey focused solely on respondents who sought some form legal assistance, as noted above. It included a screening question that asked, "During the last three years, have you or anyone in your household had any sort of problem or issue where you sought *legal* assistance?" (emphasis in original).[21] If the answer was negative, the questioner skipped the next seventeen questions, including those regarding methods of resolution. This difference in methodology prevents comparison with the COJP survey for most methods of resolution except for those incidences where an individual did seek legal advice. Even here, however, there is inconsistency in the findings. The CLNP survey concluded that 30 percent of those with a legal problem sought some form of legal assistance.[22] This is higher than in both the Justice Canada survey (11.7 percent) and the COJP survey (17.9 percent for first problem and 19.7 percent for the second problem). The reason for this difference will be examined in the final section below.

The Justice Canada survey explored responses to legal problems in a slightly different manner than the COJP survey. Where the latter presented a list of possible methods of resolution and asked respondents to identify all that applied, the former first asked whether respondents did something to resolve the problem and, if so, followed up by asking whether they attempted to resolve it on their own or sought assistance, whether legal or non-legal.[23] The Justice Canada survey does not elaborate on what is meant by "resolved the problem on their own," but presumably this would include talking to the other side and searching the Internet for information, the two main self-help methods identified in the COJP survey. Similarly, the Justice Canada survey's category of non-legal assistance would presumably include such methods identified in the COJP survey as talking to family and friends as well as seeking advice from a third-party organization. The Justice Canada survey found that the most common response to a justiciable issue was to "handle the problem on own" (44 percent). It also found that more people sought non-legal forms of assistance (22.1 percent) than legal forms of assistance (11.7 percent).[24] Bearing the differences in the questionnaires in mind, this finding affirms the narrative established by the COJP survey, which suggested that most people try to resolve their legal problems through informal self-help methods, and whereas some will turn to informal advice, only a small minority will seek out formal legal advice.

In terms of formal adjudication, the Justice Canada survey noted that 14.9 percent of respondents appeared in a court or a tribunal to resolve their problems.[25] This is notably higher than in the COJP survey (5.9 percent) and is interesting as both asked the identical question: "Did you have to appear at a court or other tribunal because of this problem?"[26] This difference may be due to the fact that the COJP survey asked respondents how they resolved up to two problems, whereas the Justice Canada survey asked about up to three problems, thereby capturing a greater problem set specifically among those who had experienced multiple legal problems. It is reasonable to posit that individuals with multiple legal problems may make use of the court system more frequently, but more data would be required to confirm this. The more likely explanation, however, may be related to the higher rate of individuals in the Justice Canada survey who reported doing nothing to resolve their problem. Many of these individuals likely engaged in informal methods of resolution, such as searching for information online, but did not report them because they did not consider them viable methods. As will be discussed below, by excluding many individuals who may have engaged in informal self-help, the Justice Canada survey may have overrepresented those who took formal action.

Cost of Civil Legal Problems

Cost to Individual
Although significant in themselves, the rate of and type of response to justiciable issues among Ontarians paint only part of the picture. What gives this narrative

more depth is an understanding of the costs associated with legal needs. The most obvious impact that legal problems may have is on an individual's pocketbook. However, those who experience legal problems may also incur costs beyond those that are monetary in nature. An individual's employment, housing, health, and family may also be affected by legal problems. The state may also incur costs when individuals experience legal problems, for example, when citizens are forced to utilize social programs or visit the hospital, or when they can no longer pay taxes.

Monetary

The COJP survey found that only about one-third of Ontarians (35.5 percent) who had legal problems spent money attempting to resolve them. This is not completely surprising given that the most common method of resolution was some form of self-help. Among those who did spend money, most (about 38.9 percent) spent less than $1,000 (Figure 5.4). A little over a quarter of Ontarians (27.4 percent) spent between $1,000 and $4,999, and the percentage of those who spent between $5,000 and $9,999 was roughly the same as those who spent $20,000 or more (12.0 and 12.6 percent, respectively). The mean dollar amount spent resolving a legal problem in Ontario was $8,362.95.[27]

The most common costs incurred by Ontarians include lawyers' fees (paid by 22.6 percent of those who incurred costs), purchasing of materials and photocopying (14.5 percent), fees for advisers or mediators (13.0 percent), transportation costs (13.0 percent), and court fees (11.4 percent). Other less

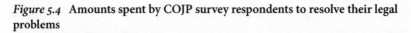

Figure 5.4 **Amounts spent by COJP survey respondents to resolve their legal problems**

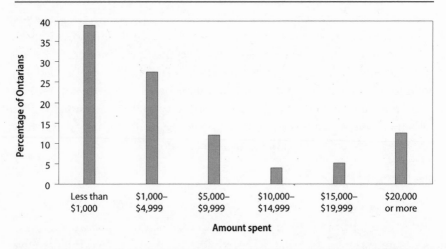

commonly cited costs include those for long distance calls or faxes (5.2 percent) and child care (3.6 percent).

Employment

It is not difficult to imagine one's employment being affected by civil legal needs. An individual working a standard workday who needs to meet with a lawyer or attend court will likely have to take time off work. Even if the individual does not need to take time off from work, legal problems that are stressful may distract from work duties and affect productivity. In the most dramatic cases, legal problems could cause a person to lose his or her job. In Ontario, 7.8 percent of those who had experienced a legal problem stated that problem caused or contributed to their loss of employment. This has a direct cost to the state as a high proportion of such individuals apply for and obtain employment insurance (39.5 percent in Ontario). The mean length of time on employment insurance was 19.9 weeks and the median was fifteen weeks; one individual reported being on employment insurance for as long as fifty-two weeks. In addition, some individuals reported that their legal problem caused them to access other social benefits or insurance plans: 1.3 percent of all respondents who experienced a legal problem stated that it caused them to go on social assistance. Another 7.5 percent were required to make a claim for insurance, with just over half (57.1 percent) receiving an insurance payout to cover their loss.

Health and Family

In terms of non-monetary consequences of legal problems, respondents were asked the fairly broad question of whether their legal problem caused or contributed to other health, social, or family problems in their life. Over one-third (34.1 percent) of respondents answered in the affirmative. Among them, 66.3 percent stated that their legal problem affected their physical health, 50.5 percent that it affected their mental health or caused extreme stress, and 23.8 percent that it caused social, family, or personal issues or made existing issues worse. Common social, family, and personal problems that were exacerbated by the legal problem include marital problems or problems with a partner (20.3 percent), relationship problems with a parent, grandparent, or child (14.8 percent), relationship problems with other family members (25.8 percent), child behaviour problems (4.7 percent), and problems with alcohol (2.3 percent). As with employment, these problems are not limited to individual families and have a direct impact on society as a whole. For example, almost two-thirds (65.1 percent) of those who stated that the legal problem affected their physical health also stated that they were required to visit their doctor and use the healthcare system more than before. Likewise, 40.6 percent of those who stated that the problem affected their mental health or caused extreme stress said they visited the doctor or used counselling services more than before. It has been estimated that the additional use of the healthcare system by Canadians who experience a legal problem costs the state approximately $101 million annually.[28]

Housing

The loss of housing is a rarer consequence of having a civil legal need: only 1.8 percent of Ontarians who experienced a civil legal problem stated that the problem caused or contributed to their losing their housing. It is certainly a dramatic and traumatic consequence, however. The mean length of time for being without housing was 7.5 weeks, and the median was four weeks. One individual reported being without housing for thirty-two weeks.

Comparison with Other Surveys

Both the CLNP survey and the Justice Canada survey examined costs associated with legal problems to varying degrees. Whereas the former focused on pecuniary costs as a barrier to legal representation, the latter was concerned primarily with social and health costs. Both surveys therefore provide data for comparison.

The CLNP survey did not examine the social costs of problems, but it did note that approximately three-quarters of those who reported a legal problem experienced some disruption in their daily lives as a result.[29] While this is a broad statement, and as such is not directly comparable to the COJP survey, it does confirm how disruptive legal problems can be. In terms of direct pecuniary costs, the CLNP survey found that about 42 percent of respondents cited cost as a barrier to affording a lawyer.[30] While it found that only a third of respondents who retained a lawyer spent over $1,000 on legal representation, this figure is a rather limited representation of the cost of resolving a legal issue as it does not take into account other costs associated with resolving legal problems, such as transportation, child care, time off from work, and court fees.[31] The COJP survey's finding that individuals spend on average over $8,000 to resolve a legal problem presents a more complete picture of the actual pecuniary costs involved.

The Justice Canada survey was concerned primarily with four consequences associated with legal problems: consequences for physical and mental health, impact on alcohol or drug use, the occurrence of violence in family and personal life, and feelings of personal safety and security.[32] The survey noted that 38.1 percent of Canadians who had a legal issue reported having a health or social problem directly attributable to a justiciable issue;[33] 77.9 percent of those who experienced a physical health problem caused by a legal issue stated that it resulted in an increased number of visits to the doctor or other health facility.[34] Though these numbers are somewhat higher than those reported by Ontarians in the COJP survey, the two surveys' findings are still close enough to be comparable.

Discussion: How Ontarians Experience the Law

While the data presented above may be interesting in and of themselves, they tell only part of the story, and further explanation is needed to understand what these statistics mean and why some of the differences between the surveys arise.[35] It would be helpful to situate the findings in a legal consciousness framework.

Legal consciousness is a theory that is primarily concerned with how the law is practised and understood by laypersons as opposed to legal experts.[36] When "law" is spoken of in this context, it refers to both formal doctrines and legal institutions, as well as the informal relationships or common understandings that develop within a community.[37] Patricia Ewick and Susan Silbey argue that legality is a structural component of society consisting of cultural schemas and resources that shape social relations such that one's understanding of the law – both formal and informal – is produced in what people do and say.[38] In other words, one's understanding of rights and obligations develops outside the formal legal system and arises from lived community relationships such as the interactions between neighbours, family members, or businesses.

When the COJP survey is compared with the CLNP and Justice Canada surveys, two notable discrepancies between the findings are seen. Fundamentally these discrepancies are the result of how the survey questions were framed, but they also provide insight into how Ontarians understand and interact with the law. The first discrepancy has to do with the types of problems that Ontarians view as being legal in nature. Whereas both the COJP and Justice Canada surveys found that the three most common types of legal problems were consumer, debt, and employment problems, the CLNP survey found that those problems were all relatively uncommon. Rather, according to that survey, the vast majority of legal problems were associated with family law, wills and powers of attorney, and housing or land. Methodologically, this difference arises from the questions being asked. To identify incidence rates, the CLNP survey asked a single open-ended question:

> There are many different problems or issues that might cause a person to need legal assistance. What are the most likely reasons you can think of for why you or someone in your household might need legal assistance in the near future?[39]

In contrast, the COJP and Justice Canada surveys asked questions about specific problems and did not explicitly frame them as legal in nature. For example, to find incidences of debt problems, the Justice Canada survey asked each respondent whether they were harassed by a collection agency, were unfairly refused credit due to inaccurate information, had a dispute over a bill or invoice, or had problems collecting money.[40] Similarly, the COJP survey asked respondents eight questions relating to debt, such as whether the respondent declared personal bankruptcy or was harassed by a collection agency. These types of problems may not be viewed by non-experts as having a legal element because one does not commonly engage the formal legal system to deal with them. Conversely, the open-ended CLNP question requires the respondent to recall a problem, recognize that it had a legal element, and be able to express it as such. This discrepancy demonstrates that when given this type of latitude, lay individuals will more commonly recognize only those problems that are typically resolved within the formal legal system as being legal in nature, while commonly disregarding other legal problems.

Consider the CLNP survey's conclusion that 30 percent of all civil justice problems were related to family relationship problems, with only 5 percent being related to debt problems and 2 percent to consumer problems.[41] The reason for this is that those experiencing family breakdowns are much quicker to recognize the legal element inherent in the situation than those facing problems related to debt or consumer issues. Canadian and Ontario law is structured in such a way that the formal legal system oversees so many aspects of a family breakdown. In order to obtain a divorce, one *has* to apply to the court. Once this happens, issues of custody, support, and division of property are also often overseen by courts. Thus, family problems are clearly seen as a civil legal need.[42] Other problems, such as debt or consumer, can be resolved without the use of lawyers or courts and therefore are less likely to be recognized by non-experts as having a legal element. Similarly, wills and powers of attorney generally require one to visit a lawyer and thus are clearly seen by non-experts as having a legal element, so it makes sense that the CLNP survey found that wills and powers of attorney were the second most common legal need of Ontarians.

From comparing the three surveys, we can conclude that Ontarians are more likely to recognize a legal need as one that requires formal access to either courts or a lawyer. This conclusion helps us understand why both the Justice Canada and COJP surveys reported a higher proportion of individuals having problems associated with consumer and debt than the CLNP survey. Those surveys did not require the respondent to recognize the legal element of a problem in order to report it and were therefore able to capture different types of problems. This conclusion would likewise help explain why the Justice Canada and COJP surveys noted an overall higher incidence of civil legal problems, since asking specific questions about issues not traditionally seen as having a formal legal element would capture a broader set of incidences. This conclusion also has an impact on how we understand who is seeking legal representation. As noted above, the CLNP survey found that far more respondents sought legal advice than the other two surveys. The most likely explanation is again methodological, as the CLNP survey allowed respondents to define legal issues narrowly. The result was that those issues that more typically require a lawyer – such as divorce or wills – were far more representative in that survey's dataset than other types of legal problems.

A second discrepancy that provides insight into how Ontarians understand the law has to do with the differing rates of inaction among those with legal problems. The Justice Canada survey found a greater number of respondents who took no action to resolve their legal problems than did the COJP survey.[43] Again, the reason for this discrepancy is most likely methodological. The Justice Canada survey asked all respondents who experienced one or more legal problems the following open-ended question: "Did you do something or attempt to do something to resolve this problem?" Conversely, the COJP survey asked all respondents who experienced one or more legal problems the following question: "People do a number of things to try to resolve problems. Please tell me if you did any of the following to resolve the [problem identified] you had. Did you ...?" The survey then provided a list of five possible actions – talk to the other party, talk with friends or relatives, search the Internet for information, contact an organization, or contact a lawyer – and concluded with the following open-ended question: "Did you do anything else?" While the Justice Canada survey found that 22.2 percent of individuals took no action to resolve the problem, the COJP survey found that only 5.3 percent took no action. This difference shows that respondents may not conceptualize certain actions – such as talking to the other side or searching for information online – as possible methods of resolving a legal problem and therefore may not have reported it, instead claiming that they did nothing. By suggesting possible methods of resolution, the COJP survey was better able to identify respondents who took informal means to resolve their problems rather than dismiss them as doing nothing. This discrepancy shows that Ontarians may not conceptualize informal paths to resolution as a legitimate means of resolving legal problems.

Other insights into how Ontarians interact with the law are evident when examining the similarities between the surveys. Perhaps the most important similarity is the finding that legal problems are ubiquitous among Ontarians. The COJP survey found that just over half of Ontarians experienced one or more legal problems during the three-year reference period, which is consistent with the Justice Canada survey's finding of 49.4 percent. While the CLNP survey found a smaller incidence rate – only 38 percent over the three-year reference period – the difference most likely has to do with how that survey allowed the respondents to define legal issues themselves, which, as discussed above, means that fewer legal problems are caught. Had the CLNP survey asked respondents about issues that they would not normally consider legal in nature, it would likely have found a higher rate of incidence.

As approximately half of Ontarians experience one or more civil legal problems during a three-year time frame, it is reasonable to take this finding a step further and postulate that almost all Ontarians will experience one or more civil legal problems at some point during their life. This pervasiveness and universality of legal problems in the lives of Ontarians should raise concerns when one considers the costs incurred as a direct result of the legal issue experienced. As stated above, over one-third of those with a legal problem had to spend money to resolve it, and while most spent less than $5,000, about a third ended up spending over $5,000, a not insignificant amount. One reason these figures are not more dramatic is that Ontarians generally do not recognize many civil problems – such as consumer or debt – as requiring formal access to the courts or a lawyer and therefore more commonly utilize informal and inexpensive methods of resolution. While it may be a good thing that Ontarians seek to resolve their legal problems through less expensive means, such as by talking to the other party directly, this presumption is dependent on Ontarians' having a meaningful choice in their path to resolution. The finding that about one-third of those with a legal problem suffered from some form of physical or mental health issue as a direct result of their problem – a finding confirmed by the earlier Justice Canada survey – suggests that this is not the case. Indeed, if individuals understood the legal implications of the problem and were able to get assistance, many of the physical and mental health problems, such as extreme stress, problems with alcohol or drugs, and problems with family, may be tempered. Less common but no less serious repercussions are that about 7.8 percent of those with a justiciable issue lost their employment as a direct result of the issue, and about 1.8 percent lost their housing. Here, too, it is not unreasonable to suggest that these repercussions could be avoided if Ontarians had a better understanding of the legal implications of their problem and how to resolve them.

The costs of legal problems go beyond individuals and their immediate families, as society will also bear some of the costs, most obviously through greater use of social services such as healthcare or employment insurance, but also due to harder-to-measure factors such as loss of productivity. These serious implications demonstrate that policy makers must ensure that Ontarians have access to meaningful ways to resolve their legal problems. This discussion, however, needs to be informed by two realities made evident in this chapter. First, many Ontarians do not recognize the legal elements inherent in many of the more common legal problems, and second, many of them take paths to resolution that may not involve the formal legal system. Those advocating more meaningful access to justice cannot ignore the problems that do not end up before the formal legal system simply because of these realities.

Notes

1 This premise is generally accepted as valid by the Canadian legal and academic community. See, e.g., Ab Currie, *The Legal Problems of Everyday Life: The Nature, Extent and Consequences of Justiciable Problems Experienced by Canadians* (Ottawa: Department of Justice Canada, 2009); Action Committee on Access to Justice in Civil and Family Matters, *Access to Civil and Family Justice: A Roadmap for Change* (Ottawa: Action Committee on Access to Justice in Civil and Family Matters, 2013), online: Canadian Forum on Civil Justice <http://www.cfcj- fcjc.org/sites/default/files/docs/2013/AC_Report_English_Final.pdf>; Trevor C.W. Farrow, "What Is Access to Justice ?" (2015) 51 Osgoode Hall LJ 957; Michael Trebilcock, Anthony Duggan, & Lorne Sossin, eds, *Middle Income Access to Justice* (Toronto: University of Toronto Press, 2012).
2 See, e.g., Pascoe Pleasence & Nigel J. Balmer, "Caught in the Middle: Justiciable Problems and the Use of Lawyers" in Trebilcock, Duggan, & Sossin, *supra* note 1 at 31. The authors provide a table of twenty-three national surveys of legal problems conducted by thirteen separate countries since 1993.
3 Trevor C.W. Farrow et al, *Everyday Legal Problems and the Cost of Justice in Canada: Overview Report* (Toronto: Canadian Forum on Civil Justice, 2016), online: Canadian Forum on Civil Justice <http://www.cfcj-fcjc.org/sites/default/files//Everyday%20Legal%20Problems%20and%20the%20Cost%20of%20Justice%20in%20Canada%20-%20Overview%20Report.pdf> [*Everyday Legal Problems*].
4 For a complete discussion of the methodology, see David Northrup et al, *Design and Conduct of the Cost of Justice Survey* (Toronto: Canadian Forum on Civil Justice, 2016).
5 Farrow et al, *Everyday Legal Problems, supra* note 3 at 8.
6 One notable exception would be bankruptcy and insolvency problems, which fall under federal jurisdiction.
7 Currie, *supra* note 1.
8 Environics Research Group, *Civil Legal Needs of Lower and Middle-Income Ontarians: Quantitative Research* (Toronto: Environics Research Group, 2009).
9 Ontario Civil Legal Needs Project, *Listening to Ontarians: Report of the Ontario Civil Legal Needs Project* (Toronto: Ontario Civil Legal Needs Project Steering Committee, 2010).
10 Out of the 1,191 Ontarians surveyed, 630 reported experiencing one or more legal problems within the three-year reference period.
11 Currie, *supra* note 1 at 16.
12 Ontario Civil Legal Needs Project, *supra* note 9 at 18 and 21.
13 Currie, *supra* note 1 at 14. This report does not break down the frequency of problem categories by province.
14 Ontario Civil Legal Needs Project, *supra* note 9 at 21.
15 Out of the 562 Ontarians who were asked about resolution, 30 stated that they took no action to resolve their legal problem. Ontarians who experienced seven or more legal problems were not asked about resolution. See Northrup et al, *supra* note 4 at 7.

16   The problems for further inquiry were randomly selected and were not chosen based on factors such as seriousness, costs, or timing.

17   See, e.g., Trevor C.W. Farrow et al, "Addressing the Needs of Self-Represented Litigants in the Canadian Justice System: A White Paper Prepared for the Association of Canadian Court Administrators" (2012) at 16, online: Canadian Forum on Civil Justice <http://www.cfcj-fcjc.org/sites/default/files/docs/2013/Addressing%20the%20Needs%20of%20SRLs%20ACCA%20White%20Paper%20March%202012%20Final%20Revised%20Version.pdf>. See also Julie Macfarlane, "The National Self-Represented Litigants Project: Identifying and Meeting the Needs of Self-Represented Litigants, Final Report" (May 2013) at 8, online: <https://lawsocietyontario.azureedge.net/media/lso/media/legacy/pdf/s/self-represented_project.pdf>.

18   Environics Research Group, *supra* note 8 at 48 and Appendix: Questionnaire 8.

19   Currie, *supra* note 1 at 55.

20   For the first 446 interviews, respondents were asked follow-up questions for up to three problems; however, because the length of interviews was deemed excessive, the remaining interviewees were asked follow-up questions for only up to two problems. See Northrup et al, *supra* note 4 at 7.

21   Environics Research Group, *supra* note 8, Appendix: Questionnaire 3.

22   Ontario Civil Legal Needs Project, *supra* note 9 at 23.

23   Currie, *supra* note 1 at 102–4.

24   *Ibid* at 56.

25   *Ibid* at 65.

26   *Ibid* at 104.

27   There were two incidences where the individual reported having spent over $1 million to resolve a problem; both were considered outliers and removed from the analysis.

28   Farrow et al, *Everyday Legal Problems, supra* note 3 at 19.

29   Ontario Civil Legal Needs Project, *supra* note 9 at 22.

30   *Ibid* at 32.

31   *Ibid* at 25.

32   Currie, *supra* note 1 at 73.

33   *Ibid.*

34   *Ibid* at 76.

35   Roderick MacDonald, "Access to Civil Justice" in Peter Cane & Herbert M. Kritzer, eds, *The Oxford Handbook of Empirical Legal Research* (Oxford: Oxford University Press, 2010) 493 at 517.

36   Patricia Ewick & Susan S. Silbey, *The Common Place of Law: Stories from Everyday Life* (Chicago: University of Chicago Press, 1998) at 17. See also, e.g., Ellen Berrey, Steve G. Hoffman, & Laura Beth Nielsen, "Situated Justice: A Contextual Analysis of Fairness and Inequality in Employment Discrimination Litigation" (2012) 46:1 Law & Soc'y Rev 1; Tom Tyler, *Why People Obey the Law* (Princeton, NJ: Princeton University Press, 2006); Lesley A. Jacobs, *Privacy Rights in the Global Digital Economy: Legal Problems and Canadian Paths to Justice* (Toronto: Irwin Law, 2014).

37   See, e.g., Jacobs, *supra note* 36 at 44–46.

38   Ewick & Silbey, *supra* note 36 at 43–46.

39   Environics Research Group, *supra* note 8, Appendix: Questionnaire 2.

40   Currie, *supra* note 1 at 94.

41   Ontario Civil Legal Needs Project, *supra* note 9 at 21.

42   Even though some legal problems, such as those dealing with family issues, may be viewed as more legal in nature, the fact is that most people still do not seek legal advice and will

attempt to resolve a problem through self-help methods. For a discussion of why individuals tend not to seek legal advice, see Matthew Dylag, "Informal Justice: An Examination of Why Ontarians Do Not Seek Legal Advice" (2018) 35 Windsor YB Access Just 363.

43 *Ibid* at 55.

6
Truth, Reconciliation, and the Cost of Adversarial Justice

Trevor C. W. Farrow

> *After all, I'm a storyteller. You can have it if you want ... Do with it what you will ... Just don't say in the years to come that you would have lived your life differently if only you had heard this story. You've heard it now.*
>
> – THOMAS KING, "AFTERWORDS: PRIVATE STORIES"

> *It is hard to re-build or restart relationships. It starts with seeing each other. It starts with acknowledging what needs to be repaired.*
>
> – SHAWN ATLEO AND HEATHER ATLEO[1]

THAT INDIGENOUS PEOPLE IN Canada were victimized for well over a century by the residential schools system for Aboriginal children is not in question.[2] The system, which amounted to an "assault on child and culture," was designed to "kill the Indian in the child."[3] Whether the legal system – purporting to provide some form of compensation in the context of claims by survivors and their families – has provided justice is a much more open question. The costs – financial, social, health, time, and so on – associated with pursuing the resolution of residential schools claims through the justice system have been enormous. These costs feed skepticism about the commitment of the justice system to the process of truth and create immense barriers to progress towards reconciliation.

The point of this chapter, part of the body of Costs of Justice research,[4] is primarily to call out some of the problematic steps in the various residential schools claims processes that have resulted in and allowed for those costs,[5] and to situate those processes and costs in current ongoing truth and reconciliation efforts in Canada. In addition to the residential schools litigation, I will briefly mention several other problematic cases and contexts to make the point that, when thinking about access to justice, the residential schools litigation is not an isolated incident but rather part of a continuum that many see as costly, unequal, and alienating justice in Canada.[6]

Residential Schools

Because the Truth and Reconciliation Commission so carefully and import-antly documented the dark and tragic truth of the residential schools program in its 2015 report, I will not try to provide any kind of meaningful analysis of that shameful history here.[7] Put very simply, for over a century, Aboriginal families and communities were ripped apart as their children were taken from them and forced into residential schools. It is well documented that the experi-ence of Aboriginal children was characterized by "violent" and "traumatic" treatment.[8] Taking children from their families and communities was part of a purposeful strategy designed "to eliminate Aboriginal people as distinct peoples and to assimilate them into the Canadian mainstream against their will."[9] Canada's residential schools program amounted to a system of "cultural genocide."[10] It is a program that the federal government has since acknowledged is "a sad chapter in our history," "was wrong," and "caused great harm."[11]

Dispute Resolution Process

In response to the tragedies inflicted by the residential schools program, thou-sands of survivors brought claims against the government and church organ-izations that were involved in running the program.[12] As of 2006, approximately 15,000 claims were ongoing, involving an estimated 80,000 people.[13] Many of the claims were being brought as individual civil litigation claims,[14] a number were being advanced through class actions,[15] and the balance were brought forward through the dispute resolution process initially set up by the federal government pursuant to the 2003 National Resolution Framework.[16] Given the challenges in bringing multiple claims individually, by class action, and also through the dispute resolution framework,[17] an effort was made to develop a process by which all outstanding claims could be resolved. An agreement in principle was reached in November 2005,[18] and a national settlement was ap-proved by nine courts across Canada in December 2006.[19] The settlement regime included a common experience payment (CEP) (amounting to at least $1.9 billion), funds for an individual assessment process (IAP) (which could exceed the CEP), the creation of a Truth and Reconciliation Commission (TRC), re-sources for commemorative events and healing processes (funds for these three initiatives amounted to $205 million), funds and in-kind services from various church organizations for victims and family initiatives, and a legal fees agreement.[20]

Problems and Costs Associated with Adversarial Claim Resolution

Notwithstanding the comprehensive procedural framework that was established to resolve all outstanding claims as efficiently and fairly as possible, many claimants experienced heavy-handed, unfair, and costly treatment from all sides in the context of trying to access the system and resolve their claims. If the government, religious organizations, and even legal regulators knew (or acknowledged) then what they know now, much cost, pain, and revictimization experienced through the dispute resolution process and justice system could have been avoided or at least minimized. Because I have documented many examples of problematic behaviour elsewhere,[21] I will only briefly discuss several examples in this chapter.

Problematic Defendant-Side Conduct

First, on the defendant side, it is clear that the government and church organizations generally took culturally disconnected and adversarial – as opposed to healing or reconciling – approaches in the context of the survivors and their claims. There was a general refusal on the part of the government and the church organizations to apologize or take responsibility for their involvement in the residential schools program.[22] Even though apologies came later,[23] although not by all,[24] a failure to take responsibility early in the process has been acknowledged as a mistake on the part of the institutional organizations.[25] Further, the initial federal government alternative dispute resolution process was condemned as culturally disconnected, costly, slow, arbitrary, disrespectful, and humiliating.[26] At the same time, the more adversarial, tort-based approach to resolving individual and class claims through the civil justice system was disconnected from any notion of restoration, cultural sensitivity, or reconciliation.[27]

As for specific problematic strategies and conduct, limitation periods were raised by the government and church organizations as shields against potential direct and vicarious tort liability claims in cases where causes of action often involved historic abuse and sexual abuse claims.[28] In addition to limitation defences, several different adversarial strategies for limiting liability and damages – for example, the "thin skull" or "crumbling skull" rules – were raised by the government and church defendants. Defendants would make the argument that – based on pre-existing conditions – they should not be responsible for making a plaintiff better off than he or she originally was.[29] The irony is that various pre-existing conditions – anxiety, alcoholism, lack of higher education, and others – were caused at least in part by the very residential school programs and experiences at issue in the litigation.[30]

In addition to "blame-the-victim" strategies, the government and church organizations also used "blame-each-other" strategies in order to limit or deny responsibility for any residential school–related damage.[31] The institutional defendants also actively sought to contest amounts, forms, and bases of liability and damage. This included defences against punitive damages,[32] arguments that abuse by a lay employee could not form the basis of vicarious liability claims,[33] and efforts to insulate church defendants from damage claims based on charitable status.[34]

Finally, institutional defendants also raised a number of evidentiary and other procedural challenges to limit or avoid liability. In terms of evidentiary challenges, for example, social science evidence regarding the effect of government approaches to educating Aboriginal children was called into question in the context of individual claims.[35] Individual claimant credibility was also regularly challenged by church and government defendants.[36] Further, institutional defendants sought to limit the definitional scope of "residential schools" in order to limit potential coverage and liability.[37] The federal government also sought to strike out affidavits and resist document production.[38] As for procedural challenges, for example, the adequacy of pleadings was questioned by requesting particulars (which, while not in theory problematic on its face, in this context raises the potential of revictimization).[39] In the context of class actions, certification was vigorously resisted by church and government defendants.[40]

Problematic Plaintiff-Side Lawyer Conduct

Problematic conduct was not limited to the defence of these cases. The legal representation of survivor claimants also involved problematic and unprofessional behaviour. For example, counsel for numbers of IAP claimants purported to provide their clients with loans that were never received, often with unreasonably high interest rates.[41] Other cases, as I have documented elsewhere,[42] involved insensitive and at times misleading client solicitations;[43] exaggerated promises of success;[44] improper disclosure to consulting non-lawyers of confidential information;[45] the unauthorized practice of law;[46] failure to properly prepare and meet with clients;[47] conflicts of interest;[48] unacceptable correspondence, arrangements, and termination letters;[49] failure to press for full compensation amounts;[50] disregard for important terms of the alternative dispute resolution (ADR) settlement process;[51] and misleading, incorrect, and falsely completed IAP forms.[52] Overall, according to one judge, "claimants were ... treated not as individual people who had in many cases suffered traumatic personal experiences ... but rather as claims, requiring little lawyer interaction,"[53] or more directly, "claims became abstracted from claimants."[54]

Costs

The costs associated with the litigation and dispute resolution processes, on all sides, have been massive. Court administration costs alone have amounted to "huge sums" of government money.[55] On the defendant side, the government and church organizations have spent millions on legal and related expert, research, and archival fees.[56] For example, in 1999 alone, it was estimated that the total legal fees paid by church organizations in connection with residential schools litigation totalled approximately $10 million.[57] The time and money spent by government lawyers supported by their experts, researchers, and consultants litigating these cases has also been massive, not to mention the agreement to pay a portion of the plaintiff-side lawyer fees under the settlement process. Much of this money could have been saved – and redirected towards more restorative initiatives – if the many aggressive and ultimately unsuccessful adversarial government and church positions had not been advanced.

Costs on the plaintiff side were also often extremely high – sometimes outweighing any meaningful benefit from the litigation or settlements.[58] In some cases, contingency fees were above the allowable rates provided for in the settlement agreement;[59] in others – particularly early in the process – half of recovered amounts reportedly went to lawyers.[60] It is important to acknowledge that not all cases and not all lawyers' billing arrangements involved problematic fees.[61] However, the examples documented above and elsewhere[62] are certainly not unique or isolated incidents. According to one report, the fees paid to some lawyers were seen as "unethical practices or greed" and "nothing short of gouging," and amounted to "revictimization" and "taking advantage of the wounded and the weakest."[63]

In addition to financial costs, all of the adversarial strategies and conduct discussed above, including the use of appeals to resist or limit claims, resulted in other psychological and emotional costs. For example, the appeal by the Anglican Church in the *F.S.M.* case damaged the survivor claimant's healing process. According to the survivor, "The healing and closure that the trial judgment provided ... was threatened by the Anglican appeal" and made the survivor feel "abused all over again."[64] Similar revictimization concerns arose in the context of other procedural challenges raised by institutional defendants,[65] as well as the unprofessional conduct of plaintiff-side lawyers. According to one victim plaintiff, her lawyer's conduct resulted in the return of "traumatic feelings she had experienced earlier in her life," which also led to a feeling of "shame."[66] Overall, as summarized in the Truth and Reconciliation Commission's report (the *TRC Report*), the residential schools litigation was "especially difficult for the Survivors, many of whom were revictimized through explicit questioning and adversarial treatment by the Government of Canada, the churches, and even their own lawyers."[67] Taken together, the "arduous" process of adversarial litigation had significant negative impacts on litigant survivors.[68]

None of these costs, of course, take into account the failure of the Canadian legal system to address non-abuse claims, including individual and collective loss of language, family relationships, and culture, among others, not just for survivors but for their parents, children, and communities.[69] These costs also do not take into account the further damage caused by the residential schools litigation and settlement process to the already broken institutional and social relationships between Indigenous people and the federal government, religious organizations, and, generally, the rest of Canada.

In the end, significant sums of money have been paid out in connection with residential schools claims. The TRC successfully completed its mandate, some apologies have been made, and important truth and reconciliation work has begun. However, the costs associated with the damage claims and overall settlement arrangements – through early litigation and class actions, through the initial ADR process, and even under the final settlement agreement – have been extremely high, and in some cases so high as to amount to the victimization of surviving claimants all over again.[70]

Ongoing Challenges

In addition to the problematic legacy of the various residential schools dispute resolution processes, there have been and continue to be other problematic cases and events involving Canada's Indigenous communities and its justice system. Although not the primary focus of this chapter, they – like the residential schools dispute resolution legacy – form part of the overall and ongoing problematic and costly treatment that Indigenous people and their communities often face through Canada's justice system when pursuing claims for violations of basic human rights.

For example, the "Sixties Scoop" – the systematic government-initiated removal of thousands of Indigenous children from their families and their placement in non-Indigenous families (in the period between approximately 1965 and 1984)[71] – continues to resonate negatively in Indigenous families, communities, and the overall Canadian public, and in the child protection system in particular.[72] As recognized by the Divisional Court in *Brown v Attorney General of Canada,* the fallout from this government program involved claims that "these children were deprived of their culture, customs, traditions, language and spirituality," which "led them to experience loss of self-esteem, identity crisis and trauma in trying to re-claim their lost culture and traditions."[73] Although another example of costly and failed attempts procedurally to dispose of Indigenous claims prior to trial in an adversarial fashion,[74] these harms and these claims – and in particular the government's responsibility for these harms – have been recognized by the courts.[75] The settlements of the claims – specifically including the legal fees – have not been favoured by all. For example, according to one class member, who described some of the lawyers involved as "cultural vultures," the settlement in his case "exploits Indigenous Peoples and enriches the lawyers."[76] Further, the overall initiative has now been acknowledged by the federal government as a "dark and painful chapter in Canada's history."[77]

In many cases related to or because of the residential schools and the Sixties Scoop, there continues to be an overwhelming number of Indigenous children and young people in child welfare and protection programs across Canada. According to a 2011 Statistics Canada survey, 3.6 percent of all First Nations children under fifteen years old were in foster care (compared with 0.3 percent of non-Aboriginal children), and almost half of all children under fifteen years old in foster care were Aboriginal children.[78] In 2017, Jane Philpott, the federal government's former Minister of Indigenous Services, described the ongoing and vastly disproportionate number of Indigenous children in the system as a "humanitarian crisis."[79] While significant challenges exist for Indigenous parents[80] – many of which developed as a result of experiences they suffered as part of the residential schools and the Sixties Scoop[81] – there is no doubt that the vast overrepresentation of Indigenous children in the child welfare system stems in large part from systemic unfairness, bias, ignorance, inadequate education, poverty, discrimination, and racism.[82] The resulting costs, in terms of broken individuals, families, and lost relationships, are tragic and significant.[83]

Unfortunately, although this chapter largely focuses on civil justice, we know that very similar problems exist in the criminal justice system. First, it is well known that Aboriginal men, women, and young people are vastly overrepresented in Canada's prisons and youth custody facilities.[84] For example, in 2015–16, according to Statistics Canada, 26 percent of adults admitted to provincial and territorial correctional services were Aboriginal, although Aboriginal people represented only 3 percent of the Canadian adult population.[85] The same is true for young people. According to Shawn Atleo, former National Chief of the Assembly of First Nations, Aboriginal children "are more likely to end up in jail than to graduate from high school."[86] For example, in 2015–16, Aboriginal youth represented 35 percent of admissions to correctional services, while Aboriginal youth between the ages of twelve and seventeen made up approximately 7 percent of the youth population in reporting jurisdictions.[87] Further, 43 percent of all female youth admitted into correctional services were Aboriginal.[88]

Former Supreme Court of Canada Justice Frank Iacobucci, also noting the overrepresentation of First Nations people in prison populations, reported that "the justice system generally as applied to First Nations peoples ... is quite frankly in a crisis."[89] In addition to problematic issues of overincarceration, Iacobucci reported a serious lack of representation by Aboriginal people in all aspects of the justice system: "Overrepresented in the prison population, First Nations peoples are significantly underrepresented, not just on juries, but among all those who work in the administration of justice in this province, whether as court officials, prosecutors, defence counsel, or judges."[90] This lack of representation has added to an overall sense of exclusion and distrust by First Nations people when it comes to all aspects of the justice system.[91]

High-profile acquittals in murder cases involving the deaths of Indigenous young people[92] have only served to further alienate members of Indigenous communities.[93] Particularly where juries have been selected to include only white jurors (purposely excluding potential Indigenous jurors),[94] significant concerns about the fairness of justice have been raised by a range of Indigenous and non-Indigenous communities and voices in this country,[95] including by the Prime Minister and former Justice Minister.[96] All of these points of alienation and distrust, coupled with the challenges faced by and findings of the National Inquiry into Missing and Murdered Indigenous Women and Girls,[97] lead to a serious and very troubling erosion in the trust and confidence that all people – particularly members of Indigenous communities – have in Canada's justice system. According to the mother of Colton Boushie, a young Aboriginal murder victim, "This racism is dividing us ... I already knew it was a kangaroo court."[98] As former Chief Justice of Canada Beverley McLachlin stated, "If people are excluded from the system, if they conclude it exists only to serve the interests of the elites, they will turn away. Respect for the rule of law will diminish, and our society will be the poorer."[99] The costs of distrust and alienation should not be underestimated.

Signs of Change?

The *TRC Report* included a number of important justice-related Calls to Action.[100] While several specifically addressed governments, some focused on other actors in the justice sector, including lawyers and law schools.[101] Although much work remains to be done in the justice system to acknowledge and understand the tragedy of the residential schools and their legacy, and to start the transformational healing work of reconciliation (contemplated by the Calls to Action), signs of positive change are emerging across the justice sector.

For example, starting with the federal government, a new "Rights Framework" was announced by the Prime Minister in February 2018.[102] According to the

government, it "will include new legislation and policy that will make the recognition and implementation of rights the basis for all relations between
Indigenous Peoples and the federal government going forward."[103] It will also
support the "rebuilding" of Indigenous governments and nations and advance
self-determination.[104] According to the Prime Minister, recognizing and implementing Indigenous rights "will chart a new way forward ... and undo decades
of mistrust, poverty, broken promises, and injustices."[105] The federal government
has also promised to "fully implement" all Calls to Action in the *TRC Report*[106]
and to reduce the incarceration rate of Indigenous people, who are overrepresented in Canada's prisons.[107] Some of these commitments can be seen, for
example, in budgetary allocations contained in the 2018 Federal Budget.[108]
Others can be seen, for example, in new legislative proposals introduced to
eliminate the use of discriminatory peremptory jury challenges.[109] Provincial
ministries are also actively looking at ways to respond to the *TRC Report* and
reframe how governments acknowledge destructive past practices, as well as
at how governments can move forward to promote and champion a culture of
reconciliation and reform.[110]

As for law societies and bar associations, the Law Society of Ontario (LSO),
for example, approved its *Indigenous Framework*,[111] which is designed to guide
the LSO's work to realize Call to Action 27, particularly in an effort to promote
access to justice and equity.[112] Other organizations have also responded positively to the Calls to Action.[113]

Law schools have also been actively taking up the invitation in Call to Action
28 to reflect on and reform their curricular approaches, offerings, and programs
as they relate to Aboriginal law and Indigenous people.[114] For example, the
University of Victoria created a joint Canadian common law and Indigenous
Legal Orders JD/JID degree.[115] Other law schools are also looking at significant
ways of embracing indigenization of their programs, both in and out of the
formal classroom.[116] For example, in addition to its Anishinaabe Law Camp,[117]
Osgoode Hall Law School recently added an Indigenous and Aboriginal Law
Requirement to its JD program.[118]

Courts and judges are also looking at ways of positively addressing the TRC's
Calls to Action and related issues involving Aboriginal law and Indigenous
legal traditions. According to Chief Justice of Canada Richard Wagner, "We
have begun the process of reconciliation with our indigenous co-citizens, with
the goal of building a new relationship. The process is difficult, as it has to be;
the scars run deep. We cannot change the past, but we can recommit ourselves
each day to right the wrongs that we can. It will take time. But we will do the
work. We are committed."[119] As for specific initiatives, the National Judicial
Institute continues to provide judicial training on issues related to Aboriginal

law and cultural context.[120] The Federal Court–Aboriginal Law Bar Liaison Committee developed specific practice guidelines for litigation involving Aboriginal Peoples.[121] The Federal Court has also started to issue some rulings in Cree and Dene.[122]

Judges themselves are also taking up the issues in individual cases. For example, in a case involving a young Aboriginal woman without a criminal record who pleaded guilty to drug smuggling charges, Justice Hill of the Ontario Superior Court of Justice was asked to consider the constitutionality of a minimum two-year sentence for such drug-related offences. When describing the accused, he commented that she "is very much the face of many Aboriginal offenders whose background has played a real role ... in their presence before the criminal courts in this country."[123] In finding the minimum sentence to be a "grossly disproportionate punishment"[124] and in ordering a sentence of less than two years, Justice Hill specifically highlighted that the "Supreme Court of Canada, the TRC, and numerous other resources have recognized, in respect of Canada's Indigenous peoples, the state's contribution to cultural genocide, the intergenerational effects of colonialism, discrimination, unfulfilled promises, and a 'tragic history' of the treatment of Aboriginal peoples within the Canadian criminal justice system."[125] Further, he acknowledged that the "courts are not isolated from the ongoing process of reconciliation and meaningful nation-to-nation dialogue involving Canada's Aboriginal peoples."[126]

Conclusion

Whether or not Canadians previously knew about the depth and breadth of the residential schools tragedy, we certainly know about it now – thanks in particular to the transformative work of the TRC. The same can be said about the justice system's challenged, often problematic, and typically very costly (financial and otherwise) handling of the residential schools claims: we have "heard [about] it now."[127] Documenting some of the problems and related costs of the residential schools claims in this chapter is part of the process of "acknowledging what needs to be repaired" in an effort to start "seeing each other."[128]

The justice-related Calls to Action in the *TRC Report* are clear. Much needs to be done in all parts of the justice system, there appears to be significant good will, and at this stage, positive signs of change are emerging. As the Chief Justice of Canada stated, the process will be difficult,[129] but reforming the justice system in line with the TRC's Calls to Action must be done. As the TRC itself made clear, the "continued failure of the justice system denies Aboriginal people the safety and opportunities that most Canadians take for granted."[130] The cost of doing nothing is far too high. As former Supreme Court Justice Frank Iacobucci commented in the context of his recommendations for jury reform,

"I realize that many of my recommendations will involve costs, but ... when principles of justice and fairness for thousands of people are involved, the financial aspects of the matter should not trump those fundamental principles ... Moreover, the costs of doing nothing will likely be more than the costs of implementing these recommendations."[131] As recent return on investment and social return on investment research confirms,[132] not only is investing in justice the right thing to do, it also makes significant economic and social sense as well – for Indigenous communities, for the justice system, and for all Canadians.

Notes

1 Shawn Atleo and Heather Atleo, "After 154 Years, a New Narrative for the Tsilhqot'in and Canada," *Globe and Mail* (26 March 2018) at A13, recalling the words of Shawn Atleo's late grandmother, who, having just listened to former Prime Minister Stephen Harper express an apology on behalf of Canada in 2008 to her and all who were impacted by residential schools, said: "They are just beginning to see us."

2 See generally Truth and Reconciliation Commission of Canada, *Honouring the Truth, Reconciling the Future: Summary of the Final Report of the Truth and Reconciliation Commission of Canada* (Ottawa: Truth and Reconciliation Commission of Canada, 2015), online: TRC <http://www.trc.ca/assets/pdf/Honouring_the_Truth_Reconciling_for_the_Future_July_23_2015.pdf>.

3 *Ibid.*

4 For a general description of this body of research, see Canadian Forum on Civil Justice, "Cost of Justice," online: Canadian Forum on Civil Justice <http://www.cfcj-fcjc.org/cost-of-justice>.

5 Several of the issues discussed in this chapter were raised in an earlier article: Trevor C.W. Farrow, "Residential Schools Litigation and the Legal Profession" (2014) 64 UTLJ 596 ["Residential Schools Litigation"].

6 See Trevor C.W. Farrow, "What Is Access to Justice?" (2014) 51 Osgoode Hall LJ 957.

7 See generally Truth and Reconciliation Commission, *supra* note 2. See also J.R. Miller, "Troubled Legacy: A History of Native Residential Schools" (2003) 66 Sask L Rev 357.

8 Royal Commission on Aboriginal Peoples, *Report of the Royal Commission on Aboriginal Peoples* (Ottawa: Government of Canada, October 1996), vol 1, *Looking Forward, Looking Back*, s 10.3 ("Residential Schools") at 349, online: Government of Canada <http://data2.archives.ca/e/e448/e011188230-01.pdf>. For an earlier discussion, see Farrow, "Residential Schools Litigation," *supra* note 5 at 596–97. See further Jennifer J. Llewellyn, "Dealing with the Legacy of Native Residential School Abuse in Canada: Litigation, ADR, and Restorative Justice" (2002) 52 UTLJ 253; Law Commission of Canada, *Restoring Dignity: Responding to Child Abuse in Canadian Institutions – Executive Summary* (Ottawa: Minister of Public Works and Government Services, 2000), online: Government of Canada <http://publications.gc.ca/collections/collection_2008/lcc-cdc/JL2-7-2000-1E.pdf>.

9 Truth and Reconciliation Commission, *supra* note 2 at 3.

10 *Ibid.* The residential schools program is part of what the Honourable Frank Iacobucci called the "tragic history of Aboriginal peoples" – part of a long history of "mistreatment, lack of respect, [and] unsound policies" experienced by First Nations people. Hon. Frank Iacobucci, *First Nations Representation on Ontario Juries: Report of the Independent Review Conducted by the Honourable Frank Iacobucci* (February 2013) at para 5, online: Ontario

Ministry of the Attorney General <http://www.attorneygeneral.jus.gov.on.ca/english/
about/pubs/iacobucci/pdf/First_Nations_Representation_Ontario_Juries.pdf>.

11 Rt. Hon. Stephen Harper, PC, MP, "Statement of Apology to Former Students of Indian
Residential Schools" (11 June 2008), online: Government of Canada <https://www.rcaanc
-cirnac.gc.ca/eng/1100100015644/1571589171655>.

12 For an earlier discussion, see Farrow, "Residential Schools Litigation," *supra* note 5 at
592–93.

13 *Baxter v Canada (Attorney General)* (2006), 83 OR (3d) 481 at paras 4, 13 [*Baxter*].

14 See, e.g., *Blackwater v Plint*, [2005] 3 SCR 3 [*Blackwater SCC*].

15 See, e.g., *Cloud v Canada (Attorney General)* (2004), 73 OR (3d) 401 (CA), leave to appeal
to SCC refused, [2005] SCCA No 50 [*Cloud*]; *Baxter*, *supra* note 13; *Richard v British
Columbia*, 2009 BCCA 185 (and related cases). See earlier *Re Indian Residential Schools*,
1999 ABQB 823.

16 See, e.g., Indian Residential Schools Resolution Canada, *National Resolution Framework*
(2003).

17 See, e.g., House of Commons, Standing Committee on Aboriginal Affairs and Northern
Development, *Study on the Effectiveness of the Government Alternative Dispute Resolution
Process for the Resolution of Indian Residential School Claims*, 38th Parl, 1st Sess, 4th report
(adopted by the Committee on 24 March 2005, presented to the House on 7 April 2005,
concurred in by the House on 12 April 2005) (Chair: Nancy Karetak-Lindell), which
describes the ADR process as an "excessively costly and inappropriately applied failure."
See further Assembly of First Nations, *Report on Canada's Dispute Resolution Plan to
Compensate for Abuses in Indian Residential Schools* (Ottawa: Assembly of First Nations,
2004) at 11, online: <http://epub.sub.uni-hamburg.de/epub/volltexte/2009/2889/pdf/
Indian_Residential_Schools_Report.pdf>. For a discussion of the shortcomings of the
dispute resolution framework, see Kathleen Mahoney, "The Settlement Process: A Personal
Reflection" (2014) 64:4 UTLJ 505. See further Canadian Bar Association, *The Logical
Next Step: Reconciliation Payments for All Indian Residential School Survivors* (Ottawa:
Canadian Bar Association, 2005).

18 *Agreement in Principle* (20 November 2005), online: Indian Residential Schools Settlement
– Official Court Website <http://www.residentialschoolsettlement.ca/aip.pdf>.

19 See *Baxter*, *supra* note 13; *Northwest v Canada (Attorney General)*, 2006 ABQB 902
[*Northwest*]. See further *Fontaine v Canada (Attorney General)*, 2012 BCSC 839 at para 2
[*Fontaine BCSC 2012*]; *Law Society of Manitoba v Tennenhouse*, 2011 MBQB 279 at para
10 [*Tennenhouse II*].

20 See *Northwest*, *supra* note 19 at paras 15–16; *Baxter*, *supra* note 13 at paras 53–55 (specifically
regarding legal fees). For a further summary, see *Canada (Attorney General) v Fontaine*,
[2017] 2 SCR 205 at paras 5–11 [*Fontaine SCC*]; *J.W. v Canada (Attorney General)*, 2019
SCC 20 [*J.W.*]. See further Government of Canada, "Indian Residential Schools" (21
February 2019), online: Government of Canada <https://www.rcaanc-cirnac.gc.ca/eng/
1100100015576/1571581687074#sect1>. For information on the status of claims, payments,
and funding under the Residential Schools agreement, see Government of Canada,
"Statistics on the Implementation of the Indian Residential Schools Settlement Agreement" (19 February 2019), online: Government of Canada <https://www.rcaanc-cirnac.
gc.ca/eng/1315320539682/1571590489978> (and now see the recently created Indigenous
Services Canada, online: Government of Canada <https://www.canada.ca/en/indigenous
-services-canada.html>).

21 Farrow, "Residential Schools Litigation," *supra* note 5 at 599–611.

22 *Ibid* at 602–3.

23 See, e.g., Harper, *supra* note 11. See further subsequent apology to former students of residential schools in Newfoundland and Labrador: Rt. Hon. Justin Trudeau, PC, MP, "Remarks by Prime Minister Justin Trudeau to Apologize on Behalf of the Government of Canada to Former Students of the Newfoundland and Labrador Residential Schools" (24 November 2017), online: Justin Trudeau, Prime Minister of Canada <https://pm.gc.ca/eng/news/2017/11/24/remarks-prime-minister-justin-trudeau-apologize-behalf-government-canada-former>.

24 The Pope continues to resist the opportunity to provide an apology, notwithstanding a call to do so in Call to Action 58 in Truth and Reconciliation Commission, *supra* note 2. For the Pope's position, see Lionel Gendron, President of the Canadian Conference of Catholic Bishops, "Letter of the CCCB President to the Indigenous Peoples of Canada" (27 March 2018), online: CCCB <http://www.cccb.ca/site/images/stories/pdf/Letter_to_Indigenous_Peoples_-_27_March_2018_-_en.pdf>.

25 See, e.g., comments from Reverend James Scott, United Church of Canada, cited in Farrow, "Residential Schools Litigation," *supra* note 5 at 602, n 30.

26 See, e.g., House of Commons, Standing Committee on Aboriginal Affairs and Northern Development, *supra* note 17; Assembly of First Nations, *supra* note 17 at 11; Canadian Bar Association, *supra* note 17, pt 11.

27 See Farrow, "Residential Schools Litigation," *supra* note 5 at 601. See generally Mayo Moran, "The Role of Reparative Justice in Responding to the Legacy of Indian Residential Schools" (2014) 64:4 UTLJ 529; Kent Roach, "Blaming the Victim: Canadian Law, Causation, and Residential Schools" (2014) 64:4 UTLJ 566 ["Blaming the Victim"].

28 See, e.g., *Blackwater SCC, supra* note 14 at para 82; *MM v Roman Catholic Church*, 2001 MBCA 148, leave to appeal to SCC refused, [2002] SCCA No 8. See also *Cloud, supra* note 15 at para 61. See further Truth and Reconciliation Commission, *supra* note 2 at 167. See generally Farrow, "Residential Schools," *supra* note 5 at 603–4.

29 For a discussion of the "crumbling skull" rule, see, e.g., *Athey v Leonati*, [1996] 3 SCR 458 at para 34, cited in *TWNA v Clarke*, 2003 BCCA 670 at para 27 [*TWNA*]. See further *Blackwater SCC, supra* note 14 at paras 74–87; *MA v Canada (Attorney General)*, 2001 SKQB 504, var'd 2003 SKCA 2, leave to appeal to SCC refused, [2003] SCCA No 151. See further Farrow, "Residential Schools Litigation," *supra* note 5 at 604–6; Roach, "Blaming the Victim," *supra* note 27 at 572.

30 See, e.g., *Blackwater v Plint*, 2001 BCSC 997 at para 376, var'd [2003] BCJ No 2783 (CA), aff'd *Blackwater SCC, supra* note 14.

31 See, e.g., *Blackwater v Plint*, [1998] BCJ No 1320 at paras 16–18 (*sub nom WRB v Plint*), var'd [2003] BCJ No 2783 (CA), aff'd *Blackwater SCC*, supra note 14; *F.S.M., Sr v Anglican Church of Canada*, 2004 BCCA 23 [*F.S.M.*].

32 See, e.g., *TWNA, supra* note 29 at paras 103–30.

33 See, e.g., *EB v Order of the Oblates of Mary Immaculate in the Province of British Columbia*, [2005] 2 SCR 45.

34 See, e.g., *Blackwater SCC, supra* note 14 at paras 39–44. See further Farrow, "Residential Schools Litigation," *supra* note 5 at 607; Moran, *supra* note 27 at 536–39.

35 See, e.g., *Blackwater SCC, supra* note 14 at para 9.

36 See, e.g., *FH v McDougall*, [2008] 3 SCR 41. See further Roach, "Blaming the Victim," *supra* note 27, pts II–III.

37 See, e.g., *Fontaine v Canada (Attorney General)*, 2012 BCSC 313; *Fontaine v Canada (Attorney General)*, 2013 BCSC 756. See further Farrow, "Residential Schools Litigation," *supra* note 5 at 608.

38 See, e.g., *Fontaine v Canada (Attorney General)*, 2013 ONSC 684; *Fontaine v Canada (Attorney General)*, 2014 ONSC 283.
39 See, e.g., *Re Indian Residential Schools, supra* note 15.
40 See, e.g., *Cloud, supra* note 15.
41 See, e.g., *Fontaine BCSC 2012, supra* note 19 at paras 17, 48–54, 59, 77–78, 164. See further Paul Barnsley and Kathleen Martens, "Judge Punishes Lawyer for 'Loan Scheme' Targeting Residential Schools Survivors," *Aboriginal Peoples Television Network* (6 June 2012), online: <http://aptnnews.ca/2012/06/06/judge-punishes-lawyer-for-loan-scheme-targeting-residential-school-survivors/>; Farrow, "Residential Schools Litigation," *supra* note 5 at 609.
42 Farrow, "Residential Schools Litigation," *supra* note 5 at 609–11.
43 See, e.g., *Fontaine BCSC 2012, supra* note 19 at paras 15–16, 55–58, 79; *Law Society of Saskatchewan v Merchant*, [2000] LSDD No 24 at paras 24, 53 [*Merchant I*], aff'd 2002 SKCA 60 [*Merchant II*]. For commentary on the *Merchant* cases, see Alice Woolley et al, eds, *Lawyers' Ethics and Professional Regulation*, 3d ed (Toronto: LexisNexis, 2017) at 156–63.
44 See, e.g., *Merchant I, supra* note 43 at para 47.
45 *Fontaine BCSC 2012, supra* note 19 at paras 18, 75.
46 *Law Society of Manitoba v Tennenhouse* (21 February 2012) Case 11-09 (Discipline Panel) [*Tennenhouse III*].
47 *Fontaine BCSC 2012, supra* note 19 at para 76.
48 *Tennenhouse v Law Society of Manitoba*, 2011 MBQB 73 at para 10 [*Tennenhouse I*].
49 *Fontaine BCSC 2012, supra* note 19 at para 22.
50 For a report of this practice, see Gloria Galloway, "Few Survivors Succeed with Full Claims," *Globe and Mail* (30 November 2017) at A6.
51 *Fontaine BCSC 2012, supra* note 19 at paras 146–49.
52 *Ibid* at paras 62–68. See also *Merchant I, supra* note 43 at paras 88, 92, 94.
53 *Fontaine BCSC 2012, supra* note 19 at para 163.
54 *Ibid* at para 161.
55 Llewellyn, *supra* note 8 at 263.
56 *Ibid.*
57 *Ibid* at 263–64, n 44 (citation omitted).
58 *Ibid* at 268–76.
59 For example, according to several reports, the Merchant Law Group expected to receive somewhere between $28 million and $100 million for work done on residential schools files. For initial concerns about these arrangements, see, e.g., Jonathan Gatehouse, "White Man's Windfall," *Maclean's* (11 September 2006), online: <https://archive.macleans.ca/article/2006/9/11/white-mans-windfall>; Geoff Kirbyson, "The Big Picture," *Canadian Lawyer* (7 August 2007), online: <http://www.canadianlawyermag.com/author/na/the-big-picture-114/>. See further *Baxter, supra* note 13 at paras 53–78. More recently, see *Canada (Attorney General) v Merchant Law Group LLP*, 2017 SKCA 62, leave to appeal to SCC refused, [2017] SCCA No 394. See further *Tennenhouse I, supra* note 48 at para 10; *Tennenhouse II, supra* note 19 at paras 17, 35, 42, 47; *Tennenhouse III, supra* note 46; *Fontaine BCSC 2012, supra* note 19 at para 171; *Merchant II, supra* note 43 at paras 132–33; Erin Anderssen, "Lawyers Swoop to Cash In on Native Claims," *Globe and Mail* (10 July 1999) A1.
60 Llewellyn, *supra* note 8 at 269. See further Farrow, "Residential Schools Litigation," *supra* note 5 at 610–11.

61 Farrow, "Residential Schools Litigation," *supra* note 5 at 611.
62 *Ibid* at 610–11.
63 See Gloria Galloway, "Lawyers Accused of 'Greed' in Fees from Residential-School Victims," *Globe and Mail* (23 October 2017) A1 at A1 and A7. See further *Merchant I, supra* note 43 at paras 28, 88, 92, 94; Anderssen, *supra* note 59 at A1, A7.
64 *F.S.M., supra* note 31 at para 7. See also *Fontaine Estate v Canada (Attorney General),* 2017 MBCA 54, appeal to SCC granted, 2019 SCC 20. See further Farrow, "Residential Schools Litigation," *supra* note 5 at 601, 606–7.
65 See, e.g., *Re Indian Residential Schools, supra* note 15 (raising pleading inadequacy concerns); *Fontaine BCSC 2012, supra* note 19 at para 96.
66 *Merchant I, supra* note 43 at para 28.
67 Truth and Reconciliation Commission, *supra* note 2 at 167.
68 Llewellyn, *supra* note 8 at 269. For a general discussion of financial and non-financial costs connected with legal problems, see Trevor C.W. Farrow et al, *Everyday Legal Problems and the Cost of Justice in Canada: Overview Report* (Toronto: Canadian Forum on Civil Justice, 2016), online: Canadian Forum on Civil Justice <http://www.cfcj-fcjc.org/sites/default/files//Everyday%20Legal%20Problems%20and%20the%20Cost%20of%20Justice%20in%20Canada%20-%20Overview%20Report.pdf>.
69 Truth and Reconciliation Commission, *supra* note 2 at 166.
70 See, e.g., *supra* notes 39 and 65–66 and surrounding text. For further recent cases that continue to deal with issues under the settlement process, see *Fontaine v Canada (Attorney General),* 2018 BCSC 63; *Fontaine v Canada (Attorney General),* 2018 ONSC 103; *Fontaine v Canada (Attorney General),* 2018 ONSC 357; *Fontaine v Canada (Attorney General),* 2018 ONSC 24.
71 See Truth and Reconciliation Commission, *supra* note 2 at 138. For a brief background description, see, e.g., Indigenous and Northern Affairs Canada, "Sixties Scoop Agreement in Principle: Backgrounder" (7 November 2017), online: Government of Canada <https://www.canada.ca/en/indigenous-northern-affairs/news/2017/10/sixties_scoop_agreement inprinciple.html>.
72 See, e.g., Truth and Reconciliation Commission, *supra* note 2 at 137–44; National Collaborating Centre for Aboriginal Health, "Indigenous Children and the Child Welfare System in Canada" (September 2017), online: National Collaborating Centre for Aboriginal Health <https://www.ccnsa-nccah.ca/docs/health/FS-ChildWelfareCanada-EN.pdf>. For commentary, see, e.g., Gloria Galloway, "Sixties Scoop Deal in Jeopardy as More Potential Claimants Object," *Globe and Mail* (5 March 2018), online: <https://www.theglobeandmail.com/news/politics/sixties-scoop-deal-in-jeopardy-as-more-potential-claimants-object/article38216223/>.
73 See *Brown v Attorney General of Canada,* 2014 ONSC 6967 at para 2.
74 *Ibid.*
75 See *Brown v Canada (Attorney General),* 2017 ONSC 251 at para 86; *Brown v Canada (Attorney General),* 2018 ONSC 3429. See further *Riddle v Canada,* 2018 FC 641; *Thompson v Manitoba (Minister of Justice of Manitoba),* 2017 MBCA 71; *Native Child and Family Services of Toronto v C.R.,* 2017 ONCJ 440.
76 Doug George-Kanentiio, "Sixties Scoop Settlement a Rotten Deal for Survivors but a Windfall for Lawyers," *CBC News* (21 April 2018), online: <https://www.cbc.ca/news/indigenous/opinion-sixties-scoop-rotten-deal-for-survivors-1.4626936>.
77 Indigenous and Northern Affairs Canada, *supra* note 71.
78 Statistics Canada, *Aboriginal Peoples in Canada: First Nations People, Métis and Inuit* (National Household Survey, 2011) (Ottawa: Minister of Industry, 2013) at 19, online: Statistics

Canada <http://www12.statcan.gc.ca/nhs-enm/2011/as-sa/99-011-x/99-011-x2011001-eng. pdf>, cited in Truth and Reconciliation Commission, *supra* note 2 at 138.

79 Reported in Jorge Barrera, "Indigenous Child Welfare Rates Creating 'Humanitarian Crisis' in Canada, Says Federal Minister," *CBC News* (2 November 2017), online: <http://www. cbc.ca/news/indigenous/crisis-philpott-child-welfare-1.4385136>.

80 Truth and Reconciliation Commission, *supra* note 2 at 139.

81 *Ibid* at 135–36.

82 *Ibid* at 137–40. See also Iacobucci, *supra* note 10 at paras 27, 214.

83 Truth and Reconciliation Commission, *supra* note 2 at 137–40.

84 *Ibid* at 170.

85 Julie Reitano, *Adult Correctional Statistics in Canada, 2015/2016* (Ottawa: Minister of Industry, 2017), online: Statistics Canada <https://www.statcan.gc.ca/pub/85-002-x/2017001/ article/14700-eng.htm>. See also Truth and Reconciliation Commission, *supra* note 2 at 170.

86 Shawn Atleo, "There Is an Election On, Isn't It Time We Talked?" *CBC News* (13 April 2011), online: <http://www.cbc.ca/news/canada/there-is-an-election-on-isn-t-it-time-we -talked-1.1071765>, cited in Jeffrey Paul Ansloos, *The Medicine of Peace: Indigenous Youth Decolonizing Healing and Resisting Violence* (Halifax and Winnipeg: Fernwood Publishing, 2017) at 4.

87 Jamil Malakieh, *Youth Correctional Statistics in Canada, 2015/2016* (Ottawa: Minister of Industry, 2017), online: Statistics Canada <https://www.statcan.gc.ca/pub/85-002-x/ 2017001/article/14702-eng.htm>. See also Truth and Reconciliation Commission, *supra* note 2 at 177.

88 See further Truth and Reconciliation Commission, *supra* note 2 at 177.

89 Iacobucci, *supra* note 10 at paras 4, 14.

90 *Ibid* at para 14.

91 See, e.g., *ibid* at paras 27–28, 209, 211, 214–15.

92 For example, Gerald Stanley, a non-Indigenous man, was charged with the murder of Colten Boushie, a young Aboriginal man. Stanley was acquitted of all charges by an all-white jury. For one of several applications in the matter, see *R v Stanley*, 2018 SKQB 27. For comments on a different case, see Hon. Carolyn Bennett, quoted in Cameron MacLean, "Jury Finds Raymond Cormier Not Guilty in Death of Tina Fontaine," *CBC News* (22 February 2018), online: <http://www.cbc.ca/news/canada/manitoba/raymond-cormier -trial-verdict-tina-fontaine-1.4542319>. See generally Kent Roach, *Canadian Justice, Indigenous Injustice: The Gerald Stanley and Colten Boushie Case* (Montreal and Kingston: McGill-Queen's University Press, 2019).

93 See, e.g., Paul Seesequasis, "A Made-in-Saskatchewan Crisis," *Globe and Mail* (13 February 2018) A17; Carrie Tait, "Alberta Calls on Ottawa to Amend Justice System," *Globe and Mail* (3 March 2018) A6.

94 Peremptory challenges are available under the *Criminal Code*. See *Criminal Code*, RSC 1985, c C-46, s 634. In the Stanley case, however, it appeared that the only consistent basis for the challenges was the fact of a prospective juror's Indigenous appearance. For comments on the jury selection process in the Stanley case, see, e.g., Joe Friesen & Sean Fine, "The Ins and Outs of Juries, Challenges and Potential Reforms," *Globe and Mail* (13 February 2018) A12. In his report, Iacobucci recommended that powers of peremptory challenge be reviewed in order to prevent their use to discriminate against First Nations people serving on juries. Iacobucci, *supra* note 10, recommendation 15. Some limits already exist with respect to jury selection (particularly in respect of the Crown). See, e.g., *R v Gayle* (2001), 54 OR (3d) 36 (CA), leave to appeal to SCC refused, [2001] SCCA No 359. Now

see Canada, Bill C-75, *An Act to amend the Criminal Code, the Youth Criminal Justice Act and other Acts and to make consequential amendments to other Acts*, 1st Sess, 42nd Parl, 2019, ss 271–72 (assented to 21 June 2019) [Bill C-75].

95 See, e.g., Alex McKeen, "Thousands Gather to Protest Verdict," *Toronto Star* (11 February 2018) A4.

96 Rt. Hon. Justin Trudeau, PC, MP, reported in John Ibbitson, "You and I Can Question the Stanley Verdict – Politicians Should Not," *Globe and Mail* (13 February 2018) A13; Hon. Jody Wilson-Raybould, PC, MP, reported in Ibbitson, *ibid.*

97 See generally online: National Inquiry into Missing and Murdered Indigenous Women and Girls <http://www.mmiwg-ffada.ca/>. For the inquiry's final report, see *Reclaiming Power and Place: The Final Report of the National Inquiry into Missing and Murdered Indigenous Women and Girls* (June 2019), online: <https://www.mmiwg-ffada.ca/final-report/>.

98 Debbie Baptiste in Joe Friesen, "Boushie Family Moves from Anger to Action in Wake of Acquittal," *Globe and Mail* (12 February 2018) A1 at A6.

99 Rt. Hon. Beverley McLachlin, PC, former Chief Justice of Canada, "Remarks to the Council of the Canadian Bar Association at the Canadian Legal Conference" (Ottawa, 11 August 2016), online: Supreme Court of Canada <https://www.scc-csc.ca/judges-juges/spe-dis/bm-2016-08-11-eng.aspx>.

100 See Truth and Reconciliation Commission, *supra* note 2, Calls to Action 25–42.

101 *Ibid*, Calls to Action 27–28.

102 Government of Canada, News Release, "Government of Canada to Create Recognition and Implementation of Rights Framework" (14 February 2018), online: Government of Canada <https://pm.gc.ca/en/news/news-releases/2018/02/14/government-canada-create-recognition-and-implementation-rights>.

103 *Ibid.*

104 *Ibid.*

105 *Ibid.*

106 Rt. Hon. Justin Trudeau, PC, MP, "Statement by Prime Minister on Release of the Final Report of the Truth and Reconciliation Commission" (15 December 2015), online: Justin Trudeau, Prime Minister of Canada <https://pm.gc.ca/eng/news/2015/12/15/statement-prime-minister-release-final-report-truth-and-reconciliation-commission>.

107 Rt. Hon. Justin Trudeau, PC, MP, "Minister of Justice and Attorney General of Canada Mandate Letter" (12 November 2015), online: Justin Trudeau, Prime Minister of Canada <https://pm.gc.ca/eng/minister-justice-and-attorney-general-canada-mandate-letter>.

108 Government of Canada, "Budget Plan" (2018), c 3, online: Government of Canada <https://www.budget.gc.ca/2018/docs/plan/toc-tdm-en.html>.

109 See Canada, Bill C-75, *supra* note 94, ss 271–72.

110 See, e.g., Ontario, Ministry of Indigenous Affairs, "Working to Ensure a Better Future for First Nations, Inuit and Métis People" (7 August 2019), online: Government of Ontario <https://www.ontario.ca/page/ministry-indigenous-affairs>.

111 Law Society of Upper Canada (as it then was), Equity and Indigenous Affairs Committee, "Indigenous Framework, Report to Convocation" (29 June 2017), online: Law Society of Ontario <http://www.lsuc.on.ca/uploadedFiles/For_the_Public/About_the_Law_Society/Convocation_Decisions/2017/Convocation-June2017-Equity-Indigenous-Affairs-Committee-Report.pdf>.

112 *Ibid* at para 7.

113 See, e.g., the Advocates' Society, Indigenous Bar Association, and Law Society of Ontario, *Guide for Lawyers Working with Indigenous Peoples* (8 May 2018), online: Advocates'

Society <http://www.advocates.ca/Upload/Files/PDF/Advocacy/BestPractices Publications/Guide_for_Lawyers_Working_with_Indigenous_Peoples_may16.pdf>; Canadian Bar Association, "Responding to the Truth and Reconciliation Commission's *Calls to Action*" (March 2016), online: Canadian Bar Association <http://www.cba.org/ CMSPages/GetFile.aspx?guid=6aa3e794-551d-4079-b129-e9b7be414b26>; Canadian Bar Association, "Answering the Call," online: Canadian Bar Association <http://www.cba. org/Truth-and-Reconciliation/Resources/Answering-the-Call>; Federation of Law Societies of Canada, News Release, "Federation of Law Societies Commits to Effective Response to TRC Report" (11 March 2016), online: Federation of Law Societies of Canada <http://docs.flsc.ca/TRC-March-2016.pdf>.

114 See, e.g., Jeffrey G. Hewitt, "Decolonizing and Indigenizing: Some Considerations for Law Schools" (2016) 33:1 Windsor YB Access Just 65; Patricia Barkaskas & Sarah Buhler, "Beyond Reconciliation: Decolonizing Clinical Legal Education" (2017) 26 J L & Soc Pol'y 1.

115 University of Victoria, Faculty of Law, "Joint Degree Program in Canadian Common Law and Indigenous Legal Orders JD/JID" (2018), online: University of Victoria <https://www. uvic.ca/law/about/indigenous/jid/index.php>.

116 Jeremy Webber (Council of Canadian Law Deans), "The Law Schools and the Future of Indigenous Law in Canada," online: (4 August 2015) Slaw <http://www.slaw.ca/2015/08/04/ the-law-schools-and-the-future-of-indigenous-law-in-canada/>.

117 See, e.g., Osgoode Hall Law School, "The Anishinaabe Law Camp," online: Osgoode Hall Law School <https://www.osgoode.yorku.ca/programs/juris-doctor/experiential -education/anishinaabe-law-camp/>.

118 See Osgoode Hall Law School, "Degree Requirements – Indigenous and Aboriginal Law Requirement (IALR)," online: Osgoode Hall Law School <https://www.osgoode.yorku. ca/programs/juris-doctor/jd-program/degree-requirements/>.

119 Rt. Hon. Richard Wagner, PC, Chief Justice of Canada, "Official Welcome Ceremony for the New Chief Justice: Remarks" (5 February 2018), online: Supreme Court of Canada <https://www.scc-csc.ca/judges-juges/spe-dis/rw-2018-02-05-eng.aspx>.

120 See generally National Judicial Institute, "Judicial Education in Canada," online: National Judicial Institute <https://www.nji-inm.ca/index.cfm/judicial-education/judicial -education-in-canada/>.

121 Federal Court–Aboriginal Law Bar Liaison Committee, *Practice Guidelines for Aboriginal Law Proceedings* (April 2016), online: <https://www.fct-cf.gc.ca/content/assets/pdf/base/ Aboriginal%20Law%20Practice%20Guidelines%20April-2016%20(En).pdf>.

122 For a discussion of the initiative, see, e.g., David Thurton, "In a Canadian First, Federal Court Issues Decision in Cree and Dene," *CBC News* (29 May 2019), online: <https://www. cbc.ca/news/politics/federal-court-dene-cree-languages-1.5153427>.

123 *R v C.S.*, 2018 ONSC 1141 at para 144.

124 *Ibid* at para 145.

125 *Ibid* at para 136.

126 *Ibid* at para 137. See generally *J.W., supra* note 20.

127 Thomas King, "Afterwords: Private Stories" in *The Truth about Stories: A Native Narrative* (Toronto: House of Anansi Press, 2003) at 167.

128 Atleo & Atleo, *supra* note 1.

129 Wagner, *supra* note 119.

130 Truth and Reconciliation Commission, *supra* note 2 at 164.

131 Iacobucci, *supra* note 10 at para 351. See generally Jessica Clogg, "Upholding the Law of the Land," online: (13 February 2018) Slaw <http://www.slaw.ca/2018/02/13/upholding-the -law-of-the-land/>.

132 Lisa Moore and Trevor C.W. Farrow, *Investing in Justice: A Literature Review in Support of the Case for Improved Access* (Toronto: Canadian Forum on Civil Justice, August 2019), online: Canadian Forum on Civil Justice <https://cfcj-fcjc.org/wp-content/uploads/Investing-in-Justice-A-Literature-Review-in-Support-of-the-Case-for-Improved-Access-by-Lisa-Moore-and-Trevor-C-W-Farrow.pdf>.

7

The Costs of Justice in Domestic Violence Cases
Mapping Canadian Law and Policy

Jennifer Koshan, Janet Mosher, and Wanda Wiegers

DOMESTIC VIOLENCE CASES IN Canada present unique access to justice challenges due to complex power dynamics, structural inequality, and the fact that victims, offenders, and children must often navigate multiple legal systems to resolve the many issues in this context.[1] The complexity of these cases has both personal and systemic impacts. Different legal systems – for example, criminal, family, child protection, social welfare, and immigration – have differing objectives and personnel with varying levels of expertise in domestic violence. Conflicting decisions by different courts and tribunals with overlapping jurisdiction may impair the safety of victims and children, and may require multiple court appearances to resolve. Victims may face contradictory messages about how seriously adjudicators will treat domestic violence, and offenders can use the existence of different systems to perpetuate abuse. These issues are gendered, as women are the primary victims of domestic violence, and the concerns may be heightened among marginalized women. The issues may also differ across Canadian provinces and territories and on First Nations reserves, given the application of different laws, policies, and dispute resolution models.

This chapter explores how the access to justice crisis in Canada manifests itself in domestic violence cases.[2] It reviews the literature on access to justice and domestic violence, adopting a broad definition of access to justice to inform the analysis. It then documents and compares the legal and policy provisions and systems affecting litigants in domestic violence cases across Canadian jurisdictions, highlighting legal reforms as well as the systemic barriers in seeking justice that victims, offenders, and children confront. A hypothetical case study is then used to explore how the complex interaction of multiple laws, policies, and dispute resolution processes may impact victims of domestic violence. This comparative mapping analysis is a first step towards identifying the systemic reforms necessary to enhance access to justice in domestic violence cases.

Defining Access to Justice in Domestic Violence Cases

Access to justice provides an important conceptual framework for examining the justice system's response to domestic violence, given its place as a fundamental principle and goal of the Canadian legal system.[3] Realizing access to justice requires the creation of a truly equal justice system, which in turn requires conceptualizing access to justice from the perspective of those most affected, especially those marginalized by social institutions such as law.[4]

Access to justice may incorporate notions of substantively fair or just outcomes and of the social and economic costs of justice.[5] In our specific context, a federal report estimated the total economic costs of domestic violence for a one-year period to be over $7 billion, $545.2 million of which was borne by the justice system.[6] Access to justice may also intersect with principles of democracy, equality, judicial independence, the rule of law, and social justice, and have distributive and symbolic components.[7] Feminist literature on access to justice emphasizes women's particular needs: access to legal advocates in light of power and financial disparities; information about rights; spiritual, cultural, and financial supports; and access to safe, independent, and accountable processes.[8]

Access to justice also has procedural dimensions. For example, a growing body of literature documents the lack of effective and equitable access to justice in the civil justice system, including the family law realm.[9] Specific issues identified in this context include lack of legal representation, services, and access to information; costs, complexity, and delays; the prevalence and impact of unmet legal needs; challenges presented by litigants' social locations; pressures to settle family disputes; lack of judicial oversight; and enforcement problems.[10] While this literature typically emphasizes barriers to the resolution of disputes using courts and lawyers, access to justice concerns may also arise from settlement initiatives such as alternative dispute resolution (ADR) processes and multi-disciplinary approaches.[11]

The literature also identifies a number of barriers unique to domestic violence, which often arise because of power imbalances and safety issues. These barriers vary according to legal context but may include a reluctance to engage with the legal system because of fear of violent retaliation or child protection consequences; routine screening out of domestic violence issues by legal actors, often due to a limited understanding of the dynamics of abusive relationships; and the fact that self-representation in court, tribunal, and ADR processes is particularly onerous for domestic violence victims.[12] Because of a lack of information and institutional support, victims may withdraw from proceedings or agree to outcomes adverse to themselves and their children.[13] Settlement-oriented dispute resolution methods may also create access to justice concerns for victims of domestic violence.[14] These processes are pervasive and are being increasingly employed in cases characterized by domestic violence, without consensus as to their appropriateness or methodology.[15]

Although not always recognized by law and policy makers, these barriers to accessing justice have a gendered dimension because women are the primary victims of domestic violence.[16] Moreover, the barriers within and tensions between different systems may be heightened for women from marginalized groups, including Indigenous women, lesbian women, immigrant women, women refugee claimants, women with disabilities, and women living in poverty, given high rates of domestic violence and/or justice system involvement.[17] Barriers may also arise for persons accused of domestic violence, including women seeking to defend themselves,[18] and may have a detrimental impact on children.[19]

Mapping Domestic Violence Laws and Policies

A comparison of the legislative treatment of domestic violence across areas of law and between jurisdictions will bring into focus the impact of discrete statutory frameworks, as well as how access to justice issues arise and are dealt with at points of intersection, a question that is only beginning to be explored in the domestic violence context in Canada.[20]

Across Canadian jurisdictions, multiple and intersecting justice system components may have diverse effects on access to justice in domestic violence cases. Some legal issues fall within federal jurisdiction, others within provincial/territorial jurisdiction, and the legal issues faced by Indigenous peoples are even more complicated jurisdictionally. As a result, diverse laws and dispute resolution models exist in different provinces and territories, and may apply in different ways to different groups.[21]

Federal Laws and Policies

Canada's criminal law does not contain any specific prohibitions related to domestic violence, but the *Criminal Code* includes several offences that may be generally applicable.[22] Other countries have prohibited domestic violence specifically, including the offence of coercive control.[23] The *Criminal Code* does identify intimate partner violence as an aggravating factor for interim release and sentencing purposes, and provides restitution for household expenses for some victims of domestic violence.[24] Orders may also provide that offenders have no contact with their intimate partners (and sometimes their children), and that they refrain from being at particular places as a condition of interim release, probation, conditional sentences, and peace bonds.[25] Where offenders are convicted of or discharged for an indictable offence in which violence was used, threatened, or attempted against their intimate partner, the court must prohibit the person from possessing any weapon during a specified period.[26] Section 127 of the *Criminal Code* provides a general offence of breaching a court order and may be used for breaches of provincial/territorial civil protection and restraining orders where the legislation does not include specific breach provisions.[27] At the enforcement level, the federal government has since 1983 maintained a pro-charging and pro-prosecution policy for offences in the domestic violence context that applies to the RCMP and federal prosecutors.[28]

The federal government also has jurisdiction over divorce and related matters, including child and spousal support and parenting issues corollary to divorce.[29] There is no presumption in favour of any particular parenting outcome, and until recent amendments come into force, the *Divorce Act* does not explicitly require the consideration of domestic violence.[30] These amendments will require that primary consideration be given to achieving physical, emotional, and psychological safety and security for children, and will add family violence as a relevant factor in making orders that allocate parenting time and decision-making responsibility.[31] However, judges will also be required to consider providing as much parenting time with each spouse as is consistent with a child's best interests (widely interpreted as a maximum parenting time principle under the current act) and to consider a parent's "willingness to support the development and maintenance of the child's relationship with the other spouse" (a "friendly parent" provision).[32] Disclosures of domestic violence may thus come with the risk that, if they cannot be substantiated, victims will be viewed as unfriendly parents and their own claims to custody may be placed in jeopardy.

The revised *Divorce Act* will also require parties to try to resolve their dispute through negotiation, mediation, or collaborative law processes "to the extent that it is appropriate to do so," and will require legal advisers to encourage their clients to do so "unless the circumstances of the case are of such a nature that it would clearly not be appropriate."[33] There is no express recognition that ADR may not be advisable in light of family violence and no requirement that professionals be trained in and undertake screening for family violence. Persons who wish to change their residence or relocate will also be expected to give notice of the move or apply to court to waive or amend notice requirements.[34] Failure to give notice or apply for an exemption will be considered in determining whether to authorize the relocation.[35] Although court applications can be made without notice to the other party, these requirements may be difficult to meet where survivors need to change residence or relocate immediately to ensure their and their children's safety and where they lack access to timely and affordable legal assistance.

Other federal family-related laws illustrate the complexity of overlapping laws for Indigenous Peoples in Canada. *An Act respecting First Nations, Inuit and Métis Children, Youth and Families* affirms the inherent jurisdiction of Indigenous Peoples to legislate in relation to child and family services and sets minimum standards for an assessment of the best interests of Indigenous children in all such matters across Canada.[36] Mandatory considerations include the direct or indirect impact of family violence on the child and "the physical, emotional and psychological harm or risk of harm to the child," as well as any civil or criminal proceedings, orders, or measures relevant to the safety and well-being of the child.[37] Such factors are to be interpreted in accordance with Indigenous laws, "to the extent that it is possible to do so."[38] The *Family Homes on Reserves and Matrimonial Interests or Rights Act (FHRMIRA)* also authorizes First Nations to develop their own laws for the possession of family homes and the division of property interests, and establishes provisional rules that govern until such laws are enacted.[39] These rules allow a spouse or partner who is a victim of family violence to apply *ex parte* to a "designated judge" either in person or by telecommunication to obtain an order for exclusive possession of the family home or other relief for up to ninety days if needed for their immediate protection or that of their property.[40] Few First Nations have enacted their own matrimonial property laws under the *FHRMIRA*, and only three provinces have designated judges, leaving many Indigenous victims of violence on reserves without access to emergency orders for exclusive possession of their homes.[41]

Also important federally in the domestic violence context is the *Immigration and Refugee Protection Act (IRPA)*.[42] Among the methods of entry to Canada is the family class, in which a Canadian citizen or permanent resident may apply to sponsor a spouse or common-law partner. Although presumptively this occurs, and permanent resident status is granted, before the sponsored spouse or partner arrives in Canada, in some circumstances the sponsorship application may be initiated from within Canada. In these circumstances, the sponsorship application can be withdrawn at any time prior to the granting of permanent resident status.[43] An extensive literature documents threats by abusive men to revoke the sponsorship application and to have their intimate partners deported, making it very difficult for women to leave such relationships.[44] If the sponsorship is withdrawn, in limited circumstances a refugee claim may be available, but usually the only route to permanent resident status is through a humanitarian and compassionate (H & C) application.[45] This is a highly discretionary form of relief that is not routinely granted, and many of the factors to be considered in exercising this discretion – a history of stable employment, a pattern of sound financial management, integration into the community – work against success on such applications for abused women precisely because of the nature of the abuse they have experienced. While immigration officers are instructed to be "sensitive to situations in which the spouse ... leaves an abusive situation and, as a result, does not have an approved family class sponsorship," the further instruction to consider court documents, police or incident reports, conviction certificates, letters from shelters, and medical reports fails to appreciate that many abused women do not have access to these forms of verification.[46] In July 2019, the federal government introduced a fee-exempt temporary resident permit for verified victims of family violence (broadly defined) whose status in Canada is dependent upon their abusive spouse/partner. While a welcome development, such permits are temporary in nature, usually for a minimum of six months and to a maximum of three years.[47]

Other provisions of the *IRPA* also raise issues of concern. A foreign national (a person who is neither a citizen nor a permanent resident) who is convicted of an indictable offence – with all hybrid offences deemed indictable – is inadmissible to Canada and subject to removal proceedings with no right of appeal.[48] Even a permanent resident may be subject to removal if convicted of an offence in Canada for which the maximum term is at least ten years or where the actual term of imprisonment imposed is more than six months.[49] The potential for removal in these situations is particularly concerning where abused women without citizenship status are inappropriately charged criminally. While the Canadian literature is sparse on this issue, some evidence indicates that abusive men will manipulate the police and criminal justice system response, resulting in charges against the victim with the attendant possibility of removal from Canada.[50] A further provision bars a Canadian citizen or permanent resident from being a sponsor if convicted of an offence that caused bodily harm to a conjugal partner or family member.[51] For abused women who are dependent upon their spouse's sponsorship, the potential loss of the sponsorship may result in reluctance to seek help.

Provincial/Territorial Laws and Policies

Given the presence of thirteen provinces and territories in Canada, with broad jurisdiction over matters including the administration of criminal justice, civil protection orders, family law, property and housing, social assistance, and employment laws, the legislative and policy picture is complex. Here, we take a look at the provincial and territorial legislation, policies, and justice system components relevant to domestic violence and compare differences across jurisdictions to gain a sense of the complex intersections facing victims and offenders in this context (see Table 7.1).[52]

In the administration of criminal justice, all provinces have pro-charging and pro-prosecution policies for domestic violence offences that apply to provincially regulated police forces and prosecutors.[53] Most jurisdictions have specialized domestic violence courts that hear criminal matters in some locations, although the scope of these courts differs greatly within and between jurisdictions. Toronto has an integrated domestic violence court (IDVC) that allows some family law cases and criminal charges to be heard by a single judge. The IDVC operates at the provincial court level, excludes divorce, family property, and child protection matters, and hears only summary conviction criminal matters.[54]

Some jurisdictions have victims of crime legislation providing for various rights, including rights to be informed of proceedings, to be granted absence from work for justice system appearances, and to be kept apart from the offender to ensure safety.[55] Most have legislation providing compensation or restitution for victims of domestic violence crimes either explicitly or implicitly.[56] Some of these jurisdictions limit the extent to which compensation is available where victims contributed to their injuries, engaged in conduct detrimental to their health or safety, or failed to report the matter or to cooperate with law enforcement authorities.

Civil domestic violence protection order legislation exists in most provinces and territories across Canada, except Ontario and Quebec.[57] This legislation is generally intended to make protection orders more accessible and extensive than restraining orders. Victims are able to obtain emergency and longer-term protection orders where "domestic," "family," or "interpersonal" violence or abuse, as defined by the legislation, has occurred or the victim has a reasonable fear that it will occur. A key difference across jurisdictions is whether emotional, psychological, and financial abuse are included. Most statutes limit the availability of orders to victims who have resided together in a family, spousal, or intimate relationship and to parents of children regardless of whether they have cohabited. Emergency orders may be issued *ex parte* by courts, and in some jurisdictions by justices of the peace via telecommunication, if an immediate order is needed for protection of the victim. Protection orders may give the applicant exclusive possession of a family home, order the removal of the respondent, and require no contact or attendance at or near specified places. Breaches may be dealt with specifically through powers of arrest and offence provisions, or, if the legislation is silent on breaches, s 127 of the *Criminal Code* will apply.

Some provinces have recently passed domestic violence disclosure laws.[58] These laws are intended to provide information that a person might use in deciding to avoid or leave a relationship with someone who could be violent, although the details have been left to regulations that have not yet been developed or not as yet proclaimed in force.

In the area of family law, many jurisdictions stipulate that domestic violence is to be considered in assessing the best interests of children and determining parenting, custody, access, and/or contact orders, but how domestic violence is defined varies widely across these jurisdictions.[59] At the same time, many jurisdictions presume the equal division of parental authority where the parents have cohabited, subject to a court order, agreement, or, in some jurisdictions, consent or acquiescence of one parent to the child's residence with the other. Many also include a maximum contact or friendly parent principle similar to that in the *Divorce Act*. Only British Columbia explicitly excludes a presumption of equal parenting responsibility and equal time in making court orders. That province also provides that a denial of parenting time or contact with a child is not considered wrongful where the guardian reasonably believed that the child might suffer violence if contact was exercised.[60] Although the inclusion of domestic violence as a mandated factor is positive, disclosures by victims could still jeopardize their own claims to custody if the violence cannot be proven.

For cross-border disputes, all provinces and territories incorporate the *Hague Convention on the Civil Aspects of International Child Abduction,* which secures the return of children wrongfully removed to states that are party to the *Convention*. The *Convention*'s "grave risk" exception – which has been found to exist in some cases of domestic violence – can be invoked where the court finds the child would be exposed to a grave risk of physical or psychological harm or otherwise be placed in an intolerable situation if returned to the child's habitual residence.[61]

Under child welfare legislation, most provinces and territories explicitly define children to be in need of protection or intervention where they may be physically or emotionally harmed by family or domestic violence.[62] All jurisdictions create a duty to report on persons who have reasonable and probable grounds to believe that a child may be in need of protection or intervention. For mothers, a disclosure of domestic violence to virtually anyone will increase the risk of reports being made to child welfare authorities and the risk of child apprehension.[63]

Statutes dealing with property division upon the breakdown of a spousal relationship do not identify domestic violence as a relevant factor, but courts are authorized to grant exclusive possession of the family home in various circumstances, including domestic violence.[64] Exclusive possession or orders for use of the family home can also be tied to parenting, child, or spousal support, and made in other circumstances. In addition, most jurisdictions have amended their residential tenancy legislation to allow tenants to terminate leases early without the usual consequences where they must vacate the premises because of domestic violence.[65] In jurisdictions without these amendments, civil protection legislation may provide other tenancy-related remedies. Regardless of these protections, however, residential tenancy legislation typically prohibits tenants from changing locks, requires them to pay rent until the end of the tenancy, and allows landlords to terminate tenancies where a tenant has caused damage to the property or adversely affected the security of another occupant, making it difficult for domestic violence victims to remain in rented premises.[66]

Procedurally, several provinces and territories encourage or mandate mediation or other forms of ADR for family disputes, but only a few require dispute resolution professionals to take domestic violence training and screen for family violence or exempt victims of domestic violence from ADR requirements.[67] Most jurisdictions provide legal aid for protection orders and family law disputes involving domestic violence, but this typically involves financial eligibility requirements and is done in policy documents, allowing coverage to be easily changed over time.[68]

In the context of social benefits laws and policies, several jurisdictions explicitly or implicitly include domestic violence in providing financial supports for moving, transportation, and other costs and/or in assessing income, assets, needs, and eligibility. Some jurisdictions also consider domestic violence in the allocation of subsidized housing and may exempt victims of abuse from the usual obligations related to social assistance eligibility, such as work search requirements and the obligation to pursue support from an ex-spouse or under an immigration sponsorship.[69]

With regard to employment law, the occupational health and safety legislation of some provinces explicitly includes domestic violence as a workplace hazard and requires employers to take all reasonable precautions for the protection of workers who may be exposed to physical injury in the workplace. Additionally, several jurisdictions permit employees to take domestic violence leave from employment to obtain medical attention, counselling, or victim services; to seek legal or law enforcement assistance; and/or to relocate.[70]

Most provinces and territories have also removed or extended limitation periods for civil claims relating to sexual assault and/or assault and battery where the claimant was living in an intimate relationship with the person who committed the assault or battery.[71]

This comparison of jurisdictions is relatively high level but still illustrates the complexity of laws, policies, and processes confronted by domestic violence victims across Canadian jurisdictions. Different terms – domestic, family, and interpersonal violence – are used and defined differently in different jurisdictions, and sometimes within jurisdictions.[72] Making matters more complicated, access to information and privacy legislation may restrict information sharing

Table 7.1 Comparison of provincial/territorial laws including domestic violence

Territorial laws	Province												
	BC	AB	SK	MB	ON	QC	NB	NS	PE	NL	YK	NT	NU
Civil domestic violence protection orders	×	×	×	×			×	×	×	×	×	×	×
Family: parenting orders	×	×	[x]	×	×			×	×	×	×	×	×
Family: child welfare	×	×	×	×		×	×	×	×	×	×	×	
Alternative dispute resolution (ADR)¹	×		×	[x]	×	×				×			
Residential tenancies	×	×	×	×	×	×	[x]	×		×		×	
Social benefits and/or social housing	×	×	×	×	×	×	×	×		×			
Employment	×	×	×	×	×	×	×	×	×	×		×	
Limitations	×	×	×	×	×	×	×	×		×	×	×	×

Note: This table includes statutes or regulations that explicitly reference domestic or family violence or related terms but does not include such references in policy documents or where those terms are read in by interpretation. Square brackets indicate that the relevant provisions were not fully in force as of March 2020.

1 Domestic violence is identified as a factor in deciding whether ADR is required and/or in requiring training on domestic violence issues for at least some ADR professionals.

across systems unless disclosure is necessary to protect a person's mental or physical health or safety, or for law enforcement purposes.[73] This leads to a siloed approach to the legal issues raised in domestic violence cases that can compromise safety in the absence of information-sharing protocols.[74]

Domestic Violence and Access to Justice across Intersecting Legal Systems

Victims, offenders, and children must frequently engage with multiple legal forums and processes in domestic violence cases, including those related to the legislation discussed earlier.[75] Though definitive information on the extent of sequential or overlapping processes is lacking, there is evidence that at least one-third of domestic violence cases with family law issues also include criminal charges, and the number of cases engaging multiple legal processes is likely much higher when other legal issues are factored in, especially those resolved before trial.[76] These legal matters are scattered across inferior, superior, unified, specialized, and integrated court systems, as well as mandatory mediation and other informal settlement processes. Domestic violence issues may also intersect with immigration, housing, and social assistance systems and tribunals.[77] Many of these issues require ongoing contact between the parties due to changing circumstances and enforcement problems, leading to continuing conflict and legal disputes.[78]

Navigating these multiple systems may impede access to justice and impair safety. Parties may have to appear before multiple courts on multiple days in multiple locations, with different lawyers, different judges, and differential access to services, legal representation, and remedies. Besides the resulting confusion, victims and children may have to tell their stories repeatedly, resulting in possible revictimization as well as child care and absenteeism issues. Delays in resolving issues and added expenses for the parties may also result from multiple and ongoing proceedings within and across systems.[79] Systemically, different legal systems have varying objectives, which may create inter-system tensions. For example, family courts are generally mandated to encourage the resolution of conflicts, avoid attributions of fault, and facilitate contact between parents and children. In contrast, courts hearing criminal matters are mandated to focus on victim safety and offender accountability, which may favour limited contact.[80] Different systems have varying legal rules on evidence, document disclosure, and privacy and confidentiality, leading to inconsistent access to information on matters such as the risk of future violence. The relevant personnel – including judges, lawyers, mediators, custody evaluators, social workers, and immigration and welfare officers – may also have varying levels of expertise and varied conceptual frameworks for understanding domestic violence.[81]

These differing objectives, priorities, rules, and levels of expertise, combined with a lack of coordination among different service providers and decision makers, may lead to contradictory norms and cultures and piecemeal and disparate outcomes for individuals, compromising access to justice. Inconsistent information, settlements, decisions, and enforcement practices within and across systems, along with system silos, may also result in conflicts and gaps that impair safety and require further court appearances to resolve.[82] More generally, victims may face contradictory pressures and messages about how their actions in response to domestic violence will be treated by decision makers.[83]

Perpetrators of domestic violence may leverage these different legal systems as a means of furthering their power and control. They may initiate multiple applications to vary parenting orders, instigate investigations of women based on false reports of child abuse or welfare fraud, or report women to immigration authorities.[84] While the sharing of information between systems can sometimes enhance safety, in other circumstances it can be used to amplify the power of abusers.[85] These contradictory effects of information sharing may dissuade some women from disclosing domestic violence and seeking help.

The Costs of Seeking Justice for a Domestic Violence Victim

The following case scenario illustrates the complex interplay of various legal systems. While it builds upon a single jurisdiction, it also illuminates why and how the details of specific legislative and regulatory regimes matter for access to justice.

Nazifa came to Canada in 2014 on a visitor's permit to see her fiancé, a Canadian citizen. With his promise to initiate a spousal sponsorship, Nazifa remained in Canada after the expiry of her permit. They married in 2015 and their son was born in 2016. They resided in an apartment in Toronto, and both had signed the lease. Nazifa's husband regularly complained about her cooking, her care of their son, and her appearance. He controlled her access to the telephone and computer, and installed cameras to ensure that she did not leave home without his permission. His physical violence began shortly after their marriage and continued to escalate. When her injuries required medical attention, Nazifa's husband always accompanied her and he did the talking. He repeatedly threatened to withdraw his sponsorship application and told her that he would ensure she was deported. Nazifa did her best to hide the abuse and violence from her son. She disclosed the abuse to no one, fearful that if the police became involved, the violence would escalate, child welfare authorities might take their son, and she would be deported.

One evening in August 2019, two male police officers arrived at their apartment, saying that a neighbour had called to report a domestic disturbance.

Nazifa's husband told police that she had assaulted him. Fortunately, the officers took Nazifa to a police station, provided an interpreter, and ensured that a female police officer conducted the interview. Nazifa's husband was arrested and charged. As required, the police officers notified the Children's Aid Society. At the time of his arrest, Nazifa's husband told the police that Nazifa was "illegal." The police learned shortly thereafter that Nazifa's husband had initiated a sponsorship application in 2018 but withdrew it immediately after he was charged. Although he was released on no-contact conditions, he regularly contacted Nazifa, promising to restart the sponsorship application if she dropped the assault charge. He also told her that if he was convicted, he would be precluded from sponsoring her. As a result, she begged the Crown prosecutor to drop the charge, but the prosecutor refused to do so. At the trial, Nazifa testified that she could not recall anything about the incident, and her husband was acquitted. Nazifa also denied the abuse when interviewed by the Children's Aid Society, and the society closed its file, noting that the abuse had not been verified.

The police response has important implications for access to justice: whether an interpreter is provided, whether charges are laid, and whether the moment of contact with the criminal justice system is seized as an opportunity to provide information, supports, and resources. Assuming this opportunity was seized and Nazifa was provided with relevant, up-to-date information and resources, she would have learned that if she chose to leave the relationship, she could get out of the lease with twenty-eight days' notice. She would also have learned that the procedure is very straightforward; she needs to complete two forms: a notice to vacate early and a "statement about sexual or domestic violence and abuse" (the statement is included on the form; all that was required was her signature). Significantly, her access to early termination was not dependent upon verification of the abuse by others.[86] While this would have enabled her to get out of the existing lease, obviously she would have needed access to other housing.

Nazifa would also have learned that in Ontario domestic violence victims have access to a priority wait-list for social housing. However, once the sponsorship was withdrawn, Nazifa was without immigration status and ineligible to apply for social housing.[87] Moreover, without status, she was also ineligible for social assistance benefits.[88] She would have been advised that, if she were able to verify that she was a victim of family violence, she would be eligible for a fee-exempt temporary resident permit (TRP) for a period between six months and three years and a work permit. The TRP is by nature temporary, and it remains the case that unless Nazifa were to stay in the relationship with her abusive husband and he were to restart the spousal sponsorship (which he would not have been able to do if convicted), her only route to permanent resident status would be through the highly discretionary H & C application process, the outcome of which is anything but assured. However, with the initiation of the H & C application, Nazifa would have been eligible to apply for both social assistance and social housing.

Yet Nazifa would have encountered additional hurdles to access priority social housing; she would have needed to provide a record verifying the abuse prepared by a listed professional (among them a doctor, lawyer, nurse, law enforcement officer, or social services provider). The only professionals from whom Nazifa could have requested a verification report were the law enforcement officers who intervened in August 2019. Whether she was able to reach them, and whether they were prepared to provide the report, would have impacted Nazifa's access to the priority wait-list for social housing.[89] While the verification sources to access a TRP are more expansive, they too focus on police records and reports from various professionals, as well as criminal and family court documents.

In the meantime, imagine that in this scenario, Nazifa's husband started a family law proceeding seeking sole custody of their child. Nazifa is very concerned for her son's well-being, given her husband's behaviour. Although judges are required to consider any violence or abuse against a spouse in assessing the ability to act as a parent, apart from the police intervention and charge (which did not result in a conviction), Nazifa has no corroborating evidence. Moreover, her testimony in the criminal trial may be used against her in the family law proceeding. Raising the abuse poses the risk that if her account is not accepted, she may be characterized as an "unfriendly" parent at best or, worse, as manipulative or alienating. But the complexity does not end there. Even assuming that Nazifa initiated an H & C claim, this would not bar removal proceedings against her. If an immigration order was issued for her removal, she could be removed without her son – in the immigration context, the best interests of a child is but one consideration among many, unlike the family law context, where it is determinative. The jurisprudence is clear that the family courts will not issue custody orders as a means of circumventing an immigration order. Rather, the court will determine the best interests of a child, taking into account the existence of a removal order against a parent. Courts will consider, among other factors, the relative educational and social advantages a child may have in Canada compared with the country to which the parent is being removed; the stability of remaining in Canada; the child's citizenship; and the child's social ties and networks. All of these factors are likely to work against a custody order in Nazifa's favour, and there is a very real possibility that she will be deported and her son will remain in Canada.[90] If Nazifa applies for and receives a TRP, this narrows the possibility of removal, but again, this is a temporary measure.

Nazifa's refusal to testify against her husband or disclose the abuse to child protection authorities may mean that she does not have the verification needed to access social housing, social assistance, or the TRP. It may also mean that her account of abuse will not be seen as credible in the family law proceeding. Yet even if she had all of the critical information about the harms of not disclosing, her decision may have been no different given the limited options open to her to secure permanent resident status. Without access to expert legal information, advice, and representation, it is difficult to imagine how Nazifa could navigate these multiple systems in a way that best ensures safety for her and her child.

Conclusion

As Nazifa's story makes clear, access to justice for survivors of domestic violence requires addressing the common obstacles faced by litigants – costs, delay, lack of information, and culturally and linguistically inaccessible services. But her story also reveals additional impediments.

For domestic violence victims, access to justice is rendered more complex not only by the need to engage multiple legal systems – criminal, family, child welfare, immigration, housing, and social assistance, for example – but by how these systems interact (or fail to do so). As noted earlier, and as illustrated by Nazifa's story, these various legal systems are shaped by different, and sometimes inconsistent, statutory mandates. In some instances, the result is that women are subject to contradictory court orders that render compliance virtually impossible. In other instances, steps taken and decisions made in one legal forum will, unknown to victims, have significant implications for decisions in another legal forum. An acquittal (or conviction) in the criminal arena, for example, will reverberate in the family, child welfare, and immigration contexts. Nazifa's story also reveals that the sharing of information across systems – by police with child welfare or immigration authorities, for example – can itself operate as a barrier to accessing justice, and that this potential is exploited by abusive men. In other instances, the sharing of information will yield a more complete picture of risk that creates the potential for more responsive safety planning.

Access to justice is also compromised by the failure to prioritize safety. Statutes that define domestic violence solely as physical violence, that fail to identify domestic violence as a relevant consideration (for example, in relation to parenting orders or access to housing), or that mandate participation in ADR processes without adequate attention to power imbalances are one such manifestation. Another is the verification of domestic violence required by statute or policy, or simply insisted upon by a decision maker before a woman's account of violence is believed and her access to benefits, such as subsidized housing, social assistance, or the early termination of a lease, is enabled. The failure to centre the safety of women and children can also be traced to the lack of knowledge among legal actors of the dynamics of abusive relationships and to the ready equation of harm with serious physical injuries, with coercive, controlling behaviour dismissed as inconsequential.

Troublingly, women's access to justice is all too often dependent upon the jurisdiction in which they reside, the treatment of domestic violence within the statute(s) governing their legal issue(s), and whether the legal professionals they encounter – lawyers, judges, mediators, and so on – have a deep understanding of domestic violence and its harms and are alive to the complex interactions between multiple legal systems. In domestic violence cases, accessing legal systems occurs in the context of ongoing inequalities of power. All too often, the result of access to legal systems, which is how access to justice has traditionally been framed, is not justice but rather the exacerbation of inequalities between victims and their abusers. Abusive men may access legal systems to further their power and control, and in these instances women are reluctantly drawn into legal systems.[91] Women's initiation of engagement with various legal systems can also be fraught with risk: of retaliatory violence, of the loss of child custody or social assistance, or of adverse immigration consequences.

Domestic violence imposes a tremendous financial burden on women, and on society more generally. The costs take the form of both expenditures – for example, to improve health, access housing, or participate in the justice system – and lost opportunities for women, in some instances undermining their capacities as workers. These lost opportunities are but one manifestation of a more profound and troubling form of cost – that is, the cost to women and children's sense of safety, of self, and of belonging.[92] Access to justice must be reframed in a way that ensures that women's interactions with various legal systems reduce rather than exacerbate these costs. Reframing of this sort points towards access to justice initiatives such as a systematic review of legislation to assess its implications for women and children's safety,[93] new approaches to judicial and legal education, and further research to better ensure that legal systems work together seamlessly in support of safe, equitable, and fair outcomes.

Notes

Our research is supported by grants from the Social Sciences and Humanities Research Council of Canada and the Law Foundation of Ontario's Access to Justice Fund, for which we are grateful. We also thank our research assistants Ellen Bolger, Elysa Darling, Kristin McDonald, Irene Oh, and Andrea Vitopoulos, and Trevor Farrow for his helpful comments on an earlier draft.

1 We use the term "domestic violence" to capture abuse in adult intimate relationships. We are especially interested in coercive controlling violence, a conceptualization that builds

upon earlier feminist work documenting tactics of power and control. Coercive control encompasses the range of tactics used to isolate, control, demean, and dehumanize women, as distinct from a decontextualized approach focused narrowly on discrete acts of physical violence. For an overview, see Jane Wangmann, "Different Types of Intimate Partner Violence – an Exploration of the Literature" (Australian Domestic and Family Violence Clearinghouse, 2011), online: OPUS <https://opus.lib.uts.edu.au/handle/10453/19466>. We use the terms "victim" and "offender" for ease of reference, recognizing that not all domestic violence cases are resolved in the justice system or with findings of culpability.

2 Our SSHRC project, *Domestic Violence and Access to Justice Within and Across Multiple Legal Systems,* consists of several phases, including legislative/policy mapping, case law research, and qualitative interviews with service providers and justice personnel. Wendy Chan and Michaela Keet are co-investigators.

3 Action Committee on Access to Justice in Civil and Family Matters, *Meaningful Change for Family Justice: Beyond Wise Words. Final Report of the Family Justice Working Group* (Ottawa: Action Committee on Access to Justice in Civil and Family Matters, 2013) [*Meaningful Change*]; Canadian Bar Association, *Reaching Equal Justice: An Invitation to Envision and Act* (Ottawa: Canadian Bar Association, 2013), online: Canadian Bar Association <http://www.cba.org/CBA-Equal-Justice/Equal-Justice-Initiative/Reports> [*Reaching Equal Justice*].

4 Action Committee on Access to Justice in Civil and Family Matters, *Meaningful Change, supra* note 3; Canadian Bar Association, *Reaching Equal Justice, supra* note 3; Trevor Farrow, "What Is Access to Justice?" (2014) 10 Osgoode Hall LJ 12.

5 Trevor Farrow, Lesley Jacobs, & Diana Lowe, *The Cost of Justice: Weighing the Costs of Fair and Effective Resolution to Legal Problems* (Toronto: Canadian Forum on Civil Justice, 2012), online: Canadian Forum on Civil Justice <http://www.cfcj-fcjc.org/sites/default/files/docs/2012/CURA_background_doc.pdf>; Patricia Hughes and Janet E. Mosher, "Foreword" (2008) 46 Osgoode Hall LJ xxi; Michael Trebilcock, Anthony Duggan, & Lorne Sossin, eds, *Middle Income Access to Justice* (Toronto: University of Toronto Press, 2012).

6 Ting Zhang et al, *An Estimation of the Economic Impact of Spousal Violence in Canada, 2009* (Ottawa: Department of Justice Canada, 2012) at x (including $320.1 million to the criminal justice system and $225.1 million to the civil justice system).

7 Canadian Bar Association, *Access to Justice Metrics: A Discussion Paper* (Ottawa: Canadian Bar Association, 2013); Mary Eberts, "Future of Law Conference: 'Lawyers Feed the Hungry': Açcess to Justice, the Rule of Law, and the Private Practice of Law" (2013) 76 Sask L Rev 115; Genevieve Painter, "Thinking Past Rights: Towards Feminist Theories of Reparations" (2012) 30 Windsor YB Access Just 1.

8 Joseph Roy Gillis et al, "Systemic Obstacles of Battered Women's Participation in the Judicial System: When Will the Status Quo Change?" (2006) 12 Violence against Women 1150; Rosemary Hunter, "Feminist Explorations of Access to Justice" (2002) 11 Griffith LR 263; Debra Parkes et al, "Listening to Their Voices: Women Prisoners and Access to Justice in Manitoba" (2008) 26 Windsor YB Access Just 85.

9 Canadian Bar Association, *Reaching Equal Justice, supra* note 3; Farrow, Jacobs, & Lowe, *supra* note 5.

10 Action Committee on Access to Justice in Civil and Family Matters, *Access to Civil and Family Justice: A Roadmap for Change* (Ottawa: Action Committee on Access to Justice in Civil and Family Matters, 2013), online: Canadian Forum on Civil Justice <http://www.cfcj-fcjc.org/sites/default/files/docs/2013/AC_Report_English_Final.pdf> [*Roadmap*]; Action Committee on Access to Justice in Civil and Family Matters, *Meaningful Change, supra* note 3; Rachel Birnbaum, Nicholas Bala, & Lorne Bertrand, "The Rise of

Self-Representation in Canada's Family Courts: The Complex Picture Revealed in Surveys of Judges, Lawyers and Litigants" (2013) 91 Can Bar Rev 67; Farrow, *supra* note 4; Law Commission of Ontario, *Increasing Access to Family Justice through Comprehensive Entry Points and Inclusivity* (Toronto: Law Commission of Ontario, 2013); Julie Macfarlane, "The National Self-Represented Litigants Project: Identifying and Meeting the Needs of Self-Represented Litigants, Final Report" (May 2013), online: <https://lawsocietyontario. azureedge.net/media/lso/media/legacy/pdf/s/self-represented_project.pdf>; Michael Saini, Rachel Birnbaum, & Nicholas Bala, "Access to Justice in Ontario's Family Courts: The Parents' Perspective" (2016) 37 Windsor Rev Legal Soc Issues 1; Noel Semple & Carol Rogerson, "Middle Income Access to Justice: Policy Options with Respect to Family Law" in Trebilcock, Duggan, & Sossin, *supra* note 5 at 413.

11 Linda C. Neilson, "At Cliff's Edge: Judicial Dispute Resolution in Domestic Violence Cases" (2014) 52 Fam Ct Rev 529; Federal-Provincial-Territorial Ad Hoc Working Group on Family Violence, *Making the Links in Family Violence Cases: Collaboration among the Family, Child Protection and Criminal Justice Systems* (Ottawa: Department of Justice Canada, November 2013), c 8 [*Making the Links*].

12 Pamela Cross, *Through the Looking Glass: The Experiences of Unrepresented Abused Women in Family Court* (Oshawa, ON: Luke's Place, 2008) [*Through the Looking Glass*]; Pamela Cross, *It Shouldn't Be This Hard: A Gender-Based Analysis of Family Law, Family Court and Violence against Women* (Oshawa, ON: Luke's Place, 2012); Jennifer Koshan & Wanda Wiegers, "Theorizing Civil Domestic Violence Legislation in the Context of Restructuring: A Tale of Two Provinces" (2007) 19 CJWL 145; Donna Martinson & Margaret Jackson, "Family Violence and Evolving Judicial Roles: Judges as Equality Guardians in Family Law Cases" (2017) 30 Can J Fam L 11; Linda C. Neilson, *Enhancing Safety: When Domestic Violence Cases Are in Multiple Legal Systems (Criminal, Family, Child Protection)* (Ottawa: Department of Justice Canada, 2013) [*Enhancing Safety*].

13 Nicholas Bala, "Reforming Family Dispute Resolution in Ontario: Systemic Changes and Cultural Shifts" in Trebilcock, Duggan, & Sossin, *supra* note 5 at 271; Semple & Rogerson, *supra* note 10.

14 Bala, *supra* note 13; Lene Madsen, "A Fine Balance: Domestic Violence, Screening, and Family Mediation" (2012) 30 Can Fam LQ 343; Wanda Wiegers & Michaela Keet, "Collaborative Family Law and Gender Inequalities: Balancing Risks and Opportunities" (2009) 46 Osgoode Hall LJ 733.

15 Neilson, *Enhancing Safety, supra* note 12; Legal Aid Ontario, *Consultation Paper: Development of a Domestic Violence Strategy* (Toronto: Legal Aid Ontario, 2015).

16 Canadian Centre for Justice Statistics, *Family Violence in Canada: A Statistical Profile, 2018* (Ottawa: Minister of Industry, 2019), s 2 (females represented 79 percent of police-reported intimate partner violence victims in 2017 and are at higher risk of intimate partner homicide).

17 In 2014, 10 percent of Aboriginal women self-reported victimization by spousal violence compared with 3 percent of non-Aboriginal women: Canadian Centre for Justice Statistics, *Family Violence in Canada: A Statistical Profile, 2014* (Ottawa: Minister of Industry, 2016) at 15. Eleven percent of lesbian and bisexual women reported spousal violence, compared with 3 percent of heterosexual women (*ibid* at 14). For discussions of spousal violence against marginalized women, see Rupaleem Bhuyan et al, *Unprotected, Unrecognized: Canadian Immigration Policy and Violence against Women, 2008–2013* (Toronto: Migrant Mothers Project, University of Toronto, 2014); Sheryl Burns, *Single Mothers without Legal Status in Canada: Caught in the Intersection between Immigration Law and Family Law* (Vancouver: YWCA, 2010); Jane Ursel, "Over Policed and Under Protected:

A Question of Justice for Aboriginal Women" in Mary Ruclos Hampton & Nikki Gerrard, eds, *Intimate Partner Violence: Reflections on Experience, Theory and Policy* (Toronto: Cormorant Books, 2006) at 80.

18 Cheryl Fraehlich & Jane Ursel, "Arresting Women: Pro-Arrest Policies Debates and Developments" (2014) 29 J Family Violence 507; Jennifer Koshan, "Investigating Integrated Domestic Violence Courts: Lessons from New York" (2014) 51 Osgoode Hall LJ 989; Shoshana Pollack et al, *Women Charged with Domestic Violence in Toronto: The Unintended Consequences of Mandatory Charge Policies* (Toronto: Woman Abuse Council of Toronto, 2005); J. Poon et al, "Factors Increasing the Likelihood of Dual and Sole Charging of Women for Intimate Partner Violence" (2012) 20 Violence against Women 1447.

19 See, e.g., Nicholas Bala, Rachel Birnbaum, & Donna Martinson, "One Judge for One Family: Differentiated Case Management for Families in Continuing Conflict" (2010) 26 Can J Fam L 395.

20 For a longer version of this paper with reference to all relevant legislation, see online: SSRN <https://ssrn.com/abstract=3598277> ["Koshan, Mosher and Wiegers"]. See also, e.g., Nicholas Bala & Kate Kehoe, "Concurrent Legal Proceedings in Cases of Family Violence: The Child Protection Perspective" (Ottawa: Department of Justice Canada, n.d.), online: Department of Justice Canada <http://www.justice.gc.ca/eng/rp-pr/fl-lf/famil/fv-vf/child_protection.pdf>; Rachel Birnbaum, Michael Saini, & Nicholas Bala, "Canada's First Integrated Domestic Violence Court: Examining Family and Criminal Court Outcomes at the Toronto IDVC" (2017) 32 J Family Violence 621; Hon. Bonnie Croll, "The Intersection between Criminal Law, Family Law and Child Protection in Domestic Violence Cases" (8 May 2015), online: FREDA Centre <http://www.fredacentre.com/wp-content/uploads/2010/09/Croll-J.-The-Intersection-Between-Criminal-Law-Family-Law-and-Child-Protection-in-Domestic-Violence-Cases-May-8-2015.pdf>; Federal-Provincial-Territorial Ad Hoc Working Group on Family Violence, *Making the Links, supra* note 11; Margaret Jackson & Donna Martinson, *Risk of Future Harm: Family Violence and Information Sharing between Family and Criminal Courts* (Fredericton: Canadian Observatory on Intimate Partner Violence, 2016); Donna Martinson, *Judicial Coordination of Concurrent Proceedings in Domestic Violence Cases* (Vancouver: FREDA Centre, 2012); Janet E. Mosher, "Grounding Access to Justice Theory and Practice in the Experiences of Women Abused by Their Intimate Partners" (2015) 32 Windsor YB Access Just 149 ["Grounding Access"]; Neilson, *Enhancing Safety, supra* note 12; Mary Ellen Turpel-Lafond, *Honouring Kaitlynne, Max and Cordon: Make Their Voices Heard Now* (Victoria: BC Representative for Children and Youth, 2012); Woman Abuse Council of Toronto, *Policies Matter: Addressing Violence against Women through Reflection, Knowledge and Action* (Toronto: Woman ACT, 2013).

21 Ongoing research includes a case law review and qualitative interviews in selected jurisdictions with justice system personnel and service providers.

22 *Criminal Code*, RSC 1985, c C-46, was amended by Canada, Bill C-75, *An Act to amend the Criminal Code, the Youth Criminal Justice Act and other Acts and to make consequential amendments to other Acts,* 1st Sess, 42nd Parl, 2018, to include several provisions related to intimate partner violence referenced here.

23 See, e.g., *Serious Crime Act 2015* (UK) c 9, s 76.

24 *Criminal Code, supra* note 22, ss 515(3)(a), 515(6)(b.1), 718.2(a)(ii), 718.201, 718.3(8), 738(1)(c).

25 *Ibid,* ss 501(3)(d), 501(3)(e), 515(3)(a), 516(2), 732.1(3)(a.1), 742.3(2)(a.3), 810(3.2).

26 *Ibid,* s 109(1)(a.1); see also s 110(2.1).

27 *Ibid,* s 127.

28 *Final Report of the Ad Hoc Federal-Provincial-Territorial Working Group Reviewing Spousal Abuse Policies and Legislation* (Ottawa: Department of Justice Canada, 2003) at 100–1,

online: Department of Justice Canada <https://www.justice.gc.ca/eng/rp-pr/cj-jp/fv-vf/pol/spo_e-con_a.pdf>. Pro-charging policies require the police to lay charges where they have "reasonable" or "reasonable and probable" grounds to do so. Pro-prosecution policies require prosecutions to proceed where there is a reasonable likelihood of conviction and it is in the public interest to do so.

29 *Divorce Act*, RSC 1985, c 3 (2d Supp).
30 Parental conduct has generally been relevant only to the extent that it affects a person's ability to parent: *ibid*, s 16(9), now s 16(5).
31 *Ibid*, ss 16(2), 16(3)(j), 16(4), as revised by Canada, Bill C-78, *An Act to amend the Divorce Act*, 1st Sess, 42nd Parl, 2018. Family violence is defined broadly to include psychological and financial abuse and coercive control as well as direct and indirect exposure of children to violence (s 2(1)). Any relevant civil or criminal proceedings or orders must also be considered (ss 16(3)(k), 7.8(2)).
32 *Ibid*, ss 16(3)(c), 16(6), formerly s 16(10).
33 *Ibid*, ss 7.3, 7.7(2)(a).
34 *Ibid*, ss 16.8(3), 16.9(3), 16.96(3).
35 *Ibid*, s 16.92(1)(d).
36 *An Act respecting First Nations, Inuit and Metis Children, Youth and Families*, SC 2019, c 24.
37 *Ibid*, s 10(3)(g) and (h).
38 *Ibid*, s 9(4).
39 *Family Homes on Reserves and Matrimonial Interests or Rights Act*, SC 2013, c 20.
40 *Ibid*, ss 7, 16(1).
41 "List of First Nations with Matrimonial Real Property Laws and the List of Jurisdictions with Designated Judges" (28 June 2019), online: Indigenous Services Canada <https://www.sac-isc.gc.ca/eng/1408981855429/1581783888815>.
42 *Immigration and Refugee Protection Act*, SC 2001, c 27 [*IRPA*]. See generally Bhuyan et al, *supra* note 17. IRPA provisions relevant to domestic violence and refugee claims are beyond the scope of this chapter.
43 *Immigration and Refugee Protection Regulations*, SOR/2002-227, s 126 [*IRPR*].
44 See, e.g., Janet Mosher, "The Complicity of the State in the Intimate Abuse of Immigrant Women" in Vijay Agnew, ed, *Racialized Migrant Women in Canada: Essays on Health, Violence and Equity* (Toronto: University of Toronto Press, 2009) 41 ["Complicity"].
45 Pursuant to s 25(1) of the *IRPA*, the Minister may exempt a foreign national from any of the requirements of the act (including that a person apply from outside of Canada) and may grant permanent resident status if of the opinion that "it is justified on humanitarian and compassionate considerations relating to the foreign national, taking into account the best interests of a child directly affected."
46 See Immigration, Refugees and Citizenship Canada, "The Humanitarian and Compassionate Assessment: Dealing with Family Relationships," online: Government of Canada <https://www.canada.ca/en/immigration-refugees-citizenship/corporate/publications-manuals/operational-bulletins-manuals/permanent-residence/humanitarian-compassionate-consideration/processing/assessment-dealing-family-relationships.html>; and "Abuse: Assessing Evidence," online: Government of Canada <https://www.canada.ca/en/immigration-refugees-citizenship/corporate/publications-manuals/operational-bulletins-manuals/service-delivery/abuse/evidence.html>.
47 See Immigration, Refugees and Citizenship Canada, "Temporary Resident Permit (TRP) for Victims of Family Violence," online: Government of Canada <https://www.canada.ca/en/immigration-refugees-citizenship/corporate/publications-manuals/operational-bulletins-manuals/temporary-residents/permits/family-violence.html>.

48 *IRPA, supra* note 42, ss 36(2)(a), 36(3)(a). A hybrid offence is one in which the Crown can elect to proceed either by way of summary conviction (maximum penalty of less than two years) or indictment.

49 *Ibid,* s 36(1)(a).

50 Pollack et al, *supra* note 18.

51 *IRPA, supra* note 42, s133(1)(e)(ii).

52 See Koshan, Mosher, & Wiegers, *supra* note 20, for more detail on the relevant laws and policies. This section is current to March 31, 2020.

53 See *Final Report of the Ad Hoc Federal-Provincial-Territorial Working Group Reviewing Spousal Abuse Policies and Legislation, supra* note 28 at 1–2.

54 See Birnbaum, Saini, & Bala, *supra* note 20.

55 See Koshan, Mosher, & Wiegers, *supra* note 20.

56 *Ibid.*

57 See Table 7.1. For analysis of this legislation across Canada, see Linda Neilson, *Enhancing Civil Protection in Domestic Violence Cases: Cross Canada Checkup* (Fredericton: Muriel McQueen Fergusson Centre for Family Violence Research, 2015). Quebec's *Code of Civil Procedure,* CQLR c C-25.01, s 509, provides for protection orders generally in circumstances of violence.

58 See Koshan, Mosher, & Wiegers, *supra* note 20.

59 See Table 7.1.

60 For a discussion of the BC provisions, see Susan B. Boyd & Ruben Lindy, "Violence against Women and the BC Family Law Act: Early Jurisprudence" (2016) 35 Can Fam LQ 101.

61 *Hague Convention on the Civil Aspects of International Child Abduction,* 25 October 1980, Hague XXVIII, art 13(b) (entered into force 1 December 1983).

62 See Table 7.1. *The Child and Family Services Act,* CCSM, c C80 in Manitoba and Ontario's *Child, Youth and Family Services Act, 2017,* SO 2017, c 14 do not explicitly include domestic violence, but provisions relating to harm or injury due to the domestic environment (Manitoba) or emotional harm (Ontario) have been interpreted as including exposure to domestic violence (Manitoba, s 17; Ontario, s 74(2)).

63 See, e.g., Judith Mosoff et al, "Intersecting Challenges: Mothers and Child Protection Law in BC" (2017) 50:2 UBC L Rev 435.

64 A married spouse must typically apply for relief before a divorce is granted, and an unmarried cohabiting spouse must apply within a specified time period after cohabitation ends.

65 See Table 7.1. See also Jonnette Watson Hamilton, "Reforming Residential Tenancy Law for Victims of Domestic Violence" (2019) 8 Annual Review of Interdisciplinary Justice Research 248.

66 Watson Hamilton, *supra* note 65.

67 See Table 7.1.

68 Koshan, Mosher, & Wiegers, *supra* note 20.

69 See Table 7.1.

70 *Ibid.*

71 *Ibid.*

72 See, e.g., Alberta, where dating relationships and psychological/emotional abuse are included as "domestic violence" for residential tenancy and employment legislation, but not as "family violence" under civil protection legislation.

73 This legislation also typically restricts access to personal information where safety issues would arise from disclosure. Some jurisdictions also have legislation creating torts for the non-consensual distribution of intimate images. See Koshan, Mosher, & Wiegers, *supra* note 20.

74 For a discussion of promising coordination practices among systems, see Federal-Provincial-Territorial Ad Hoc Working Group on Family Violence, *Making the Links, supra* note 11.

75 See, e.g., *ibid;* Jackson & Martinson, *supra* note 20; Linda Neilson, *Responding to Domestic Violence in Family Law, Civil Protection and Child Protection Cases,* 2017 Can LII Docs 2.

76 Federal-Provincial-Territorial Ad Hoc Working Group on Family Violence, *Making the Links, supra* note 11 at 26–27.

77 See, e.g., Bhuyan et al, *supra* note 17; Burns, *supra* note 17; Mosher, "Complicity," *supra* note 44; Pollack et al, *supra* note 18.

78 Bala, Birnbaum, & Martinson, *supra* note 19.

79 See, e.g., Martinson, *supra* note 20.

80 *Ibid;* Noel Semple, "Whose Best Interests? Custody and Access Law and Procedure" (2010) 48 Osgoode Hall LJ 287.

81 Jackson & Martinson, *supra* note 20; Neilson, *Enhancing Safety, supra* note 12.

82 Bala, Birnbaum, & Martinson, *supra* note 19; Jackson & Martinson, *supra* note 20; Neilson, *Enhancing Safety, supra* note 12.

83 Marianne Hester, "The Contradictory Legal Worlds Faced by Domestic Violence Victims" in Evan Stark and Eve S. Buzawa, eds, *Violence against Women in Families and Relationships,* vol 2, *The Family Context* (Denver: Praeger, 2009) 127.

84 Cross, *Through the Looking Glass, supra* note 12; Heather Douglas, "Legal Systems Abuse and Coercive Control" (2018) 18 Criminology & Criminal Justice 84; Martinson, *supra* note 20; Janet Mosher, Patricia Evans, & Margaret Little, "Walking on Eggshells: Abused Women's Experience of Ontario's Welfare System" (5 April 2004), Commissioned Reports, Studies and Public Policy Documents, Paper 160, online: Osgoode Digital Commons <https://digitalcommons.osgoode.yorku.ca/reports/160/>; Neilson, *Enhancing Safety, supra* note 12; Andrea Vollens, *Court-Related Abuse and Harassment* (Vancouver: YWCA, 2010); David Ward, "In Her Words: Recognizing and Preventing Abusive Litigation against Domestic Violence Survivors" (2016) 14 Journal for Social Justice 429.

85 Jackson & Martinson, *supra* note 20; Neilson, *Enhancing Safety, supra* note 12; Mosher, "Grounding Access," *supra* note 20.

86 *Residential Tenancies Act, 2006,* SO 2006, c 17, ss 47.1–47.3, and see Form N15. Most other jurisdictions require verification of abuse by a professional unless a no-contact order is in place. See Watson Hamilton, *supra* note 65.

87 O Reg 367/11, s 24(1)(a) (made under the *Housing Services Act, 2011,* SO 2011, c 6).

88 O Reg 134/98, s 6 (made under the *Ontario Works Act, 1997,* SO 1997, c 25, Sched A).

89 O Reg 367/11, *supra* note 87, s 58(1).

90 See *Patterson v Osazuma,* 2015 ONCJ 454; and *JH v FA,* 2009 ONCA 17.

91 See the references at *supra* note 84.

92 For a quantification of other costs associated with access to justice, including increased reliance on social assistance, public housing, and health services, see Trevor C.W. Farrow et al, *Everyday Legal Problems and the Cost of Justice in Canada: Overview Report* (Toronto: Canadian Forum on Civil Justice, 2016), online: Canadian Forum on Civil Justice <http://www.cfcj-fcjc.org/sites/default/files//Everyday%20Legal%20Problems%20and%20the%20Cost%20of%20Justice%20in%20Canada%20-%20Overview%20Report.pdf>.

93 See, e.g., Australian Law Reform Commission, *Family Violence and Commonwealth Laws: Improving Legal Frameworks,* Report 117 (November 2011), online: <https://www.alrc.gov.au/publication/family-violence-and-commonwealth-laws-improving-legal-frameworks-alrc-report-117/>.

Part 3
Legal Services and Paths to Justice

8

Paralegals and Access to Justice for Tenants
A Case Study

David Wiseman

A PROPOSAL THAT OFTEN arises in the pan-Canadian debate about how to improve access to justice is to expand the pool of legal services providers, which is currently largely restricted to lawyers, by creating or regularizing the provision of legal services by non-lawyer "paralegals," including allowing paralegals to serve as representatives in some formal dispute resolution processes.[1] This proposal is commonly based on the assumption that they offer a more affordable, "user-friendly" alternative to lawyers.[2] Among Canadian jurisdictions other than Quebec (which has a distinctive self-regulating profession of notaries with a uniquely broad scope of practice), Ontario has gone the furthest in formalizing the regulation of paralegals, establishing them as an independent branch of the self-regulating legal profession and providing them with the widest scope of practice.[3] This chapter seeks to shed light on the access to justice potential of paralegals by reporting and reflecting upon a case study of paralegal representation in landlord-tenant disputes in a region of Ontario. Ultimately, since it is found that paralegals perform a significant and perhaps increasing share of landlord representation but hardly ever represent tenants, it is concluded that the Ontario model of paralegal regularization does not appear to be improving access to justice for tenants.

Considering the access to justice potential of paralegals requires attention to two issues in particular: first, the quality or effectiveness of paralegal services; and, second, affordability and other determinants of the user-friendliness of paralegal services. From an access to justice perspective, expanding the availability of paralegal services is justified if they can provide services that are sufficiently effective, as well as sufficiently affordable and otherwise user-friendly. In using the term "user-friendly," I refer to the factors, other than cost, that impact consumption or use of legal services by those in need of legal assistance, such as the geographic or technical convenience of access points for services and the range of languages in which services are available.[4] To date, there has been relatively little empirical analysis of the access to justice potential of paralegal services, especially in Canada. What empirical analysis there is has tended to focus on effectiveness rather than affordability and user-friendliness. A leading US study has empirically demonstrated that non-lawyers can provide legal representation at levels of effectiveness comparable to or better than lawyers in certain dispute resolution contexts,[5] but it has also been empirically demonstrated, in a leading Canadian study, that they have not done so in other contexts.[6] Those studies do not examine affordability and user-friendliness, and there is scant other information or analysis. Consequently, the assumption that paralegals offer lower costs of justice and are otherwise user-friendly is largely untested. The case study reported and reflected upon in this chapter casts some doubt on the reasonableness of that assumption, at least in relation to tenants. As we shall see, the case study raises questions about how the problem of lack of access to justice is understood and about how proposals for addressing that lack are framed. I suggest that lack of access to justice needs to be understood, at least for tenants, as a problem of legal (dis)empowerment, and that improving access to justice requires measures that are more proactive and community-oriented than the approach that paralegals currently appear to be taking.

Paralegals as Legal Professionals in Ontario

In Ontario, the legal profession is self-regulating under the auspices of the Law Society of Ontario (formerly the Law Society of Upper Canada).[7] The Law Society has a long history of responsibility for the regulation of lawyers in Ontario, who, until 2007, enjoyed a near-monopoly on the entitlement to provide legal services in the province. It was a *near*-monopoly in the sense that there existed some specific legislative permissions for non-lawyers to provide legal services in particular circumstances or forums, but the preponderance of legal services were formally and practically restricted to being provided by lawyers. One of the more significant areas of permission entitled non-lawyer "agents" to appear in criminal matters involving provincial offences or summary proceedings,[8] with a series of court decisions establishing that agents could be strangers to the accused (rather than only friends or family) and could be compensated.[9] In the area of residential tenancy disputes, when a quasi-judicial tribunal was first established for such disputes in Ontario in 1997, it too permitted representation by agents, similarly defined.[10]

Concerns about the lack of regulation of agents prompted a number of inquiries, reports, and recommendations that eventually led to the establishment of the paralegal branch of the legal profession via the *Access to Justice Act (AJA)*.[11] The creation of the paralegal profession was justified as a means for improving access to justice in Ontario, with an emphasis on consumer protection and choice (with "choice" apparently signalling affordability considerations).[12] The

AJA brought paralegals into the self-regulatory structure of the Law Society and at the same time expanded the legislative specification of its regulatory mission to expressly include a responsibility to "facilitate access to justice."[13] The Law Society was largely responsible for working out the details of the regulatory framework applicable to the training and licensing of paralegals (which ultimately substantially imitated the framework applicable to lawyers), as well as defining paralegal scope of practice (which essentially matched that which had been enjoyed by non-lawyers prior to establishment of the paralegal profession).[14] The package of legislative reforms did not include any direct measures to ensure affordability of the services provided by paralegals, and neither did the regulatory framework subsequently put in place by the Law Society, which, for lawyers and paralegals alike, relies upon market forces to determine the costs of justice.

The assumption as to the relative affordability of paralegals is based on a two-part line of reasoning that is clear and simple enough. First, the costs of qualifying for licensing for paralegals will tend to be lower than for lawyers. A regulatory provision for "grandfathered" licensing of eligible non-lawyer agents who were active at the time the paralegal profession was established meant many such agents faced little or no new costs of formal training to be eligible for licensing as paralegals. For newcomers to the paralegal profession, the requirements for formal training are limited to successful completion of a two-year college diploma program.[15] The direct cost of such a program pales in comparison to the direct costs of the required formal training for lawyers, which includes both a university undergraduate degree (often four years in duration) and then a three-year university law degree.[16] Consequently, it is reasoned, newly licensed paralegals will incur lower costs on the path to establishing their practices. To the extent that the price of legal services is determined by a need or desire to recoup such costs (as may especially be the case with an accumulated debt), paralegals ought to be able to offer their services at relatively lower prices.[17] Second, due to both the nature of their training and regulatory limits, the practices of paralegals will be oriented to the provision of legal services that are less time-consuming and less complex, enabling them to attain substantive and process experience and expertise relatively quickly and, in turn, permitting them to achieve an economically sustainable level of efficiency and productivity despite offering relatively lower prices for their services.

Since commencing its role as regulator of paralegals, and despite having to undertake a self-review of the regulatory performance after five years, the Law Society has paid no direct attention to whether the assumption as to the affordability of paralegal services has been realized in practice.[18] Affordability was also ignored in the parallel process and report of an independent expert appointed by the Attorney General of Ontario.[19] Some light can be shed on the issue by considering the findings of a survey commissioned by the Law Society and made public as an appendix to its self-review report. The survey included information on the reasons why clients chose paralegals as their service providers, with the most cited reason, at 46 percent, being "cost less than a lawyer."[20] This was closely followed by "simple matter/not requiring a lawyer," at 41 percent. Other reasons were that a paralegal had represented themselves as very experienced or a specialist in the relevant area (33 percent); a paralegal was easier to hire or manage than a lawyer (23 percent); and the respondent had a personal relationship to a paralegal (8 percent). Although these findings provide some empirical support for the assumption that paralegals are more affordable than lawyers, a number of limitations must be recognized. First, there may be a difference between client perceptions of whether paralegals are cheaper than lawyers and actual cost differentials, especially since it may be difficult for a client to be certain that the costs they are comparing are actually for comparable services. Second, the findings do not tell us anything about the magnitude of cost savings, which might be a relevant factor if it is important to consider the broader question of whether paralegal services represent good value for money.[21] Finally, an indication that paralegals are generally cheaper than lawyers does not provide sufficient information to determine whether paralegals are cheap enough to provide an affordable option for a significant proportion of the people who regard themselves as unable to afford lawyers. Of course, even if paralegals only offer a newly affordable option for a relatively small segment of the population who would otherwise lack access to justice, that may be regarded as a worthwhile improvement. But it should also bring into focus the question of what other measures might be needed to reach other segments of the population, especially those who are more socio-economically disadvantaged, as well as the question of where the priorities of the state and other legal regulators should lie.

Paralegals and Residential Tenancy Disputes

The impetus for this case study was anecdotal evidence arising from a tenant-oriented Housing Justice Project (HJP) operated through a partnership between the Ottawa chapter of ACORN, a low-income persons' membership-based community organization, and the Faculty of Law at the University of Ottawa. The HJP provided a vehicle for law students, under legal supervision, to provide legal assistance to existing and prospective ACORN members experiencing residential tenancy problems. Given the existing availability, albeit limited, of low- or no-cost legal assistance for tenants facing eviction – primarily through publicly funded lawyers providing services as tenant duty counsel or from community legal clinics – the main focus of the HJP was tenant problems with the habitability of their rental units, usually due to lack of maintenance, repairs, or pest control. Over time, students involved in the HJP noticed that landlords seemed to be frequently, and perhaps increasingly, represented by paralegals. This raised a concern that, to the extent that paralegals might be improving access to justice in landlord-tenant disputes, they might be doing so only for landlords and not for tenants. To test that concern, a research case study was designed and pursued under the umbrella of the Cost of Justice research project of the Canadian Forum on Civil Justice. This part of this chapter reports on the case study, including the data and methodology, as well as the findings. As a precursor to doing so, the first sub-part sketches some key elements of the context of paralegals and residential tenancy disputes as everyday legal problems.

Context

The survey of everyday legal problems conducted by the Cost of Justice research project found that in the preceding three years, approximately 2.5 percent of adult Canadians, or almost 590,000 people, experienced one or more problems relating to housing that they considered to be serious and difficult to resolve. Given the incidence of multiple problems, the total number of housing problems was estimated at approximately 1.16 million. In inquiring about "housing" problems, the survey canvassed a range of housing-related problems, covering both renters and owners. Rental situations gave rise to the vast majority of problems, at just over 1 million, or about 86 percent. In terms of rental housing problems, the survey directed respondents to consider the occurrence of a specified list of seven problems, all of which were framed from the perspective of tenants. For example, in the last three years, "have there been arbitrary changes to your rent?" or "were you evicted or threatened with eviction?" However, there was also a catch-all question enabling respondents to specify any other problems. This provided both landlords and renters an opportunity to identify problems that were not included in the survey's questions on housing-related problems.[22] By no means are rental-housing problems the most prevalent type of everyday legal problem. Housing problems rank equal ninth, with personal injury problems, in the overall incidence of everyday legal problems – well behind the top three: consumer (22.6 percent), debt (20.8 percent), and employment (16.4 percent). Nevertheless, at just over 1 million problems per three-year period, rental-housing problems are not quantitatively insignificant.

In Ontario, the Landlord and Tenant Board (LTB) is the formal mechanism available for resolving rental-housing problems. The creation and operation of quasi-judicial administrative tribunals like the LTB are often justified by the notion that administrative processes can offer better access to justice for everyday disputes than the court system.[23] Over the five years of data relevant to this case study, the total caseload of the LTB averaged around 80,000 applications annually, with landlord applications typically accounting for around 90 percent.[24] For the Eastern Region, the total caseload was usually around 8,000 applications.[25] Nevertheless, being relatively more accessible than the court system does not necessarily mean that the legal rules and processes of the LTB are accessible enough, especially in the absence of legal assistance.[26] State-funded legal assistance for residential tenancy disputes in Ontario, in the form of funding for duty counsel services, community clinic legal staff, and private bar legal aid certificates, is quite limited. A recent review of the Tenant Duty Counsel Program makes it clear that state-funded services, although valuable to and effective for tenants who can access them, do not reach a significant portion of the total legal needs of tenants.[27] Meanwhile, private lawyers are generally regarded as too expensive. Without representation, the legal rules and processes appear to be complicated enough to leave many low-income tenants struggling to enter or navigate the dispute resolution system on their own.

Given this situation, the possibility of accessing effective, affordable, and user-friendly legal assistance through paralegals could be a significant benefit for low-income tenants. It is clear that residential tenancy disputes are one area in which Ontario paralegals offer legal assistance, as did unregulated non-lawyers previously. The survey commissioned by the Law Society as part of its five-year self-review of paralegal regulation included information on the major areas of practice of paralegals. Paralegals cited residential tenancy disputes as the third most frequent area of practice, with 27 percent of paralegals performing work in this area, with the more frequent practice areas being small claims court work (43 percent) and provincial offences work (37 percent).[28] On the surface, then, it would appear arguable that paralegals are contributing to access to justice in residential tenancy disputes. However, looking below the surface of the frequency of paralegal work in the area of residential tenancies, as this case study does, it becomes apparent that the reality is more complicated.

Data and Methodology

This research case study gathered and analyzed all reported decisions (through the Canadian Legal Information Institute [CanLII] website) of the Ontario Landlord and Tenant Board for the Eastern Region (which includes hearings in Ottawa as well as in Kingston, Brockville, and other smaller communities) for the six years spanning the period from 2009–10 to 2014–15. Each year spanned the period from April to the following March. The starting year was selected for two reasons. First, it corresponded with the introduction of a new database system for the LTB, which prevented access to older data. As will be explained below, access to information in the database was required for the research, and so the earliest date for data collection was the calendar year 2009. Second, by the beginning of 2009, the Law Society's regime for licensing paralegals had been in operation for just over eighteen months (since May 2007), which was regarded as sufficient time for the newly designated legal professionals, especially those who were grandfathered into paralegal licensing, to be evident in LTB dispute resolution.

The total number of case files in the dataset was initially 948 decisions, although there was significant variation in the.number of decisions available from year to year (see *n* values in Table 8.1). Indeed, the number of cases reported through CanLII for the Eastern Region of the LTB for 2014–15 was unusually small (*n* = 24), and so, although not revealing any meaningful inconsistency with the rest of the dataset, that year of cases was excluded from the project. Thus, the final dataset consisted of 924 reported decisions. Since many claims do not reach the decision stage, and since only a modest proportion of decisions are reported, the total number of decisions gathered is only a small subset of the total number of claims filed with, and resolved through, the LTB for the Eastern Region. The decisions included claims filed by both landlords (typically for eviction) and tenants (typically for maintenance and, relatedly, rent abatements).

It should be noted that the annual datasets are generally not large enough to be treated as representative samples. Moreover, the small subset of reported decisions is itself not necessarily representative; indeed, a representative of the LTB itself informed the author that there is no systematic approach to the reporting of decisions, which therefore appears to be ad hoc. Nevertheless, these cases are all that is publically available, and analysis of them at least indicates potentially significant attributes that, if representative, would warrant consideration.

The dataset was coded for a variety of attributes. For present purposes, the relevant attributes were type of party (landlord or tenant) and type of representation (e.g., paralegal). Other coded attributes included type of application (landlord or tenant), type of claim (eviction, maintenance, and so on), and type of result (applicant success, respondent success, mixed/partial success, and other variations). The coding was undertaken by a number of research assistants and subject to verification on the aspects reported here. Identification of type of representative was more complicated than originally anticipated, owing to the fact that the LTB adopted a practice of using the label of "Legal Representative" to refer to both lawyers and paralegals in its decisions. In order to distinguish these types of legal representatives, it was first necessary to compile a list of all case files in which a legal representative appeared and then to seek the names (personal and business) of the representatives by utilizing the *Freedom of*

Information and Protection of Privacy Act.[29] Once the names were obtained, they were entered into the electronic directories of licensees maintained by the Law Society in order to determine whether the named persons were lawyers or paralegals. Where necessary to clarify or confirm professional status, personal and business names were searched on the Internet more broadly. Ultimately, a variety of types of representatives were identified.

For landlords, the types were:

- *self-representation*
- *non-legal* – a corporate officer or employee of a corporate landlord or of a property management business retained by a landlord, but sometimes a real estate agent
- *paralegal*
- *lawyer*
- *agent* – other representatives, possibly family or friends, who could not be confirmed as belonging to any of the preceding categories or clearly did not belong to those categories.

Technically speaking, where corporate landlords are involved and are represented by non–legally qualified corporate officers or employees, the corporate landlords are engaged in a form of self-representation. Practically speaking, however, this form of representation is being undertaken by individuals who have a formal business responsibility, as a corporate officer or employee, to perform representational duties. In many instances, they would also either have training, repeat experience, or corporate guidance in relation to acting as a representative – especially where the corporate landlord owns property with multiple dwelling units. Thus, it was deemed important to provide some distinction between non–legally qualified corporate officers or employees representing corporate landlords and non-corporate individual landlords who represent themselves. By the same token, it must be acknowledged that non-corporate individual landlords may also have repeat experience to draw upon, and so this distinction is somewhat fluid.

For tenants, the types were:

- *self-representation*
- *duty counsel* – publicly funded lawyer assistance, located on-site in Ottawa and on-site or nearby at other Eastern Region locations
- *public lawyer* – non–duty counsel publicly funded lawyers, typically housed in community legal clinics

- *private lawyer* – other lawyers who could be identified as in private practice or whose practice context could not be confirmed; may include some private lawyers appearing on the basis of legal aid certificates
- *paralegal*
- *legal worker* – publicly funded, neither licensed lawyers nor paralegals, typically housed at community legal clinics
- *agent* – other representatives, possibly family or friends, who could not be confirmed as belonging to any of the preceding categories or clearly did not belong to those categories.

Using these categories of types of representatives, the data were analyzed for both the prevalence of the different types of representatives for each type of party – landlord or tenant – and also for the prevalence of different types of head-to-head representation dyads.

Prevalence of Different Types of Representation

The tables and figures below report the prevalence of different types of tenant and landlord representation for each of the five years from 2009–10 to 2013–14.

Table 8.1 reports on tenant representation, in both percentage terms and relative rank (R#). It is important to note that the category of "Duty counsel" representation captures only a portion of the representation assistance, and none of the other types of assistance, provided by publicly funded duty counsel lawyers to tenants. Specifically, casework statistics on the Eastern Region duty counsel program provided by the Advocacy Centre for Tenants Ontario show that duty counsel, who usually assist around 25–30 percent of total tenants, provide summary advice to around 90 percent of the tenants they assist but provide representation services to only 30–50 percent of assisted tenants. Moreover, not all duty counsel representation services are necessarily identifiable in the written decisions and orders that constitute the dataset.

Table 8.1 reveals a number of significant points. First, the prevalence of self-representation among tenants was never below 50 percent and typically over 60 percent. Second, leaving aside self-representation, the main type of representation utilized by tenants is consistently duty counsel (with a range of 13–26 percent), which clearly plays a significant role in assisting tenants, especially considering that many tenants who are officially identified as self-represented will have consulted with duty counsel prior to their hearing. Third, lawyers, both public and private, also consistently play a role in representing tenants. Fourth, and most importantly in terms of the focus of this case study, paralegals

Table 8.1 **Prevalence of different types of tenant representation at Ontario LTB, Eastern Region (2009–10 to 2013–14)**

Tenant representation	2009–10 (n = 155) %	R#	2010–11 (n = 216) %	R#	2011–12 (n = 118) %	R#	2012–13 (n = 344) %	R#	2013–14 (n = 91) %	R#
Self	62.0	1	62.5	1	54.0	1	69.7	1	61.0	1
Duty counsel	19.0	2	17.5	2	26.0	2	13.6	2	18.6	2
Lawyer	11.0	3	11.1	3	13.5	3	7.8	3	14.0	3
Public	5.8		6.0		7.5		3.8		8.5	
Private	5.2		5.1		6.0		4.0		5.5	
Agent	4.5	4	3.2	5	3.3	4	4.3	4	5.4	4
Legal worker	2.5	5	4.6	4	1.6	5	3.4	5	1.0	5
Paralegal	0.6	6	0.4	6	0.8	6	0.8	6	0	–

Note: R# = relative rank.

Figure 8.1 **Types of tenant representation at Ontario LTB, Eastern Region (2009–10 to 2013–14)**

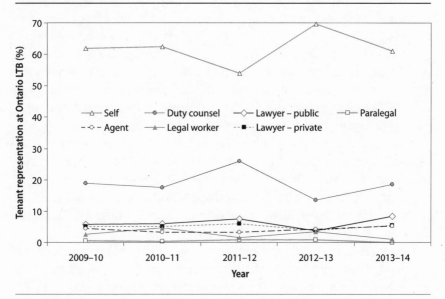

play a consistently very marginal role in tenant representation, less than 1 percent in all years. The relative prevalence of the different types of tenant representatives over the five years is visually depicted in Figure 8.1.

Table 8.2 and Figure 8.2 report on landlord representation over the five years and also reveal some significant points. First, throughout this period, landlord

Table 8.2 Prevalence of different types of landlord representation at Ontario
LTB, Eastern Region (2009–10 to 2013–14)

Landlord representation	2009–10 (n = 155)		2010–11 (n = 216)		2011–12 (n = 118)		2012–13 (n = 344)		2013–14 (n = 91)	
	%	R#	%	R#	%	R#	%	R#	%	R#
Self	29.0	2	34.7	1	27.3	2	31.0	1	32.0	1
Non-legal	30.3	1	15.2	3	17.0	4	20.6	3	13.1	4
Paralegal	21.2	3	28.2	2	32.0	1	29.0	2	28.5	2
Lawyer	15.0	4	12.0	4	17.7	3	12.7	4	17.5	3
Agent	4.5	5	9.7	5	6.0	5	6.7	5	8.7	5

Note: R# = relative rank.

Figure 8.2 Types of landlord representation at Ontario LTB, Eastern Region
(2009–10 to 2013–14)

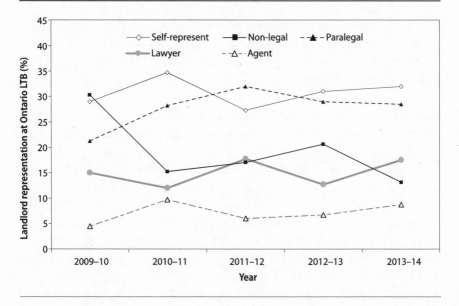

self-representation remained constant at around 30 percent. Second, both
paralegal and non-legal representatives have consistently played a significant
role in landlord representation, and lawyers have made a consistent contribution
as well. At no less than 21 percent and consistently closer to 30 percent, paralegals
obviously play a far larger role in representing landlords than they do in representing tenants. Third, there may have been a significant switch from the use

of non-legal representatives to paralegals. The use of paralegals rose from 21 percent in 2009–10 to 28 percent in 2010–11, and has remained at around that level since, whereas the use of non-legal representatives declined from 30 percent in 2009–10 to 15 percent in 2010–11, and has remained well below 30 percent, although fluctuating significantly, in subsequent years.

A caveat needs to be lodged regarding the indication of a significant switch in landlord representation from non-legal representatives to paralegals. Since the prevalence of paralegal representation has remained fairly consistent since 2010–11, it may be that the lower prevalence in 2009–10 was merely a quirk in the dataset. In other words, the baseline for prevalence of paralegal representation might be better indicated by the four later years of data than by the initial year of data. On the other hand, if this is not a data quirk and the switch is real, then the data indicate that paralegals quickly established a newly significant role in landlord representation in the Eastern Region of the LTB. Moreover, since non-legal representatives are typically employees of corporate landlord entities or the property management businesses more commonly used by larger or corporate landlords, the switch would suggest that corporate landlords are the main beneficiaries of any greater prevalence of paralegals in the residential tenancy dispute system.

Prevalence of Head-to-Head Representation Dyads
The data were also analyzed for prevalence of different types of representational dyads – in other words, different types of head-to-head representation dynamics. This analysis examined the dataset as a whole, including the small set of cases available for 2014–15. In the most frequent representation dyad, which occurred in 22.5 percent of cases, both landlord and tenant were self-represented. In the next most frequent, at 15.5 percent, the landlord was represented by a paralegal while the tenant was self-represented. This was followed by non-legal representation for the landlord versus a self-represented tenant, at 11.8 percent, and then lawyer-for-landlord versus self-represented tenant, at 8.1 percent. All told, 65 percent of self-represented tenants faced a represented landlord. In contrast, only 39 percent of self-represented landlords faced a represented tenant. By the same token, of the situations where self-represented landlords faced represented tenants, 71 percent of the tenant representatives were lawyers (including duty counsel). In contrast, of the situations where self-represented tenants faced a represented landlord, only 20 percent of the representatives were lawyers (with 39 percent being paralegals, 30 percent being non-legal, and 10 percent being agents).

Given that the frequency of self-representation among tenants (around 60 percent) was consistently twice that among landlords (around 30 percent), it is not surprising that tenants more often find themselves in a one-sided representation dynamic where they are self-represented against a represented landlord. The case study did not aim to undertake the much more complicated analytical task of assessing whether there is any relationship between the type of head-to-head representational dynamic and the fairness of process or outcome. Nonetheless, it seems reasonable to speculate that there is at least a possibility that the mere fact of being on the unrepresented side of a one-sided representation dynamic is a disadvantage and that tenants are bearing a heavier burden of that disadvantage.

Paralegals and Access to Justice for Tenants
The case study findings suggest three main points in relation to access to justice in landlord-tenant disputes. First, it appears that paralegals are not sufficiently affordable or otherwise user-friendly for tenants and so offer them no direct access to justice improvements. Second, it appears that paralegals are sufficiently affordable and user-friendly for landlords, especially larger or corporate landlords, perhaps increasingly so. This indicates that paralegals are playing a role in maintaining or improving access to justice for landlords. Third, to the extent that corporate landlords may be benefiting from greater use of paralegals, there is the danger that this may be directly detrimental to tenants who, especially where they are self-represented, may be facing relatively more effectively represented opponents. Any such detriment to tenants may amount to a decrease in their access to justice.

Self-represented tenants are in the greatest danger of experiencing a decrease in their access to justice due to the possibility that paralegals are providing relatively more effective representation to landlords. One basis for discerning a potential disadvantage in a one-sided lack of representation is a difference in capacity to effectively manage and participate in the hearing itself. However, another potential disadvantage exists in the recognition that, generally speaking, it can be expected that a represented party will also be better prepared than a self-represented party for a dispute resolution process. Moreover, relative differences in degrees of preparation may also be a factor in other types of representation dyads that, on their face, do not seem so potentially unfair to tenants. For instance, the data reveal that of the 70 percent of cases where a landlord was represented, the opposing tenant was represented by duty counsel in 20 percent of those cases. While the presence of duty counsel would be expected to contribute to levelling the playing field for the tenant, it is important to recognize that duty counsel is often involved only at the eleventh hour of disputation and so may not be able to entirely compensate for any prior lack of preparation by tenants.

The possibility that paralegals are contributing to more effective representation for landlords relative to tenants may also mean that already existing power imbalances are being exacerbated. This may be especially the case for the proportion of tenants who are members of socially and economically disadvantaged groups. The 2016 review of the Tenant Duty Counsel Program observed that it "has been amply demonstrated in prior research that tenants as a group tend to have higher rates of low income than homeowners, and are more likely to be members of equity-seeking and disadvantaged groups."[30] It went on to observe that many clients who access the duty counsel program exhibit "extreme vulnerability."[31] The report also identifies an example of how landlord representatives can unethically exploit their relatively more powerful position, namely, by entering into side-negotiations with tenants who are ill informed about their procedural and substantive rights and responsibilities.[32] By the same token, as newly minted members of the legal profession, paralegals are subject to clear ethical obligations that may mean they are less inclined than non-legal landlord representatives to engage in exploitative behaviour.

What about the role of paralegals in improving access to justice? Should the role they appear to be playing in maintaining or improving access to justice for landlords be regarded as a socially significant improvement in access to justice more generally? When it comes to addressing deficits in access to justice in residential tenancy disputes, it would seem reasonable to suggest that improving the situation of tenants, who tend to be relatively more disadvantaged and disempowered, ought to be given greater priority in social and legal policy initiatives than improving the situation of landlords.

This leads back to the point made earlier that paralegals would appear not to be sufficiently affordable or otherwise user-friendly for tenants and so offer them no direct access to justice improvements. For tenants, it is not enough that paralegals may be more affordable than lawyers – they are apparently not affordable enough for tenants.

Affordability, however, is only one factor conditioning the use of paralegal services. User-friendliness is another. A clue that this might be a factor lies in the fact that tenants do utilize publicly funded lawyers, especially those who serve as duty counsel and who work in community legal clinics. Duty counsel are typically located at or near LTB hearing locations, where tenants have to attend. Community legal clinics are usually known to the neighbouring populace and to social service providers who work with these potential clients; they typically also engage in community-oriented public legal education and outreach. Thus, whether statically, as with duty counsel, or dynamically, as with clinic lawyers and legal workers, providers of publicly funded legal services are able to draw the attention of tenants. There is an element of proactivity to these sources of legal assistance, in possible contrast to paralegals, who may be unable or unwilling to operate proactively to attract the attention of potential tenant clients.

A capacity to proactively engage with disadvantaged and vulnerable populations in need of legal assistance is a characteristic closely associated with the idea and effectiveness of "community lawyering."[33] At a deeper level, this characteristic is related to the idea of legal empowerment, which has emerged over the last two decades or so from law and development literature and practice. According to a pioneer in the field, Stephen Golub, "[L]egal empowerment can be characterized as the use of rights and laws specifically to increase disadvantaged populations' control over their lives."[34] In general, legal empowerment initiatives focus directly on the needs of disadvantaged populations and develop programs that proactively serve those needs, in contrast to traditional rule of law approaches in law and development that focus more on the operation of legal institutions such as courts and meet the needs of disadvantaged populations only indirectly, if at all.[35] A number of recent studies of legal empowerment initiatives note that community-based programs of paralegal assistance are prevalent and promising, but those studies emphasize the need to embed paralegals in the communities they are to serve.[36] In other words, a key attribute of the legal empowerment approach to improving access to justice is proactivity.

As a final reflection, therefore, I suggest that the issue of access to justice for tenants may benefit from being reconceived as an issue of legal empowerment, and that initiatives aimed at improving access to justice for tenants may be more effective if they generally adopt the approach of legal empowerment and utilize proactive methods of providing service to tenants.

Conclusion

The analysis of the data gathered for this case study of residential tenancy disputes in the Eastern Region of the Ontario Landlord and Tenant Board reveals that paralegals, who might be expected to have the potential to offer more affordable and user-friendly legal services than lawyers, are making a significant contribution to the resolution of residential tenancy disputes, but only for landlords, and mostly for corporate landlords. Paralegals are playing almost no role at all in maintaining or improving access to justice as representatives for tenants. Moreover, in their role as representatives for landlords, they may be exacerbating the power imbalances that favour landlords in this context and may in fact be contributing to a worsening in access to justice for tenants. Consequently, to the extent that paralegals are presented as a potential means of improving access to justice in residential tenancy disputes and similar processes, this analysis indicates a need to more fully explore and assess *who* provides legal services, *whose* legal needs are met by those services, and *whether,* or to what extent, meeting those needs counts as meaningfully improving access to justice. In the case of paralegals and residential tenancy disputes, provision of legal services by paralegals appears thus far to have improved affordability and user-friendliness only for landlords while potentially exacerbating the access to justice problem of tenants.

All of this is not to say that, because of the inability of paralegals to improve access to justice for tenants, proposals to expand the scope of legal service provision by paralegals should be rejected. Even if paralegals are not affordable enough for tenants, they are nevertheless more affordable than lawyers, so measures such as supplements or complements to bridge the affordability gap for tenants need to be considered. Similarly, if the inability of paralegals to meet the needs of tenants can be attributed to a lack of user-friendliness or a lack of proactivity, there is a need to draw on the ideas and approaches of community lawyering and legal empowerment to reframe the problem of lack of access to justice for tenants and the approach to solutions in a more community-based and proactive direction.

Ontario's regularization of the formal status of paralegals as legal professionals has the potential to improve access to justice for tenants, but it should be regarded as only a first step. If additional supplementary or complementary steps are not taken to address problems with affordability and user-friendliness, the path of paralegal service provision will lead in the wrong direction for tenants.

Notes

I am grateful to the Social Sciences and Humanities Research Council of Canada and the directors of the Cost of Justice Project for funding support for the research case study reported in this chapter. Many thanks to the group of dedicated and diligent law students who provided research assistance (and in most cases were also committed participants in the Housing Justice Project): Guida Heir, Mark Trischuk, Daniel Tucker-Simmons, Evan Barz, Eric Girard, and Josh Smith. Preliminary findings of the case study have been presented at conferences of the Canadian Association of Law Teachers and the Australasian Law Teachers Association.

1   The extent to which non-lawyers are permitted to provide any of the forms of legal assistance, including representation, varies among Canadian jurisdictions. For example, notaries in British Columbia may provide a much broader range of services than their counterparts in Ontario (compare *Notaries Act,* RSBC 1996, c 334 with *Notaries Act,* RSO 1990, c N.6), but notaries in Quebec can deliver an even broader range of services than their namesakes in both of those provinces and have a scope of practice that, in terms of substantive areas, although not adjudicative forums, exceeds that of paralegals in Ontario (see *Notaries Act,* c N-6).

For an overview of the historically evolving meaning of the ideal of access to justice, identifying access to legal representation for dispute resolution as the defining characteristic of the "first wave" of access to justice, see Roderick Macdonald, "Access to Justice in Canada

Today: Scope, Scale and Ambitions" in Julia Bass, William A Bogart, & Frederick H. Zemans, eds, *Access to Justice for a New Century – The Way Forward* (Toronto: Law Society of Upper Canada, 2005) at 20.

2   An example of an argument for improving access to justice via non-lawyers that is part of an effort to also address other dimensions of the broader debate is Canadian Bar Association, *Reaching Equal Justice: An Invitation to Envision and Act* (Ottawa: Canadian Bar Association, 2013) at 99 and 106, online: Canadian Bar Association <http://www.cba. org/CBA-Equal-Justice/Equal-Justice-Initiative/Reports>. See also Alice Woolley & Trevor C.W. Farrow, "Addressing Access to Justice through New Legal Service Providers: Opportunities and Challenges (2016) 3 Tex A&M L Rev 549. Earlier examples include Macdonald, *supra* note 1 at 46.

3   Ontario paralegals are "independent" in the sense that they can operate autonomously from lawyers. In contrast, paralegals operating in other Canadian provinces are either unregulated (as in Alberta) or dependent on lawyer supervision (as in British Columbia). Moreover, a recent inquiry into improving access to justice in the area of family law in Ontario has recommended allowing paralegals to add that area to their scope of permitted legal practice. See Recommendation 4 in Justice Annemarie Bonkalo, *Family Legal Services Review* (Toronto: Ministry of the Attorney General, 2016), online: <https://www.attorney general.jus.gov.on.ca/english/about/pubs/family_legal_services_review/>.

4   For an overview of a range of factors that impact the extent to which people engage legal services in search of access to justice, see Macdonald, *supra* note 1 at 26–29.

5   Herbert Kritzer, *Legal Advocacy* (Ann Arbor: University of Michigan Press, 1998) examined the effectiveness of lawyers and non-lawyers in four dispute resolution forums in the United States and found that, since effectiveness can often depend more on specialized process experience and specific knowledge expertise rather than on formal legal training, lawyers are not necessarily more effective than non-lawyers and, indeed, that non-lawyers can be as or more effective than lawyers, or at least some lawyers, depending on the context.

6   Sean Rehaag, "The Role of Counsel in Canada's Refugee Determination System: An Empirical Assessment" (2011) 49 Osgoode Hall LJ 71, in which non-lawyer immigration consultants were found to generally provide less effective representation than refugee lawyers. But low-quality lawyering can also be found in the refugee system: Julianna Beaudoin, Jennifer Danch, & Sean Rehaag, "No Refuge: Hungarian Romani Refugee Claimants in Canada" (2015) 12 Osgoode Hall LJ 705. Given the different representational forum examined by Rehaag, his results are not necessarily inconsistent with those of Kritzer, *supra* note 5.

7   *Law Society Act,* RSO 1990, c L.8.

8   This was allowed under the *Provincial Offences Act,* RSO 1990, c P.33, s 82 (repealed in 2006) and under the *Criminal Code,* RSC 1985, c C-46, ss 800 and 802.

9   See *R v Lawrie,* 1987 CanLII 4173 (ONCA), and *R v Romanowicz,* 1999 CanLII 1315 (ONCA).

10   *Tenant Protection Act,* SO 1997, c 24 (superseded by *Residential Tenancies Act,* SO 2006, c 17). The term "agent" is not defined in the *Tenant Protection Act,* but the *Act*'s provisions contain a number of references to appearance by agent, such as ss 172(2) and 190(3).

11   *Access to Justice Act,* SO 2006, c 21. For a discussion of the road to paralegal regulation in Ontario that also raises disturbing questions about perverse impact on access to justice, see S. Bouclin, "Regulated Out of Existence: A Case Study of Ottawa's Ticket Defence Program" (2014) 11 JL & Equality 35.

12   Upon introducing the *Access to Justice Act* to the legislature, the Attorney General stated: "The regulation of paralegals would increase access to justice by giving consumers a choice

in the qualified legal services they use, while protecting those who receive legal advice from non-lawyers." Michael Bryant, Ontario, Legislative Assembly, *Official Report of Debates (Hansard)*, 38th Parl, 2nd Sess, L011-41 (27 October 2005) (Michael Bryant), online: Ontario Hansard <http://hansardindex.ontla.on.ca/hansardespeaker/38-2/l011-41. html>.

13   *Law Society Act, supra* note 7, s 4.1.2.

14   It should be noted, though, that some specific permissions still remain for provision of legal services by non-lawyers/non-paralegals.

15   Law Society of Ontario, By-Law 4, s 13.

16   *Ibid*, s 9.

17   This line of reasoning is suggested by Woolley & Farrow, *supra* note 2 at 550.

18   Law Society of Upper Canada, *Report to the Attorney General of Ontario, Pursuant to Section 63.1 of the Law Society Act* (Toronto: Law Society of Upper Canada, 2012).

19   David J. Morris, *Report of the Appointee's Five-Year Review of Paralegal Regulation in Ontario* (Toronto: Ontario Ministry of the Attorney General, 2012).

20   Stratcom Strategic Communications, *Five Year Review of Paralegal Regulation: Research Findings*, appendix to Law Society of Upper Canada, *supra* note 18 at 36–37.

21   This point is illustrated by the findings of the one empirical analysis of the fee levels of lawyers and paralegals that appears to have been done in Canada, by the Law Society of Alberta: "The cost of hiring a lawyer is perceived to be too high; however, polling data indicates that the average mean cost differential on the final bill to the client for a lawyer and a non-lawyer providing legal services was not substantially different, at approximately $350." See Alternative Delivery of Legal Services Committee, *Alternative Delivery of Legal Services Final Report* (Edmonton: Law Society of Alberta, 2012) at 14.

22   Five respondents indicated that they experienced other housing problems; three of them were landlords.

23   For a critical appraisal of the extent to which improving access to justice for tenants genuinely informed the introduction of the tribunal system in Ontario, see Elinor Mahoney, "The Ontario Tenant Protection Act: A Trust Betrayed" (2001) 16 JL & Soc Pol'y 261.

24   See Tribunals Ontario, *Social Justice Tribunals Ontario: Annual Report, 2013–14* (Toronto: Tribunals Ontario, 2015), online: Tribunals Ontario, Social Justice Division <http://www. sjto.gov.on.ca/documents/sjto/2013-14%20Annual%20Report.html>.

25   *Ibid.*

26   For an overview of access to justice issues in administrative law and in relation to administrative tribunals, see Lorne Sossin, "Access to Administrative Justice and Other Worries," in Colleen Flood & Lorne Sossin, eds, *Administrative Law in Context* (Toronto: Emond Montgomery, 2013).

27   Emily Paradis, *Access to Justice: The Case for Ontario Tenants – Final Report of the Tenant Duty Counsel Review* (Toronto: Advocacy Centre for Tenants Ontario, 2016), online: Advocacy Centre for Tenants Ontario <http://www.acto.ca/assets/files/TDCP_FinalReport_ -Nov7.pdf>.

28   Stratcom Strategic Communications, *supra* note 20 at 19.

29   RSO 1990, c F.31.

30   Paradis, *supra* note 27 at 46.

31   *Ibid.*

32   *Ibid* at 50 and 62.

33   For a discussion of the notion of community lawyering in a Canadian context, which identifies "collaborating with the community" as one of three core skills, see S. Imai, "A

Counter-Pedagogy for Social Justice: Core Skills for Community Lawyering" (2002) 9 Clinical L Rev 195.

34 Stephen Golub, "Introduction: Legal Empowerment's Approaches and Importance" in Open Society Justice Initiative, *Justice Initiatives: Legal Empowerment* (September 2013) at 5, online: Open Society Foundations <https://www.opensocietyfoundations.org/publications/justice-initiatives-legal-empowerment>.

35 See Stephen Golub, "Beyond Rule of Law Orthodoxy: The Legal Empowerment Alternative" (2003) Carnegie Endowment for International Peace Working Paper No 41, online: Carnegie Endowment for International Peace <http://carnegieendowment.org/2003/10/14/beyond-rule-of-law-orthodoxy-legal-empowerment-alternative-pub-1367>.

36 *Ibid* at 12; Stephen Golub, ed, *Legal Empowerment: Practitioners' Perspectives* (Rome: International Development Law Organization, 2010), online: International Development Law Organization <http://www.idlo.int/publications/legal-empowerment>; Law and Development Partnership, "Developing a Portfolio of Financially Sustainable, Scalable Basic Legal Service Models" (2015) Law and Development Partnership Briefing Paper, online: International Development Research Centre <https://www.idrc.ca/sites/default/files/sp/Documents%20EN/resources/bls-briefing-paper-en.pdf>.

9

Court-Ordered Family Legal Information Sessions in Ontario
A Path to Justice Approach

Lesley A. Jacobs and Carolyn Carter

A CENTRAL PILLAR OF meaningful access to justice for families is the idea that when people face legal problems, they need adequate assistance and support to help them navigate the family justice system to address their difficulties. The provision of more and better legal information and education for persons with family legal problems is widely viewed as a valuable form of such assistance and support. Yet we know relatively little about the extent to which this form is effective: for what types of clients, for which kinds of family justice problems, and in what circumstances can more and better legal information and education assist and support users of family legal services? In Canada, over the past two decades, most provinces have adopted some form of mandatory family law information session for parents involved in family law disputes in the courts in order to provide them with assistance and help improve court sessions if and when they get there. To what extent are these information sessions effective at advancing access to justice for families?

The research context for the discussion in this chapter is provided by a large longitudinal study of the impact of legal information on the quality of people's interactions with the justice system in Ontario and British Columbia. The Evolving Justice Services Research Project (EJSRP) study is led by Community Legal Education Ontario and the Institute for Social Research at York University and funded by the Law Foundation of Ontario.[1] The study is designed to track and assess the usefulness of legal information in helping people with everyday legal problems over a three-year period. This study involved people dealing with civil justice problems in three areas: Family Law Problems in Ontario and British Columbia (58 percent of participants); Rental Housing Problems in Ontario (35 percent); and Discrimination/Human Rights Violations in Ontario (7 percent). All participants encountered some legal information and tried to deal with their problem. The study initially recruited 600 individuals early in their engagement with the civil justice system and followed them for up to three years as they encountered the legal system and accessed justice services. Because of attrition, the database is comprehensive for almost 400 participants. This study is the largest panel empirical research project undertaken in Canada on civil justice services.

This chapter focuses specifically on the experiences of the EJSRP participants who attended the court-ordered Mandatory Information Program (MIP) for users of Ontario's family justice system. It reports new empirical findings designed to provide insights into the effectiveness of the MIP in advancing meaningful access to justice for those users. Five stories based on in-depth follow-up interviews with five EJSRP participants who attended a MIP show how the information sessions impacted their encounters with family justice services. They show that people with legal problems follow various paths to justice and that specific information is needed at specific points along those paths. Acknowledging this path to justice approach in family law, and refocusing the MIP accordingly, is a necessary step to achieving meaningful access to family justice.[2]

The Landscape for Mandatory Information Programs

Traditionally, the strength and adequacy of the assistance provided to users of family courts have been measured in terms of representation by a lawyer. It is well documented, for example, that when divorce lawyers meet with their clients, this changes significantly how clients understand their family law problem, their expectations for resolution, the process for reaching resolution, and their ability to reach resolution.[3] Much of the public spending in the past has focused on providing individuals with representation by a lawyer. Legal Aid Ontario (LAO), for example, has long made family legal issues its second-highest priority after representation in criminal matters. In 2017–18, LAO issued 51,675 certificates for representation in the case of new criminal charges, 19,334 domestic family law certificates, and 5,924 certificates for child protection.

The emphasis on legal representation as the key to meaningful access to justice for families has come under increasing scrutiny, however. In part, this is a reflection of the growing belief that family justice requires the attention of a multidisciplinary professional practice that includes more than just lawyers.[4] However, the reality is that within the justice system, many people with family problems lack legal representation. In Ontario, for example, Justice Annemarie Bonkalo in her 2016 review of Family Legal Services for Ontario's Ministry of the Attorney General reported that 57 percent of litigants in family court were unrepresented in 2014–15.[5]

This context has encouraged important new public policy developments across Canada to advance meaningful access to justice for families with legal problems.[6] The provision of more and better legal information has been widely viewed as a possible substitute – rather than a replacement – for legal representation.[7] An important innovative program that has been implemented in many provinces has been some sort of court-ordered mandatory family law information session for parents involved in family law disputes in the courts. These programs are also widespread in other countries, especially the United States, where forty-six states have mandatory education programs for divorcing parents. In general, such programs have been found to be beneficial.[8] For example, they may reduce the harmful effects of divorce on children,[9] and, in at least one American jurisdiction, they have been found to reduce post-divorce conflict.[10]

There is similar, though far less, research in Canada. A study by Desmond Ellis and Dawn Anderson published in 2003 found that in Ontario a pilot for mandatory legal information sessions reduced court resources spent on motions and case conferences, as well as trial duration.[11] A more comprehensive evaluation of the mandatory Parents After Separation program in British Columbia undertaken for the Family Justice Service Division of the Ministry of Attorney General found that over 80 percent of participants reported a very high level of satisfaction and learning from the program.[12] The study found little evidence, however, that the program reduced engagement with the justice system and that only about 10 percent of the participants were diverted from the system.[13] A survey of litigants who attended the MIP session in Ontario found that only "42% reported that it was very helpful or somewhat helpful for learning about the family justice process."[14]

Court-Ordered Family Law Information Sessions in Ontario

In Canada, the largest and most extensive court-ordered program of family law information sessions operates in Ontario. Under the authority of Rule 8.1 of the Family Law Rules, the Ministry of the Attorney General implemented the MIP on 18 July 2011. The program is designed to provide parties to family law cases with information about the impact of separation and divorce on parents and children, options available for resolving disputes, including alternatives to going to court, legal issues, the family law court process, and community services (legal and non-legal) for children and adults experiencing separation and divorce.[15] If a spouse or parent has started a family court case, both spouses or parents must attend the program as the first step in the case. Although the program is mandatory for parties involved in family court proceedings, adults who have family justice problems but are not involved in court proceedings are also encouraged to attend.[16]

The MIP service providers are private vendors chosen through a competitive procurement process administered by the Ministry of the Attorney General's

Family Policy and Programs Branch, which also provides oversight, policy support, and financial accountability. The MIP is largely delivered in person at local courthouses where parties are involved in legal proceedings.[17] The three-hour sessions are led by a team of two or three instructors. At least one instructor is a member of the local family law bar. The team presents information about separation and the legal process on topics such as the options available for resolving differences, alternatives to going to court, the impact of divorce and separation on children, and resources available to deal with problems arising from family breakdown. An explicit objective is to deliver information to assist families in obtaining quicker resolutions to family court issues.[18]

The need for better legal education and information to promote access to family justice in Ontario is well established. The Law Commission of Ontario observed in 2013 that there was not "sufficient information and assistance to enable family members involved in family disputes to make a decision about whether they want to enter the family legal system and if so, how to take subsequent steps."[19] In its major study of the family justice system, the Law Commission of Ontario found that "it is important that the needs of those whose lack of familiarity with the system and whose circumstances make the system particularly confusing and difficult to navigate be identified and addressed in how information is delivered and in the availability of appropriate intermediaries, for example."[20] In response, the MIP was developed to provide legal education and information to help people resolve their family legal challenges and problems.

Seeing the MIP as a measure to fill a needs gap in the family justice system fits with the broader emphasis the Ministry of the Attorney General has placed on the importance of access to justice. Indeed, the Attorney General stated in 2017 that "access to justice is the most central and relevant challenge facing the legal community today."[21] This acknowledges the importance of having user-focused justice system reforms and initiatives, which are important pillars of meaningful access to civil justice.[22] The primary purpose of the MIP is to support accessible, fair, timely, and effective justice services for those commencing family law proceedings, which in turn facilitates meaningful access to family justice.[23]

What Happens at a Mandatory Legal Information Session?
MIP sessions occur daily all over Ontario. One such session took place in a mid-size city in southern Ontario in 2015. It was delivered in a large room in the city's main courthouse. The room could accommodate 150 people. At the front was a reception area where a variety of printed material such as brochures,

pamphlets, and information sheets were available for participants. The three presenters – one male lawyer and one male and one female mediator – all worked at the courthouse. The lawyer was an advice counsel at the Family Law Information Clinic (FLIC) and duty counsel on court hearing days. The two mediators worked for the private mediation company that held the contract to operate the FLIC and deliver the MIP in the region. There were twenty-eight participants, eighteen women and ten men. All were white except for one Black male. Five attendees were also participants in the Evolving Justice Services Research Project.

When all were seated, one of the male presenters approached the podium and read from the MIP set script for fifteen minutes. The script explains the impact of separation on parents and children, options available for resolving disputes between parents, including alternatives to going to court, family legal issues, the court process, and resources available to deal with problems arising from separation. The presenter did not introduce himself or make eye contact with the audience. The other male presenter took over where the first one left off. He introduced himself and read for approximately twenty minutes. The two men took turns reading the MIP script for another two hours and forty-five minutes.

At no point did the presenters make eye contact with the participants, ask them whether they understood what was being read, or allow questions to be asked. Their technique for delivering the script appeared deliberate. One of the research participants subsequently said that his general impression was that the presenters "just wanted to get through the script – they didn't care if we were there."

None of the participants asked the presenters any questions before, during, or after the three-hour session. Nearly half of the twenty-eight participants slept through it, while others busied themselves with their mobile phones. Participants later reported that the session was a "waste of time" because the presentation was "boring" and the presenters "made them fall asleep."

Findings of the Evolving Justice Services Research Project

The EJSRP collected extensive data over a three-year period from May 2015 to April 2018 for 400 people as they encountered the civil justice system and utilized a diverse range of justice services. Participants included 130 people in Ontario with family law problems. Of these:

- Sixty-nine percent were women, 31% were men.
- Thirty-two percent were 35 years of age or younger, 57% were between 36 and 55, 11% were 56 years of age or older.

- Thirty-five percent reported that they were single, 20% married, 8% in common law relationships, 23% separated, 13% divorced, and 1% widowed.
- Six percent reported no children, 26% one child, 51% two children, and 3% three or more children.
- Forty-four percent reported being employed full-time.
- Twenty-eight percent reported an annual individual income of less than $20,000, 45% between $20,000 and $50,000, and 27% over $50,000.
- For annual household incomes, 17% reported an income of less than $20,000, 33% between $20,000 and $50,000, and 50% over $50,000.
- Forty-three percent reported owning their homes, 43% reported renting, the rest reported some other arrangement.
- Fifty percent reported at least some college or university, 25% reported high school completion.
- Fifteen percent reported a serious health issue, 6% a physical disability.
- Seventy-eight percent reported being born in Canada.
- Eighty-five percent reported that English was their primary language at home.
- One hundred percent reported having ready access to the Internet.

Among the participants, there was a range of reported problem types (Table 9.1). Access, custody, and support were the most common family law problems.

Of the 130 participants, 29 reported attending a MIP session for family legal information in Ontario. All did so because their attendance was court-mandated. Most attended the MIP session in the early stages of the EJSRP. Each EJSRP

Table 9.1 Family law problem types among participants in the Evolving Justice Services Research Project

Family law problem type	Percentage of participants
Divorce decree	12
Separation agreement	7
Dispute over access to children	25
Other custody issues	38
Late or stopped child support payments	13
Other support payment issues	32
Family violence	6
Restraining order	5
Children's Aid Society	2
Criminal issue	2
Family home or property issues	4

participant who attended a MIP session was asked about their general impressions of the experience, how much they learned about the justice system process and next steps for them, and the information provided to them about substantive law. Not all of the twenty-nine participants answered the three questions.

Some participants recognized that a central message during the MIP session was early stage dispute settlement. Others identified concern about the best interests of children involved as an important message. Most felt that they learned little about the justice system process or how the law applied in their own specific situation.

Stories of Five MIP Participants

Our examination of how well Ontario's MIP sessions actually serve the users of the family justice system draws on both EJSRP data and in-depth follow-up interviews with some participants who attended one of the MIP sessions. The research provided a perspective on how those individuals understood "meaningful access to family justice" and the possibilities for legal information and education. As Richard Delgado explains, "stories create their own bonds, represent cohesion, shared understandings, and meaning."[24] The voices of users of Ontario's family justice system who attended an MIP session suggest that the program may ultimately be a barrier to meaningful access to family justice rather than a conduit.

In follow-up interviews four months after they attended the MIP session, five EJSRP participants were asked open-ended questions about the nature of their legal problem, the information they learned at the session, and their impression of how the information assisted them as users of the family justice system in Ontario.

Michael's Story

Michael is a forty-eight-year-old Canadian-born Black male. He has been separated for three years from his wife of fifteen years. When asked how long he and his ex-partner have been in litigation, Michael said, *"She has been dragging me to court for three years now ... as soon as one problem gets resolved, she creates another."* He retained a lawyer after he was separated because he thought that they would resolve their legal problems *"within three months or so."* He also said that *"after the first year of fighting, I paid over $56,000 in legal fees."* Michael went on to say, *"It was only after my money ran out that I decided to represent myself and seek help from the FLIC lawyers and Duty Counsel."*

Michael said that he was a respondent to his ex-partner's current application for property division, child custody, child support, and spousal support. He explained that his ex-partner accused him of feeding their older son gluten, which she characterized as child abuse, the reason for her custody application. He said that his ex *"is making stuff up because my son does not have any food allergies."* Michael said that it was *"insulting and hurtful"* to know that his ex-partner wanted him to have supervised visits with his children because she thought that he could not be trusted to feed them properly. *"What reason would I have to serve food to my children that I know is harmful to them? Does that make sense to you? She is crazy ... and the court allows her to carry out her craziness."*

With regard to child support, Michael reported, *"We verbally agreed to an amount after we separated. I have been giving her that money every month and she never complained, until now ... Even the spousal support application is a joke. She earns more than me! ... So, I should be the one asking for spousal support. And furthermore, she lives in our house with her new man, so she's just being unreasonable."*

Michael attended a scheduled MIP session just one day before his hearing date. He reported: *"I thought that they would talk about how to prepare for court and tell us what to expect in court – when you don't have a lawyer ... I wanted to learn about property division because my ex is living in the house with the 'man,' so I wanted to know if he is entitled to a share of the property and they didn't talk about that. So no, the session did not make a difference for me. It was a waste of time ... I definitely did not learn how to navigate the legal system."*

Sally's Story

Sally is a thirty-two-year-old white woman with three children under the age of eighteen. She separated from her husband of four years because he sexually and physically abused her *"for way too long"* and he traumatized their children for over two years. Sally filed an application in family court for a separation agreement, child support, spousal support, and property division. She said, *"I am sure that my ex would not agree to mediation."*

Sally found the MIP session *"too long and extremely boring, but it was kind of helpful."* She explained: *"Well, the presenters just read the information from beginning to end and to be honest, they were not very good readers, so that was boring. But the parenting information was good. It was helpful to be reminded that I should focus on the best interest of the children and don't focus too much on emotions."* Sally added: *"[T]he information was general. They did not provide specifics. At least not specific to my issues. Honestly, I thought that they would talk about the legal system – like how the court works and what to expect in court and so on, but they didn't ... definitely did not help me with navigating the Family Law system."*

Robert's Story

Robert is a forty-five-year-old white man with a high school education. He is the custodial father of four children – one over the age of eighteen – and he has been separated from his wife for two years. His ex-wife accused him of preventing the children from seeing her, but he denies doing so. He is a respondent to her application for child access and spousal support. Robert said that he does not believe that he should be made to pay spousal support because his wife is healthy and able to work.

Robert found the MIP session *"a waste of time."* When asked to explain, he said, *"It did not help. I did not learn anything. I thought that they could help me, but they said that they can't give me any legal advice, I have to talk to Duty Counsel ... They said that they couldn't help me, I will have to talk with a lawyer. And I wanted to leave early, but they said that I have to wait until the end, so that I can get my certificate to give to the judge."* When asked whether the information session helped him navigate the family justice system, Robert said, *"Nope. It was a waste of time."*

Shelly's Story

Shelly is a forty-eight-year-old divorced white mother of two teenagers. She filed an application in family court because her ex-husband failed to pay child support. Shelly reported that the MIP session *"was so boring. And to be honest with you, I slept through most of it."* She also said that she did not know if the information session script was well matched to her legal problems because *"I slept through most of it."* She felt that the information session did not help her navigate the family justice system.

Brandon's Story

Brandon is a twenty-six-year-old white father of two children under the age of eighteen. He has separated from his common law partner, with whom he lived for four years. He has been paying child support, but his ex-partner thinks that he can and should pay more and, for this reason, is preventing him from seeing his children. Brandon was a respondent to his ex-partner's application for child support, and he filed a counter application for child access. He attended the MIP session just one day before his court hearing.

Brandon found the information session *"very informative."* He explained: *"The instructions were good ... they reminded me to put the kids first ... I am a child of divorced parents, so I understand what it's like ... I could relate. But they didn't give any legal information. They just told us what not to do and so on. It's the kind of information that everyone should know, but some people don't know."* He didn't feel that the session helped him navigate the family justice system.

Common Themes

What can be learned from this one MIP session and the five follow-up stories about meaningful access to justice for users of family legal services? We think that it provides a useful window into the potential strengths and weaknesses of MIP sessions, it opens up thinking around potential reforms to the MIP, and it provides a research design model for follow-up research. More specifically, through this research, a persistent theme has emerged that the MIP session is boring in its delivery. Both monotone reading of the MIP script and presenters' lack of connection with the audience have been cited as being of significant concern. When participants were asked to explain what they meant by "boring," they chose commonly used terms and expressions such as "not interesting," "repetitive," "uninspiring," "lifeless," "I couldn't stop yawning," and "they made me fall asleep." Others believed that the presenters did not care whether participants paid attention to the presentation because they were more interested in getting to the end of the script. Participants also said that because the session was so "boring" they could not focus, and for that reason they did not learn much, if anything. It should be noted, however, that the way the information was delivered was a distinct issue from the content of the material delivered.

Since many participants had been denied legal aid for one reason or another, they believed that the session would provide legal information similar to that from a lawyer. Some thought that they would get to watch videos on how to navigate the court; others thought that they would receive hands-on training on how to complete court forms and receive professional instructions on how to present themselves to the judge and what to expect in court, among other things. They felt that their expectations were reasonable because the Ministry of the Attorney General promised that the session would help them better understand their legal problems and navigate the family law system – but it failed to do so.

Many felt confused about the purpose and timing of the session because they were quite far along in the legal process or were attending their court hearing the following morning, so that no matter what the presenters might have said, there was no way for them to change the path they were on. Others felt that the information provided was far too general for their needs; what they needed was information that pertained to their specific situation or problem.

Although all the participants expressed disappointment that the session did not provide much useful legal information, they were less in unison about the value of the material provided in the MIP session. Several but not all the participants appreciated the fact that the session included a focus on good parenting and concerns about the well-being of children caught in the middle of a separation or divorce. One participant said, *"My parents divorced when I was 10 years old, so I have firsthand knowledge about what works and what doesn't. So I don't want to be told how to parent after a separation – I already know that. You know, they should help us fill out the forms, and things like that ... But to have us sit there for 3 hours ... not good."* Others felt that the emphasis on parenting was disingenuous and that the advertisements for the session were misleading.[25]

Recalibrating the MIP for Paths to Justice

It is clear that from the perspective of these users of family legal services, the script for the MIP should include more useful legal information, and the information could be delivered in a multimodal manner that includes media-like videos and scenario-based role plays. Important questions include: What constitutes useful legal information *for these users?* What kinds of assistance and support would improve meaningful access to justice for *these specific individuals?*

A central insight of recent socio-legal research on access to civil and family justice is that users of legal services follow particular paths to justice and that on those journeys they encounter critical junctures where they make decisions that significantly impact the paths they take and the appropriateness of those paths for addressing their legal problems.[26] The relevant point is that users of family legal services need assistance and support at these critical junctures and that the legal information provided through an MIP should be calibrated to these critical junctures. This requires, at least in part, mapping of the possible critical junctures during a person's journey through a family legal challenge or problem when legal information can be especially impactful. This kind of mapping is not new; rather, it is already a well-explored topic of research in Ontario that needs to be further applied in the MIP setting.[27]

The critical junctures in the pursuit of meaningful family justice that are especially worth highlighting include entering the family legal system, opting for mediation, hiring a lawyer, new motions and applications, responses, case conferences, and settlement conferences. At these critical junctures, the legal information needed is both substantive (what are the legal issues at stake, possible remedies, costs and benefits, and so on?) and process-oriented (what are the possible next steps, which applications and forms need to be completed, how are they submitted, and so on?). This information can be both general and concrete. It is often best delivered in a format that includes a glossary and a frequently asked questions section.

What we do know from the five stories reported here is that the MIP in Ontario is in many cases not providing legal information calibrated in this tailored way. These findings are corroborated by the Ministry of the Attorney General's *Court Services Division Annual Report 2012–13,* which found no evidence that the information sessions were causing participants to take advantage of dispute resolution mechanisms other than litigation to resolve their legal problems, nor was it helping them navigate the family law system.[28] This is consistent with findings from other jurisdictions, such as British Columbia, that offer similar family justice information programs.

Ultimately, our point is that MIP sessions in Ontario have the potential to assist and support users of family legal services, but in order to realize that potential, the delivery of the program requires a script and a format that provide legal information that reflects a paths to justice approach, and the information provided should be calibrated towards assisting and supporting users at specific critical junctures on those paths. In our view, this recalibration will provide meaningful access to justice for those with family problems in Ontario.

Notes

This chapter originated in graduate field research conducted by Carolyn Carter, supervised by Les Jacobs. The research was funded by the Law Foundation of Ontario and the Mitac Accelerate Fellowship Program.

1 The three principal investigators are Lesley Jacobs (York University) and Julie Mathews and Joanna Birenbaum (both at Community Legal Education Ontario).

2 See further Hazel Genn, *Paths to Justice* (Oxford: Hart Publishing, 1999). For a general discussion of meaningful access to justice, see the Introduction to this volume.

3 For the classic American research, see Austin Sarat and William L.F. Felstiner, *Divorce Lawyers and Their Clients: Power and Meaning in the Legal Process* (New York: Oxford University Press, 1998), and Lynn Mather, Craig McEwen, & Richard Maiman, *Divorce Lawyers at Work* (New York: Oxford University Press, 2001).

4 Brenda Jacobs & Lesley Jacobs, "Multidisciplinary Paths to Family Justice: Professional Challenges and Promising Practices" (Research paper prepared for the Law Commission of Ontario's family law reform project, Best Practices at Family Justice System Entry Points: Needs of Users and Response of Workers in the Justice System, June 2010), online: <http://www.lco-cdo.org/wp-content/uploads/2010/11/family-law-process-call-for-papers-jacobs.pdf>.

5 Justice Annemarie Bonkalo, *Family Legal Services Review* (Toronto: Ministry of Attorney General, 2016). See also Julie Macfarlane, "The National Self-Represented Litigants Project: Identifying and Meeting the Needs of Self-Represented Litigants, Final Report" (May 2013), online: <https://lawsocietyontario.azureedge.net/media/lso/media/legacy/pdf/s/self-represented_project.pdf>; Rachel Birnbaum, Nicholas Bala, & Lorne Bertrand, "The Rise of Self-Representation in Canada's Family Courts: The Complex Picture Revealed in Surveys of Judges, Lawyers and Litigants" (2013) 91 Can Bar Rev 67.

6 Good examples include the establishment of Family Legal Information Centres in Ontario, Parenting After Separation sessions in British Columbia, and family court counsellors in Alberta.

7 See Noel Semple & Nicholas Bala, *Reforming Ontario's Family Justice System: An Evidence-Based Approach* (Toronto: Association of Family and Conciliation Courts, Ontario Chapter, 2013) at 33–43.

8 For broad reviews of the American research over a thirty-year period, see Susan Pollett & Melissa Lombreglia, "A Nationwide Survey of Mandatory Parent Education" (2008) 46:2

Fam Ct Rev 375; Tamara Fackrell, Alan Hawkins, & Nicole Kay, "How Effective Are Court-Affiliated Divorcing Parents Education Programs? A Meta-Analytic Study" (2011) 49:1 Fam Ct Rev 107.

9 Denise Brandon, "Can Four Hours Make a Difference? Evaluation of a Parent Education Program for Divorcing Parents" (2006) 45:2 J Divorce & Remarriage 171.

10 M.N. Criddle, S.M. Allgood, & K.W. Piercy, "The Relationship between Mandatory Divorce Education and Level of Post-Divorce Parental Conflict" (2003) 39:1 J Divorce & Remarriage 99.

11 Desmond Ellis & Dawn Anderson, "The Impact of Participation in a Parent Education Program for Divorcing Parents on the Use of Court Resources: An Evaluation Study" (2003) 21 Conflict Resolution Quarterly 169.

12 Catherine Tait Consulting, *Evaluation of Online Parenting after Separation* (Victoria: BC Ministry of Attorney General, 2013) at 31–39.

13 *Ibid* at 50.

14 Birnbaum, Bala, & Bertrand, *supra* note 5 at 85.

15 Ontario, Ministry of the Attorney General, "Family Justice Services: Mandatory Information Programs (MIPs)," online: Ministry of the Attorney General <https://www.attorney general.jus.gov.on.ca/english/family/family_justice_services.php#mip> ["MIPs"].

16 *Ibid*.

17 Legal Aid Ontario also offers an online version of the MIP script.

18 Ontario, Ministry of the Attorney General, "MIPs," *supra* note 15.

19 Law Commission of Ontario, *Increasing Access to Family Justice through Comprehensive Entry Points and Inclusivity: Final Report* (Toronto: Law Commission of Ontario, 2013) at 1.

20 *Ibid* at 2.

21 Ontario, Ministry of the Attorney General, *Putting Justice within Reach: A Plan for User-Focused Justice in Ontario* (Toronto: Ministry of the Attorney General, 2017) at 10.

22 See the Introduction to this volume.

23 Ontario, Ministry of the Attorney General, *Court Services Division Annual Report 2012–13* (Toronto: Government of Ontario, 2013) [*Annual Report 2012–13*].

24 Richard Delgado, "Storytelling for Oppositionists and Others: A Plea for Narrative" (1989) 87 Mich L Rev 2411 at 2411.

25 It is notable that in Ontario the program is called an information session, whereas in British Columbia a similar mandatory program is explicitly titled "Parenting After Separation."

26 See Genn, *supra* note 2. For Canadian applications, see Lesley Jacobs, *Privacy Rights in the Global Digital Economy: Everyday Legal Problems and Canadian Paths to Justice* (Toronto: Irwin Law Books, 2014), as well as the Introduction to this volume.

27 See Jacobs & Jacobs, *supra* note 4; Law Commission of Ontario, *supra* note 19.

28 Ontario, Ministry of the Attorney General, *Annual Report 2012–13*, *supra* note 23.

10

The Value of Class Actions

Catherine Piché

THE VALUE OF CLASS actions as a path to justice has long been controversial.[1] This chapter focuses on the desirability, economic utility, and effectiveness of class actions in Canada. It shows that class actions are instruments for compensation of class members but that this compensation remains imperfect in terms of the numbers of members compensated, the extent to which they are compensated, and the exorbitant costs of bringing such actions. In this chapter, I highlight the significant lack of data in Canada about class action activity; discuss the objectives of class action law, as these objectives must be met for the class action procedure to be successful and legitimate; define the value of class actions and show how the measure of success in class actions relates to how "optimal" the class action is; and provide the measure of class action value based on recent data from the province of Quebec. Overall, I establish a framework of analysis of class action monetary outcomes based on a novel approach to compensation.

My discussion draws on the preliminary data of an ongoing empirical project at the University of Montreal's Faculty of Law Class Actions Lab that addresses member compensation through class actions (the Class Action Compensation Project). The project began in the summer of 2015 and is scheduled to conclude in 2022.[2] It is unique because it is conducted in partnership with judges, lawyers, public servants, and governmental agents – all actors in the judicial system – notably, the Quebec Bar Association, the Quebec Superior Court and Superior Court judges, the Fonds d'aide aux actions collectives, Educaloi, Soquij and Options Consommateurs, and the Law Commission of Ontario, among many others.

The first phase of the project involved a thorough analysis of class action files introduced in Quebec between 2004 and 2016. It also included a compilation and comparison of participation and take-up rates in various class action files, as well as per-plaintiff recovery data.[3] The project has sought to measure the end product of class action litigation, the value and benefit of this kind of litigation, and, incidentally, its costs as assumed by the parties and the system. It has identified specific parameters that can be used to evaluate empirically class action costs and benefits, and a significant list of criteria directly associated with higher rates of participation and compensation. This is the first Canadian study of its kind.[4]

Context: Significant Lack of Class Action Data in Canada

There is a dearth of data on judicial activity in Canada in all sectors of litigation, including class actions.[5] In fact, apart from the limited and rather informal data gathered by the provinces' superior court class action judges, court registries, bar association registers, and informal, often impressionistic numbers circulating within the class action bar and among judges,[6] no one can reliably draw any conclusions as to class action activity in Canada. Consequently, it is difficult to know whether the class action system is truly effective, fair, and efficient. How can or should the law move forward, evolve, and be reformed in this context?

The principal reason for the lack of data is that throughout North America parties have not traditionally been required to report back on class distributions.[7] However, since the adoption of the reformed 2016 Province of Quebec *Code of Civil Procedure (CPC)*[8] and its related court rules, class action distributions must be reported back to the court at the conclusion of every class action case.[9] This requirement was integrated into Quebec Superior Court rules of practice in early 2016[10] as a result of judicial training activities I conducted through the Class Actions Lab as well as specific recommendations I made to judges and court administrators for better and more systematic reporting of distributions data.

The Canadian Class Action Legal System and Its Objectives

Overview of the Law of Class Actions in Canada

The Federal Court of Canada and all Canadian provinces except Prince Edward Island have class action legislation.[11] Apart from the underlying differences in the common law system (which applies to all Canadian provinces except Quebec, which has a largely civil law–driven system), Canadian class action legislation is modelled on the American Federal Rule 23.[12] Quebec, however, requires that the action be "authorized" pursuant to four criteria listed under Article 575 of the *CPC*.[13] In terms of these class action certification criteria, the main distinctions between Quebec and the rest of Canada are that the Quebec provisions do not require that the class action be the "preferable procedure," nor do they mandate a litigation plan from the class representative.[14]

The nature of the relief available to members in the class action procedure throughout Canada generally amounts to compensatory damages for pecuniary losses. Injunctions may also be awarded, although they are less frequent. When a class action case ends in trial, an assessment is made of aggregate awards, and sampling evidence is used to award damages to the class collectively, on an average or proportional basis.[15] In all Canadian jurisdictions, individuals can participate in claim recovery distributions individually or collectively.[16] In cases where collective recovery is ordered, individual liquidation of the class members' claims can be provided, or distribution of an amount to each class member can be ordered.[17] Reparatory measures are also possible and frequent.[18] The court will dispose of any remaining balance in the same manner as when remitting an amount to a third person, while always taking into consideration the members' interests.[19] In a case where the individual liquidation of the class members' claims or the distribution of an amount to each class member is impracticable, inappropriate, or too costly, the court determines the balance remaining and orders the amount to be remitted to that third designated person.[20] Finally, class action litigation financing considerations are also similar in the different provinces, but the costs of litigation and liability are much lower in Quebec as they are capped to foster greater access to justice.[21] In addition, governmental funds in the provinces of Ontario and Quebec help finance class litigation. For instance, the Quebec fund, called the Fonds d'aide aux actions collectives, finances one-third of all Quebec class action cases.[22]

Objectives of Canadian Class Actions
This chapter is about defining class action measure and value and providing data relative to measure and value. I argue here that the desirability and legitimacy of the class action device must be evaluated in light of its objectives and whether they are accomplished. I also propose a new framework for analysis of class action outcomes based upon a novel approach to class compensation, which is one of the three class action objectives.

Under Canadian law, class actions seek to achieve the following objectives: (1) providing access to the courts for all (including to the less favoured) by rendering the process more cost-effective (at least in theory); (2) compensating injured parties for modest but non-trivial losses suffered by widely dispersed individuals who are in similar circumstances, in ways that cannot be practically achieved through individual litigation; and (3) enforcing the law and deterring or modifying the injurious behaviour of wrongdoers.[23] The approach I have taken in my own work is to recognize that while class actions serve the three stated purposes, these purposes are not always fulfilled together in the same case, and that some cases may serve principally to provide compensation while others may merely deter the defendants without providing any form of compensation.

Access to Justice

The access to justice objective has traditionally been considered to be the most important prerequisite and benefit of the class action mechanism and a principal objective of class action statutes.[24] In *Dutton,* the Supreme Court of Canada explained that class actions improve access when fixed litigation costs are divided over a large number of class members because they make "economical the prosecution of claims that would otherwise be too costly to prosecute individually."[25] For the court, "[w]ithout class actions, the doors of justice remain closed to some plaintiffs, however strong their legal claims. Sharing costs ensures that injuries are not left unremedied."[26] Accordingly, the access to justice argument supposes that without the class action, important numbers of low-value claims would never be brought before the courts.[27]

Compensation

The second class action goal is compensation. The aim of compensation across the common and the civil law is to restore and redress the balance of justice, to place the victim in the position he or she would have been in if not for the wrongdoer's contravention of the law.[28] There are various types of compensation, such as means-replacing compensation and ends-replacing compensation.[29] Importantly, those persons who are entitled to compensation must "actually receive compensation and in the amount to which they are entitled."[30] In a collective redress or class action context, once the parties conclude a settlement, or a final judgment on the merits is issued against one or more defendants, the plaintiff representative and the class members whom he or she has represented and who have suffered a similar loss are entitled to compensation.

How accurate does the compensation of class members have to be? How much inaccuracy in compensation is acceptable for the sake of collective or class recovery? I argue in favour of a collective approach to compensation, one that requires that a substantial majority of the class members – viewed as an "entity," the class – be compensated appropriately in order to meet the objective.

Deterrence and/or Behaviour Modification

Class action lawsuits are believed to impact the behaviour of defendants forced to compensate victims. When defendants compensate class members – and necessarily a large number of them – they are in fact acting as though they admit liability. As a result, the argument is that they are then deterred from acting wrongly in the future. The deterrence view is that "the primary purpose of class litigation is not so much to redress injured plaintiffs as to deter wrongful conduct on the defendant's part by forcing them to disgorge their unlawful gains or by restructuring his behavior through the use of injunctions."[31] A crucial question that arises, however, is whether defendants truly feel so disinclined to act injuriously in the future, and, if that is the case, how a causal relationship may be proven to exist between the fact of class litigation and its related consequences (such as the duty to pay damages and/or the reputational effects), and the deterrence and/or behaviour modification effects.

Measuring the Value of Class Actions

Value and Success Perceived Collectively: The *Optimal* Class Action
The class action's purpose is to allow an entity to be collectively compensated through a peculiar, unique procedure. Generally recognized as a regular procedure that does not – and should not – change the substantive law, the class action has, in fact, impacted the development of the substantive law by better defining its limits and by permitting novel applications of the law in increasingly different contexts and cases.[32] Class actions are indeed in a class of their own in this regard.[33] With the advent of the class action, substantive and procedural laws are on an equal footing, such that the class procedure can encroach upon the remedial law. Recoveries in the form of damages may then be appreciated collectively or globally. Accordingly, I argue that when it comes to appreciating outcomes and the degree of success of these kinds of actions, individual litigation values and objectives do not matter.

The class action is justifiable because it provides justice to the masses, collective justice to an entity: the class. Instead of being an individual form of justice conducted in the aggregate, it is a purely aggregative procedural tool that provides a form of collective justice. The North American class action has evolved to accept the principles of collective causality, common prejudice, and common proof through collectively appreciated evidence. Significant progress has been made towards conceptualizing the class action as a peculiar procedure unlike any other, rather than an "idealized version of individual litigation."[34] Indeed, class actions have traditionally been justified as consistent and necessary in light of "rough justice" considerations.[35]

Since the class action claims recovery process is organized according to collective justice considerations,[36] accuracy of distribution schemes is less important than efficiency. Indeed, the greater the fine-tuning of settlement allocations, the greater the costs incurred.[37] Accordingly, "the more intricate the calculation, the greater the delay in having a settlement distributed to class members."[38] For these reasons, averages, approximations, and lump sum payments are resorted to whenever possible at the distributions design stage. Ultimately, an appropriate balance must be achieved between the efficient and speedy distribution of claims and administrative feasibility. Attention must be paid to individual claims to ensure that the settlement is fair to the members. Favouring efficiency over accuracy, and approximate justice and sometimes imperfect distributions over lengthy and complex distributions, has thus become justifiable to achieve fairness in class actions.

Trial is our paradigm of how civil disputes should be resolved. In reality, however, only a small fraction of litigated class action cases are carried through to judgment; most cases are resolved through settlement.[39] Parties believe that a bad settlement is probably better than a good trial; thus, public policy favours settlement. As the parties and lawyers argue their case and the judge applies the substantive law, there is an expectation of substantive accuracy of result, that the outcome will reflect the correct result, based on the substantive law.[40] By contrast, in out-of-court settlements, what matters more than substantial accuracy is agreement and consent without coercion, which gives legitimacy to the negotiated outcome.[41] This line of reasoning supports a collective and less accurate appreciation of outcomes.

At the fairness hearing, courts have to test the settlement fairness and reasonableness "in light of the best possible recovery and in light of the risks the parties would face if the case went to trial."[42] When evaluating the reasonableness of proposed settlements in cases where monetary damages are sought, courts will "compare the amount of the proposed settlement with the present value of the damages plaintiffs would likely recover if successful, appropriately discounted for the risk of not prevailing."[43] Thus, the final compensation awarded to the members in a settlement context necessarily remains imperfect. The settlement approved is considered to be the best settlement for the parties, even if it is imperfect. It is considered to be the best possible alternative to trial, viewed collectively, and in the best interests of the class members as a whole.[44]

Considering that most class action cases settle through this micro-judgment process, the appreciation of the value, outcome, and overall success of the class action depends largely on whether the conditions of the contract are respected. Thus, once the take-up rate has notably been calculated (if possible) and it is clear that a substantial majority of class members have participated in the settlement and received a form of monetary relief, pursuant to the judge's order and a process established contractually, my view is that the class action may largely be considered "successful." As for class action cases ending with a judgment on the merits with the judge ordering a form of collective monetary distribution, the same reasoning applies, and a successful class action will see the entity compensated – that is, the substantial majority of class members have received monetary relief.

For all these reasons, I believe that a novel framework for analyzing the success of class action outcomes is warranted. Determining the value and success of class actions requires focusing on what the *optimal* class action might be in light of its underlying objectives. This optimal class action provides access to justice, deterrence, and compensation or, alternatively, access and deterrence and/or compensation. One can imagine two different measures of the optimal class action: an aggregate or "vertical" measure by which the optimal settlement provides the most generous total distribution to the class, and a distributional or "horizontal" measure that argues that the optimal settlement is the one that provides compensation to the largest numbers of members.

From my own perspective, assuming that the focus is on compensation and access to justice understood as access to compensation in one form or another, success will have been achieved *when a substantial majority of the class members receive monetary relief, even if minimal.* I thus choose the horizontal approach, thereby recognizing that these small-value (or negative-value) class actions with minimal payouts make compensation a secondary goal, with deterrence being the primary objective.

Empirical Value of Class Action Compensation

The Class Actions Lab's Class Action Compensation Project

Research Method
Phase I of the Class Action Compensation Project began in 2015 with a review of data in forty files at the Fonds d'aide aux actions collectives.[45] Phase II followed in 2016 with a review of all closed class action cases from a list provided by the Quebec Ministry of Justice from 2004 to 2016. These closed cases were reviewed by accessing both a database of official court summaries and the physical case files. The research team gathered information about the time frame of each action and of each significant procedural step, the substantive law and claims at stake, the recovery process applied, the methods chosen for reaching out to the class members, the contents of notices and claim forms, and judicial fees. I conducted the subsequent analysis of the accomplishment of compensatory objectives. Regarding monetary awards, the total amount paid directly to all class members was identified, as well as the actual or estimated total number of class members, the number of class members who received payments, the average amount paid directly to all class members, and class counsel and claims

administrator fees. Take-up and participation rates were calculated.[46] Different factors that in my view serve to influence take-up rates were identified.

Tables 10.1 to 10.5 summarize my principal findings according to the six most fundamental factors: take-up rates, participation rates, total monetary award, total costs and attorney fees, proportion of total amount received by the members, and amount of leftover distributions. Importantly, within the 450 files reviewed during the two phases, only 60 were found to contain data relative to monetary distributions. Upon a closer review, only 52 files were chosen for reporting as these files contained the relevant numbers for calculating monetary distributions and take-up rates, which were prioritized for the project's purposes. Cases that did not allow me to draw conclusions about take-up rates or that contained uncertain or incomplete information were excluded for these purposes.

My analysis focused on the definition of compensation. For each given class action, I asked: "What was the actual recovery achieved for the benefit of the class"?[47] I considered member recovery to involve the amounts distributed by defendants to each member, by way of cheque, money transfer, or other form of payment, through individual liquidation of collective damages, for those damages suffered.[48] Important leftover amounts provided by settlement or by way of final judgment, or amounts remaining after class distributions, were highlighted. One question that arose was whether leftover or *cy-près* distributions, transferred to public entities benefiting the class members indirectly rather than directly, contributed to the supposed "success" of the class action. Within the chosen range of cases, compensation sometimes took the form of coupons, discounts, or other indirect (non-monetary) benefits to the members and to future customers, sometimes independently of their membership in the class. These indirect modes of compensation were excluded from the analysis because they benefit the members in a way that is inconsistent with traditional compensatory goals.

Challenges

In this project, I sought to calculate the *actual* monetary benefit of class actions to class members. Measuring class action value, as well as the procedure's economic utility and effectiveness, is inherently challenging. During the physical review of the case files, my team and I were surprised to find reports and distributions data in files that were in fact closed (and for which distributions were completed) but that had initially appeared to be open upon mere consultation of the docket. Another surprise was to come across largely generic and imprecise reports and accountings that did not provide distribution numbers, the progress made in distributions, and/or the details of the claims recovery process. Reports of class distributions were often incomplete, obscure, or simply absent from the case file. Additional confusion resulted from the absence of certainty within the file regarding the scope of the class size. In fact, the confidential nature of the data was on occasion dictated within the settlement agreement, upon agreement between settling counsel and/or as provided in confidentiality agreements. Nonetheless, I was comforted by the fact that I was actually able to find data relative to compensation in class action files when the data are largely non-existent in other Canadian jurisdictions such as Ontario.

Calculating Rates

Measuring class action value involved calculating the actual direct economic benefit to the class members following class action settlement or judgment. For this purpose, the calculations included a take-up rate for each file reviewed. The take-up rate is defined, as indicated above, as the portion of class members who file a claim for recovery and are compensated pursuant to a class action settlement or judgment divided by the total number of class members estimated or confirmed. This rate reflects the number of members who ultimately received compensation – in other words, the number of members who actually benefited from the class action. Take-up rates are important because "high take-up rates are evidence to the courts, policymakers and the general public that the class being represented really does care about their case and that they are being compensated for the wrongs they suffered."[49] As the Ontario Court of Appeal recently noted, take-up rates reflect "the actual benefit to the class" and "an appropriate measure of the results achieved."[50]

Accordingly, in addition to take-up rates, I calculated a *participation rate*. As mentioned above, this rate compares the number of claims filed with the number of claims accepted, thereby attesting to the difficulty and the general effectiveness of the claims process as well as the access to a system of compensation. With respect to additional fees, my research team sought to evaluate counsel and claims administrator fees, the costs of notice, and the extrajudicial costs. Leftover or *cy-près* distributions were identified as well; these are considered to be a form of indirect distribution to members, and I have chosen to include them in the analysis to better evaluate the many forms of monetary compensation available.

I also attempted to calculate a *compensation rate* for each file. This required dividing the total amount paid for the benefit of the class (the settlement fund made available to the members, or the total payout) by the total amount of damages suffered. The compensation rate helps measure whether the amounts awarded to the members were significant considering how much money they lost at the outset, thereby indicating the actual direct economic benefit to the members. Unfortunately, very few cases disclosed the amount of damages initially suffered by the plaintiffs, which made the calculation of a compensation rate for each file unrealistic.

Observations and Findings

The observations and findings reported in this chapter stem from Quebec court case files where a monetary award was distributed directly to the members, during the period 2004–16. For this purpose, I excluded from my case sample those cases where monetary rebates or credits were awarded to the class members exclusively from any other form of monetary compensation. In cases where take-up rates varied between one amount and another, and only a range of rates was determinable, I provided in the tables below an average rate in order to be more prudent and conservative in my calculations. In addition, I acknowledge that there were many instances of overcompensation, leading to rates over and above 100 percent. In this chapter, my results appear in a general table, Table 10.6 in the Appendix, and are reproduced in the more specific Tables 10.1 to 10.5.

Generally speaking, the calculated take-up rates were much more impressive than expected. This first impression can be explained by the general climate favouring class actions in Quebec, and the fact that the Supreme Court of Canada has unanimously reaffirmed the broadness and flexibility of Quebec's conditions for class action certification.[51] A more conservative reason for these positive results could be that the large majority (forty-seven out of fifty-five) of the cases studied were private bargaining cases for which negotiated settlements led to class distributions; thus, these cases were negotiated dispositions in which the parties were able to reach results (i.e., class distributions) that did not always accurately reflect the applicable law or rules but instead were coherent with the individual values and preferences of the parties and counsel. The results of the empirical analysis of case files also showed mixed outcomes in terms of the great diversity of take-up rates found, varying from 0 to 100 percent and more (see Table 10.6).

The most important conclusion of this project is that although take-up rates vary tremendously between the case files studied, *class actions do compensate Quebec citizens.* Table 10.1 provides a summary overview of the results and highlights the differences between settlement and judgment outcomes in terms of the average take-up rate, the average total award paid by the defendant, the average administration fees (including fees paid to representatives, symbolically or not, for their involvement in the action), the average attorney fees, and the average leftover amounts. Row 1 provides the average take-up rates, whether the monetary compensation followed a class action settlement or a class action judgment on the merits, while row 2 provides the average amount paid by the

Table 10.1 Summary of take-up rates and monetary distributions following class action settlement or judgment

	Case outcome		
	Judgment (8)	Settlement (47)	All cases (55)
Average take-up rate (%)	68.75	52.33	54.76
Average total amount paid by defendant ($)	3,264,988	5,867,701	5,503,321
Average administration fees ($)	379,472	452,872	444,717
Average attorney fees ($)	1,123,883	1,100,767	1,103,849
Average leftover/*cy-près* ($)	1,733 341	340,545	608,391

defendant(s) following a settlement or a judgment on the merits. Row 3 provides average fees paid to claims administrators and class representatives, and row 4 the average fees paid to attorneys. Row 5 provides the average leftover and *cy-près* distributions, which arguably are considered indirect forms of compensation.

What Table 10.1 principally indicates is that an average of **roughly 55 percent of class members are compensated.**[52] Quebec class actions do serve to compensate a majority of class members in the case sample, and this result supports the proposition that class actions serve their compensatory objective.

How successfully are class members compensated? Table 10.2 shows a breakdown of the take-up rates found. In column 1, take-up rates are separated in 25 percent brackets. Column 2 shows the number of cases within the take-up rate bracket, and column 3, the percentages of cases found in each bracket.

Table 10.2 shows that 46 percent of class action cases have a take-up rate of less than 50 percent. More significantly, however, approximately 54 percent of cases compensate at least 50 percent of all members (between 50 percent and over 100 percent, to be precise). Put differently, in more than half of this sample of Quebec cases, class actions compensate a majority – and much more! – of the class member population.

Table 10.2 Comparison of overall take-up rate levels

Take-up rate	Number of cases	% of cases
Lower than 25%	17	31.48
Between 25% and 50%	8	14.81
Between 50% and 75%	12	22.22
Between 75% and 100%	12	22.22
Over 100%	5	9.26

I wondered whether settlements could provide for more appropriate, generous, and adequate compensation of class members than court judgments and their distribution orders. In other words, would these out-of-court agreements provide enhanced distributions, since they are reached through negotiations between the parties? Table 10.3 separates the results found in Table 10.2 into settlement and judgment categories. Again, column 1 shows take-up rates separated into 25 percent brackets, while column 2 indicates the number of judgments per bracket, followed by their percentage in column 3. Columns 4 and 5 show the same results for class settlements.

Table 10.3 shows that 25 percent of cases ending in judgments have take-up rates lower than 25 percent and that 37 percent of such cases have take-up rates of 50 percent or less. For cases ending in out-of-court settlements, the numbers are slightly higher, with 33 percent of settlements showing take-up rates lower than 25 percent and 48 percent showing take-up rates of 50 percent or lower. Table 10.3 also shows that 62 percent of cases ending with a judgment on the merits have a take-up rate of over 50 percent.[53] Correspondingly, 51 percent of cases ending in settlements have a take-up rate of over 50 percent. Only 31 percent of cases ending in settlement compensated over 75 percent of the members.[54] One interesting conclusion is that class members appear to be better compensated following a judgment.

What I have found in my more detailed individual study is that high take-up rates are achieved when a series of favourable factors in the action are present. In most of the files where take-up rates exceeded 75 percent, class members tended to be already identified or to be readily identifiable. Compensation is greatest in instances where class members are simple to trace and reach, which is mainly the case in consumer protection cases. Otherwise, higher take-up rates will generally be achieved when the parties have made significant efforts to trace and notify class members. These efforts are seen when, for instance, companies put in place programs, online or otherwise, that help reach members

Table 10.3 Comparison of take-up rate levels between settlement and judgment outcomes

Take-up rate	Judgments N	%	Settlements N	%
Lower than 25%	2	25	15	33
Between 25% and 50%	1	12	7	15
Between 50% and 75%	2	25	10	22
Between 75% and 100%	2	25	10	22
More than 100%	1	12	4	9

and facilitate compensation. In future reform efforts, therefore, defendants should be held to the highest standards of good faith and collaboration in terms of their efforts during claims distribution processes.

I have also found in my analysis of individual cases that higher take-up rates are correlated with direct distributions. Put differently, the less the effort required by individuals to obtain compensation, the greater the chances that members will actually be compensated and that many of them will be so. When simpler distribution systems are put in place, with automatic distributions or distributions following easy-to-follow or easy-to-use claims procedures and simple, plain language claims forms – ideally without requiring proof of damages suffered – members are more readily compensated and in greater numbers. Accordingly, one of my original hypotheses, that complex claims processes and complicated forms have a negative impact on distribution processes, was partially confirmed. Intricate claims procedures and forms generally have a negative effect on take-up rates, especially in cases where the amount recoverable is low. Thus, I firmly believe that technologies and social networks should be used to facilitate simpler claims distribution processes.

The reality, however, is that despite the existence of advanced communication technologies, newspapers continue to be the preferred way to notify class members, except where members are individually identifiable and reachable. In several consumer cases, the costs invested in massive newspaper notice campaigns are disproportionate, given the data relative to class members' participation and take-up rates. The use of new communication tools such as social media ventures was not favoured in many of the cases reviewed, even though, as I have written elsewhere,[55] take-up rates are enhanced significantly when technology is used for notification.

Incidentally, in my analysis of the class action files, I sought to calculate participation rates (defined earlier as the relation between the number of claims filed and the number of claims accepted), to test the odds that a claim filed would be accepted by the claims administrator, defendant administrator, or court clerk. Although the data are not entirely reliable, I found that participation rates varied between 63 and 100 percent, which suggests that members who choose to eventually file a claim will most frequently be compensated. This finding demonstrates that class members should be encouraged to file claims, even when the effort required to do so appears excessive or disproportionate to the financial advantages sought.

One observation that raises concerns is that only in 9 percent of the cases studied did the take-up rates reach 100 percent or higher, with all of the class's members being compensated. While this can be interpreted to mean that class actions do not generally compensate all the members of a given class, my own interpretation is that class actions do not aim for accuracy of outcomes, and that such discrepancies are to be expected.[56]

Do higher promised individual awards lead to higher take-up rates? Will class members make greater efforts to claim distribution amounts when potential awards are more significant? Logic would suggest that when higher payouts are at stake, members will more readily choose to participate in claims distributions processes. In five of the files providing potential awards of less than $50, only one evidenced a take-up rate of over 25 percent. This seems to suggest that lower payouts are less interesting to the members and provide less incentive to participate, thereby reducing take-up rates.

How much are the members awarded relative to the costs of the case, including administration and lawyer's fees? In other words, how much does it cost to bring and try or settle a class action file compared with the total award paid by the defendant? Legal fees and other disbursements, as well as costs of the case – administration and otherwise – were impressive in most of the cases analyzed. Table 10.4 presents the average proportion of the costs of the case relative to the total amount paid by the defendant following judgment or settlement. Column 2 shows the cost of administrating the case (including any and all payments made to external firms, to consultants, to representatives for their special efforts, etc.), as well as attorney fees, divided by the total award paid by the defendant for each file. The percentage obtained represents the rough cost of instituting the action from beginning until the final outcome. Unfortunately, while settlements show an average of 38 percent of the total award representing the costs of the case, this does not mean that the balance (62 percent) represents class member distributions. Members will often receive a minimal portion of the total award, and leftover amounts are impressive, as seen in Table 10.5.

What Table 10.4 demonstrates is that costs of the case are a significant portion of the total amounts paid by defendants, varying between 36 percent (in judgment outcomes) and 39 percent (in settlement outcomes) of the total amounts disbursed by these defendants. Interestingly, in my case sample, settlement outcomes involved higher costs than judgment outcomes. In addition, these percentages, which consider attorney fees and case administration fees,

Table 10.4 **Average proportion of costs of case relative to total award paid by defendants**

Case outcome	Proportion of costs of case relative to total award (%)
Judgment	35.67
Settlement	38.51
All cases	38.14

are much higher than the stated average percentages reserved for attorney fees as provided in Quebec case law, which vary at the time of writing from 25 to 35 percent of the total case award. In a decision issued by the Superior Court of Quebec in the matter of *Option Consommateurs v Amex Bank of Canada*, Justice Claudine Roy refused to approve class action settlements and deemed that the class counsel fees were not fair and reasonable.[57]

My case samples contained a significant number of prohibitively high attorney fee payments. In twelve out of forty-five cases with data regarding attorney fees, fees paid to Quebec counsel varied between \$1,100,000 and \$11,622,587. Fourteen cases saw payments of over \$500,000, and thirty cases saw payments higher than \$100,000. In several instances, attorney fees represented over half the amount of member distributions. These numbers seem to suggest that in many instances, class members may not be getting the larger part of the settlement and that the case may not be managed optimally to produce the best possible outcomes for the members.

Another surprising conclusion deriving from the case data analysis is that leftover amounts and *cy-près* distributions are not only frequent but also important, indicating the degree of indirect compensation in the cases studied. I was surprised to see an average amount of \$608,391 for this indirect compensation and, more significantly, that among the twenty-four cases where indirect compensation was awarded (of the fifty-five cases studied), eleven had dedicated \$100,000 or more to indirect distributions in the form of external charities or otherwise. This high number is alarming, considering that the class action's primary purpose is to provide access to justice through compensation of the class members. If thousands of dollars do not find their way directly into the hands of the members – as in one-fifth of all cases studied – then a broad reform of our laws to require closer scrutiny of class settlements and distributions is warranted.

In Table 10.5, I compare the amounts distributed directly to the members with these forms of leftover or indirect *(cy-près)* distributions. Row 4 provides the average proportion (in judgment and settlement outcomes) of indirect compensation relative to the total award provided, thereby showing that in my sample, settlements appear to generate lower indirect distributions than judgments. This conclusion may need to be validated further, considering that take-up rates also appear to be much less favourable in a settlement context than in a judgment context.

I also attempted to identify the impact, if any, of holding an external assessment process by a claims administrator of the merits of the claims presented. The existence of such a process does not seem to impact the members' compensation, considering the high participation rates in the majority of cases (in

Table 10.5 **Indirect versus direct distributions**

	Case outcome		
	Judgment	*Settlement*	*All cases*
Average take-up rate (%)	68.75	52.33	54.76
Average total award paid by the defendant ($)	3,264,988	5,867,701	5,503,321
Average leftover or *cy-près* ($)	1,733,341	340,545	608,391
Average % leftover or *cy-près* relative to total award	23.14	17.61	18.67

most cases, participation rates reaching over 95 percent). In fact, the administrators' denial of compensation is often due to the duplication of claims or the non-eligibility of a member rather than other factors of non-conformity. One might think that the lack of adequate proof to support a potential claim would prevent compensation of the members. Instead, I found only one case in which the unavailability of documentary proof constituted a barrier to the administrator's approval of the claim. High participation rates confirmed that the lack of documentary proof does not prohibit compensation, especially given that long periods of time often separate the event that gives rise to damages and the time of the compensation, reducing the likelihood that members will still have documentary proof to support their claim.

Another question that arose in the project was whether it is possible to establish a causal relationship between the length of class action proceedings and take-up rates. While the cases studied generally took between two and five years to be resolved judicially or out of court, the only two cases that lasted longer than ten years are both characterized by lower than 4 percent take-up rates. These cases suggest that the passage of time has a negative impact on compensation.[58]

In addition, my review of the physical files and the correspondence within those files has led me to conclude that a judge's close involvement in the process decisively and positively influences the success of the class action by enhancing distributions. Several cases were actively managed by judges, who ordered searches for additional class members or required the publication of an additional notice to the members. These measures were resorted to in hopes of raising the take-up rates or in response to requests for progress reports detailing the distributions process. In at least five of the case files studied, I found evidence of dynamic, above-average judicial involvement in the management of the case, leading to enhanced take-up rates ranging from 58 to 100 percent.

Conclusion

The Class Action Compensation Project and empirical analysis of class action files dating from 2004 to 2016 has shown that a majority of class actions within the case sample compensated Quebec citizens, as seen in the take-up rate of 50 to 100 percent of the class member population. Accordingly, a collective approach to compensation applied to the data analysis supports a conclusion that class actions compensate people. If class actions compensate people, then access to justice can be said to be provided to citizens of the province. With enhanced access to justice and accomplishment of at least one goal of the class action – that of compensation – the class action can be considered a legitimate, desirable, and effective procedural tool.

Appendix

Table 10.6 **Measuring class action value in monetary award cases from Quebec (2004–16)**

Case outcome	Take-up rate (%)	Total award paid by defendant ($)	Administration fees ($)	Attorney fees ($)	Leftover/ cy-près ($)
Judgment	80	1,580,000	71,000	501,000	582,000
Settlement	139	1,150,000	86,000	242,000	–
Settlement	93	3,250,000	750,000	–	–
Settlement	112	1,028,020	12,465	257,000	70,525
Settlement	45	13,490,000	1,098,000	3,000,000	–
Settlement	84	83,885	–	–	–
Settlement	–	375,000	6,077	93,750	–
Settlement	67	4,146,670	–	351,000	–
Settlement	35	2,880	–	320	1,800
Settlement	149	29,526,000	171,275	472,133	833
Settlement	68	6,000,000	–	–	–
Settlement	91	74,918	–	25,000	–
Settlement	58	500,000	141,386	–	35,000
Settlement	1	109,620	38,924	31,721	19,108
Settlement	98	–	900	25,000	–
Settlement	4	83,606	–	80,423	–
Settlement	86	10,181,297	281,059	331,769	–
Judgment	76	568,824	–	394,524	–
Settlement	98	55,000,000	–	11,622,587	362,550
Settlement	100	80,650	4,468	55,128	–
Judgment	41.5	4,397,316	212,422	1,467,775	824,531

Case outcome	Take-up rate (%)	Total award paid by defendant ($)	Administration fees ($)	Attorney fees ($)	Leftover/ cy-près ($)
Settlement	26	–	1,400,000	–	–
Settlement	31	977,000	55,078	309,018	311,210
Settlement	80	27,000,000	3,941,155	3,289,175	–
Settlement	0	550,000	–	189,709	180,146
Settlement	73	280,000	2,000	205,894	19,567
Settlement	54	5,000,000	–	1,300,000	–
Judgment	72	2,416,000	–	700,603	9,377
Judgment	71	359,527	–	123,711	22,679
Settlement	44	4,397,316	219,671	25,065	824,531
Settlement	4	225,000	–	80,000	–
Settlement	26	302,500	20,000	83,125	–
Settlement	16	350,000	–	–	–
Settlement	70	7,803,824	–	2,500,000	1,068,988
Settlement	73	6,100,000	–	1,100,000	3,588,093
Settlement	1	109,620	38,924	31,721	38,219
Judgment	2	6,281	–	–	–
Settlement	9	373,324	500	350,000	25,000
Settlement	16	1,000,000	–	223,970	–
Settlement	1	4,200,000	–	2,750,000	–
Settlement	73	280,000	2,000	205,894	9,784
Settlement	93	3,570,488		377,655	149,651
Settlement	54	4,960,175	185,000	1,261,316	364,964
Settlement	23	–	–	–	–
Settlement	11	–	–	–	–
Judgment	195.5	–	–	–	–
Settlement	0	272,000	–	90,000	–
Settlement	34	43,452,502	1,130,354	9,612,323	32,371
Settlement	0	8,750,000	283,696	366,773	–
Settlement	73	6,057,171	1,000,000	1,424,372	–
Settlement	98	793,775	–	427,384	16,527
Judgment	12	13,526,967	854,993	3,555,685	7,228,120
Settlement	1	250,000	–	95,000	492
Settlement	75	113,885	–	30,000	–
Settlement	20	60,000	–	13,671	32,089
Average	54.6	5,503,321	444,717	1,103,849	608,391

Note: More than 450 class action files were analyzed. In 55 class action files, a monetary award was paid to class members and a take-up rate could be calculated. The figures shown in this table are for those 55 files.

Notes

I would like to extend a warm thank you to my LLM student, Me Shana Chaffai-Parent, at the University of Montreal, for being an incredibly helpful research assistant and for all her hard work at the Class Actions Lab.

1 Arthur Miller, "Of Frankenstein Monsters and Shining Knights: Myth, Reality, and the 'Class Action Problem'" (1979) 92 Harv L Rev 664.

2 I must highlight here that my much more extensive data collected over the course of a twenty-five-year period in Quebec have led to the publication of a book on the topic: Catherine Piché, *L'action collective: ses succès et ses défis* (Montreal: Éditions Thémis, 2019) [*L'action collective*].

3 The take-up rate is defined as the portion of class members who file a claim for recovery and are compensated pursuant to a class action settlement or judgment divided by the total number of class members estimated or confirmed. This rate reflects the number of members who ultimately received compensation – in other words, the number of members who actually benefited from the class action.

4 For a comparable American study, see Brian T. Fitzpatrick & Robert C. Gilbert, "An Empirical Look at Compensation in Consumer Class Actions" (2014) 11 NYUJ L & Business 767. Also see Brian T. Fitzpatrick, "Do Class Actions Deter Wrongdoing?" (September 12, 2017) Vanderbilt Law Research Paper No 17-40, online: SSRN <https://ssrn.com/abstract= 3020282>.

5 Catherine Piché, "Le recouvrement et l'indemnisation des membres dans l'action collective" [Member compensation and distribution in class actions] (2016) 94 Can Bar Rev 171; Catherine Piché & André Lespérance, "L'action collective comme outil de prévention, d'évitement et de dissuasion" [The class action as a tool to prevent, to avoid, and to deter] in *National Collective Action Seminar – Recent Developments in Québec, Canada, and the United States* (Cowansville, QC: Yvon Blais, 2006) at 61.

6 See Ward Branch & Greg McMullen, "Take-Up Rates: The Real Measure of 'Access to Justice'" (Paper delivered at the 8th Annual Symposium on Class Actions, Toronto, 2011) at 4.

7 Most empirical studies rely on a set of anecdotal cases. See Alon Klement & Keren Weinshall-Margel, "Cost-Benefit Analysis of Class Actions: An Israeli Perspective" (2016) 172 J Institutional & Theoretical Economics 75; Fitzpatrick & Gilbert, *supra* note 4 at 775; Nicholas M. Pace & William B. Rubenstein, "How Transparent Are Class Action Outcomes?" (2008) RAND Corporation Working Paper No WR-599-ICJ, cited in Fitzpatrick & Gilbert, *supra* note 4 at 772; Deborah R. Hensler et al, *Class Action Dilemmas: Pursuing Public Goals for Private Gain* (Santa Monica, CA: RAND Corporation, 2000) at 55, online: RAND Corporation <http://www.rand.org/pubs/monograph_reports/MR969. html> (referring to the "worth it" test); Nicholas M. Pace et al, *Insurance Class Actions in the United States* (Santa Monica, CA: RAND Corporation, 2007); Janet Cooper Alexander, "Do the Merits Matter? A Study of Settlements in Securities Class Actions" (1991) 43 Stan L Rev 497 at 567.

8 *Code of Civil Procedure*, SQ 2016, c C-25.01 [*CPC*].

9 *Règlement de la Cour supérieure du Québec en matière civile* [Rules of the Superior Court of Quebec in Civil Matters], r 0.2.1, c C-25.01, (Can Que), Rule 59.

10 *Ibid.*

11 *An Act Respecting the Class Action*, RSQ, c R-2 (Can); *Code of Civil Procedure*, RSQ 1977, c C-25, ss 999–1051 (old Quebec Code of Civil Procedure); *Class Proceedings Act*, RSO 1992, c 6 (Can Ont) [*CPA Ontario*]; *Class Proceedings Act*, RSBC 1996, c 50; *Class Actions Act*, RSS 2001, c 12.01 (Can Sask); *Class Actions Act*, RSNL 2001, c C-18.1 (Can); *Rules Amending the Federal Court Rules*, SOR 98-106 (Can); *The Class Proceedings Act*, CCSM, c C130 (Can

Man); *Class Proceedings Act,* RSA 2003, c. C-16.5 (Can Alta); *Class Proceedings Act,* RSNS 2007, c 28 (Can NS).

12 *Federal Rules of Civil Procedure* (USA), Rule 23.

13 *CPC, supra* note 8, art 575.

14 See *Vivendi Can., Inc. v Dell'Aniello Canada,* 2014 SCC 1 [*Vivendi*].

15 This is possible, for example, through the application of the Ontario *Class Proceedings Act, CPA Ontario, supra* note 11, ss 23–24. See also *Markson v MBNA Canada Bank,* 2007 ONCA 334 at para 45 (statistical sampling possible without proof of individual claim).

16 *CPC, supra* note 8, art 595; *CPA Ontario, supra* note 11, ss 24 and 25.

17 See *CPC, supra* note 8, art 596.

18 *Ibid,* art 598.

19 *Ibid.*

20 *Ibid,* art 597.

21 Catherine Piché, "Public Financiers as Overseers of Class Proceedings" (2016) 12 NYUJ L & Business 776.

22 *Ibid.*

23 See the following Supreme Court of Canada trilogy: *Hollick v Toronto (City),* 2001 SCC 68 [*Hollick*]; *W. Can. Shopping Ctrs. v Dutton,* 2001 SCC 46 [*Dutton*]; *Rumley v British Columbia,* 2001 SCC 69.

24 See Catherine Piché, "The Cultural Analysis of Class Action Law" (2009) 2 J Civil & Legal Studies 101 at 127 ["Cultural Analysis"]; *Hollick, supra* note 23 at 19; Frank Iacobucci, "What Is Access to Justice in the Context of Class Actions?" (2011) 53 Sup Ct L Rev (2d) 17.

25 *Dutton, supra* note 23.

26 *Ibid.*

27 F. Paul Morrison & H. Michael Rosenberg, "Missing in Action: An Analysis of Plaintiff Participation in Canadian Class Actions" (2011) 53 Sup Ct L Rev 97, reprinted in Jasminka Kalajdzic, gen ed, *Accessing Justice: Appraising Class Actions Ten Years after Dutton, Hollick & Rumley* (Markham, ON: LexisNexis, 2011).

28 Robert Goodin, "Theories of Compensation" (1989) 9 Oxford J Legal Stud 56 at 59.

29 *Ibid* at 60.

30 *Ibid.* Indeed, compensation requires that the defendant provide the plaintiff with the equivalent of his or her loss (at 59).

31 Note, "Defendant Class Actions" (1978) 91 Harv L Rev 630 at 632–33.

32 See Élodie Falla, "Les dommages de masse: proposition pour renforcer l'efficacité de l'action en réparation collective" [Mass damages: proposal to enhance the effectiveness of collective redress] (PhD Thesis, Université de Montréal and Université Libre de Bruxelles, 2016) [unpublished; on file with author].

33 Catherine Piché, "L'emprise des cinq doigts de Frankenstein: réflexion en cinq temps sur l'action collective" [Frankenstein's five fingers: a five-step reflection on collective action] (2016) 2 RIDC 1.

34 *Ibid.*

35 Ethan E. Litwin & Morgan J. Feder, "European Collective Redress: Lessons Learned from the US Experience" in James Langenfeld, ed, *The Law and Economics of Class Actions* (Bingley, UK: Emerald Group Publishing, 2014) 209 at 237.

36 Piché & Lespérance, *supra* note 5.

37 Michael Legg, "Class Action Settlement Distribution in Australia: Compensation on the Merits or Rough Justice?" (2016) 16 Macquarie LJ 89 at 99: "[C]osts incurred by solicitors (and possibly by experts) [and claims administrators] to design the distribution scheme may reduce the settlement funds available for group members or increase the legal costs

and disbursements that are incurred and usually paid by the respondent as part of a settlement."

38 *Ibid* at 100.

39 Catherine Piché, *Fairness in Class Action Settlements* (Toronto: Carswell, 2001).

40 Cooper Alexander, *supra* note 7 at 498.

41 *Ibid* at 499.

42 *Ibid.*

43 *Ibid.*

44 *Ibid;* see also Samuel Issacharoff & Richard A. Nagareda, "Class Settlement under Attack" (2008) 156 U Pa L Rev 1649.

45 The Fonds d'aide aux actions collectives is an organization whose mission is to contribute to the financing of class actions during first instance and in appeal, as well as to distribute information relating to the exercise of the class action. For more information, see "Fonds d'aide aux actions collectives," online: Portail Québec <http://www4.gouv.qc.ca/fr/Portail/citoyens/programme-service/Pages/Info.aspx?sqctype=mo&sqcid=211>.

46 This rate compares the number of claims filed with the number of claims accepted, thereby attesting to the difficulty and the general effectiveness of the claims process, as well as the access to a system of compensation.

47 This consideration is inspired by the Ontario Court of Appeals case in *Lavier v MyTravel Can. Holidays Inc.,* 2013 ONCA 92 [*Lavier*].

48 Piché, "Cultural Analysis," *supra* note 24, citing Mauro Cappelletti, "La protection d'intérêts collectifs et de groupe dans le procès civil (Métamorphoses de la procédure civile)" [The protection of collective and group interests in the civil process], (1975) 27 RDIC 571 at 597.

49 Branch & McMullen, *supra* note 6 at 4.

50 *Lavier, supra* note 47 at para 57.

51 See *Vivendi, supra* note 14.

52 It is also worth mentioning here that members are sometimes overcompensated (over 100% take-up rate); the original class in these cases is modified and a larger class is indemnified through a negotiated outcome.

53 There is a margin of error and rounding of 1 percent here.

54 There is, again, a margin of error and rounding of 1 percent.

55 See, e.g., Catherine Piché, "The Coming Revolution in Class Action Notices: Reaching the Universe of Claimants through Technologies" (2018) 16 CJLT 227.

56 See Mancur Olson, *The Logic of Collective Action* (Cambridge, MA: Harvard University Press, 2009) at 2.

57 *Option Consommateurs c Banque Amex du Canada,* 2017 QCCS 200.

58 This issue is further discussed at length in c 3, s 3.4 in my book *L'action collective, supra* note 2.

11

Social Enterprise, Social Innovation, and Access to Justice

Lorne Sossin and Devon Kapoor

THIS CHAPTER SEEKS TO illustrate that social enterprise and social innovation are ideally suited to improving access to justice in Canada. Quite simply, social enterprise describes legal entities engaged in socially oriented economic activity for the purpose of generating revenue to be used to advance a social mission. Meanwhile, social innovation, a broader and more inclusive concept, describes solutions of all forms that are more effective and sustainable than existing solutions and that create value primarily for society as a whole. As we elaborate below, we believe that social enterprise and social innovation fill an important gap in the justice system. There are three rationales in particular for seeing these concepts as a piece of the access to justice puzzle. First, while courts and tribunals typically focus on legal needs once disputes have arisen and need to be resolved, social enterprise and social innovation can intervene at other junctures in the life cycle of legal programs and prevent those problems from ever becoming the kind of disputes for which courts and tribunals are needed. Second, social enterprise and social innovation are better able to innovate in legal services and dispute resolution; they can run experimental pilots, incorporate novel design principles, and "fail" in ways that would be intolerable for traditional justice providers such as law firms, courts, tribunals, or government-funded programs. Finally, social enterprise and social innovation are able to meld the nimbleness and responsiveness of the private sector with the values and principles of the public interest and social good. In this way, they can incorporate the creativity, energy, adaptability, and resilience so often missing from the state-administered justice system, without the inherent conflicts of for-profit motivations that attach to market-based solutions to legal problems.

The importance, then, of social enterprise and social innovation to access to justice lies in their ability to envision new ways of addressing existing problems. In other words, they serve as creative paradigms through which innovators, lawyers, governments, and other public and private bodies can examine and approach the complex and ubiquitous obstacles preventing individuals from fully exercising their legal rights.

We begin with a discussion of the access to justice problem and its merits as an essential pursuit for the legal community and (legal) entrepreneur. We then show that, because of their unique qualities, social enterprise and social innovation can address important gaps in the justice system by intervening across the life cycle of legal problems, innovating in ways that traditional justice providers cannot, and combining the flexibility of private sector organizations with the social dedication of public interest organizations. We conclude by outlining a conception of the life cycle of legal problems and examining existing social enterprise and social innovation initiatives operating at its various stages. The aim here is to provide insight into the capacity of social enterprise and social innovation to tackle the breadth of the access to justice problem. We also offer practical suggestions for how social enterprise and social innovation can act as catalysts for, and expand the capacity of, access to justice.

The Justice Problem

Access to justice may be conceived of as access to lawyers and courts. In this view, services such as *pro bono* legal services and legal aid provide a means for individuals to receive counsel in disputes or for transactional issues where they would otherwise be unable to do so. Another example is the waiver of court hearing fees for individuals without the financial means to pay, thus giving everyone access to the courts.[1]

A broader conception, however, is that access to justice is not "just about access to the courts but also about access to markets and regulatory regimes that would lessen the need for access to the courts."[2] This leaves the door open for mechanisms and services such as online access to informal dispute resolution, accessible public legal information and culturally or linguistically responsive advice centres, formal state-administered dispute resolution, and dispute resolution and restorative justice programs that provide an alternative to the courts. Further, this broader approach embraces the adoption of innovations in the traditional justice system such as small claims courts, class actions, and other tools, such as the Civil Resolution Tribunal (an online small claims tribunal),[3] that allow a greater number of individuals to seek legal remedies.[4] Broad approaches to access to justice also highlight the importance of both public and private regulatory bodies, which set and enforce standards that protect consumers and those affected by a range of economic and social activity.[5]

Finally, a further, even broader conception is that access to justice refers to any mechanism or service that directly (or perhaps even indirectly) enhances opportunities for individuals to understand, access, or shape the legal system. Access to justice is not only about enabling individuals to access means of legal remedies (as with the first two conceptions) but also about breaking down the barriers that often prevent people from maximizing their legal rights. Under this view, a great many things improve access to justice: wheelchair accessibility at courthouses, translation services, Indigenous sentencing circles, text-to-speech programs for the blind, or free and well-organized sources of legal information. Additionally, data collection and transparency about the justice system itself enhance access.[6]

Regardless, however, of what particular view one takes on the scope of access to justice, the problem of underserved and under-equipped communities exists. In order to fully understand the justice problem, it is important to grasp three key points: (1) a significant number of Canadians experience legal problems, particularly vulnerable individuals; (2) a significant number of Canadians do not truly understand how to appropriately deal with their legal problems (due to over-complexity and a lack of accessible and digestible information);[7] and (3) dealing with legal problems is often prohibitively expensive and time-consuming.

The first thing that one must understand about the justice problem is that legal needs are ubiquitous. According to a 2013 report by the Action Committee on Access to Justice in Civil and Family Matters, nearly 12 million Canadians will experience at least one legal problem in a given three-year period.[8] Further, "lower income individuals and members of vulnerable groups experience more legal problems than higher income individuals and members of more secure groups."[9] To make matters worse, there is evidence that legal problems have "momentum" and that individuals who experience one issue have a greater likelihood of experiencing others (for instance, domestic violence issues can lead to divorce proceedings and custody issues).[10] In other words, not only do a significant number of Canadians experience legal problems, but it is those most vulnerable in society who are more prone to encountering them.[11]

The second key notion to understand is that many Canadians do not truly understand how to handle their legal problems. For instance, in Canada, "over 20% of the population take no meaningful action with respect to their legal problems, and over 65% think that nothing can be done, are uncertain about their rights, do not know what to do, think it will take too much time, cost too much money or are simply afraid."[12] Legal education, access to relevant and timely legal information, and awareness of legal options are all seriously lacking. For most people, "legal problems" are just problems until they learn that the legal system might provide a solution. For example, losing a job is just a problem unless (and until) one learns that it might constitute wrongful dismissal or violate employment standards or one's employment contract, and that for each of these potential breaches, there is recourse through the legal system. Some of the most serious and common access to justice gaps result from people whose rights are never protected because legal information is too scarce when and where people need it most.

Third, it is important to understand that the cost and time-consuming nature of legal services constitute a barrier to justice for many. Research has shown that for individuals who do not seek legal assistance, cost is often the overriding factor in their decision to refrain from action.[13] And, in many instances, the perceived high cost of legal services is justified – lawyers' fees can range on average from $195 to $380 per hour, and trials can range from $13,000 to over $120,000 depending on the length.[14] Further, while many may see legal aid as a solution for those in need, the program is available only to those of extremely modest means – according to a Statistics Canada report, in 2013/2014, only 64.8 percent of legal aid applications across Canada were approved for full service. In raw numbers, 252,587 of the 717,943 applications were denied full service. Reasons included financial ineligibility, coverage restrictions (particularly in areas outside of criminal justice), and lack of merit.[15] All of this is to show that when one encounters a legal issue, handling it through traditional channels can be prohibitively expensive and time-consuming.

As former Chief Justice of Canada Beverley McLachlin once observed: "Do we have adequate access to justice? I think the answer is no. Among those hardest hit are the middle class and the poor. We have wonderful justice for corporations, and for the wealthy."[16] That Canada has an access to justice crisis is not seriously disputed; the current systems are too complex, expensive, and time-consuming to offer adequate assistance to the vast number of Canadians dealing with legal issues. What is needed is a drastic change in the way we approach access to justice.

The Potential of Social Enterprise and Social Innovation to Improve Access to Justice

Can social enterprise and social innovation facilitate the kind of change needed to provide access to justice to those with unmet legal and dispute resolution needs? In this section, we explore how they might address important gaps in the justice system by intervening across the life cycle of legal problems, by experimenting with new mechanisms for delivering services that traditional justice system providers cannot, and by combining the flexibility of private sector organizations with the social dedication of public interest organizations.

Although we do not approach social enterprise or social innovation as neatly defined concepts, a full exploration of the scope of each is beyond the needs of this study. For our purposes, social enterprise may be understood as a "legal entity engaged in socially responsible economic activity for the purpose of generating revenue which is to be used to advance a social mission."[17] For instance, Ecosia, a US social enterprise, is "a search engine that plants trees with its ad revenue."[18] Other examples include Blackboard Marketing, a "full-service creative marketing agency providing hands-on career training and experience to youth and disadvantaged, marginalized and underserved communities," and Interpreter Services Toronto, which "offers interpretation and translation services for interviews, investigations, medical appointments, court cases, [and] labour arbitrations."[19] The common element between these various organizations is the presence of an underlying social goal to their business – they are not principally interested in profit but rather in generating revenues in a socially responsible manner for the greater purpose of giving back to society. Thus, social enterprises occupy a hybrid space between non-profit and for-profit enterprises.

Beyond their capacity to improve society in general, social enterprises also have – as a result of their hybrid qualities – the unique potential to improve access to justice. One reason for this is their ability, in ways less restricted than non-profits, to seek revenue-generating programs, raise capital, and distribute earnings. This ability is important when one considers the difficulties inherent in attempting to tackle issues such as the provision of advising and dispute resolution services to lower- and middle-income communities that do not have enough resources to attract market-based services and at the same time do not meet eligibility thresholds for legal aid clinics and services. These are not simple problems, and solutions can require significant amounts of capital. Because social enterprises are expected to generate revenue, they can become self-sustaining and may attract more capital than initiatives that simply disburse funds to address needs.

Another reason that social enterprises are uniquely situated to improve access to justice is that, unlike for-profit entities, they are dedicated to making a positive social impact. For instance, in British Columbia, a "community contribution company" (a legal form for social enterprise) must include in its memorandum of association a statement confirming its community purpose – meaning a purpose beneficial to society at large or a segment of society broader than the company itself, and includes providing health, social, environmental, educational or other services.[20] Thus, they are likely to be more reliable actors than for-profit corporations, which are obliged to satisfy shareholder demand for profit (this is particularly true in the case of public companies). Although for-profit entities can certainly provide social benefit through corporate social responsibility initiatives, these efforts are often incidental to the mission and priorities of the organization, and geared as much (or more) towards improving brand perception as towards making a meaningful impact on the community. In this sense, for example, while the Royal Bank of Canada's Youth Mental Health Project[21] represents a significant investment in important programs and services, which may well help address access to justice issues, the goal of the bank is to generate surpluses for its shareholders through commercial banking transactions. Ultimately, if the bank has to allocate priorities, it is not likely to put youth mental health ahead of generating shareholder value in banking. By contrast, social enterprises revolve around a social mission. That social mission is why the social enterprise exists, and it is key to its priorities. Even where a social enterprise also seeks to generate revenue, the purpose of that revenue is to enhance and advance that social mission. It is these qualities – significant financial freedom (unlike non-profits) and social dedication (unlike commercial enterprises) – that make social enterprise ideally suited to improving access to justice.

While we believe social enterprises have distinct features well suited to access to justice initiatives, they form part of a broader movement of initiatives often organized under the rubric of social innovation. For our purposes, social innovation includes any "novel solution to a social problem that is more effective, efficient, sustainable, or just than existing solutions and for which the value created accrues primarily to society as a whole rather than private individuals." A social innovation "can be a product, production process, or technology, but it can also be a principle, an idea, a piece of legislation, a social movement, an intervention, or some combination of them."[22]

Social innovation may comprise many forms of organization, whether social enterprises, non-profit organizations, or those associated with the broader public sector entities, such as universities, colleges, hospitals, or prisons. While social enterprises are examples of social innovation that operate in and through markets, other forms of social innovation operate in civil society. For example, the Toronto Community Foundation has started a new after-school program, Beyond 3:30, that "brings recent teachers' college grads and local non-profits right into the schools to provide non-traditional activities geared specifically to middle-school students." Now operating in eighteen schools, Beyond 3:30 provides improved nutritional practices, homework support, and physical activity in a safe environment for the kids.[23] While a social innovation program of this kind has to support itself financially, it does so outside the market, with a mix of public, social, and philanthropic funding. In other words, Beyond 3:30 is not a business in the way a social enterprise would be, but rather an innovative social program that relies on non-market-based forms of revenue to perform its social mission.

Another example of social innovation of this kind, with an environmental focus, is the repurposing of decommissioned elevated railways in New York City and Chicago into "linear parks." These new green spaces, such as the High Line and The 606, "revitalize working class neighbourhoods and produce new public spaces frequented by locals and visitors alike."[24] Social innovation is thus a broad movement that is leading to change in all areas of society, particularly spheres where both the state and market have been ineffective in meeting social needs. Indeed, it is possible to see the significant growth of experiential learning in universities and the rise of clinics and *pro bono* projects in law schools as expressions in support of social innovation and its potential for improving access to justice.[25]

The Life Cycle of Legal Problems and the Impact of Social Enterprise

For purposes of this analysis, we see social innovation and social enterprise as relevant in the three junctures of a legal dispute: (1) the conflict avoidance period, in which disputes and legal problems can be avoided or dealt with quickly and affordably through one or more pieces of relevant and accessible legal information, summary advice, or facilitated negotiations; (2) the conflict resolution period, in which disputes and legal problems require some form of informal and/or formal dispute resolution mechanism where some form of expertise or legal assistance is often necessary to achieve success; and (3) the conflict restoration period, in which disputes and legal problems, particularly but not exclusively those of a criminal nature, may resurface and place additional burdens on both the individuals and the justice system.

At each of these critical junctures in the life cycle of legal problems, social innovation and social enterprise may enhance the capacity of the justice system to meet legal needs. Their effectiveness is closely tied to the legal design movement, which seeks to marry methodologies from the human-centred design sector (user-focused, beta-tested, holistic, responsive to adaptation, etc.) with the legal and justice systems, as illustrated by the design focus of several examples highlighted below.[26]

The Conflict Avoidance Period

The best way to address legal problems is to prevent them from arising in the first place. To quote the oft-invoked metaphor of the person falling off the cliff, it is much more time-consuming, complex, expensive, and uncertain to rush an effective ambulance to the scene than to simply build an effective rail at the top so people do not fall in the first place. Applying this metaphor to the access to justice context, smart and responsive regulation may be the best response in areas such as consumer protection, breach of labour and environmental standards, and many aspects of family justice, especially the protection of children. Governments may also implement policies that expressly preclude certain kinds of disputes. For example, with the stroke of a pen, the introduction of no-fault auto claims removed from the dockets thousands of cases arising annually from disputes over who caused car accidents.[27]

Another useful method is to ensure that vulnerable people are aware of their rights and to provide other forms of public legal education and summary advice that can help them avoid disputes. By empowering people to advocate for their own interests more effectively, we can take great strides in easing the burden on the traditional justice system. It is in this space that social innovation and social enterprise may have the most significant and positive impact.

Below we explore several examples of social innovation and social enterprise active in this aspect of the conflict life cycle, with the twofold goal of demonstrating the ways in which they represent a distinct and discrete sphere of access to justice activity and exploring the potential advantages of this sphere, as outlined above.

The Hague Institute for the Internationalization of Law (HiiL)

Operating at the juncture before legal problems escalate, HiiL is a not-for-profit social enterprise based in The Hague that collects data on the needs and satisfaction of the users of justice systems across the world and devises and invests in new, innovative procedures geared towards improving access to justice.[28] It has provided various forms of access to justice to more than 1.4 million people across twelve countries since 2012 and has a goal of assisting 150 million people by 2030.[29] One of its projects, ACT (Action, Collaboration, Transformation), "supports major brands and retailers in their interactions with trade unions representing workers in the clothing industry. The goal is to develop a system of collective bargaining that will lead to a living wage." This initiative is important because it offers a proactive means of addressing legal issues before they reach a stage where courts and review boards are necessary to adjudicate the disputes.

Another project is Burenrechter, a resolution method for neighbour disputes. The program is an online platform where "people who face disputes with their neighbours can login and describe their issues."[30] These issues are then documented, and the program suggests a dialogue between the parties to help negotiate a solution. Similarly, HiiL has launched Rechtwijzer 2.0, an "online-based dispute resolution platform that supports people through their justice journey." The platform provides information about legal options and puts users in control when dealing with their disputes. The program was launched at the end of 2014 and has been used in the Netherlands, the United Kingdom, and British Columbia for divorce and separation procedures. It was well received and was used to settle roughly 600 cases across the three zones in 2016.[31] Nevertheless, HiiL dissolved the program in 2017 in the face of limited public subsidies and rising costs in order to focus its efforts on the Dutch family law market with a new digital service.[32]

Here, the innovation lies in these programs' ability to provide a far less complex and tedious solution to everyday legal problems. Rather than having to spend time and money on lawyers and in traditional mediation or the family law system, individuals can work at their own pace and at a reduced cost. Similar products available throughout Canada could well serve to release the pressures on small claims courts, "low-stakes" mediation, and the family law system. As Shannon Salter has argued, these areas also highlight the significant potential of technology and digital forms of access to legal services and dispute resolution.[33]

Legalswipe

As indicated above, a key cause of inaccessible justice is the lack of relevant and responsive legal information when and where people need it most. Legalswipe was dedicated to addressing such deficits by bringing legal information to a person's smartphone. When Legalswipe was first launched in Toronto in 2015, its servers could not keep up with demand. It received high-profile coverage in particular because its launch coincided with heightened awareness of police "carding" and the importance of people's knowing their rights in relation to police encounters.[34]

Legalswipe is an example of the blend between public and private revenue and ideas. The technology on which it operates was privately funded through advertisement revenue and organizations such as Dreammaker Ventures and the Ontario Presenter for Excellence, while its legal education workshops were supported by donations and grants from public organizations such as the Ontario Trillium Foundation. The mix of private capital, public grants, and non-profit public interest activities presents significant potential while at the same time raising potential concerns. To what extent will knowledge gained from the Legalswipe charitable foundation be used by its private revenue-generating arm? What proportion of revenue generated from advertising will fund Legalswipe's public interest work? These questions are common in the realm of social enterprise and social innovation and speak to the heightened importance of transparency and the development of metrics for consistent and comparative evaluation in this sector, particularly in justice-related initiatives.

While social innovation already has a relatively well-defined place in the justice sector, the role and potential of social enterprise is just becoming apparent. It is not yet clear whether social enterprises like Legalswipe will (or should) be measured by how much they are used, how many gaps in access they fill, how many breakthroughs in technology they facilitate, the extent to which they shift cultures of legal and justice services, or how much revenue or investment they are able to attract.

Winkler Institute for Dispute Resolution

Another key addition provided by social innovation and social enterprise is a new approach or methodology to tackle access to justice issues. In this vein, the Winkler Institute for Dispute Resolution runs two programs based on the application of human-centred design methodology to the justice system:[35] the Justice Innovation and Access to Justice Program, and the Justice Design Project, both of which are geared towards offering law and post-secondary students the chance to learn about the issues and potential solutions relating to the justice problem. More specifically, the Justice Innovation and Access to Justice Program offers courses for JD candidates that focus on the "theory and tools needed to promote innovation in the legal field," how to apply these tools in case studies and simulations, and how to build partnerships with community organizations in order to improve real-world access to justice. Similarly, the Justice Design Project is a week-long workshop for post-secondary students that offers hands-on learning about innovation and its applications in the justice sector. The value of these initiatives is their establishment of a culture of innovation and awareness of access to justice issues in young lawyers; if the justice problem is to be solved in a sustainable fashion, it will be necessary for the next generation of lawyers to be comfortable with and committed to the issues.

In addition to its initiatives in creating awareness and knowledge surrounding access to justice, the Winkler Institute also runs a number of projects geared towards improving the existing processes and procedures at work in the justice system. For instance, through a workshop with the Yukon Courts, the Yukon Department of Justice, and the Family Law Information Centre, the institute helped develop a completely redesigned family law statement of claim form that addressed the various pain points normally associated with complex legal documents.[36] Another design-oriented project, Improving Ontario's Family Justice System through Technology, is engaging with family justice sector participants, such as litigants, court staff, legal professionals, and judges, to develop a technology-based product to improve the family law system in Ontario. A project called Indigenous Youth: Designing a Better Justice System is geared towards creating technology solutions to "build a justice system that is reflective of Aboriginal experiences and responsive to Aboriginal traditions."[37]

The importance of these initiatives lies in the fact that they seek to adapt the existing processes and elements of the justice system to be more accessible and digestible for those with serious legal problems, and that they introduce new ideas and approaches. In this way, social innovation and social enterprise can serve as a laboratory for improving the justice system.

Legal Innovation Zone

The Legal Innovation Zone (LIZ) is a tech incubator launched in 2015 with a focus on legal service delivery. Hosted at Ryerson University in Toronto, LIZ provides co-working space, resources, and supports for companies and individual start-ups that may be for-profit or not-for-profit, in addition to mentorship services for those with legal services concepts that have not yet matured into start-ups. One of the eighteen start-ups hosted by LIZ is Clausehound, an annotated legal library of legal agreements, sample contracts, and drafting software aimed at small businesses and entrepreneurs.[38] In addition, LIZ matches interested students and others who wish to get involved with start-ups.[39]

One of the key areas where university-based social innovation hubs such as LIZ can complement other justice system resources is in being a catalyst for new concepts. In 2016, for example, LIZ, in partnership with the Ontario Ministry of the Attorney General, hosted a province-wide challenge for ideas to enhance access to justice. From the twenty-nine applications, six start-up ideas were selected and given four months to be developed. At the end of the four-month incubation period, three start-ups were awarded a combined total of $50,000 in seed funding to continue developing their businesses. As exemplified by LIZ, this incubation/acceleration role for social innovation and social enterprise provides an invaluable mechanism for moving concepts towards concrete reality and providing more and better justice services to the public.

Once again, LIZ reflects a blend of broader public sector initiatives that may give rise to more private sector activity. While not every start-up within LIZ is a social enterprise, the goal of facilitating greater innovation in the justice system to reach middle- and lower-income communities itself constitutes a form of social innovation.

The Conflict Resolution Period

Once a conflict has emerged (either because conflict avoidance measures were not in place or not appropriate or effective in the circumstances), some kind of external dispute resolution mechanism is necessary to resolve the legal problem.

Here, as well, social innovation and social enterprise can serve important gap-filling and capacity-enhancing roles.

National Self-Represented Litigants Project

The National Self-Represented Litigants Project (NSRLP), housed at the University of Windsor Faculty of Law and funded by the Law Foundation of Ontario, is an example of social innovation arising out of an academic research project conducted by Dr. Julie Macfarlane from 2011 to 2013.[40]

In light of the fact that court and tribunal systems can represent harsh and challenging environments for people representing themselves, the NSRLP both advocates for systemic changes to improve the experience of SRLs in the justice system and develops concrete resources for SRLs to enhance their capacity to navigate that system. The NSRLP also publishes ongoing data on the demographics and narratives of self-represented litigants. One of the tools it provides, the Canadian Legal Information Institute (CanLII) primer, introduces SRLs to the public database of judicial and tribunal decisions and how they can use it to fashion their submissions.[41] Other resources focus on building relationships with opposing counsel and how to approach settlement negotiations.[42] Thus, although the mandate of the NSRLP itself is not revenue generating, it is a social innovation paving the way for subsequent social enterprises.

DoNotPay

DoNotPay, a robot lawyer chatbot designed and developed by Stanford University student Joshua Browder, applies the potential of machine learning algorithms for interactive, automated information and summary advice, and is an example of the experimental and innovative potential of conflict resolution tools.[43] To date, DoNotPay has been applied most notably to traffic tickets. The program first works out whether an appeal is possible through a series of simple questions, such as whether there were clearly visible parking signs, and then guides users through the appeal process.

By 2016, the Chatbot had been successfully used to contest 160,000 parking tickets across London and New York for free;[44] and by the summer of 2017, it had expanded to all fifty US states and had overturned 375,000 such cases.[45] In its first twenty-one months, the free service, then available only in London and New York, was used in 250,000 cases (the 160,000 "winning" cases thus translated into a success rate of 64 percent, with $4 million saved in parking tickets).

Additional applications for the program include refugee asylum applications and homeless benefits. In early 2017, Browder developed another version of

DoNotPay that helps the homeless apply for government housing in the United Kingdom. It works with the Facebook Messenger app in a similar way to the DoNotPay website (by asking users questions to learn more about their case and then generating an appeal letter).

Also in 2017, Browder expanded the chatbot to Facebook Messenger to help refugees in the United States, the United Kingdom, and Canada claim asylum. "Ultimately, I just want to level the playing field so there's a bot for everything," he told *Business Insider*.[46] "I originally started with parking tickets and delayed flights and all sorts of trivial consumer rights issues," he added. "But then I began to be approached by these non-profits and lawyers who said the idea of automating legal services is bigger than just a few parking fines. So, I've since tried to expand into doing something more humanitarian."[47]

In the summer of 2017, Browder announced a massive expansion of the chatbot to tackle 1,000 legal areas, including consumer and workplace rights (all free of charge). He envisions the chatbot tackling more complex legal processes like marriages, divorces, and bankruptcies. Reflecting a mix of social enterprise and corporate social responsibility (CSR) initiatives, IBM has offered its Watson technology for free to DoNotPay, making it possible for users to express their legal questions in natural language.[48]

DoNotPay illustrates how social innovation and social enterprise do not operate in silos – they interact with and influence the direction of both business enterprises and the government justice sector (for example, in 2017, the City of Toronto launched an online portal for challenging parking tickets).[49]

The Conflict Restoration Period
One of the most promising and least scrutinized aspects of the life cycle of legal problems is what occurs after they are resolved. In the criminal justice sector, the focus is often on recidivism, the parole system, housing and employment barriers, the mental health system, and what happens after the release of those convicted of criminal offences and incarcerated. On the family side, this may relate more to the psychological consequences of family breakdown and family justice dispute resolution. Every legal problem and dispute, however, has consequences for those involved, and the ripple effects of negative experiences with the legal system can often persist well into the future. The social enterprise and social innovation sector has been active in addressing these distinct challenges, which also call for more holistic approaches, blending an understanding of the legal system with cognate disciplines and sources of knowledge and insight. In our view, a successful strategy for access to justice must be holistic in reflecting people's experience with the justice system and the life cycle of legal problems.

Homelessness Partnering Strategy (HPS)

Operating at the tail end of the life cycle of legal problems, the Homelessness Partnering Strategy (HPS) is "aimed at preventing and reducing homelessness in Canada."[50] Under this initiative, five social enterprise projects were developed with a goal of exploring "how social enterprises can contribute to labour market integration for individuals exiting the criminal justice system who are homeless or at risk of homelessness."[51] The projects include the Rideau Social Enterprise program, which assists "former prisoners successfully secure and sustain meaningful employment outcomes after release" by providing them with "job training, employment placement ... and the coordination of housing and other support services such as addiction and mental health counselling." Another organization is the Asphalt Gals Social Enterprise, an asphalt shingle recovery social enterprise that creates "suitable employment for women leaving the corrections system."[52]

The impact of these initiatives on the welfare of participating individuals appears to have been positive, with 48 percent of individuals maintaining employment with their social enterprise, finding external employment, or pursuing education. This can be compared with the 42.5 percent of individuals who experienced a "negative" trajectory, which entails a loss of employment due to immigration issues, a lack of interest in the programs, mental health and substance abuse issues, or a breach of conditions. In some ways, it seems difficult to view these numbers as positive (as the "negative" numbers almost equal the positive ones). However, given the complexity of the task (as well as the difficulty of even establishing a baseline for understanding how to measure success with recidivism[53]), they seem to be having an overall positive impact. The importance of these kinds of organizations lies in the fact that they not only assist individuals to maintain employment and transition back into society but also alleviate the pressure placed on state-run programs of a similar nature.

The HPS reflects the goals of conflict restoration due to its work in helping prevent previously incarcerated individuals from re-entering the criminal justice system – a result that would place further burdens on an already overburdened system. Since a distinctive feature of the justice problem is the "momentum" of legal problems, the likelihood of further interactions with the law must be reduced if our justice systems are to function adequately. Of course, each of the phases of conflict interacts with the others; in this sense, conflict restoration initiatives like HPS also may be seen through the lens of conflict avoidance.

Emma's Acres

Similar to HPS, Emma's Acres in Mission, British Columbia, is a social enterprise aimed at improving the reintegration of former prisoners, but it goes further and seeks to bring together offenders and victims in a shared agricultural enterprise aimed at enhancing food security. Founded by Glen Flett, who spent twenty-three years behind bars, the Emma's Acres farm is an experiment in restorative justice, which aims to promote healing as well as provide life and job skills. Flett describes the goal of Emma's Acres in the following way:

> Originally, we wanted to get people in prison working, making some money to give to the families of victims. But after a few years, we realized we could generate profits to fund our mission. We wanted a sustainable farm that would help inmates along their journey and also support victims of violent crime.[54]

In 2013, with a grant of $75,000 from a credit union and generous lease terms with the district, Flett and his wife, Sherry, obtained an eight-acre forested plot of land and launched Emma's Acres. Approximately twenty-four inmates on community service passes from nearby federal penitentiaries tend the farm's gardens, and the produce is sold at the Mission City Farmers Market. Profits are used to fund a part-time support worker, and produce is given free every week to survivors of violent crime. Sherry Flett describes the impact of Emma's Acres as transformative:

> We just didn't expect the kind of effect this would have on survivors ... It's incredible how much joy the offenders have in helping other people. The survivors see this joy and are deeply impacted. Everyday interactions over food really have the potential to transform lives.[55]

Emma's Acres made $25,000 from food sales in 2015, and expansion plans will see the enterprise move into beehives, chickens, and goats. Flett's ultimate goal is to use farm profits to fund a healing centre for victims of serious crimes.[56]

*

While distinct in their specific goals, all of these initiatives provide services beyond those available in the public justice institutions (courts, tribunals, legal aid, etc.). Additionally, they all respond to gaps in the justice system, where specific needs have gone unmet. While the state views the justice system as encompassing the resolution of conflict, social enterprises and social innovations are able to intervene across a broader spectrum of the life cycle of conflicts, focusing on conflict avoidance and restorative justice in addition to conflict resolution. Whether addressing these upstream or downstream aspects of the problem, they are products of human-centred design and respond to the lived experience that people have with the justice system.

Conclusion

In this brief study, we have argued that social innovation and social enterprise can complement the justice system, extend its reach, and address gaps in access to justice. We have identified several advantages that they have, including broader coverage of the life cycle of disputes; greater ability to innovate, experiment, and learn from trial and error; and a greater degree of nimbleness in using both revenue-generating and public interest strategies to achieve greater access to justice.

Too often we confuse access to justice with access to lawyers or access to courts and tribunals. The social determinants of justice are broader and do not conform neatly to disciplinary boundaries. For instance, where does the failure of the mental health system end and the failure of the justice system begin in relation to the overrepresentation of people with mental health needs in prisons? Are failures of access to justice a consequence or cause of social marginalization and poverty?

Access to justice is about having the means to solve problems. Ideally, those solutions happen quickly and cheaply. Solutions may require legal assistance but will often flow from more widely available legal information. They may require a dispute resolution mechanism, but that may be mediation or negotiation rather than litigation and adjudication, and it may be more effective to provide access from a phone than from a downtown building. Social innovation and social enterprise can achieve greater flexibility and greater responsiveness to this array of solutions, and provide them for segments of society without the market power to attract market resources from businesses and firms.

The public justice system of courts and tribunals has boundaries. The Ministry of the Attorney General's portfolio is similarly bounded. If it turns out that people are deprived of access to justice because they lack education or mental health resources or because of poverty, these are viewed as matters over which other ministries of government (education, health, social services, etc.) have jurisdiction. Social enterprises and social innovations, by contrast, have no such constraints, and can blend services and resources across the complete lifespan of conflicts, from those that can help people avoid the need for courts and tribunals to those that help them recover from the impacts of court and tribunal proceedings.

The ambition and conclusions of this study have been modest. Our hope is to see additional study and analysis of the current and potential impacts of social innovation and social enterprise in relation to the justice system. While they will not render either public resources or private lawyers and paralegals redundant, we believe they have a key and growing role to play if access to justice is to become a reality.

Notes

1 *Trial Lawyers Association of British Columbia v British Columbia (Attorney General)*, 2014 SCC 59, 3 SCR 31.
2 Kent Roach & Lorne Sossin, "Access to Justice and Beyond" (2010) 60 UTLJ 373 at 374.
3 Civil Resolution Tribunal, online: <https://civilresolutionbc.ca/>; Shannon Salter, "Online Dispute Resolution and Justice System Integration: British Columbia's Civil Resolution Tribunal" (2017) 34:1 Windsor YB Access Just 112.
4 Roach & Sossin, *supra* note 2 at 376.
5 See Michael Trebilcock, Anthony Duggan, & Lorne Sossin, eds, *Middle Income Access to Justice* (Toronto: University of Toronto Press, 2012).
6 See Chapter 2 of this volume.
7 See, e.g., Ontario Civil Legal Needs Project, *Listening to Ontarians* (Toronto: Ontario Civil Legal Needs Project Steering Committee, May 2010).
8 Action Committee on Access to Justice in Civil and Family Matters, *Access to Civil and Family Justice: A Roadmap for Change* (Ottawa: Action Committee on Access to Justice in Civil and Family Matters 2013) at 2, online: Canadian Forum on Civil Justice <http://www.cfcj-fcjc.org/sites/default/files/docs/2013/AC_Report_English_Final.pdf>.
9 *Ibid.* In Canada, there is a serious problem with the overincarceration of Indigenous people – Aboriginal people make up only 4 percent of the Canadian population, yet, as of February 2013, they make up 23.2 percent of the federal inmate population. Further, the "over-representation of Aboriginal people in Canada's correctional system continued to grow in the last decade," increasing from 17 percent in 2000 to 23.2 percent in 2013. Office of the Correctional Investigator, "Aboriginal Offenders – A Critical Situation (16 September 2013), online: Office of the Correctional Investigator <http://www.oci-bec.gc.ca/cnt/rpt/oth-aut/oth-aut20121022info-eng.aspx>.
10 Action Committee on Access to Justice in Civil and Family Matters, *supra* note 8 at 3.
11 This correlation relates to specific kinds of legal problems. For example, vulnerable people may be far less likely to experience disputes involving financial investments and securities. With respect to legal problems that may have the most significant impact (e.g., loss of housing, loss of immigration status, loss of employment, criminal prosecutions, etc.), the correlation may be especially strong.
12 Action Committee on Access to Justice in Civil and Family Matters, *supra* note 8 at 4.
13 *Ibid.* See also Ontario Civil Legal Needs Project, *supra* note 7 at 32.
14 Action Committee on Access to Justice in Civil and Family Matters, *supra* note 8 at 4. See also Michael McKiernan, "The Going Rate: The 2015 *Canadian Lawyer* Legal Fees Survey Shows Litigation Fees Have Returned to Pre-Recession Rates," *Canadian Lawyer* (June 2015) 33, online: <https://www.canadianlawyermag.com/staticcontent/images/canadian lawyermag/images/stories/pdfs/Surveys/2015/CL_June_15_GoingRate.pdf>.
15 Statistics Canada, "Legal Aid in Canada, 2013/2014" (30 November 2015), online: Statistics Canada <http://www.statcan.gc.ca/pub/85-002-x/2015001/article/14159-eng.htm>.
16 Michael McKiernan, "Lawyers Integral in Making Justice Accessible: McLachlin," *Law Times* (21 February 2011), online: <http://www.lawtimesnews.com/author/michael-mckiernan/lawyers-integral-in-making-justice-accessible-mclachlin-8327/>.
17 Lorne Sossin & Devon Kapoor, "Social Enterprise, Law and Legal Education" (2017) 54:4 Osgoode Hall LJ 997.
18 Ecosia, "How It Works," online: Ecosia <https://info.ecosia.org/what>.
19 Toronto Enterprise Fund, "Who We Fund," online: Toronto Enterprise Fund <http://www.torontoenterprisefund.ca/what-we-do/sustain-existing-eses/who-we-fund>.
20 *Business Corporations Act*, SBC 2002, c 57, ss 51.91–51.93.

21 Royal Bank of Canada, "Supporting Youth," online: Royal Bank of Canada <http://www.rbc.com/community-sustainability/commitment-to-youth/index.html?tab=health-project>.
22 James A. Phills Jr., Kriss Deiglmeier, & Dale T. Miller, "Rediscovering Social Innovation" (2008) 6:4 Stanford Social Innovation Rev 34 at 39. There are many other useful definitions of social innovation. For instance, Mark Goldenberg defined social innovation as "the development and application of new or improved activities, initiatives, services, process, or products designed to address social and economic challenges faced by individuals and communities": Mark Goldenberg et al, "Social Innovation in Canada: An Update" (2009) Canadian Policy Research Networks Research Report at 3, online: Social Sciences and Humanities Research Council of Canada <https://www.sshrc-crsh.gc.ca/about-au_sujet/publications/social_innovation_report_E.pdf>.
23 Toronto Foundation for Student Success, "Beyond 3:30," online: Toronto Foundation for Student Success <http://tfss.ca/our-programs/beyond-330>.
24 John Lorinc, "What Are We Talking about When We Talk about Social Innovation?" online: The Philanthropist <http://thephilanthropist.ca/2017/01/what-are-we-talking-about-when-we-talk-about-social-innovation/>.
25 See Lorne Sossin, "Law School as Social Innovation" (2017) 48 VUWLR 225.
26 See Lorne Sossin, "Designing Administrative Justice" (2017) 34:1 Windsor YB Access Just 87.
27 See Erik S. Knutsen, "Deconstructing Automobile Insurance Coverage in Canada" (1 September 2008), online: SSRN <https://ssrn.com/abstract=1262084>.
28 HiiL, "About Us," online: HiiL <https://www.hiil.org/who-we-are/>.
29 *Ibid*; HiiL, "Annual Report and Accounts 2016" at 4, online: HiiL <https://www.hiil.org/wp-content/uploads/2018/07/HiiL_Annual_Report_and_Accounts_2016.pdf> ["Annual Report 2016"].
30 HiiL, "Burenrechter: State-of-the-Art Resolution for Neighbour Disputes," online: HiiL <https://www.hiil.org/projects/burenrechter-state-of-the-art-resolution-for-neighbour-disputes/>.
31 HiiL, "Annual Report 2016," *supra* note 29 at 17.
32 See Roger Smith, "Goodbye, Rechtwijzer: Hello, Justice42," online: Law, Technology and Access to Justice <https://law-tech-a2j.org/advice/goodbye-rechtwijzer-hello-justice42/>.
33 Salter, *supra* note 3.
34 Marco Chown Oved, "Lawyer-in-Your-Pocket App Helps during Police Carding," *Toronto Star* (2 July 2015), online: <https://www.thestar.com/news/gta/2015/07/02/lawyer-in-your-pocket-app-helps-during-police-carding.html>.
35 See also the Legal Design Lab, online: <http://www.legaltechdesign.com/>.
36 Winkler Institute for Dispute Resolution, "Yukon Simplified Court Forms," online: Winkler Institute for Dispute Resolution <https://winklerinstitute.ca/projects/featured-content-center/>.
37 Winkler Institute for Dispute Resolution, "Indigenous Youth: Designing a Better Justice System," online: Winkler Institute for Dispute Resolution <https://winklerinstitute.ca/projects/aboriginal-youth/>.
38 See Legal Innovation Zone, "Clausehound," online: Legal Innovation Zone, <http://www.legalinnovationzone.ca/startup/clausehound/>.
39 See Legal Innovation Zone, "Year in Review," online: Legal Innovation Zone <http://www.legalinnovationzone.ca/wp-content/uploads/2016-17-Year-in-Review-Postcard-.pdf>.
40 Julie Macfarlane, "The National Self-Represented Litigants Project: Identifying and Meeting the Needs of Self-Represented Litigants, Final Report" (May 2013), online: <https://

lawsocietyontario.azureedge.net/media/lso/media/legacy/pdf/s/self-represented_
project.pdf>.

41 National Self-Represented Litigants Project, "The CanLII Primer: Legal Research Principles
and CanLII Navigation for Self-Represented Litigants," online: <http://representing
yourselfcanada.com/wp-content/uploads/2016/11/NSRLP-CanLII-Primer-V1.pdf>.

42 Julie Macfarlane, "'Settlement Smarts' for Self-Represented Litigants: How to Use Settlement Processes Knowledgeably and Effectively" (July 2014), online: <https://representing
yourselfcanada.com/wp-content/uploads/2016/11/SettlementSmarts.pdf>.

43 Legal Design Lab, "Robot Lawyer Expert Chat Bot," online: Legal Design Lab <http://legal
techdesign.com/access-innovation/robot-lawyer-expert-chat-bot/>.

44 Samuel Gibbs, "Chatbot Lawyer Overturns 160,000 Parking Tickets in London and New
York," *The Guardian* (26 June 2016), online: <https://www.theguardian.com/technology/
2016/jun/28/chatbot-ai-lawyer-donotpay-parking-tickets-london-new-york>.

45 Leanna Garfield, "The Free Robot Lawyer That Appealed $3 Million in Parking Tickets Is
Now Available in the US," *Business Insider* (13 July 2017), online: <http://www.business
insider.com/robot-lawyer-chatbot-2017-7>.

46 Mark Malloy, "'Robot Lawyer' That Overturned 160,000 Parking Tickets Now Helping
Refugees," *The Telegraph* (7 March 2017), online: <http://www.telegraph.co.uk/technology/
2017/03/07/robot-lawyer-overturned-160000-parking-tickets-now-helping-refugees/>.

47 *Ibid.*

48 John Mannes, "DoNotPay Launches 1,000 New Bots to Help You with Your Legal Problems," *TechCrunch* (12 July 2017), online: <https://techcrunch.com/2017/07/12/
donotpay-launches-1000-new-bots-to-help-you-with-your-legal-problems/>.

49 CBC News, "New System to Fight Parking Tickets Will Make Process 'Faster, Easier,'"
CBC News (21 August 2017), online: <http://www.cbc.ca/news/canada/toronto/parking
-system-1.4255354>.

50 Anita Desai, *Social Enterprise and Labour Market Integration for Individuals Exiting
the Criminal Justice System: A Synthesis of Pilot Project Evaluations* (Ottawa: St. Leonard's
Society of Canada, 2015) at 1, online: <http://www.stleonards.ca/wp-content/uploads/
2013/05/SLSC_CDHPD_Social-enterprise-and-labour-market-integration-for
-individuals-exiting-the-criminal-justice-system-a-synthesis-of-pilot-project-evaluations.
pdf>.

51 *Ibid.*

52 *Ibid* at 2.

53 Correctional Service Canada, "FORUM on Corrections Research" (5 March 2015), online:
Correctional Service Canada <http://www.csc-scc.gc.ca/research/forum/e053/e053h
-eng.shtml>.

54 "Emma's Acres: Inmates and Victims Growing Food in Mission BC," online: Vancity <https://
www.vancity.com/AboutVancity/InvestingInCommunities/StoriesOfImpact/Food/
EmmasAcres/>.

55 *Ibid.*

56 BC Food Security Gateway, "Emma's Acres: An Innovative Approach to Stewarding the
Land in the Fraser Valley" (10 February 2016), online: BC Food Security Gateway <http://
bcfoodsecuritygateway.ca/emmas-acres-an-innovative-approach-to-stewarding-the
-land-in-the-fraser-valley/>.

Part 4
The Legal Profession and Meaningful
Access to Justice

12

Legal Culture as the Key to Affordable Access

M. Jerry McHale, QC

OVER THE LAST TWENTY-FIVE years, numerous reports have inquired into the problem of unaffordable and inaccessible justice in Canada. These reports have carefully explored the access problem and have made viable recommendations for ways to fix it. In fact, the quality of these recommendations is such that we can say that the ideas needed to make the system more accessible have already been identified. Over the same period, a collateral body of research has detailed the scale of unmet legal need as well as the excessively high individual and social costs that result when legal problems are not resolved. The research tells us that the public is increasingly unhappy about access barriers and that senior justice officials have declared access a top priority. The current situation, then, is that we appear to have the ideas, the motivation, the remedies, and the commitment required to solve this problem. Yet, on the ground, the justice system is less accessible now than it was twenty years ago.

Why is this so? Why, after decades of skillful analysis and promising reform initiatives, have we brought about relatively little change on the ground? What is preventing the justice system from making the changes needed? This chapter will identify a number of factors that play a role in frustrating access reform in Canada. Some of these factors – justice underfunding and lack of coordinated leadership, for example – have already received considerable attention and are fairly visible topics in the national reform conversation. The two related factors that will be considered in more detail here – what I am calling the problem of law's mandate and the problem of legal culture – have not yet received the attention they merit given their large role in frustrating access reform.

The mandate problem has to do with the fact that the demands being made on the justice system have changed and expanded enormously over the last sixty years, to the point where law is now tasked with responsibility for dealing with social problems that are well beyond its traditional expertise. The clearest examples of this are on the civil side, in family law matters, and criminally, in cases involving addicted, mentally disordered, and homeless offenders. In both areas, the system is struggling and is expending too many resources with too little effect; in both cases, the policy, program, and process changes needed to make the system work better rely on non-traditional perspectives and values that depart significantly from customary legal approaches. The reforms therefore face considerable resistance from mainstream legal culture.

The culture of any identifiable group consists of shared values and common beliefs that are expressed through attitudes and behaviours that those within the group regard as normal and that they expect to see in each other. Culture is an enormously powerful force that both defines and enforces norms. For centuries, adversarial values have been at the heart of legal culture, but more recently questions have been raised about the limits of the adversarial approach and the need for different values and additional approaches to disputing. The access reports have repeatedly suggested that the complex, competitive, and labour-intensive approaches characteristic of the adversarial model create significant barriers to justice by magnifying party differences and making legal services too complicated, too expensive, and too slow. More than twenty years ago, the report of the Canadian Bar Association's (CBA) Task Force on Systems of Civil Justice stated that "a preoccupation with gaining advantage through an adversarial approach too often has the result of displacing substantive communication, common sense and a problem-solving orientation, all of which assist in resolving disputes."[1] Accordingly, when the access reports make recommendations intended to foster a simpler, cheaper, and faster system, they often propose changes that are either explicitly non-adversarial or are otherwise at odds with the adversarial attitudes and beliefs that remain deeply and durably embedded in legal culture. The same CBA report also warned of the possibility that the entrenched legal culture would resist change and frustrate reform efforts:

> The inertia borne of comfort and familiarity with the current system has led some to suggest that the reforms possible within the constraints of local legal culture and tradition simply cannot affect significant problems such as delay, costs and lack of understanding. Under this approach only modest reforms are carried out, and improvements are correspondingly modest.[2]

This caution was prophetic. In spite of many more reports and much similar advice over the intervening years, "the constraints of legal culture" have proven to be an overriding force. While legal culture has undoubtedly been influenced by non-adversarial perspectives, and while some measure of productive headway has been made in the use of non-adversarial processes, progress has been nowhere near the scale required to move the access dial beyond the modest improvements predicted by the CBA.

This relative lack of progress raises the possibility that changing the justice system requires more than the instrumental projects like amending rules, simplifying forms, or increasing legal aid funding that reformers have focused on. Reform has focused too much on the machinery and operations of the justice system and not enough on the internal culture and mindset of the people who operate it. We need to animate reform initiatives with a new spirit, one that is bold and adopts new attitudes, new ways of thinking, and new behaviours. Reform strategies must recognize that the system will not change unless and until the people running the system change.

Background

Dozens of large-scale civil legal needs research studies over the last twenty years have provided much important information about how often people experience legal problems and what happens when they do. These studies have been supplemented by numerous academic papers and professional reports, the cumulative effect of which is to show that our justice systems are poorly aligned with the needs of people with civil and family legal problems.

The primary access barriers described in the reports are cost, delay, and complexity. These barriers impair both public access and the system's ability to produce just outcomes.[3] Of the primary barriers, complexity of substantive and procedural law is the most important. For represented parties, complexity drives time and cost; for unrepresented parties, it renders the system incomprehensible.

A 2016 legal needs study conducted by the Canadian Forum on Civil Justice concluded that over a given three-year period, nearly half of all adult Canadians will experience one or more serious and difficult-to-resolve legal problem(s).[4] About 95 percent of these people will try to do something about their problems, but less than 20 percent will seek legal advice, and only 7 percent will utilize tribunals or courts.[5] Ultimately, nearly one-third of the respondents in this study did not resolve their problems, about 15 percent resolved some but not all of their legal problems, and over half did resolve their problems.[6]

The high cost of legal services is the primary factor deterring people from seeking legal advice.[7] Some manage to resolve their legal problems informally. When that is not possible, people either walk away or attempt, always inefficiently and often unsuccessfully, to navigate the civil and family courts without legal representation.

The negative consequences flowing from inaccessible legal services have been well documented. Unresolved legal problems tend to generate more legal

problems, and they tend to cluster together with related emotional and physical problems, family and relationship problems, employment problems, and
housing problems.[8] These clusters of interrelated legal and social problems have
the potential to trigger a downward spiral away from the social mainstream
into exclusion and dependency.[9] Beyond individual impacts, there is also evidence that governments incur additional costs for healthcare, social services,
housing subsidies, and employment insurance resulting from unresolved
legal problems. Further costs are incurred in the private sector through employee
absence and diminished productivity.[10]

Numerous reports exploring these problems have been generated by lawyers,
judges, administrators, academics, auditors, and governments. Every common
law jurisdiction in the world confronts similar access problems, and virtually
all have published many reports containing extensive recommendations and
suggested reforms. The analyses are all similar, and the recommendations
have become repetitive, but the language of the reports is growing more urgent.
A Canadian report says, for example: "We need to make visible the pain caused
by inadequate access ... We need to illuminate how profoundly unequal access
to justice is in Canada. We cannot shy away from the dramatic level of change
required."[11]

Canadians live in a densely regulated and legally complex society where legal
problems are an inevitable part of everyday life. When rights and obligations
are brought into force by law, there is an implicit public expectation that the
means to exercise these rights and enforce these obligations will be available to
those whose lives are governed by them. A right without an affordable remedy is
in some respects worse than no right at all. It is, in effect, an "unfulfilled promise"
that creates a potentially corrosive inequity between those who can afford to
enforce rights and those who cannot.[12] The role of access to justice in maintaining
both public confidence and the rule of law has been well recognized in western
legal systems for hundreds of years.[13]

For all of these reasons, it is particularly troubling that access reform appears
to be at an impasse. Those leading the reform charge are trying to make sense
of the fact that in spite of several decades of studies, reports, advice, and recommendations, as well as countless legislative, procedural, program, and policy
reform initiatives, contemporary civil and family justice systems are less accessible today than they were twenty years ago.[14]

Impediments to Access Reform: The Usual Suspects
The Action Committee on Access to Justice in Civil and Family Matters[15] describes the gap between these many promising access reform recommendations

and the system's current realities as the "implementation gap," and concludes that "it is going to take more than wise advice to change the system."[16] If good ideas were sufficient, the problem would already be solved!

A cluster of factors has been identified frequently enough in reports, papers, and speeches to be characterized as the usual explanations for the gap. Each of the following five deficits contributes in a substantial way to the access problem, and each will ultimately need to be addressed as part of an effective response to the implementation gap. As will be discussed, however, these factors rest on, and to a certain extent are a product of, deeper problems that should have a prior call on our time and attention.

Lack of Resources

Access barriers are often attributed to a lack of necessary resources and underfunding of the civil justice system. Legal aid funding has been on a downward trajectory for years, and many courts have long-standing judicial vacancies. Calls for more legal aid, more judicial appointments, and more justice services are ubiquitous but largely ineffective. Justice occupies an increasingly distant third place behind health and education in government funding priorities. Realistically, even if government were to increase funding, there would never be enough money to address current levels of unmet legal need with existing service delivery models.[17]

Lack of Administrative Coordination and Coherent Leadership

The Action Committee's report observes that the administration of justice in Canada is fragmented and that the justice system lacks coordinated leadership.[18] The judiciary, government, and bar operate independently and largely within separate silos, without unified leadership and without a common vision or a coordinated plan for reform. Professor Erik Knudsen observes that "[t]he influential players in the civil justice system ... are so fragmented in their influence on the system that they appear almost institutionally designed to maintain a momentum that impedes access to justice."[19]

Lack of Essential Management Tools

The justice system has not exploited some of the modern management tools now well utilized by other disciplines. All sectors have been slow to capitalize on the benefits of information technology. As the Action Committee notes, "[w]hile technological innovations are transforming much of modern life, they appear to be bypassing the justice system."[20] Similarly, Canadian justice systems are failing to utilize metrics to measure program performance or evaluate the effectiveness of reforms. This lack of objective evidence impairs policy development, hampers effective planning, and weakens claims for justice funding.

Lack of Internal Professional Commitment to Change

Many senior leaders in the justice system have demonstrated a sincere commitment to the access reform agenda. However, below the leadership level and down to the front lines, there is much less engagement with the problem and less investment in finding a solution. Part of the explanation for this may be that many judges, lawyers, and court administrators are already too busy meeting the daily demands of their jobs. They do not think they have the time to dedicate to systemic reform, they do not see the macro-level institutional problems as their remit, and they are probably not sure what they can do about them anyway. Possibly, the high profile given the access issue by their leaders allows them to assume that the problem is being taken care of by someone else. A survey of American law firms asked "why we have not seen more dramatic changes in law firms' behavior despite widespread agreement among firm leaders that they face a host of legitimate threats and challenges that will only increase going forward."[21] The survey found that "the biggest impediment to change, identified by 64% of firm leaders, is that partners resist most change efforts" and that "part of the problem is simple lack of awareness among rank and file partners ... most partners are unaware of what they might do differently."[22]

This inaction can turn into frank opposition. Law's conservative and risk-averse culture is always wary of change, especially if it implies a threat to economic self-interest. The dominant hourly billing model, for example, endures largely untouched, even though critics have long argued that it creates perverse incentives and encourages costly and protracted litigation.[23] While the justice system is not working for most who try to use it, and it is not working as well as it once did for many lawyers, it is still working well enough for quite a few lawyers. For those insiders who believe their income and status are secure, concerns about inaccessible justice and declining public confidence are insufficient reason to engage in reform work.

Lack of Public Engagement and Political Support

There is a corresponding lack of engagement in the public and political spheres. The public is much more likely to respond to health, education, or housing concerns than to justice issues. To the extent that government resource allocations are determined by public priorities, this weakens the justice sector in the inter-ministry competition for finite government resources. When a justice issue does capture public attention, it is likely to involve criminal law. Despite the fact that more members of the public are affected by civil or family law problems, crime is more likely to mobilize greater public, media, and political attention, disadvantaging the civil and family side even further. As Hazel Genn has observed, "[T]here are plenty of votes in crime, but few in civil justice."[24]

*

Each of the five impediments to access reform just described contributes in a real and significant way to the intractability of the access problem. I suggest, however, that there are two additional factors receiving less attention but ultimately playing a larger role in frustrating access reform. The first is the mismatch between law's modern mandate and its traditional competencies; the second is legal culture's deep resistance to change. These factors lie at the core of both the need for reform and the relative ineffectiveness of reform efforts so far.

Impediments to Access Reform: The Mandate Problem

In relative terms, Canada's justice system is one of the best in the world. The 2020 Rule of Law Index ranks Canada 9 out of 128 globally and 9 out of 37 by income group.[25] This is encouraging, but as a relative measure it provides only limited comfort. What does it mean to have a superior system if it is largely inaccessible?

One of the salient features of contemporary Western justice systems is how much more extensive and complicated the justice mandate has grown over the last sixty years. Governments have expanded their legislative and regulatory reach to unprecedented levels. Complex regulatory frameworks now govern an array of personal, commercial, and social problems that for most of history were largely unregulated and effectively out of scope. And as entitlements grew, so did people's expectations about what law should do for them.

In the 1960s and 1970s, the concept of legal empowerment took root in public policy. There was a belief that law, combined with expertise from the social sciences, could manage and possibly transform social problems – even those as daunting as poverty and racism. Justice was increasingly seen as an important determinant of social well-being, and our modern attitudes towards access to justice began to take shape. Legal aid plans were created and community law clinics began to appear. It was a time of such institutional optimism that politicians were inspired to propose that governments could engineer "the great society" (in the United States) and "a just society" (in Canada).[26] In service of such aims and driven by rapidly changing social norms, legislators began to move into relatively uncharted territory. Divorce reform, for example, radically altered historical approaches to family law and created a wide path from marital discord directly to the courthouse. At a similar order of magnitude but on a different front, the *Canadian Charter of Rights and Freedoms* entrenched a broad range of rights and protections and expanded the reach and role of the courts enormously. Regulatory control expanded in areas as diverse as human rights, health and safety, the environment, worker compensation, employment, tenancy, labour, and consumer law.

The underlying assumption driving this approach was that important social and individual needs could be legislatively framed as entitlements, and that the courts would help realize these entitlements by managing the flow of rights disputes that would follow. By 1985, Lawrence M. Friedman, in reference to this "law explosion" and the "tremendous increase in certain uses of legal process," described this dynamic and its demands on the legal system as a "general expectation of justice, and a general expectation of recompense for injuries and loss," and observed that "together they make up a demand for 'total justice.'"[27]

A growing body of rights together with the public expectation of total justice generated more claims than Western justice systems had ever before handled. Initially, the systems tried to meet the demand by expanding the size and number of courts, but it was inevitable that this approach would eventually reach its fiscal limits. A range of access to justice strategies helped to increase efficiency and expand capacity, but they have never helped enough, and any gains they achieved have been more than negated by the steady and relentless growth in procedural complexity. In the long run, civil justice systems have been unable to deal with a large portion of existing justiciable issues. Meanwhile, the inventory of legislated rights continues to expand and we continue to steer rights-holders towards an inaccessible court system for enforcement.

The problem of capacity is more than just a matter of large numbers, however. It is also a question of the way in which individual cases are managed and the inefficiencies that arise from our excessive reliance on the adversarial style of resolving disputes. Adversarial values, attitudes, behaviours, and processes dominate the way nearly all justice system professionals think about and manage conflict. Adversarial theory presumes that justice flows from a strenuous clash of opposing rights. Thus, new cases fall into a process that is antagonistic and confrontational from the start. Every dispute is framed as a battle to be won, and every opposing party is regarded as an enemy to be defeated. Every case is worked up as if it will be resolved at trial, even though it almost certainly won't be. Meeting the trial-ready standard requires that every stone be turned and that costly interim skirmishes be fought in search of tactical advantage.

In terms of system capacity, there are two essential problems with this approach. First, it consumes far more time and money than is necessary to resolve most problems. The complex, contentious, and labour-intensive methods of the adversarial process needlessly magnify party differences and protract conflict, making legal process too complicated, too expensive, and too slow. Because it does not prioritize settlement, early negotiations tend to be characterized by exaggerated and inflexible demands. More serious negotiations occur only much later in the game, after the bulk of the transaction costs have been incurred.

The second problem has to do with the way the adversarial process frames the issues to be resolved. The adversarial model recognizes only rights-based legal questions. When, for example, a separating spouse seeks legal advice, her lawyer will listen to her narrative in order to identify the rights issues appropriate for adjudication. These legal issues will virtually always be a subset of a larger and more complicated human problem. The client's original concerns will include diverse substantive, psychological, interpersonal, and procedural needs or interests that remain problematic and relevant to her but are characterized as irrelevant to the legal process.

In this way, the client's problem is reframed and decontextualized. The legal issues are lifted out of the larger context that is the client's reality and the problem is redefined as the smaller, partial set of more easily answered legal questions. The client's experience is often dominated by powerful and complex emotions, and her energy is consumed by conflicted, nuanced, and often dysfunctional interpersonal dynamics, all of which she needs to see resolved. Reframing the narrative in terms of only the legal issues removes these vital elements of the human problem from consideration. This is an oversimplification that leaves information that is often essential to a workable resolution on the cutting room floor. The standard legal analysis reduces the visibility of the underlying non-legal problems but not their vitality or influence. In fact, such vitality and influence may grow as each party learns that the process is about seeing the other as an opponent to be overcome. In this way, the essential problems persist and continue to complicate the lives of the parties, even to the extent of undermining the utility of the eventual legal outcome.

Of course, the litigation system is only doing what it was designed for. It was designed to answer legal questions; it was not designed to resolve social or interpersonal problems. But society has changed, and the adversarial process does not translate adequately into the hyper-regulated, dispute-rich, and resource-strained world of the twenty-first century. The justice system needs additional methods and tools if it is to respond to modern needs and satisfy its mandate.

Processes like mediation and collaborative practice in civil and family law, and problem-solving courts and restorative justice in criminal law, are trying to implement the methods and tools the system needs. These non-adversarial (or less adversarial) processes work by recontextualizing the legal issues in order to reclaim and manage the otherwise unruly non-legal components. These processes give lawyers, judges, and parties the information and the tools they need to recognize and comprehensively manage the legal problem in the context of, and while accounting for, the nuances and complexity of the larger human problem.

After several decades of unsuccessful reform efforts, we must accept that the justice system, in its current form and absent fundamental change, is not likely to manage cases any better in the future than it does now. The justice system must either equip itself at scale with the non-adversarial theories, skills, and services needed to better manage the underlying social problems that fill its dockets or reconcile itself to the status quo for the long term. The good news is that many of the ideas and innovations needed to shift in the directions proposed above have already been identified and have been, to a considerable extent, tested and proven.[28] In the meantime, the disruption flowing from unmet legal need and self-represented litigants will continue, and to the extent that the justice system does not resolve these problems from the inside, it is likely that government, using information technology and deregulation, will attempt to fix them from the outside.

Impediments to Access Reform: Adversarial Legal Culture

Calls for Legal Culture Change

The adversarial system is built on a foundation of substantive and procedural law, ethical standards, and legal culture that is over two centuries old. While our justice systems are less purely adversarial today than in the past, fundamental aspects of the adversarial model endure because of their social utility:

> [The adversarial model's] strengths lie in the concepts of the independence of the Bar and Bench from governments, the autonomy of the parties, the power of examination and cross-examination to elicit facts, and in the fact that courts are open to scrutiny and that court officers are disinterested parties in often hotly contested and sensitive disputes.[29]

The model's weaknesses include its cost and complexity, the time it requires, its confrontational methods, its detrimental impact on relationships, its limited range of remedial options, its failure to take non-legal interests into account, and its emphasis on winning over problem solving.

In response to these limitations, the access to justice reports have made recommendations intended to mitigate the harsher impacts of adversarial procedure and promote increased reliance on collaborative values and non-adversarial dispute resolution processes. The reports are careful to avoid framing simplistic dichotomies that imply that adversarial process is bad and non-adversarial process is good. Rather, the vision is of a multi-option justice system that utilizes a range of dispute resolution processes by matching the unique nature and needs of each dispute with an appropriate resolution process. Within this vision, access to justice includes but goes beyond the courts, and litigation is regarded as a valued but last resort. This vision is not yet realized, except on a very limited scale. While traditional legal culture has unquestionably made some room to accommodate non-adversarial values and collaborative processes, especially in family law, the greater part of civil practice holds fast to adversarial values, thinking, and behaviour.

There is growing attention in the access to justice reports to the importance of changing culture. Nearly fifteen years ago, a family law access report published by the BC Justice Review Task Force (JRTF) argued that effective reform necessarily involves looking beyond administrative and procedural changes to culture:

> We conclude that changing the culture of family law involves more than changes to services, procedures, legislation and court structure. It also involves people ... changes to systems and procedures alone will not be sufficient, and in fact are secondary to changes in values, standards, principles and practices that constitute the day-to-day workings of the family justice system.[30]

More recently, the Action Committee's final report described change in legal culture as "urgently needed" and as an essential part of successful law reform. The report declared one of its three purposes to be "to identify and promote a new way of thinking – a culture shift – to guide our approach to reform."[31] This culture shift demands "a fresh approach"[32] in order to "move away from old patterns and old approaches."[33] Like other reports, it links reform, in part, to broader and deeper integration of consensual values and problem-solving approaches,[34] and it calls for increased lawyer education focused on consensual dispute resolution, alternative dispute resolution (ADR), and other non-adversarial skills.[35]

Earlier Action Committee reports made similar points. The report of the Court Processes Simplification Working Group recommended expanded use of ADR programs and called for a "culture shift at all levels of the court system."[36] The report of the Family Justice Working Group said that "the implementation gap is a function of the culture of the justice system and its incomplete embrace of non-adversarial or consensual dispute resolution processes ... we see further culture change as one of the more important options for enhanced access to family justice."[37]

None of these recommendations assumes or is meant to imply that ADR is a panacea or is appropriate for all cases. It is beyond question that there will always be disputes that require the procedural protections of litigation and that in some circumstances people could be harmed or disadvantaged through participation in informal process. That said, the justice system over-utilizes litigation, and after over thirty years of experience with ADR processes, it is clear not only that ADR can be used safely and effectively but also that we are nowhere near exploiting its full potential.

What Does Cultural Resistance Look Like?
How does legal culture resist reform, and what would a shift in legal culture look like? This question can be answered by looking at two of the recommendations repeated most frequently in the access to justice reports: the calls for streamlined civil procedure and for expanded use of collaborative dispute resolution processes. As these areas have been the focus of considerable reform effort, they are also where cultural resistance to change is most apparent.

The role of legal culture in reform of civil procedure was explicitly addressed by the Supreme Court of Canada in *Hryniak v Mauldin,* in which the court noted the growing support within the justice system for non-adversarial dispute resolution, as well as the "developing consensus that the traditional balance struck by extensive pre-trial processes and the conventional trial no longer reflects the modern reality and needs to be re-adjusted." The court called for simplified and proportionate pretrial procedures and stated that "[i]ncreasingly, there is recognition that a culture shift is required in order to create an environment promoting timely and affordable access to the civil justice system."[38]

Over the last twenty years, Canadian reports have made hundreds of recommendations relating to timely and affordable civil process. These recommendations always call for simplified and proportionate procedures, and they propose a now-familiar list of reform objectives, including prevention, triage, matching, multi-tracking, timeliness, and flexibility. Procedural suggestions typically include expedited disclosure, limits on discovery, limits on experts, increased case planning, increased judicial intervention, and increased settlement orientation. While these ideas are almost universally endorsed in access reports, they are rarely, if ever, effectively implemented. Even when they make it beyond the recommendation stage and are written into civil rules, they ultimately have very little impact on the style of practice. Litigation practice remains substantially unchanged because it continues to be informed by older attitudes and traditional beliefs about how litigation and judging are supposed to work. These beliefs include:

- the belief that more process is a guarantee of more fairness
- the assumption that litigation is the one-size-fits-all process appropriate for every dispute
- the practice of managing every case as if it will ultimately be decided by a judge at trial[39]
- the belief that the only proper advocacy is zealous advocacy
- the exploitation of court rules to play labour-intensive litigation games
- the pretrial focus on winning skirmishes rather than solving problems
- the neglect of the principle of proportionality
- the convention of the judge as a umpire presiding above the fray while counsel make their case as they see fit.

A prime example of attempted rules reform flowed from the 2006 report of a group of senior justice leaders styled as the BC Justice Review Task Force. The report, titled *Effective and Affordable Justice*, aimed high in asserting that "maintaining the status quo is not an option" and "fundamental change is necessary," and it argued for streamlined Supreme Court rules and changes in legal culture.[40] The initiative resulted in a full revision of the BC Supreme Court civil and family rules, but the original JRTF recommendations were modified and considerably diluted throughout a contentious drafting process, and the innovations that remained in the revised civil and family rules when they were promulgated in 2010 were resisted and diluted again in practice.[41] The result was that the desired fundamental reform to the rules and significant changes to legal culture were not achieved, and there has been no impact on the underlying problems of cost, delay, and complexity.

This has been the fate of virtually all attempts at rules reform, and the lesson typically learned from such efforts is that procedural reform will not come about without a corresponding shift in legal culture. A 2015 report of the American College of Trial Lawyers and the Institute for the Advancement of the American Legal System reviewed the progress of extensive civil procedure reform efforts in several American states and concluded: "As we have studied the rules and reviewed the comments and the results of the pilot projects, one thing has become very clear to us: rules reform without a change in culture will not be effective."[42]

The mediation story is similar. Beginning in the mid-1980s in Canada, mediation was promoted as a simpler, faster, and cheaper alternative to litigation. The model introduced at that time was described as a facilitated, interest-based negotiation that frames the parties as joint problem solvers, not adversaries, and works to minimize conflict and support cooperation and collaboration. By

working with the underlying interests, needs, emotions, and relational dynamics, mediation is designed to address both legal and non-legal interests in order
to generate affordable, nuanced, practical, and durable resolutions. The process
promotes self-determination and party participation and aims to have the parties, with the necessary legal support in the background, engage directly in
crafting their own agreement.

The use of mediation slowly expanded through the 1980s and 1990s, and while
it is not possible to quantify the number of mediations in the system today, it
is safe to say both that its use has grown considerably and that it has not grown
enough. General support for non-adversarial values and collaborative skills has
also grown. A growing settlement orientation, including greater use of judicial
settlement processes and the introduction of collaborative practice, also suggests
a meaningful shift in legal culture. Collaborative values have been incorporated
into some legislation.[43] As the Action Committee put it, however, "[d]espite
these changes, reports and inquiries continue to call for further reform, saying
that the changes to date, while welcome, are simply not enough."[44]

The reports emphasize that the justice system has so far failed to maximize
the potential of mediation. This failure takes three forms. First, mediation is
used too little. Litigation remains by far the first resort and the preferred
procedural option. Relative to the scale of litigation, the use of mediation is
marginal. While mediation is not appropriate for every case, its efficacy is well
established and practitioners know how to identify and manage its limitations.[45] Several Canadian reports have responded to the underutilization of
mediation by calling on governments to use legislation to require litigants to
participate in some form of ADR.

Second, when mediation is used, it is often used too late in the litigation
process. It is typically initiated during the late stages of litigation, as the case
closes in on trial and after many of the fiscal and relationship costs of litigation
have already been incurred. The potential efficacy of mediation is further
undermined to the extent that the parties are more polarized in their rights-
based positions by this point.

Third, mediation is conceived not as an alternative but as an adjunct to
the adversarial process. The form of the mediation process usually employed
has drifted far from the non-adversarial, interest-based model introduced in
the 1980s, and in the course of doing so it has taken on a decidedly adversarial
character. Rosalie Abella warned twenty years ago that "[e]ven alternate dispute
resolution mechanisms, hailed at first as the expeditious alternatives to cumber-
some court procedures, are themselves turning into procedural mimics of the
court system."[46] While many of the outer forms of mediation have been pre-
served, adversarial values have displaced much of mediation's collaborative

spirit. The model of the mediator who facilitates a cooperative negotiation aimed at helping the parties construct an agreement that responds to their underlying relational interests and psychological needs has been displaced by adversarial attitudes and strategies. Most mediations are actually facilitated distributive negotiations that move forwards not by reconciling interests but by iterative concessions, compromises, and trade-offs on rights-based positions. The process looks very much like a traditional, competitive lawyer-to-lawyer negotiation save that it is supervised by a mediator. The primary basis for settlement is not what the parties need on the facts but what a court would decide on the legal issues. Mediators readily influence the substantive terms of settlement by offering non-binding opinions on how they believe a court would dispose of matters at issue. This highly distributive and evaluative form of mediation now dominates practice. It is legitimate and useful as far as it goes – it does settle cases – but it is used too seldom, too late, and in a manner that ignores the more sophisticated relational goals of interest-based mediation while importing many of the traditional disadvantages of litigation.

The gravitational pull of the adversarial model has captured mediation and locked it into a tight orbit. Adversarial culture has excised most of the non-adversarial elements from mediation and has made it a venue that preserves the familiar strategies and customary formats of adversarial disputing. Linda Ippolito, an Ontario lawyer, asks, "What happened to the 'alternative' in 'alternative dispute resolution'?" and observes:

We have recast [ADR] in our own image, adapted it to our mindset and for our purposes rather than expanding ourselves outward to meet it. Instead of taking the opportunity to open ourselves up to the larger world of conflict resolution, we have taken these practices and adapted them to fit into the legal box ... It has been institutionalized and formularized within the profession.[47]

Mediation has been colonized by traditional litigation processes and by adversarial culture, and in the process much of its potential as an effective response to the access to justice problem has been lost. This represents not only a lost opportunity for litigants but also a lost market for lawyers and mediators. Those promoting mediation in the mid-1980s assumed that its demonstrable capacity to respond to the problems of cost, delay, and complexity and to produce quick, affordable, and practical outcomes would almost inevitably lead to rapid growth in the use of mediation and to a greater reliance on collaborative strategies in practice generally. This was a miscalculation that overestimated the impact of a good idea and underestimated the durability of adversarial values. The result, as Carrie Menkel-Meadow writes, is that "a critical challenge to the status quo has been blunted," and, in a reversal of expectations, adversarial values have shaped mediation more than mediation has managed to influence the adversarial system.[48] Menkel-Meadow describes the adversarial model as "so powerful a heuristic and organizing framework for our culture that, much like a great whale, it seems to swallow up any effort to modify or transform it."[49]

These attempts to reform civil procedure and to introduce new methods of dispute resolution are specific examples intended to illustrate the general proposition that legal culture will continue to trump reform strategies and that otherwise sensible access to justice initiatives will continue to fail unless and until legal culture achieves a much deeper and more sophisticated alignment with reform goals. Such alignment would demand the creation of a true multi-option civil justice system where disputes are seen as problems to be solved, not battles to be won, and where cases are managed to settlement, not trial. It would presume that lawyers were prepared to default to consensus-based resolution processes and would have the knowledge and skills necessary to collaborate effectively in all contexts, including litigation. It would not require the abandonment of adversarial processes, skills, or values, but it would require that they be employed only when necessary and not as a matter of course in every dispute.

Conclusion

Senior justice leaders now speak of a system that is badly broken,[50] unsustainable, and in urgent need of change.[51] The access problem is described as a crisis[52] that threatens the continuation of the legal profession's monopoly[53] and puts the survival of the system at stake.[54] Numerous studies and reports have made hundreds of viable suggestions for ways to fix this problem, but more than two decades of inability to implement these suggestions strongly suggest that we need to look somewhere new for the solution.

The lack of progress on access reform over the last two decades is substantially attributable to legal culture's refusal to accept the manifest need for new ways of doing business. This problem is compounded by the fact that the justice mandate has expanded over the last several decades to include a number of complex social problems for which law's traditional skills and methods – the old ways of doing business – are not well suited. This situation is further complicated by operational and organizational deficits that include insufficient funding, lack of coordinated leadership, failure to exploit metrics and technology, lack of internal professional engagement, and lack of public and political support. This hierarchy of challenges can be tackled effectively only from the foundation up. That is, the justice system must first address the necessary changes to legal culture in order to come to terms with its expanded mandate. Only at that point will it be positioned to effectively address its operational and organizational deficits.

Notes

1 Task Force on Systems of Civil Justice, *Report of the Canadian Bar Association Task Force on Systems of Civil Justice* (Ottawa: Canadian Bar Association, 1996) at 18.

2 *Ibid* at 18.

3 Action Committee on Access to Justice in Civil and Family Matters, *Access to Civil and Family Justice: A Roadmap for Change* (Ottawa: Action Committee on Access to Justice in Civil and Family Matters 2013) at 4, online: Canadian Forum on Civil Justice <http://www.cfcj-fcjc.org/sites/default/files/docs/2013/AC_Report_English_Final.pdf> [*Roadmap*].

4 Trevor C.W. Farrow et al, *Everyday Legal Problems and the Cost of Justice in Canada: Overview Report* (Toronto: Canadian Forum on Civil Justice, 2016) at 6, online: Canadian Forum on Civil Justice <http://www.cfcj-fcjc.org/sites/default/files//Everyday%20Legal%20Problems%20and%20the%20Cost%20of%20Justice%20in%20Canada%20-%20Overview%20Report.pdf>.

5 *Ibid* at 9.

6 *Ibid* at 11.

7 Action Committee on Access to Justice in Civil and Family Matters, *Roadmap, supra* note 3 at 4.

8 Ab Currie, *The Legal Problems of Everyday Life: The Nature, Extent and Consequences of Justiciable Problems Experienced by Canadians* (Ottawa: Department of Justice Canada, 2009) at 42.

9 *Ibid* at 47.

10 Farrow et al, *supra* note 4 at 12 and 16.

11 Canadian Bar Association Access to Justice Committee, *Reaching Equal Justice: An Invitation to Envision and Act* (Ottawa: Canadian Bar Association, 2013) at 6, online: Canadian Bar Association <http://www.cba.org/CBA-Equal-Justice/Equal-Justice-Initiative/Reports> [*Equal Justice*].

12 As stated by members of the public: "To me, legal rights are an unfulfilled promise" and "The good old dollar defines what our legal rights are." See Amanda Dodge, "Access to Justice Metrics Informed by the Voices of Marginalized Community Members: Themes, Definitions and Recommendations Arising from Community Consultations" (Report prepared for the Canadian Bar Association Access to Justice Committee, 2013) at 2, online: <http://www.cba.org/CBA/cle/PDF/JUST13_Paper_Dodge.pdf>.

13 See Graham Sharp, "The Right of Access to Justice under the Rule of Law: Guaranteeing an Effective Remedy" (2016), online: Canadian Institute for the Administration of Justice <https://ciaj-icaj.ca/wp-content/uploads/page/2016/05/the-rule-of-law-and-the-right-to-effective-access.pdf>.

14 Action Committee on Access to Justice in Civil and Family Matters, *Roadmap, supra* note 3 at 6.

15 Convened in 2008 by then Chief Justice of Canada Beverly McLachlin, the Action Committee is composed of senior justice system leaders from across Canada and is mandated to develop priorities to improve access to civil and family justice.

16 Action Committee on Access to Justice in Civil and Family Matters, *Meaningful Change for Family Justice: Beyond Wise Words. Final Report of the Family Justice Working Group*

(Ottawa: Action Committee on Access to Justice in Civil and Family Matters, 2013) at 9 [*Meaningful Change*].

17 See Gillian Hadfield, "The Cost of Law: Promoting Access to Justice through the (Un)corporate Practice of Law" (2014) 38 Int'l Rev L & Econ 43.

18 Action Committee on Access to Justice in Civil and Family Matters, *Roadmap, supra* note 3 at iii.

19 Erik S. Knutsen, Book Review of *Middle Income Access to Justice* by Michael Trebilcock, Anthony Duggan, & Lorne Sossin, eds (2013) 50 Osgoode Hall LJ 1063–70 at 1066.

20 Action Committee on Access to Justice in Civil and Family Matters, "Report of the Access to Legal Services Working Group" (May 2012) at 3, online: Canadian Forum on Civil Justice <http://www.cfcj-fcjc.org/sites/default/files/docs/2012/Report%20of%20the%20Access%20to%20Legal%20Services%20Working%20Group.pdf>.

21 Eric Seeger & Thomas Clay, *2016 Law Firms in Transition: An Altman Weil Flash Survey* (2016) at vi, online: Altman Weil Inc. <http://www.altmanweil.com/dir_docs/resource/95e9df8e-9551-49da-9e25-2cd868319447_document.pdf>.

22 *Ibid* at vi. The survey also found that "[o]nly 4% of law firm leaders rated their partners as highly adaptable to change."

23 See D.A. Ipp, "Reforms to the Adversarial Process in Civil Litigation – Part I" (1995) 69 Austl LJ 705 at 726. "Our system of civil litigation creates perverse incentives for lawyers" with the consequence that "dubious delaying tactics, claims brought for tactical reasons rather than their true merit, sham defences and unnecessary motions are frequently to be observed."

24 Hazel Genn, *Judging Civil Justice* (Cambridge: Cambridge University Press, 2010) at 39.

25 World Justice Project, *World Justice Project Rule of Law Index 2020* (Washington, DC: World Justice Project, 2019) at 21, online: World Justice Project <https://worldjusticeproject.org/sites/default/files/documents/WJP-ROLI-2020-Online_0.pdf>.

26 "The great society" described a collection of domestic programs initiated in the mid-1960s by US President Lyndon Johnson. Pierre Elliot Trudeau campaigned successfully for the federal Liberal Party leadership in 1968 on the promise to make Canada into "a just society."

27 Lawrence Friedman, *Total Justice* (New York: Russell Sage Foundation, 1985) at 5.

28 The elements of a different procedural and cultural paradigm are explored widely in the literature under topics including non-adversarial justice, interest-based negotiation, consensual dispute resolution, collaborative practice, therapeutic jurisprudence, comprehensive lawyering, procedural justice, problem-solving courts, integrated courts, traditional decision making, restorative justice, participatory justice, preventative law, and others.

29 Michael King et al, *Non-adversarial Justice* (Alexandria, NSW: Federation Press, 2009) at 1.

30 BC Justice Review Task Force, "A New Justice System for Families and Children: Report of the Family Justice Reform Working Group to the Justice Review Task Force" (May 2005) at 8 and 110, online: Government of British Columbia <https://www2.gov.bc.ca/assets/gov/law-crime-and-justice/about-bc-justice-system/justice-reform-initiatives/final_05_05.pdf>.

31 Action Committee on Access to Justice in Civil and Family Matters, *Roadmap, supra* note 3 at iii

32 *Ibid* at 6.

33 *Ibid* at 5.

34 *Ibid* at 18.

35 *Ibid* at 21 and 22.

36 Action Committee on Access to Justice in Civil and Family Matters, "Report of the Court Processes Simplification Working Group" (May 2012) at 16, 20, and 22, online: Canadian Forum on Civil Justice <http://www.cfcj-fcjc.org/sites/default/files/docs/2013/Report%20of%20the%20Court%20Processes%20Simplification%20Working%20Group.pdf>.

37 Action Committee on Access to Justice in Civil and Family Matters, *Meaningful Change, supra* note 16 at 3.

38 *Hryniak v Mauldin,* 2014 SCC 7.

39 Typically trials rates are reported at less than 2 percent of filings.

40 BC Justice Review Task Force, "Effective and Affordable Civil Justice: Report of the Civil Justice Reform Working Group to the Justice Review Task Force" (November 2006) at vii, online: Government of British Columbia <https://www2.gov.bc.ca/assets/gov/law-crime-and-justice/about-bc-justice-system/justice-reform-initiatives/cjrwg_report_11_06.pdf>.

41 See Canadian Bar Association, British Columbia Branch, "Supreme Court Rules Survey – 2014" (2014), online: Canadian Bar Association, British Columbia Branch <https://www.cbabc.org/CBAMediaLibrary/cba_bc/pdf/Surveys/SummarySupremeCourtCivilRules-Survey2014.pdf>. For example, of fifty-one respondents who commented on the principle of proportionality, which was new to the rules, "roughly half ... suggested that, while proportionality is a good concept, it is rarely applied" (at 34).

42 American College of Trial Lawyers Task Force on Discovery and Civil Justice, *Reforming Our Civil Justice System: A Report on Progress and Promise* (Denver: Institute for the Advancement of the American Legal System, 2015) at 3, online: <http://iaals.du.edu/sites/default/files/documents/publications/report_on_progress_and_promise.pdf>.

43 See, for example, *Family Law Act,* SBC 2011 c 25, pt 2, Division 1, "Resolution Out of Court Preferred."

44 Action Committee on Access to Justice in Civil and Family Matters, *Meaningful Change, supra* note 16 at 2.

45 The use of mediation is generally avoided, for example, in cases involving violence or power imbalance or where parties lack capacity or are not participating in good faith. Training programs and codes of conduct fully address such matters.

46 Rosalie Silberman Abella (then Justice of the Court of Appeal for Ontario), "Professionalism Revisited" (Opening address at the Bencher's Retreat, Law Society of Upper Canada, 14 October 1999), online: Ontario Courts <http://www.ontariocourts.ca/coa/en/ps/speeches/professionalism.htm>.

47 Linda Ippolito, "ADR Has Lost Its 'Alternative' Way," *Lawyer's Weekly* (11 September 2012).

48 Carrie Menkel-Meadow, "Pursuing Settlement in an Adversary Culture: A Tale of Innovation Co-opted or 'The Law of ADR'" (1999) 19 Fla St UL Rev 1 at 3.

49 Carrie Menkel-Meadow, "The Trouble with the Adversary System in a Postmodern, Multicultural World" (1996) 38 Wm & Mary L Rev 5 at 40.

50 Canadian Bar Association Access to Justice Committee, *Equal Justice, supra* note 11 at 13.

51 "We must make changes urgently ... The current system is unsustainable": Action Committee on Access to Justice in Civil and Family Matters, *Roadmap, supra* note 3 at iii and 6.

52 Yves Faguy, "McLachlin: Where Do We Go from Here?" *CBA National* (14 August 2015).

53 See then Governor General David Johnston, "The Legal Profession in a Smart and Caring Nation: A Vision for 2017" (Speech delivered at the Canadian Bar Association's Canadian Legal Conference, Halifax, 14 August 2011), online: <http://ismymoneysafe.org/pdf/Governor%20General%20David%20Johnston%20Speech%20-%20The%20Legal%20Profession%20in%20a%20Smart%20and%20Caring%20Nation%20Vision%20for%202017.pdf>.

54   "There is today an overwhelming consensus that if the justice system as we know it is to survive, it must undergo significant change to provide greater access to justice for the public": Hon. Warren K. Winkler, then Chief Justice of Ontario, Opening of the Courts of Ontario, September 2013, in Law Society of Ontario, Background Paper, "Access to Justice: Quotable Quotes" (October 2013) at 257, online: Law Society of Ontario <https://www.lsuc.on.ca/uploadedFiles/For_the_Public/About_the_Law_Society/Convocation_Decisions/2014/Quotable_quotes.pdf>.

13

Legal Fee Regimes and the Cost of Civil Justice

Herbert M. Kritzer

THE IDEA THAT THE legal fees charged by lawyers form a principal barrier to access to justice is widely held in Canada. This is reflected in frequent estimates about the high costs of a civil trial. For example, the influential 1995 report of the Ontario Civil Justice Review estimated that a typical three day General Division court trial would require 191 billable hours for the plaintiff, which would translate into fees of almost of $60,000, assuming fees of $300 per hour.[1] Most of these fees reflect the lawyers' time providing representation in and out of court. Often, it is argued that legal fees can be reduced by making simplistic changes to the procedural rules, institutional arrangements, and other aspects of the Canadian civil justice system, and thereby advance access to justice. My view is that such efforts are problematic because of the complexities of fee structures, what I label the "legal fee regime."

Legal fee regimes have three primary components: how the fee is computed, who pays the fee, and how fees are regulated. The dilemma for those who would change how the costs of civil justice are computed and paid, or more specifically, how the costs of representation are computed and paid, lies in the fact that all arrangements for costs and fees create incentives. Some of those incentives will be positive while others will be perverse. Predicting how the positive and perverse incentives will balance out is difficult. The difficulty is increased by the fact that, while reformers think specifically about the positives they seek to achieve, identifying the possible perverse incentives is complex and often overlooked.

Canada has few concerted examples of reforms designed to reduce the legal fees charged by lawyers for civil actions. Common law jurisdictions in other countries have, however, sought to undertake reforms intended to reduce legal fees in the civil justice system. This chapter focuses specifically on the twenty-five-year effort in England to embrace reforms of this kind. The broad lesson for Canada is that legal fee regimes are so complex that it is difficult, if not almost impossible, to advance access to justice by altering them.

The Concept of Legal Fee Regimes

To further an understanding of how fees and costs are structured, I employ the concept of legal fee regime, which I define as:

> The structure of attorney compensation for contentious work, including litigation, arbitration, administrative adjudication, and settlement of claims in the absence of any third-party processing.

Although lawyers' fees do not comprise all of the civil litigant's costs, for most cases they constitute such a large percentage that understanding the complexities of fees is a central issue. Some of the elements of fee regimes also apply to other aspects of litigation costs.

As noted previously, fee regimes involve three distinct dimensions:

1   who pays the fee
2   how the fee is computed
3   how fees are regulated and reviewed.

The complexities of fee regimes arise from the variety found within each of the three dimensions and, more importantly, from the myriad ways in which the dimensions interact.

Who Pays the Fee

Although I label this dimension "who pays the fee," it applies broadly to who pays a party's litigation costs.

The first alternative to the "who pays" dimension is that each side pays its own lawyers. This is the traditional "American" rule. Normally, when one thinks of the American rule, one thinks in terms of a litigant hiring a lawyer and paying that lawyer's fee. However, there are other ways of thinking about how each party might cover the cost of representation. Specifically, *pro se* litigation is a form in which the party covers its own cost of representation, even though that "cost" involves no out-of-pocket payment; instead the party covers the "cost" by expending its own time and effort. For the corporate party or a governmental party, representation by an in-house, salaried lawyer is another way by which a party covers its own cost of representation.

The second way fees might be paid is by the losing party in a contentious matter, the traditional English Rule, or more generically by "fee shifting." Losers might be obligated to pay the reasonable costs incurred by the winner or only some portion of those costs. There may be two-way fee shifting or only one-way fee shifting, whereby only a losing defendant incurs costs obligations vis-à-vis its opponent, a situation that exists under various US statutes and is now reflected in "qualified one-way cost shifting" in England.

Payment by a third party is the third answer to the question of who pays. Most familiar here is the liability insurer that, as part of a liability policy, pays its insured's legal expenses. A second form of insurance is what is variously labelled "legal expense insurance" or "before-the-event legal insurance," which might be sold as a stand-alone product, be included as part of some other insurance,[2] or be a kind of benefit provided by an employer or union. A third form of insurance is what is called "after-the-event" (ATE) insurance, a product that developed in England after reforms in 1995; this product covers the downside risk in a fee-shifting regime: paying the defendant's legal fees and costs should the defendant prevail.[3]

Another form of third-party payment is legal aid. Legal aid can be either a government program or a charitable program. In many countries, legal aid originally developed in the form of privately funded charities, and in some American states this type of legal aid continues to be of some importance. In some countries, legal aid is, or was, largely funded by the government, although there may also be specialized legal aid providers that exist as charities. A third way legal aid is funded is through interest on lawyer trust accounts, a system common in Canada. Lastly, legal aid might be funded by the legal profession itself, either through lawyers' *pro bono* work or contributions made in lieu of donating time.

A final form of third-party payment is the litigation funding company, which provides non-recourse funding (i.e., the funding is repaid only if damages are paid by the defendant) to lawyers and possibly to the litigants themselves. For example, in the United Kingdom, Juridica Investments obtained a capitalization of £80 million in 2007. In the United States, one finds companies such as LawCash, Law Capital Enterprises, and Omni Bridgeway, which also operates in Australia, New Zealand, Hong Kong, Singapore, and Canada.

How the Fee Is Computed

There are many ways fees can be computed, such as:

- time
- flat/fixed
- percentage of recovery
- item of service (task-based)
- value to client (value-based)

- set by court schedule or statute
- per diem
- salary or covered as part of an ongoing retainer.

Several of these require some explanation:

- "Item of service" usually refers to very specific discrete tasks (e.g., writing a letter, preparing a motion, making a court appearance, taking a deposition); however, it could also refer to what I have heard described as "phase billing," where a fee is set for each phase of an action, perhaps with the specific fee depending upon the complexity of the specific case.
- The "value to client" approach is rather vague but reflects the traditional considerations of amount of effort involved, level of expertise required, importance of the matter to the client, and results achieved.
- "Set by court schedule or statute" is the method used in Germany, where it is based on the amount that is claimed to be in controversy.[4] The "fixed recoverable cost system" introduced initially in 2003 for certain cases in England is another example of a pre-set schedule, although it works differently from the system in Germany.
- "Per diem" is a fee system where the client is billed based solely on the length of time the file is open; the fee may be computed by counting days, months, or quarters. The amount of work done does not affect the fee; it depends solely on the length of time from when the case is referred to the lawyer until the case is closed.
- Salary or ongoing retainer is most commonly the form of payment when the case is handled by someone on the staff of the litigant (i.e., an in-house lawyer). However, it could also reflect an arrangement whereby the client pays the lawyer a monthly retainer in return for handling whatever matters arise. There are also arrangements where a client contracts with a firm to purchase a fixed amount of time from the firm (i.e., a certain number of full-time equivalents of lawyer effort) and pays the firm on a contract basis; this type of outsourcing of an in-house lawyer type of arrangement is offered by the American firm Axiom, and probably other companies as well.

There are myriad ways in which these might be combined or enhanced. For example:

- contingent hourly (time plus risk enhancement/"uplift")
- fixed-fee plus bonus for success
- reduced-rate hourly plus bonus for success

- flat fee for all work up to trial preparation; hourly for trial preparation and trial itself
- time-capped flat fee in which the flat fee covers up to a maximum amount of time (typically more than what the expected hourly rate would cover), with anything above the cap billed hourly
- Item of service for certain tasks (e.g., per deposition or witness statement), hourly for other tasks.

The motivation for trying various fee arrangements is to modify incentives to the advantage of the lawyer or the client, and perhaps even both. However, the revised incentive structures may produce undesired effects, leading firms and their clients to retreat to previous arrangements.[5]

Fee Regulation and Review

The third element of a fee regime is the nature of any regulation of fees and any mechanism for reviewing the amount of the fee. Even when a specific fee arrangement is permitted, the regulations governing those fees are important. Fee regulations can be based on professional standards, legislative enactments, or common law court decisions. For example, the Law Society of Ontario has set standards regarding contingency fees. In the United States, some states place statutory limits on the percentages that can be charged as contingency fees or require that the percentage be on a sliding scale, either in general or in certain types of cases. As I will discuss below, regulations have been an important issue in the years since England began permitting percentage-based contingency fees, labelled "damages-based agreements," in 2013.

Because of fee shifting, Canada and England have long had a structure, albeit imperfect, for reviewing fees. Costs judges, taxing masters, assessment officers, taxing officers, legal services commissioners, legal ombudsmen, and similar officials have expertise in norms and regulations that they use in assessing fees for reasonableness. Law societies in Canada all have a process for handling disputes over fees. In Chapter 6, Trevor Farrow describes how fees were reviewed in the case of residential schools litigation in Canada. In Chapter 15, Noel Semple will explore how to regulate contingency fees in Canada. In England, how legal fees are reviewed has changed over time so that there is now a mixture of "fixed recoverable costs," "summary assessment" of costs, and "detailed assessment" of costs.

In contrast, there is no systematic structure for fee reviews in the United States. Courts have an inherent power to review fees, but this is seldom used except in certain special circumstances, such as when the client is not legally competent due to age or mental condition. Some states have statutes authorizing judges to review contingency fees, but there is little evidence that many such reviews occur or, when it does happen, what types of standards or bases are used to assess the reasonableness of fees. Judges do review fee petitions and formally approve or set fees in class actions and one-way fee-shifting cases.[6] In some states, the state bar association and/or the state court system provides an arbitration procedure to resolve fee disputes.[7] It is not clear how often they are used or what types of norms are employed in resolving disputes.

One broad issue regarding fee review concerns the standards that are appropriate for determining the proper amount for a fee. This can depend in part on who is paying the fee. One set of standards may be appropriate when a losing party is obligated to pay the winning party's fees. A second set of standards may be appropriate for assessing the reasonableness of what a lawyer is asking his or her own client to pay. And a third set of standards might be employed in the situation where a third party is paying the lawyer's fees. One problem that can arise for third-party payment is that the third party may limit payment in a way that constrains the lawyer to an inadequate level of effort. In the absence of limits, however, the client may want the lawyer to do everything necessary to win, even if the level of effort is unreasonable when viewed in light of what the client might gain or lose; the client may want vindication regardless of the cost to the third-party payer.

A final element focuses on "rates," particularly when the fee is based on the amount of time devoted to a matter. What kinds of hourly rates are appropriate, and who determines this? Can the market set the rate when someone other than the consumer of the service is paying the fee? How efficient is the market in determining rates, particularly for services provided to infrequent users of legal services? Should the rate depend on who is paying the fee? All these issues need to be addressed in the context of fee regulation and fee review.

The Multiple Worlds of Civil Litigation

It is not possible to dissociate the nature of the fee regime and its potential impact from the type of litigation. There are at least three worlds of litigation:[8]

- Routine everyday cases with modest to moderate amounts at stake, epitomized by most personal injury cases.
- High-value litigation involving individual claims. Defining where the routine ends and the high-value world begins can only be imprecise, but one arbitrary line that might be drawn would define this world as including cases where it makes sense for the costs of the litigation itself to reach six figures for one or more parties. This would include serious personal injuries regardless of their

cause (auto accidents, premises, medical negligence, and product liability), professional negligence (lawyers, accountants, architects, etc.), business torts, and major commercial disputes.

- Large-scale litigation, including mass torts; class actions; those that Marc Galanter has called "case congregations,"[9] which in the United States often involve "multi-district litigation" or possibly wind up in bankruptcy proceedings; and what is sometimes called "bet-your-company" litigation, where the future of the company itself is at stake.

The implications of specific fee regimes depend on which of these worlds one is considering.

This can be seen by contrasting issues of fees and costs in routine versus high-value cases. The costs and returns for both lawyers and litigants in high-value litigation change how the parties look at the process in ways that turn very heavily on the fee structure. Corporate defendants may be willing to spend more and give lawyers more leeway, particularly if there is no insurance company standing between the defendant and the lawyer (i.e., the defendant is paying their lawyer themselves rather than relying on third-party payment by an insurer). Plaintiffs' lawyers working on a no-win, no-pay basis need to be able to finance high-value litigation, which is the major reason that medical malpractice and products liability tend to be specialized areas of practice.

The nature of potential conflicts of interest between lawyers and clients can change depending on whether one is considering a routine or high-value case. In the former, the percentage-fee lawyer's short-run interest is to secure a quick settlement with relatively modest amounts of time invested; this may mean only a fractional recovery of damages to the client. As I have argued elsewhere, the lawyer's long-run interest is likely to be different, and even in the short term the percentage-fee lawyer has an incentive to try to push settlement offers up because the marginal return to the lawyer for a small amount of effort can be quite good. If the client is paying the lawyer's fee on an hourly basis, win or lose, the client is not likely to want the lawyer to make an all-out effort.[10] However, in a fee-shifting regime, or where the lawyer is paid by a third party, the lawyer's interest and the client's interest might align nicely, although there may be conflict with a third-party payer of the lawyer's fee who might question whether the cost was commensurate with the amount recovered.

In a high-value case, a (percentage) contingency fee lawyer's short-run economic interest will readily align with that of the client. It is easily worth it to the lawyer to invest more time because the potential return on that investment is very attractive. However, a lawyer handling a high-value case has more at stake in terms of what has been invested, and the risk of no return on that investment may shift some lawyers towards being somewhat risk-averse. Also, at some point, a client in a high-value case may see a substantial settlement that is nonetheless considerably less than the case is likely to bring at trial as sufficiently attractive that the client will prefer to take what is on the table because the client has only one shot at the "game." Under a fee regime where the plaintiff is paying his or her own lawyer win or lose, the plaintiff's attitude towards settlement may change as the sunk costs increase.

Fee Regimes, Incentives, and Conflicts

Fee regimes affect the incentives of those involved in both litigation and cases that never get to litigation. The previous section discussed some of these effects in the context of the multiple worlds of litigation. This section considers incentive issues more broadly, along with how fee regimes create or mitigate conflict between litigants and their legal representatives.

Fee regimes are a significant factor in the value of cases. Fee shifting can either increase or decrease the value of a case depending on the level of risk involved. For cases that are low-risk for the plaintiff, fee shifting increases case value from the perspective of the defendant. From the defendant's perspective, the value of a case is the expectation of the total of its own cost of defence, what it will pay in damages, and what it will pay for the plaintiff's costs; this equals the total of the costs multiplied by the probability that the plaintiff will win, minus the defence costs, times the probability that the defence will win. Without fee shifting, the defendant's case value is its costs plus the amount of damages, times the probability of having to pay those damages. For low-risk cases, the case valuation from the defendant's perspective is almost certainly higher with fee shifting than without. A study of fee shifting in Alaska, the one American state that has general two-way fee shifting, found that many defence lawyers saw the primary effect of fee shifting as increasing the value of cases for settlement purposes, particularly when the central issue in the case was quantum rather than liability.[11]

The analysis of case value from the plaintiff's perspective is more complex because it depends not just on whether there is fee shifting but also on whether the plaintiff is directly at risk for the fee shift. Plaintiffs may not be directly at risk for two possible reasons: either the plaintiff does not have the financial resources to pay the defendant's costs should the defendant prevail, or the plaintiff has insurance against those costs. The state of Florida briefly had a fee-shifting system in medical negligence cases, the adoption of which had been strongly backed by the medical establishment. However, the system was quickly repealed because defendants found that they were paying out more in cases in which the plaintiff prevailed while at the same time seldom being able to recover their costs because most plaintiffs had little or no resources available to pay those costs.[12]

As one would expect, the incentives for litigants are affected by the risks they face, in terms of whether they must pay their own lawyer as a case progresses and whether they are at risk for the other side's costs. This was clearly illustrated for me by the comments of a small-town solicitor in England whom I interviewed in 1987. This solicitor handled cases for both privately paying clients and clients who had before-the-event insurance. How he dealt with cases depended on who was paying him. When the case was funded by the insurance program, he did not hesitate to initiate court action; when the client was paying privately, he asked the client to cover the filing fee, which not infrequently led the client to drop the matter.[13]

Incentive issues from the litigant's perspective involve a combination of risk preference and simple cost-benefit analysis. A plaintiff who is paying a lawyer on an hourly basis will be very cognizant of the cost relative to what might be recovered. This is the same calculation that everyone makes when deciding whether to spend on things such as repairs, some types of healthcare, and the like: Is the benefit worth the cost, particularly compared with possible alternatives? One often hears in the United States that a decision by a defendant to settle was driven not by the merits of the case but by the cost of litigating the case. As I have discussed elsewhere, estimating the effects of fee shifting is complex.[14] There is some evidence that it weeds out some weaker claims, but at the same time it may increase the intensity (i.e., cost) of litigation for stronger claims as well as the amounts paid in settlement of those stronger claims.[15]

Incentives for lawyers depend on the fee regime as well. A lawyer working on a no-win, no-pay basis will make choices that are different from those made by a lawyer working on an hourly basis, and the nature of the difference will depend on whether the ultimate fee will be based on a percentage of recovery, hourly billing, or some type of flat or scheduled fee. A lawyer who is being paid by a third party will deal with cases differently from a lawyer who is being paid directly by the client. Not surprisingly, if the lawyer's fee is based on the amount recovered, the lawyer will want to focus on money in settlement negotiation, while a lawyer who is paid hourly or with a fixed fee or who is on salary will be more inclined to entertain settlements with a significant non-monetary component.[16] One might expect plaintiffs who are paying their lawyer on some basis other than a damage-based contingency fee to be more willing to consider non-monetary resolutions, in whole or in part, if costs will be recovered from the defendant.

Lawyers' decisions regarding *which* cases to pursue will depend very heavily on who is paying and how the fee will be computed. As discussed previously, many cases that can be handled on an hourly basis with the loser paying would not be financially viable on a percentage-fee basis because the amount at issue is too small. As I have described elsewhere, insurance companies and their outside lawyers have tried a variety of alternatives to the hourly fee; although the intent is typically that the lawyers will continue to work on the cases in more or less the same way that they did on an hourly basis, the firms and clients quickly find that they both change how they approach cases when the fee arrangement changes.[17] When the lawyer's fee is paid by a third party, particularly a third party such as an insurance company with which the lawyer has an ongoing relationship, the lawyer has to balance the interests of the actual client, to whom the lawyer owes his or her *professional* loyalty, with the interests of the payer of the lawyer's fee, towards whom the lawyer is likely to have an *economic* loyalty.[18] This may be further complicated if the lawyer who is representing an insured is a direct employee of the insurer, a situation that is increasingly common in the United States with the growth of "staff counsel" offices and "captive" law firms.

The basis on which any service provider's fee is calculated affects incentives vis-à-vis the service provider's efficiency. For lawyers, this incentive is very clear: being paid by the hour creates incentives for extra care and extra work; as one observer noted, "most lawyers will prefer to leave no stone unturned, provided, of course, they can charge by the stone."[19] On the other hand, if payment is by a fixed fee set in advance, the incentive is to be as efficient as possible.[20] A percentage-based contingency fee falls somewhere in between because the lawyer's incentive is to invest time as long as the marginal return to the lawyer exceeds the opportunity cost of the lawyer's time.[21]

As noted above, the lawyer's long-run interest will often mitigate these incentives: the hourly-fee lawyer working for a repeat client must be mindful of the need to get future work from that client, and excessive bills arising from over-investment can have negative long-run consequences. The flat-fee or contingency fee lawyer working for one-off clients usually needs those clients as a source of future referrals; skimping on effort on clients' cases is likely to be harmful to the lawyer's future ability to secure clients. However, the incentives also structure choices as to *how* a lawyer does something with the structure of the fee, leading the lawyer to make choices with an eye to efficiency or lack thereof. For example, a lawyer not being paid based on the amount of time expended might employ informal means of fact investigation, while a lawyer being paid hourly might be inclined to use more formal methods requiring more of the lawyer's time.[22]

As one would expect, fee regimes create and modulate conflicts between litigants and their lawyers. This is the classic principal-agent problem. Every fee structure has the potential for conflicts of interest between the client and the lawyer, between the client and a third-party payer, and between the lawyer and a third-party payer. The nature and degree of conflicts can differ depending on whether one takes a short-run or long-run perspective. Moreover, clients differ in their ability to monitor their lawyers' actions; the less able the client is in monitoring, the more likely the conflict will work to the detriment of the client.[23] Often the conflicts created by fee regimes reflect differences between lawyers and their clients regarding the tolerance for risk; the lawyer is more likely to be risk-neutral, or at least less risk-averse than the client. Another common conflict can arise when there is a third-party payer with whom the lawyer has a continuing relationship, as is often the case with lawyers retained by insurance companies to represent an insured.[24]

England's Access to Justice Act

The difficulties with reforming legal fee regimes can be seen in the effects of England's *Access to Justice Act 1999 (AJA)*.[25] Starting in 1995, English solicitors were permitted to charge a type of no-win, no-pay fee that was labelled a "conditional fee." To make such fees attractive to solicitors, solicitors were permitted to charge their clients an "uplift" to their normal fee; this uplift was limited to 100 percent of the normal fee with a recommendation by the Law Society of England and Wales that it not exceed 25 percent of the amount recovered. Although this enabled plaintiffs to pursue a case without fear of having to pay their solicitors if the claim was unsuccessful, it left the threat of having to pay the defendant's costs, which include both legal fees reasonably incurred and other expenses such as court fees and fees of expert witnesses. To solve this problem, the system of after-the-event (ATE) insurance developed, where, by paying a modest premium, the plaintiff was protected from the risk of having to pay the costs of a successful defendant. Under the 1995 system, the client had to pay both the ATE premium (presumably upfront) and the uplift, although the system evolved such that the ATE premium was not due until the end of the case and was waived if the case was not successful. Although more attractive than the system that existed prior to 1995, it was not attractive as an alternative to the then-existing legal aid system, under which a losing claimant's own lawyer was paid by legal aid and the plaintiff was generally not liable for the defendant's costs.[26]

The English conditional fee may be preferable from the lawyer's perspective for smaller, routine cases because the damages limit the amount that can be earned on a percentage basis. In contrast, for large cases, the lawyer would probably prefer a percentage-fee structure because of the potential "profit," but the client might prefer a time-based conditional fee because it would be lower than the percentage fee, even if it is higher than if the client bore the risk. From

278 Herbert M. Kritzer

the perspective of the plaintiff with a very modest claim, a conditional-fee arrangement may be better by making it easier to secure representation and thus increase access to justice, although this will depend on the level of fees that can be recovered from the opposing party.[27]

The 1999 *AJA* was intended by the government to change the English civil justice system in a way that would make conditional fees attractive to those then eligible for legal aid. It accomplished this by making both the uplift and the ATE premium payable by the losing defendant. More generally, the idea was to increase the willingness of potential plaintiffs to retain lawyers on a conditional-fee basis, particularly those plaintiffs who would otherwise qualify for legal aid. The availability of conditional fees allowed the elimination of civil legal aid for personal injury cases and would thus reduce the costs of legal aid. Prior to the *AJA,* defendant insurers had no reason to care about the size of the uplift or the cost of ATE insurance, but the client had, in theory, some incentive to try to keep both the uplift and ATE premium at a reasonable level, and ATE insurers had an incentive to price their coverage at a level that was attractive to buyers. With the adoption of the *AJA,* the client had no reason to be concerned about either the uplift or the ATE premium; although the uplift was still capped as before, the ATE premium was not limited. Now that defendant insurers were obligated to pay those costs in most cases, they were very concerned about what they had to pay as the uplift and for the ATE premium.[28] Moreover, the defendant insurers were repeat players and were willing to fight over these issues. The result was intense conflict over both the size of the uplift and the ATE premium, including whether it was appropriate to pay any ATE premium in cases where liability was clear. This issue has been fought out through a series of cases that came to be known as the "cost wars."[29]

Early research in England showed that lawyers who have clients protected from costs can be more aggressive bargainers. Studies looking at cases prior to the introduction of conditional fees and the subsequent changes that made uplifts and ATE premiums shiftable found that when faced with solicitors who have clients not at risk for costs, insurers were more likely to make settlement offers (and to make subsequent offers if an initial offer is refused) than when dealing with a solicitor whose client was paying on a private basis.[30] In my own research, I have seen evidence that the lawyer's having a direct stake in the outcome can, at least at the margins, push them to produce better outcomes for clients. One example is the effort by plaintiffs' lawyers to keep trying to push up a settlement offer even if what is on offer is acceptable to the client; a small amount of additional time can produce a nice return to the lawyer.[31] A second example was in a study of advocacy before administrative law judges handling appeals of Social Security disability claims. In the United States, lawyers often handle these claims on a no-win, no-pay basis; both salaried non-lawyers and salaried or *pro bono* lawyers also handle those cases. The most effective lawyers in this area were working on a no-win, no-pay basis, which provided a greater incentive to win for those lawyers compared with those handling cases either *pro bono* or as members of a salaried staff.[32]

The dissatisfaction with the system as it was operating after 2000 led in 2009 to the Master of the Rolls asking Sir Rupert Jackson, a Lord Justice of the Court of Appeal, to undertake a review of litigation costs and make recommendations for changes. Lord Justice Jackson considered a range of issues, including the recoverability of the uplift and ATE premium and the more general issue of "proportionality," meaning to the degree to which the costs of obtaining redress should be proportionate to what is at stake. The Jackson review produced extensive proposals for reform.[33] A subset of those reforms, known as the Jackson reforms, was adopted by the Conservative government in May 2012 as part of the *Legal Aid, Sentencing and Punishment of Offenders Act 2012 (LASPO)* and went into effect in April 2013.[34]

The issue of proportionality has been a central element of the reform agenda in England. In part this came in response to several prominent cases in which damages were modest but the costs claimed from the losing party were exorbitant in relation to those damages. A prominent example was an invasion of privacy suit filed in 2001 by supermodel Naomi Campbell against the *Daily Mirror*. At trial, she won an award of £3,500, with her lawyer saying he would seek £250,000 in costs. The *Mirror* won on appeal, and Campbell was ordered to pay £350,000 in costs.[35] Campbell then appealed to the House of Lords, which ruled in her favour and ordered the *Daily Mirror* to pay over £1 million in costs, almost £280,000 of which was a success fee because Campbell's lawyers handled the House of Lords appeal under a conditional-fee agreement.[36]

Many elements of the Jackson reforms that were implemented were directed specifically towards costs. Recoverable costs would no longer be on the basis that they were "reasonable and necessarily incurred." The new governing principle is that recoverable costs must be "proportionate" to what was at issue in the case, including the amount at stake, the importance of the case, the complexity of the issues, and the financial position of each party. Parties in most larger cases (with £25,000 or more at stake) are now required to submit cost budgets, and the courts now issue costs management orders.

Central to my discussion are the four reforms related to how litigation is funded, or how costs are determined. First, the uplift and the ATE premium are no longer recoverable; the uplift is now capped at the lesser of either 25 percent of the sum of general damages and financial loss to date or 100 percent of the base fee, but is now paid by the client. To compensate for ending recoverability, there was a 10 percent increase in the guidelines for general damages. Second, in most personal injury cases, there is now "qualified one-way cost shifting," which means that a successful plaintiff can normally recover costs, but a defendant can recover costs only in special circumstances.[37] Third, lawyers can now offer their services using the kind of contingency fee common in the United States, a straight percentage-of-recovery basis, what is labelled a "damages-based agreement" (DBA); in personal injury cases, these are capped at 25 percent of the sum of general damages and financial loss to date and at 50 percent of damages in other kinds of matters. Fourth, the application of a fixed recoverable costs regime, which began in a very limited way for traffic accidents in 2003, was extended to most other personal injury cases not long after the other Jackson reforms went into effect.[38] Under this regime, recoverable costs are set by a schedule for each stage of a case.[39] In the aggregate, these reforms represent a backing away from the traditional English Rule, under which the loser in litigation pays the winner's reasonable costs.[40]

The Impacts of the Jackson Reforms on Access to Justice in England

As of 2019, the Jackson reforms had been in place for about five years. During that period, there was a continuing perception that the goal of proportionality was yet to be met, and in 2017 Lord Justice Jackson conducted another inquiry focused on proposals to extend the fixed recoverable costs regime to cases involving as much as £250,000.[41] In July 2017, he issued a report recommending that fixed recoverable costs be extended only to claims involving a maximum of £25,000 and to claims of £100,000 for cases that can be tried in three days or less. He also recommended some additional measures intended to rein in costs, and a pilot program in which participants could opt to have a fixed costs regime for cases involving as much as £250,000.[42] Almost two years later, the Ministry of Justice finally moved towards implementing a revised version of Jackson's proposal.[43] One commentator expected the changes to probably become effective in late 2020.[44]

Lord Justice Jackson's 2017 inquiry was undertaken despite little in the way of systematic assessments of the changes or non-changes attributable to the Jackson reforms beyond some reports and discussions that occurred. About seven months after the reforms had been implemented, the *New Law Journal* published a short report on the effects on litigation trends.[45] Six months later, the Civil Justice Council (CJC) established a working group to deal with the impact of the reforms,[46] and a report by John Peyser was produced for the CJC.[47] These endeavours identified some types of effects, and other developments seem clear even without systematic research. In this final section, I examine what has and has not happened, using the insights of the fee regimes framework and drawing on several conversations that I had with knowledge-able persons during a visit to London in March 2017.

The issue of how the fee calculation affects efficiency incentives was driven home in a conversation in March 2017 with senior lawyers at a major plaintiffs' personal injury firm in England. One of the lawyers commented that they were now seeing insurers making very good offers in high-value cases early in the case's development, before the respondent's firm had put in a lot of time. In the past, any offer would have come much later, after a substantial investment of time, which in turn would be the basis of the fee that could be recovered. An early settlement meant a sharply reduced fee. Under a percentage-fee arrange-ment, the lawyer would welcome an early offer before expending a lot of time because the result would be more profitable for the lawyer.

Another important finding is that few firms decided to employ DBAs. Everyone I spoke with attributed this primarily to the regulations that were created to govern DBAs. This is based on experience after the adoption of conditional-fee arrangements (CFA), where some slight deviation from the regulations resulted in the agreements being deemed unenforceable, which, given the indemnity principle, denied the lawyer any fee and negated cost shift-ing. Solicitors expressed concern that something similar would happen with DBAs.[48] A second problem with the regulation is the prohibition on hybrid fee arrangements under which the fee is based partly on an hourly rate and partly on the amount recovered; in his 2009 report, Lord Justice Jackson recommended allowing such arrangements, but the Ministry of Justice chose not to do so. This is closely related to the third problem arising from the indemnity principle. The indemnity principle limits the amount recoverable to the amount the client is obligated to pay the lawyer. Given that the recoverable fee continues to be controlled by time-based standards, this means that if the fee produced by the percentage is less than what would be paid on an hourly basis, the plaintiff can recover only the percentage amount; hybrid fees could go a long way towards solving this problem.

It is unclear whether there would be a role for DBAs even without the regula-tory issues, given that they exist alongside CFAs. To understand this, one must keep in mind that the DBA in personal injury cases is now capped at 25 percent of general damages plus financial loss to date, with the same cap applying to the uplift on a CFA. The client might prefer a DBA in a low-value case because it might be less than what the client had to pay under a CFA. In a high-value case,[49] the lawyer might prefer a DBA because the percentage of the recovery could substantially exceed the fee that could be obtained with a CFA; the client in this situation would prefer the CFA if the uplift plus any amounts over the recoverable fee that a client agreed to pay was less than 25 percent of the recovery.

Essentially, it is unclear under what circumstances there would be mutual interest in a DBA as preferable to the CFA, even without the uplift's being recoverable.

One clear discernible impact has been on fixed recoverable costs, which almost certainly reduced, on average, the amount of recoverable costs. The Jackson reforms extended the reach of fixed recoverable costs, and the elimination of the recoverability of the uplift changed the economics of handling cases subject to fixed recoverable costs.[50] Prior to the Jackson reforms, the fixed costs plus the recoverable uplift were probably enough to keep such cases economically feasible for the recoverable costs. That changed with the elimination of the recoverability of the uplift, putting pressure on firms that specialized in handling the kinds of cases subject to fixed recoverable costs, forcing some to abandon personal injury cases or even go into "administration" (bankruptcy).[51] In theory, firms could collect the uplift from the client, but it appears that some firms are reluctant to use CFAs if the uplift is not recoverable, and this probably reflects an unwillingness to require the client pay the uplift out of the recovery.

From comments at a seminar conducted by Lord Justice Jackson and comments by a senior solicitor from a prominent personal injury firm ("AA Solicitors"), it appears that some firms have figured out how to work under the fixed recoverable costs for personal injury cases. AA has split its operation so that it handles cases subject to fixed recoverable costs at an office outside London, with much of the work done by staff who do not hold a solicitor's practising certificate. The firm structured a system sufficiently efficient to generate a profit across its portfolio of fixed recoverable cost cases. AA Solicitors is not alone in developing systems for handling a portfolio of cases subject to fixed recoverable costs in a profitable fashion, but these are generally based on volume practices designed to minimize the time expended by solicitor-level staff.[52]

Another effect may be on the cost of before-the-event (BTE) insurance, either formally as insurance or effectively in the form of a union benefit. One law firm that handles claims on behalf of union members, who receive the equivalent of BTE insurance as a union benefit, noted that the changes were putting pressure on the unions,[53] probably because the solicitors now turn to the union to cover more of the costs due to the reduction in what can be recovered. A similar problem would exist for firms hired by BTE insurers.

The overall unintended effect of the Jackson reforms has been fewer practitioners and the greater selectivity regarding which cases solicitors will take on, which is a reduction in the ability of injured parties in England to obtain redress, and therefore a decrease in access to justice. This is despite the reduction of the overall costs paid by claimants and insurers. My point is that solicitors in England have become more selective in the cases they handle because the overall economics have changed. Although in theory the claimants' lawyers could collect the same overall fee, that burden has shifted from being entirely on the defendant to being shared between the defendant and the client, unless the solicitor forgoes any uplift on a CFA and accepts only the recoverable costs as payment for the services provided. As noted above, for some solicitors this was not acceptable, and they abandoned or limited their personal injury practice. Other solicitors have become much more selective in the cases they will handle.

Conclusion

Although legal fees are often identified as a barrier to access to civil justice, removing or reducing that barrier is challenging and may have negative unintended consequences. The general lesson from England's experience with the *Access to Justice Act* and the subsequent Jackson reforms is that alterations to the legal fee regime are complex, which makes it difficult to use such reforms as a vehicle for advancing access to civil justice in Canada. Certainly, for some litigants, reforms to the legal fee regime may be beneficial. But these reductions in legal fees affect the supply of lawyers available for civil actions and their assessments of which clients they will act for, which may create new barriers to access to civil justice.

Notes

This chapter draws heavily on Herbert M. Kritzer, "Fee Regimes and the Cost of Civil Justice" (2009) 28 CJQ 344. I thank Les Jacobs, Peter Hurst, and Dominic Regan for extremely helpful comments on an earlier draft.

1   See c 11 in Civil Justice Review Team, "First Report" (March 1995), online: Ontario Ministry of the Attorney General <https://www.attorneygeneral.jus.gov.on.ca/english/about/pubs/cjr/firstreport/cost.php>.
2   See Matthias Kilian, "Alternatives to Public Provision: The Role of Legal Expenses Insurance in Broadening Access to Justice: The German Experience" (2003) 30 JL & Soc'y 31.
3   ATE insurance operated alongside a form of no-win, no-pay fee, called a conditional fee, that came into existence in England in 1995.
4   See Werner Pfennigstorf, "The European Experience with Attorney Fee Shifting" (1984) 47 Law & Contemp Probs 37 at 46, 55–56, 63. Clients remain free to negotiate other arrangements with their own attorney.
5   See Herbert M. Kritzer, "The Commodification of Insurance Defense Practice" (2006) 59 Vand L Rev 2053 at 2060–68 ["Commodification"].
6   See Task Force on Contingent Fees, "Report on Contingent Fees in Class Action Litigation" (2006) 25 Rev Litig 459; William J. Lynk, "The Courts and the Plaintiffs' Bar: Awarding the Attorney's Fee in Class-Action Litigation" (1994) 23 J Legal Stud 185; Theodore Eisenberg & Geoffrey P. Miller, "Attorney Fees in Class Action Settlements: An Empirical Study" (2004) 1 J Empirical Legal Studies 27; Theodore Eisenberg, Geoffrey P Miller, & Roy Germano, "Attorneys' Fees in Class Actions: 2009–2013" (2016), NYU Law and Economics Research Paper No 17-02, online: SSRN <https://ssrn.com/abstract=2904194>.

7   See, for example, Michael V. Gervasi & Gerald Lebovits, "Part 137: The Attorney-Client Fee-Dispute Program" (2009) 8 Richmond County Bar Assoc J 7 at 23.

8   See Deborah R. Hensler et al, *Trends in Tort Litigation: The Story behind the Statistics* (Santa Monica, CA: RAND Institute for Civil Justice, 1987).

9   Marc Galanter, "Case Congregations and Their Careers" (1990) 14 L & Soc'y Rev 371.

10 See Herbert M. Kritzer, *Risks, Reputations, and Rewards: Contingency Legal Practice in the United States* (Stanford, CA: Stanford University Press, 2004) at 222–23 [*Risks, Reputations*].

11 Susanne Di Pietro, Teresa W. Carns, & Pamela Kelley, *Alaska's English Rule: Attorney's Fee Shifting in Civil Cases* (Anchorage: Alaska Judicial Council, 1995) at 110–11.

12 See Edward A. Snyder & James W. Hughes, "The English Rule for Allocating Legal Costs: Evidence Confronts Theory" (1990) 6 JL Econ & Org 345 at 356.

13 Herbert M. Kritzer, *Let's Make a Deal: Negotiations and Settlement in Ordinary Litigation* (Madison: University of Wisconsin Press, 1991) at 110 [*Let's Make a Deal*].

14 Herbert M. Kritzer, "Lawyer Fees and Lawyer Behavior in Litigation: What Does the Empirical Literature Really Say?" (2002) 80 Tex L Rev 1943 at 1947–48.

15 James W. Hughes & Edward A. Snyder, "Litigation and Settlement under the English and American Rules: Theory and Evidence" (1995) 38 JL & Econ 225 at 243–48.

16 See Kritzer, *Let's Make a Deal, supra* note 13 at 45–46.

17 See Kritzer, "Commodification," *supra* note 5 at 2060–68.

18 See Herbert M. Kritzer, "Betwixt and Between: The Ethical Dilemmas of Insurance Defense Practice" in Leslie C. Levin & Lynn Mather, eds, *Lawyers in Practice: Ethical Decision Making in Context* (Chicago: University of Chicago Press, 2012) 131 ["Betwixt and Between"].

19 Deborah L. Rhode, "Ethical Perspectives on Legal Practice" (1985) 37 Stan L Rev 589 at 635.

20 Cyrus Tata & Frank Stephen, "When Paying the Piper Gets the 'Wrong' Tune: The Impact of Fixed Payments on Case Management, Case Trajectories, and 'Quality' in Criminal Defence Work" in Pascoe Pleasence, Alexy Buck, & Nigel J. Balmer, eds, *Transforming Lives: Law and Social Process* (London: Legal Services Commission/Thomson, Sweet and Maxwell, 2007) at 190; see also Paul Fenn, Neil Rickman, & Alastair Gray, "Standard Fees for Legal Aid: An Empirical Analysis of Incentives and Contracts" (2007) 59 Oxford Economic Papers 662.

21 See Earl Johnson Jr., "Lawyer's Choice: A Theoretical Appraisal of Litigation Investment and Decisions" (1980–81) 15 L & Soc'y Rev 567 at 585–91.

22 See Kritzer, "Commodification," *supra* note 5 at 2066; Kritzer, *Risks, Reputations, supra* note 10 at 137–38; and Tata & Stephen, *supra* note 20.

23 The classic discussion of the monitoring issue in the context of the American contingency fee is Douglas E. Rosenthal, *Lawyer and Client: Who's in Charge* (New York: Russell Sage Foundation, 1974).

24 See Kritzer, "Betwixt and Between," *supra* note 18.

25 *Access to Justice Act 1999* (UK) c 22.

26 In some circumstances, a losing plaintiff could be made to contribute to the defendant's costs.

27 Evidence from the United States shows that percentage-fee lawyers may handle large numbers of cases that are not profitable, and that the lawyer knows upfront are not likely to be profitable, because handling such cases can help build a referral network of prior clients; see Kritzer, *Risk, Reputations, supra* note 10 at 97.

28 See Annette Morris, "Deconstructing Policy on Costs and the Compensation Culture" in Eoin Quill & Raymond J. Friel, eds, *Damages and Compensation Culture* (Oxford: Hart Publishing, 2016) 125 at 135.

29 Richard Moorhead, "Cost Wars in England and Wales: The Insurers Strike Back" in Mathias Reimann, ed, *Cost and Fee Allocation in Civil Procedure: A Comparative Study* (Ius Gentium: Comparative Perspectives on Law and Justice, vol 11) (Dordrecht, Netherlands: Springer, 2012) 117.

30 See Paul Fenn & Ioannis Vlachonikolis, "Bargaining Behaviour by Defendant Insurers: An Economic Model" (1990) 14 Geneva Papers on Risk and Insurance 41; Timothy Swanson & Robin Mason, "Nonbargaining in the Shadow of the Law" (1998) 18 Int'l Rev L & Econ 121.

31 Kritzer, *Risks, Reputations, supra* note 10 at 159.

32 See Herbert M. Kritzer, *Legal Advocacy: Lawyers and Nonlawyers at Work* (Ann Arbor: University of Michigan Press, 1998) at 146–47.

33 The Rt. Hon. Lord Justice Jackson, *Review of Civil Litigation Costs: Final Report* (Norwich: HMSO, 2009).

34 *Legal Aid, Sentencing and Punishment of Offenders Act 2012* (UK) c 10. A summary of these reforms can be found at "The Jackson Reforms: What You Need to Know" (January 2015), online: Clyde & Co. <http://www.clydeco.com/uploads/Files/3565371v1.pdf>.

35 Herbert M. Kritzer, "'Loser Pays' Doesn't," *Legal Affairs* (November/December 2005) at 25.

36 The *Daily Mirror* appealed the awarding of the success fee to the House of Lords, but it was upheld; an appeal to the European Court of Human Rights on this issue produced a ruling favourable to the newspaper on the success fee issue, but that still left a bill for over £700,000. See "MGN Ltd v. United Kingdom," online: Open Society Justice Initiative <https://www.opensocietyfoundations.org/litigation/mgn-ltd-v-united-kingdom>.

37 Claimants still face the risk of some of the defendants' costs when they decline what is now called a "Part 36" offer, which is the modern equivalent of payment into court.

38 Lord Justice Jackson had recommended extending fixed recoverable costs to all cases involving claims of less than £25,000. Fixed costs apply only to cases in what is called the "fast track," which excludes clinical negligence and disease cases regardless of the amount of claimed damages.

39 See Rule 45.2 in "Part 45 – Fixed Costs," online: Justice (UK) <https://www.justice.gov.uk/courts/procedure-rules/civil/rules/part45-fixed-costs#rule45.2>. The schedule of recoverable costs was reduced by the government not long after the system went into operation. There is also a fixed recoverable cost regime that pre-exists the Jackson reforms in the specialized Intellectual Property and Enterprise Court for cases with claims of up to £50,000.

40 Arguably, England had backed off from a strict loser-pays system some time ago; see Herbert M. Kritzer, "The English Rule: Searching for Winners in a Loser Pays System" (1992) 78 ABAJ 54.

41 See "Update: Review of Fixed Recoverable Costs" (13 February 2017), online: Courts and Tribunals Judiciary (UK) <https://www.judiciary.gov.uk/publications/review-of-fixed-recoverable-costs/>. Lord Justice Jackson had previously advocated for an extension of fixed recoverable costs in a lecture given in January 2016: "Fixed Costs – The Time Has Come" (IPA Annual Lecture, 28 January 2016), online: Courts and Tribunals Judiciary (UK) <https://www.judiciary.gov.uk/wp-content/uploads/2016/01/fixedcostslecture-1.pdf>.

42 See "Review of Civil Litigation Costs: Supplemental Report – Fixed Recoverable Costs" (31 July 2017), online: Courts and Tribunals Judiciary (UK) <https://www.judiciary.gov.uk/publications/review-of-civil-litigation-costs-supplemental-report-fixed-recoverable-costs/>; for a brief summary, see "Jackson Scales Back Plans for Fixed Recoverable Costs," *New Law Journal* (31 July 2017), online: <https://www.newlawjournal.co.uk/content/jackson-scales-back-plans-fixed-recoverable-costs>.

43 See Neil Rose, "Government to Implement Jackson's Fixed Costs Blueprint" (28 March 2019), online: Litigation Futures <https://www.litigationfutures.com/news/government -to-implement-jacksons-fixed-costs-blueprint/print/>.

44 Dominic Regan, "Jackson and Fixed Costs: The Final Chapter Revisited," *New Law Journal* (4 April 2019), online: <https://www.newlawjournal.co.uk/content/jackson-fixed-costs-the -final-chapter-revisted>.

45 James Baxter, "Litigation Trends – The Jackson Effect: The Revolutionary Road," *New Law Journal* (29 October 2013), online: <https://www.newlawjournal.co.uk/docs/default -source/article_files/litigationtrendssurvey.pdf?sfvrsn=465bf55_2>.

46 See "New CJC Working Group to Deal with Impact of Jackson Reforms" (25 June 2014), online: LexisNexis <http://blogs.lexisnexis.co.uk/dr/new-cjc-working-group-to-deal -with-impact-of-jackson-reforms/>; however, as best I can tell, the Civil Justice Council issued no report or assessment of impacts.

47 John Peysner, "Impact of the 'Jackson' Reforms: Some Emerging Themes" (Report prepared for the Civil Justice Council Cost Forum, 21 March 2014), online: Courts and Tribunals Judiciary (UK) <https://www.judiciary.gov.uk/wp-content/uploads/2014/05/ impact-of-the-jackson-reforms.pdf>.

48 Lord Justice Jackson noted these fears in a keynote speech he gave before a Law Society conference; see "Commercial Litigation – Post Jackson" (24 October 2014), online: Stripes Solicitors <http://stripes-solicitors.co.uk/business-blog-2/commercial-litigation-post -jackson/>.

49 Exactly where the breakpoint is between a low-value and high-value case is imprecise. Anything under £25,000 would probably fall in the low-value category and anything exceeding £250,000 in the high-value category. In the large middle range, the preferred fee arrangement would depend on assumptions about how difficult it will be to reach a resolution (i.e., how much of the lawyer's time will be required).

50 Recoverability continues to exist for privacy and defamation cases; see art 4 of the *LASPO* (Commencement No 5 and Saving Provision) Order 2013 (SI 2013/77).

51 See Richard Lewis, "Structural Factors Affecting the Number and Cost of Personal Injury Claims in the Tort System" in Quill & Friel, *supra* note 28 at 49.

52 See Morris, *supra* note 28 at 138.

53 Thompsons Solicitors, "Submission on Impact of Jackson Reforms to CJC" (n.d.), online: Thompsons Solicitors <https://www.thompsonstradeunion.law/media/1969/cjc-on -impact-of-jackson-reforms-march-2014-thompsons-solicitors.pdf>.

14

Assessing Client Interests and Process Costs in a Litigation Risk Analysis

Michaela Keet and Heather Heavin

EARLIER CHAPTERS IN THIS book paint a picture of the cost of unresolved conflict and lack of access to responsive justice processes and legal services. We focus this chapter instead on the experience of people who have accessed legal services and are already involved in or assessing the value of civil litigation – and what they need to know in order to make informed decisions about the future. We also focus on represented clients, and the role of the lawyer as central to informed decision making in a litigation journey that, as we now know, will have multi-faceted impacts. We encourage lawyers to have client-centred conversations about litigation risk. By expanding their interview scripts and exploring the impact costs of litigation, lawyers can prepare their clients for sound decision making about the litigation process and better align with their clients' particular goals, resources, and constraints.

How Lawyers and Clients Make Decisions about Litigation

The more that is at stake for a litigant, the more difficult the decision-making process can be. According to a growing body of literature on the psychology of decision making, cognitive biases normally at work in the human brain are certain to cloud judgment.[1] These barriers can be overcome, and client decision making enhanced, with clear, predictive assessments of legal outcomes and focused dialogue about interests served inside and outside the process. Yet, lawyers are typically reluctant to make predictions about the course and outcome of litigation. They are drawn instead to "informal" approaches to risk analysis, characterized by imprecise and qualitative language.[2] Many view litigation predictions as inherently "subjective" or a "very amorphous evaluative thing"[3] and worry that formal and precise assessment of litigation risk will "scare the client away."[4] Vague discussions of litigation risk are prevalent, leaving troubling gaps in what clients hear and understand.

In our view, the tension this creates is a problem in today's justice climate. Codes of conduct require a lawyer to provide candid advice designed to enable the client to make decisions about how to proceed even at early stages in litigation.[5] The growing call for "accessible justice" invokes a client-centred orientation. Older practice models that treat the client as the passive recipient of a professional service – rather than a partner in planning and decision making – no longer fit as comfortably.[6] On the corporate side, there are increasing pressures regarding resource allocation and better alignment with corporate decision-making patterns.[7]

Clients may have difficulty predicting the impact of the legal process (as distinct from legal outcomes) on their individual lives – positive or negative. Without a *systematic way* of thinking about various impacts and valuing those, both the lawyer and client are operating on intuitive, or "quick-thinking," methods – a strategy that, in the midst of conflict and information overload, can allow cognitive errors to influence results. Experts in the psychology of human decision making confirm that multiple cognitive processes (put simply, the way that our brains allow us to see the world) will lead to overconfidence: "secure in the belief that they see the world accurately, people tend to be confident in their abilities to persuade those on the other side and neutral third parties of the merits of their position."[8] This can set in motion a *de facto* commitment to litigation, once litigation is engaged.

We have elsewhere outlined a simple framework for a litigation risk analysis.[9] We suggest, first, that lawyers need to project litigation outcomes with some precision. At the first stage of the analysis, lawyers assess the strength of the lawsuit, including the damages that would be awarded. To achieve this assessment, elements of the legal dispute must be broken down into their component parts and an assessment undertaken to determine the ability to prove each element of the case. At Stage 1, a careful consideration and quantification of all risks and uncertainties allows for a more accurate prediction of the strength or weakness of the client's case. A careful assessment of the remedies available is then required, particularly the quantum of damages that can be proven. The second stage of the analysis, however, requires an assessment of the process costs – the costs associated with attaining the outcome predicted. Our focus in this chapter is on what we view as central to Stage 2: now that a projection on outcome has been developed, the lawyer must assess the impact of "getting there," viewed from the perspective of the client.[10] Unless process impact costs are fully considered, the assessment of litigation risk is incomplete. The final calculation (subtracting overall projected costs from projected outcome) will underestimate what may have surprisingly lasting impact on the client.

How the Litigation Process Affects People

Until very recently, there has been little consideration of the social and psychological impacts civil litigation has on litigants.[11] In Canada, that is beginning to change with the National Self-Represented Litigants Project's collection of personal experiences with the justice system.[12] We already know that the litigation environment can cause chronic stress for lawyers,[13] whereas the litigant's experience – "the full extent to which litigation is stressful and what factors of litigation exacerbate or mediate psychological symptoms" – has not been well studied.[14] The health and psychology literature offers a starting point for better understanding these consequences.[15]

First, it is clear that people respond to legal process in a way distinct from its outcome.[16] Although a legal process itself can have therapeutic benefits,[17] the more common documented impact is harm – emotional and psychological harm.[18] Psychologists offer several labels, without consensus. "Critogenic (law-caused) harm" is described as the "intrinsic and often inescapable harms caused by the litigation process itself, even when the process is working exactly as it should."[19] "Litigation-response syndrome" is "made up of complaints that arise solely from the experience of being personally involved in a lawsuit, rather than the events that precipitated the litigation."[20] Finally, the general burden of stress accompanying litigation has been called "forensic stress,"[21] which in some individuals develops into "forensic stress disorder."[22] Stress can begin as early as the first notification that one is going to be sued[23] and last until well after litigation has ended.[24] It tends to intensify at critical stages or "psychological soft spots:"[25] important examinations or questioning processes, independent evaluations, pivotal hearings, and the trial itself.[26]

Psychological stress has been described as inevitable for all clients in any lawsuit in which the stakes *feel* significant to the litigant.[27] Some personality types are more vulnerable to litigation stress than others, and the pressure of litigation can even activate certain personality predispositions.[28] Included among those who may be more vulnerable to litigation stress are people who prefer to feel in control,[29] have poor communication skills[30] or dependent personality types,[31] or are already predisposed to stress, mood disorders, anxiety disorders, or substance abuse problems.[32] Individuals who have been involved in pre-litigation trauma (such as accidents) or who have post-traumatic stress disorder (PTSD) may experience more intense physical manifestations of anxiety.[33] Other capacity issues or prior experiences may also intensify the impact and counteract the restorative potential of litigation, for example, for people who are brain-injured[34] or suffer with pain disorders[35] or other chronic or debilitating physical conditions.[36] Certain kinds of cases – civil sexual assault actions and sexual harassment claims,[37] for example, may predispose claimants to higher levels of anxiety and psychological risk, competing with therapeutic benefits.[38] In these cases, litigation itself is described as an additional "crisis event" that the plaintiff may not have the skills to manage.[39]

Litigation stress may be more easily recognized in cases involving family conflict. Research indicates that most adults manage the transition of divorce with resilience.[40] However, clients usually enter divorce litigation already feeling suspicious, hurt, frightened, and confused.[41] It can be a time of crisis, disorganization, and vulnerability.[42] Due to the emotional issues and conflicts involved in marital breakdown, divorce proceedings have a substantial psychosocial, mental, and physical health impact on litigants.[43]

The links between psychological stress and physical health symptoms are recognized in the medical world.[44] When it comes to the impact of litigation, researchers list the following physical manifestations: appetite disturbances, lowered self-esteem, disruptions of attention and concentration, indecisiveness, disruptions of sexual functioning, and feelings of hopelessness and pessimism.[45] Other symptoms include anger, frustration, humiliation, indecision, and despondency.[46] Anxiety can interfere with daily life, leaving some clients thinking about their case obsessively and others trying to avoid anything associated with the lawsuit.[47] Emotional triggers can abound during litigation, causing sleeplessness, headaches, nausea, sweats, muscle tension, shakiness, or panic attacks.[48]

The legal process can also affect litigants' relationships, causing their social world to shrink and support systems to "burn out."[49] Many litigants have a compulsive need to talk about the experience that exceeds the patience of their friends and family members.[50] In this way, litigation can be a very isolating experience. Ongoing litigation enables clients to put their lives on hold and so avoid other aspects of their lives.[51] Even apart from divorce and family litigation *per se*, the stress of civil litigation has been said to have a potentially devastating impact on families, with a discernible increase in disruptiveness, disorganization, or incapacitation.[52] Social relationships can be impacted even at the community level, where certain kinds of litigation can create collective trauma and ultimately be corrosive.[53]

Although more research is needed, the following components of litigation have been noted as causing stress to litigants. The adversarial nature of the litigation process makes some level of stress inevitable.[54] From a psychological standpoint, the process has been described as "noxious,"[55] creating a damaging "aura of combat"[56] laden with complex concepts and unfamiliar language[57] ("a game disconnected from the real world"[58]). Adversarial litigation may involve delaying tactics in the hope that protracted litigation will wear the other party down.[59] It provides only limited and scripted opportunities for litigant participation.[60] Delay is identified as a major stressor,[61] preventing clients from moving on psychologically and from developing a sense of "completion"[62] or emotional closure[63] – or even preventing institutional learning.[64] Whether litigation moves too slow or too fast,[65] the timing is simply one aspect of the overarching loss of control that litigants tend to experience with litigation.[66] Even meetings with lawyers can be distressing, intimidating, or disorienting for clients.[67] So too are aspects of the building of the case, such as having to disclose information that clients know can weaken their case, and to produce information requested by the other side.[68] The requirement for a plaintiff to prove injury can be a distinct source of distress,[69] especially when the claim includes proof of emotional or psychological harm.[70] Claims that require clients to retell their story several times cause additional anxiety – where the repetition of interviews, and interview conditions, induce strain, [71] evoke emotions, and possibly activate a client's dissociative defences.[72] Generally, psychologists warn that it is therapeutic for a client to talk about trauma only under controlled circumstances – that the courtroom "is not a substitute for the therapist's couch."[73] It follows that examinations under oath are also linked with strain for the client.[74] The need to give testimony in a public trial has been described as "exquisitely painful."[75] Testifying may increase traumatic responses,[76]and litigants can feel helpless or frustrated as they are forced to listen to testimony (or arguments) that may sound unfavourable.[77] Regardless of the outcome, many litigants leave the process with a "bruised sense of personal integrity."[78]

How the Litigation Process Affects Organizations

In addition to the personal health and stress-related impacts experienced by individuals within an organization, the organization as an entity[79] is also impacted by litigation processes through loss of opportunity and reputation.[80] Opportunity costs are valued as the loss of potential gain from other alternatives when one alternative is chosen.[81] Such costs include the diversion of the organizations' productive capacity to other uses. Litigation leads to loss of opportunity within organizations as individuals are required to allocate time and resources to support the lawsuit. The time spent by employees, managers, or executives gathering, assembling, and organizing information, preparing for and attending litigation processes (including mediations, discoveries, pretrials, trials), and reporting on and making decisions pertaining to the litigation is time that could have been used to pursue the goals of the organization.[82]

Opportunity costs can be valued by looking at the costs of lost time and of loss of output that would otherwise have been achieved had the productive assets of the organization not been allocated to support the litigation. They can also include loss of enjoyment and satisfaction attributed to personal stress, and other health impacts experienced by individuals engaged in litigation that lead to reduced workplace productivity or low morale.[83]

Other intangible assets, such as a firm's reputation, may also be impacted by the process of litigation (as opposed to the litigation itself).[84] While this also results in a diversion of assets within the corporation, it has additional external effects, such as on a firm's public brand, making it vulnerable to losing market share through loss of customers or clients or loss of talent from within the organization.[85]

Weighing Litigation Process Costs: Informed Decision Making

Most lawyers are surprised by these costs, and yet are still unlikely to assess and discuss them systematically.[86] *Traditional interview frameworks, designed with fact-finding in mind, and based on "lawyer-as-expert" models of the relationship, are deficient in this regard.* "[E]xperienced lawyers often have a limited view of what is required for comprehensive representation,"[87] and use an interview "script [that] rarely changes even when the client changes."[88] The danger is the premature assumption of a *shared base of understanding*: the lawyer does not fully understand the client's priorities and limitations, and the client does not fully understand how a legal process is likely to unfold and be experienced.

We suggest that where transparency and accuracy (rigour) in decision making are vital, the lawyer has to guide the conversation with deliberation.

Focusing on Client-Centred Priorities and Impacts

Understanding the current and future priorities of clients is important in order to identify what clients may be giving up to pursue litigation. Time and energy have value insofar as they are related to the pursuit of a particular priority. By inviting clients to consider the impact litigation will have on their ability to maintain or achieve these priorities, both the lawyer and the client can anticipate and measure the pros and cons of moving forward with the process. A litigation risk assessment, therefore, should include an assessment of how litigation may affect various aspects of the client's life:

- *Financial goals and stability* – A general profile of assets, debts, and income and expenses, along with a discussion of financial goals, will shed light on capacity to fund litigation and impact of the process and outcome on current and future goals and opportunities.
- *Career, education, and "productive work"* – For individual clients, this may mean losing or delaying the opportunity to advance their career or education or to engage in other "productive work" (paid or unpaid, inside or outside the home). For organizations, this may mean delaying or forgoing business

opportunities or new initiatives, or impacting existing operations and service levels. Short- and long-term goals, including the development or maintenance of professional networks or vocational relationships, and potential impacts of time or energy siphoned away from alternative goals and options should be explored. Considerations of reputation or professional identity that are connected to an individual's productive work or an organization's mandate should be canvassed.

- *Relationships, family, and community* – Clients should consider whether litigation will damage support systems or other external relationships. Psychological research suggests that external support systems (including family supports or "communities" around the litigant) are important and are commonly affected by the strain. An assessment of potential positive and negative impacts and resources in this sphere is key.[89] This would invite clients to consider the impact of litigation (monetary and psychological) on their capacity to invest in and manage these relationships, as well as the impact on those third parties or social groups. Professional or commercial relationships may also be eroded due to reputation losses arising from publicity associated with the litigation process.

- *Health and wellness* – Most of the research on litigation impact focuses on stress and anxiety, with some information about how these translate into physical health. Within organizations, litigation stress may contribute to low employee morale and decreased work productivity, including stress-induced leaves of absence. Litigants should be invited to reflect on their expected resilience to litigation (their capacity to absorb stress in healthy ways and their personal appetite for risk). If the lawyer has questions about the client's capacity to critically reflect on these factors, or if the lawyer suspects that the client's personality or circumstances may give rise to particular vulnerabilities identified in the aforementioned research, then ensuring appropriate supports (such as counsellor or psychologist referrals) may be necessary to support the client.[90]

- *Perceptions built on litigation history and past experience* – Litigants will be operating with particular schemas that affect how they might view future litigation.[91] "[I]t can be helpful to acknowledge the reality that preexisting knowledge structures can influence perception."[92] Lawyers will have limited capacity and responsibility to investigate such histories and cognitive schemas, but at the same time, we suggest that a discussion about the client's past litigation experiences (and their impact) would be useful in predicting resilience, expectations, and risk appetite. At the very least, this may evoke a relevant comparative framework for the lawyer and allow any red flags to be identified.

When it comes to a risk assessment conversation, it is important that the lawyer employ a client-centred approach (or a team mentality[93]), with a commitment to engaged and active listening.[94] This part of the dialogue needs to be motivated by curiosity,[95] an attitude of "informed not-knowing."[96] Generally, client satisfaction increases when the client feels involved.[97] The dialogue requires a balance between information seeking and information giving. Information about how others experience litigation may help. Research shows that the accuracy of people's assessments increases when they have "surrogate knowledge" – information about how other people experienced an event.[98] The conveyance of information by lawyers to their clients can be viewed as an educational process, and – here again – it is helpful to understand how people respond to information. Presenting information in concrete rather than abstract forms, breaking it into manageable segments, and using visual aids (flowcharts and decision trees) are all considered superior communication strategies.[99] Raising possible areas of impact, and even inviting the client to take some time to reflect or map out the pros and cons,[100] will contribute to slow and systematic decision making. Clients with particular vulnerabilities may need a more targeted discussion of – and, if necessary, planning for – the litigation's "psychological soft spots."[101]

Weighing the Impact of Litigation on Client-Centred Priorities

The distinction made between estimating the value of direct legal costs and other "intangible" impact costs often focuses on the perceived ability to objectively measure and value one but not the other. Legal processes costs are often identified as more capable of valuation and, as they represent clear out-of-pocket costs to be incurred by the client, will always have an important impact on the overall anticipated value of a case. They will also be more accurately tracked, as the legal services business model depends on charging clients for the services provided. Law societies (and individual law firms) generate various templates to help lawyers identify, quantify, and communicate more precise and accurate estimates of these litigation costs for the client.[102] They also advocate for better upfront communications between the lawyer and client so that the client can fully understand and budget for the legal fees and disbursements that must be paid by the client in order to pursue the legal action. These other intangible process costs, identified above, are not tracked by law firms, however, and are often assumed to be incapable of measurement or valuation with any degree of certainty. Furthermore, measuring the value of human health, happiness, or quality of life may also elicit social or moral objection by appearing to reduce these aspects of the human experience to numerical or monetary terms.[103] The converse, however, of failing to provide any monetary value to these impacts results in treating these impacts as having zero value. While quantifying health (including mental health) expenses incurred by individuals engaged in litigation may provide some information about some aspects of intangible impact costs, they may not be readily accessible or practically useful to individual lawyers and clients.

Valuation of these impacts will always be subjective as they are dependent on factors and influences that may be unique to each client.[104] However, lawyers and clients engaged in a fulsome discussion of the impacts identified above can undertake a simple valuation by simply asking the client to attribute value personally. What value do clients place on their mental well-being? Relationships? Time? By asking clients to place a value on their time, health, priorities, and relationships, lawyers and clients can co-construct the costs associated with the sphere of impacts and ensure that the value of these impacts is not forgotten and ignored. An alternative framing of this valuation by the client would be to ask what they would pay to avoid the impact risks identified. Placing a value on avoiding future risk is a concept that underlies why people purchase insurance products. This willingness-to-pay method is also used when there is no other method available to conduct a valuation.[105] In the context of litigation, George Adams suggests that risk-averse clients may be willing to pay a "risk premium": the premium applicable to a risk-averse defendant, for example, is that amount over the expected value of the litigation the defendant would pay to be relieved of any chance of a greater loss.[106]

We view the lawyer as responsible for raising the client's awareness of potential areas of impact, and *actually valuing them* as part of assisting the client in making informed decisions about how to proceed. Lawyers who have a good grasp of their clients' priorities and limitations, who have had transparent conversations with them about the full costs of the litigation impact, and who have a good sense of how those interests balance out with the potential risks and gains of litigation as each step unfolds can make better decisions not just about settlement but also about the management of litigation itself.[107]

Conclusion

Prudent lawyers will "discuss the costs, suitability, timing ... probable outcomes and finality" of all procedural options available to the client.[108] While there is much talk in the mediation literature about the potential efficiencies and "soft gains" in the process,[109] there is little guidance on how to rigorously or systematically assess those impacts. While we focus this chapter on litigation impact costs, this approach should be used to assess process impact costs for any procedural option.[110]

Litigation has impacts beyond the financial burden of paying legal fees. Attention must be paid to the risks and inevitable impacts of the legal process *before* the client commits to a litigation path.[111] With open communication between lawyers and clients about all impact costs of pursuing a legal action, clients will be better equipped to make informed decisions about pursuing litigation, settlement, or other forms of dispute resolution, as well as to prepare themselves for the impact the litigation process will have on all spheres of their financial, emotional, and psychological well-being. Informed decision making is central to the lawyer-client relationship, and assessing and valuing all impact costs associated with pursuing litigation is a critical aspect of this decision making.

Notes

1   Andrew J. Wistrich & Jeffrey J. Rachlinski, "How Lawyers' Intuitions Prolong Litigation" (2013) 86:3 S Cal L Rev 571. See generally Daniel Kahneman, *Thinking, Fast and Slow* (New York: Farrar, Straus and Giroux, 2011); Thomas Gilovich, Dale Griffin, & Daniel Kahneman, eds, *Heuristics and Biases: The Psychology of Intuitive Judgment* (Cambridge: Cambridge University Press, 2002); Randall L. Kiser, Martin A. Asher, & Blakeley B. McShane, "Let's Not Make a Deal: An Empirical Study of Decision Making in Unsuccessful Settlement Negotiations" (2008) 5:3 J Empirical Leg Studies 551; Randall Kiser, *Beyond Right and Wrong: The Power of Effective Decision Making for Attorneys and Clients* (Berlin: Springer, 2010); Charles W. Murdock & Barry Sullivan, "What Kahneman Means for Lawyers: Some Reflections on Thinking Fast and Slow" (2013) 44 Loy U Chicago LJ 1377 at 1396.

2   See Heather Heavin & Michaela Keet, "The Path of Lawyers: Enhancing Predictive Ability through Risk Assessment Methods" (Paper delivered at the Canadian Institute for the Administration of Justice Annual Conference, 5–7 October 2016) ["The Path of Lawyers"]. See also John Wade, "Systematic Risk Analysis for Negotiators and Litigators: How to Help Clients to Make Better Decisions" (2002) 13:2 Bond L Rev 462; Jeffrey M. Senger, "Analyzing Risk" in Andrea Kupfer Schneider & Christopher Honeyman, eds, *The Negotiator's Fieldbook: The Desk Reference for the Experienced Negotiator* (Washington, DC: American Bar Association, 2006) 445 at 452.

3   Interview with Lawyer No 1 in Heavin & Keet, "The Path of Lawyers," *supra* note 2.

4   Interview with Lawyer No 6 in *ibid.*

5   Federation of Law Societies of Canada, *Model Code of Professional Conduct* (2017) (obliging lawyers to "advise and encourage a client to compromise or settle a dispute whenever it is possible to do so on a reasonable basis," r 3.2-4). This obligation is supplemented by the provisions in the *Code* setting standards for competency, quality, and candour (r 3.1-2, commentary 1-15; r 3.2-1, commentary 1-6; r 3.2-2, commentary 1-3). Alice Woolley has suggested that the duty of honesty and candour requires lawyers giving advice to "engage in reasoned explanation of their position, noting its weaknesses and any countervailing arguments": "The Lawyer as Advisor and the Practice of the Rule of Law" (2014) 47:2 UBC L Rev 743 at 773. Elsewhere, Woolley has argued that full and candid advice is at the core of lawyers' fiduciary duty to their clients: "The Lawyer as Fiduciary: Defining Private Law Duties in Public Law Relations" (2015) 65:4 UTLJ 285 at 333.

6   See Julie Macfarlane, *The New Lawyer: How Settlement Is Transforming the Practice of Law* (Vancouver: UBC Press, 2008).

7   This message came through consistently across many of the interviews: Heavin & Keet, "The Path of Lawyers," *supra* note 2. Business organizations engaged with risk management on

an operational level are familiar with decision making in the face of future uncertainty and have utilized decision analysis frameworks for operational decision making. See Douglas N. Dickson, ed, *Using Logical Techniques for Making Better Decisions* (New York: John Wiley and Sons, 1983); David Targett, *Analytical Decision Making* (London: Pitman Publishing, 1996); Peter P. Wakker, *Prospect Theory for Risk and Ambiguity* (Cambridge: Cambridge University Press, 2010).

8   Jennifer K. Robbennolt & Jean R. Sternlight, *Psychology for Lawyers: Understanding the Human Factors in Negotiation, Litigation, and Decision-Making* (Chicago: American Bar Association, 2012) at 23.

9   Heather Heavin & Michaela Keet, "Litigation Risk Analysis: Using Rigorous Projections to Encourage and Inform Settlement" (2017–18) 7:2 J Arbitration & Mediation 57 at 65–83; Heavin & Keet, "The Path of Lawyers," *supra* note 2.

10 For a general discussion about client financial interests and the idea of offsetting, see John Lande, "Good Pretrial Lawyering: Planning to Get to Yes Sooner, Cheaper, and Better" (2014–15) 16 Cardozo J Conflict Resolution 63.

11 The first large-scale empirical study of litigation costs in North America (a multi-state 1980s study) assessed the parties' view of the overall gains and costs without detailing what those might have been; see David M. Trubek et al, "The Costs of Ordinary Litigation" (October 1983) 31:1 UCLA L Rev 72 at 119–20.

12 See National Self-Represented Litigants Project, online: <https://representingyourselfcanada.com>. Reported feelings *about interactions within the justice system, including with legal professionals,* included "humiliated," "stressed," "bullied," "frustrated," "afraid," "traumatized," and others – with the most common response being "overwhelmed."

13 Dennis Portnoy, "Burnout and Compassion Fatigue: Watch for Signs" (2011) 92 Health Progress 47 at 48; Lee Norton et al, "Burnout and Compassion Fatigue: What Lawyers Need to Know" (2015–16) 84 University of Missouri–Kansas City L Rev 987 at 989.

14 Christian Diesen & Hugh Koch, "Contemporary 21st Century Therapeutic Jurisprudence in Civil Cases: Building Bridges between Law and Psychology" (January-March 2016) 2:1 Ethics, Medicine & Public Health 13 at 23.

15 For a fulsome overview of this literature see Michaela Keet, Heather Heavin, & Shawna Sparrow, "Anticipating and Valuing the Psychological Costs of Litigation" (2017) 34:1 Windsor YB Access Just 73.

16 E. Allan Lind et al, "In the Eye of the Beholder: Tort Litigants' Evaluations of Their Experiences in the Civil Justice System" (1990) 24 Law & Soc'y Rev 953 at 957.

17 Happiness, relief, confidence, and triumph: Martin Gramatikov "A Framework for Measuring the Costs of Paths to Justice" (February 2009) 2 The Journal Jurisprudence 111 at 145; Noel Semple's review of interview transcripts with self-represented litigants concluded that approximately 20 percent of the reported feelings (about process) were positive: "The Cost of Seeking Civil Justice in Canada" (2016) 93:3 Can Bar Rev 639 at 667, 668. See also benefits listed in c 28 of Alan M. Goldstein, ed, *Handbook of Psychology, Forensic Psychology,* vol 11 (Hoboken, NJ: Wiley, 2003).

18 For example, see Gary Fulcher, "Litigation-Induced Trauma Sensitisation (LITS) – A Potential Negative Outcome of the Process of Litigation" (2004) 11 Psychiatry, Psychology & L 79 at 80; J. Gutman et al, "The Psychological Impact of the Legal System on Sexually Abused Children" (2001) 8 Psychiatry, Psychology & L 174; Paul Elston et al, "Litigation Stress" (2006) 150:34 Solicitor's J 1146; R.L. Binder et al, "Is Money a Cure? Follow-Up of Litigants in England" (1991) 19 Bulletin of the American Academy of Psychiatry and the Law 151; and Edward J. Hickling et al, "The Psychological Impact of Litigation: Compensation Neurosis, Malingering, PTSD, Secondary Traumatization, and Other Lessons

from MVAS" (2006) 55 DePaul L Rev 617 at 625; Nicole M. Zapzalka, *The Psychological Impact of Civil Litigation: A Comparison of Perceived Anxiety Levels in Civil Litigation as Viewed by Trial and Alternative Dispute Resolution Litigants* (PhD Thesis, Capella University, 2007) [unpublished] at 75.

19 Thomas G. Gutheil et al, "Preventing 'Critogenic' Harms: Minimizing Emotional Injury from Civil Litigation" (2000) 28 J Psychiatry & L 5 at 6.

20 Paul R. Lees-Haley, "Litigation Response Syndrome: How Stress Confuses the Issues" (1989) 56 Def Couns J 110.

21 Larry J. Cohen & Joyce H. Vesper, "Forensic Stress Disorder" (2001) 25 Law & Psychol Rev 1 at 4.

22 *Ibid* at 4.

23 Or, for plaintiffs, stress complaints may arise as soon as they consider embarking on litigation. Lees-Haley, *supra* note 20 at 114. Overall, there appears to be no difference in anxiety levels between plaintiffs and defendants: Zapzalka, *supra* note 18 at 69.

24 Up to six months: Cohen & Vesper, *supra* note 21 at 4. Even after, unpleasant memories from the litigation experience can continue to result in stress: J. Steven Picou, "Disaster, Litigation, and the Corrosive Community" (2003–4) 82 Social Forces 1493 at 1503.

25 Captain Evan R. Seamone, "The Veterans' Lawyer as Counselor: Using Therapeutic Jurisprudence to Enhance Client Counseling for Combat Veterans with Posttraumatic Stress Disorder" (2009) 202 Mil L Rev 185 at 195; Bruce Winick, "Therapeutic Jurisprudence and the Role of Counsel in Litigation" (2000–1) 37 Cal WL Rev 105 at 110.

26 Lees-Haley, *supra* note 20 at 114.

27 *Ibid* at 112; Larry H. Strasburger, "The Litigant-Patient: Mental Health Consequences of Civil Litigation" (1999) 27 J American Academy of Psychiatry and the Law 203 at 204.

28 Herbert N. Weissman, "Distortions and Deceptions in Self Presentation: Effects of Protracted Litigation in Personal Injury Cases" (1990) 8 Behav Sci & L 67 at 68. On the other hand, certain dispositions can also mitigate litigation stress, such as the capacity for optimism and endurance: John P. Gould, "The Economics of Legal Conflicts" (1973) 2 J Legal Stud 279.

29 Cohen & Vesper, *supra* note 21 at 15.

30 Lees-Haley, *supra* note 20 at 111.

31 Cohen & Vesper, *supra* note 21 at 15. See also Norton et al, *supra* note 13 at 995.

32 Lees-Haley, *supra* note 20 at 111.

33 Cohen & Vesper, *supra* note 21 at 14. Clients suffering from PTSD can be embroiled in the psychological defence of avoidance, which is thwarted as they revisit the trauma through examinations and testimony. As the avoidance defence fails, these litigants experience a resurgence of traumatic reactions. Strasburger, *supra* note 27 at 205.

34 Anthony Feinstein, "The Effects of Litigation on Symptom Expression: A Prospective Study Following Mild Traumatic Brain Injury" (2001) 41 Med Sci Law 116 at 118.

35 Marilyn S. Jacobs, "Psychological Factors Influencing Chronic Pain and the Impact of Litigation" (2003) 1 Current Physical Medicine and Rehabilitation Reports 135 at 135: In particular, where the condition causing the pain is at issue in litigation, which is associated with increased depression, anger, frustration, anxiety, mistrust, and hopeless despair (at 139). See also Weissman, *supra* note 28 at 68.

36 J.M.S. Pearce, "Aspects of the Failed Back Syndrome: Role of Litigation" (2000) 38 Spinal Cord 63 at 63.

37 Nora West, "Rape in the Criminal Law and the Victim's Tort Alternative: A Feminist Analysis" (1992) 50 UT Fac L Rev 96 at 116; Angela K. Lawson & Louise F. Fitzgerald, "Sexual

Harassment Litigation: A Road to Re-victimization or Recovery?" 9 Psychological Injury and Law 216 at 216.

38 Which may include a sense of empowerment and control, when compared with criminal proceedings: West, *supra* note 37 at 111. Many sexual assault victims decide to litigate as a response to a crisis, such as a nervous breakdown or suicide attempt. Bruce Feldthusen et al, "Therapeutic Consequences of Civil Actions for Damages and Compensation Claims by Victims of Sexual Abuse" (2000) 12 CJWL 65 at 79. See also Rosemarie Boll, "Opening Closed Doors – The Downside of Suing Your Abuser" (2012) 36:6 LawNow 38 at 38; Angela K. Lawson, *Having Your Day in Court: The Psychological Impact of Sexual Harassment Litigation* (PhD Thesis, University of Illinois at Urbana-Champaign, 2007) at 8; L.F. Fitzgerald, "Sexual Harassment and Social Justice: Reflections on the Distance Yet to Go" (2003) 58 American Psychologist 915; Caroline Vaile Wright & Louise F. Fitzgerald, "Angry and Afraid: Women's Appraisals of Sexual Harassment during Litigation" (2007) 31 Psychology of Women Quarterly 73 at 81.

39 Lawson, *supra* note 38 at 15.

40 David A. Sbarra, "Divorce and Death: A Meta-Analysis and Research Agenda for Clinical, Social and Health Psychology" (2011) 6 Perspectives on Psychological Science 454 at 455; M. Richards, "The Effects of Divorce and Separation on Mental Health in a National UK Birth Cohort" (1997) 27 Psychological Medicine 1121 at 1121.

41 Bennett Wolfe, "The Best Interest of the Divorcing Family – Mediation Not Litigation" (1983) 29 Loy L Rev 55 at 72.

42 *Ibid.*

43 *Ibid* at 70; Richards, *supra* note 40 at 1127. See also Sbarra, *supra* note 40 at 459.

44 For example, PTSD is associated with greater general health problems over time: Maria L. Pacella, Bryce Hruska, & Douglas L. Delahanty, "The Physical Health Consequences of PTSD and PTSD Symptoms: A Meta-Analytic Review" (2013) 27 J of Anxiety Disorders 33.

45 Lees-Haley, *supra* note 20 at 113. Pacella documents the relationship between mental stress (PTSD) and physical health: Pacella, Hruska, & Delahanty, *supra* note 44.

46 Strasburger, *supra* note 27 at 204.

47 Cohen & Vesper, *supra* note 21 at 5, 16.

48 *Ibid.*

49 Strasburger, *supra* note 27 at 204.

50 *Ibid.*

51 *Ibid* at 209.

52 Joyce H. Vesper & Larry J. Cohen, "Litigating Posttraumatic Stress Disorder: Effects on the Family" (1999) 27 J Psychiatry & L 313 at 315.

53 An extreme example involves toxic torts: J. Steven Picou, "When the Solution Becomes the Problem: The Impacts of Adversarial Litigation on Survivors of the *Exxon Valdez* Oil Spill" (2009–10) 7 U St Thomas LJ 68. See also Lewis Robert Shreve, "Lessons from Exxon-Valdez: Employing Market Forces to Minimize the Psychological Impact on Oil Spill Plaintiffs" (2011) 35 Law & Psychol Rev 239 at 248.

54 Feldthusen et al, *supra* note 38 at 115; Cohen & Vesper, *supra* note 21 at 1; Lind et al, *supra* note 16 at 956.

55 Norton et al, *supra* note 13 at 995.

56 Strasburger, supra note 27 at 203.

57 Cohen & Vesper, *supra* note 21 at 4; Lind et al, *supra* note 16 at 959.

58 Brent K. Marshall et al, "Technological Disasters, Litigation Stress, and the Use of Alternative Dispute Resolution Mechanisms (2004) 26 Law & Pol'y 289 at 295.

59   *Ibid* at 302.
60   Lind et al, *supra* note 16 at 959.
61   Elston et al, *supra* note 18 at 1146; Jamie O'Connell, "Gambling with the Psyche: Does Prosecuting Human Rights Violators Console Their Victims?" (2005) 46 Harv Int'l LJ 295; Gutheil et al, *supra* note 19 at 11.
62   Elston et al, *supra* note 18 at 1147; Strasburger, *supra* note 27 at 205.
63   Gutheil et al, supra note 19 at 12. Especially true of wrongful death claims, which can suspend the grief process, resulting in debilitating consequences for the claimant: Daniel W. Shuman, "When Time Does Not Heal: Understanding the Importance of Avoiding Unnecessary Delay in the Resolution of Tort Cases" (2000) 6 Psychology, Public Policy and Law 880 at 890.
64   Such as in the case of medical malpractice claims: Seth A. Seabury et al, "On Average, Physicians Spend Nearly 11 Percent of Their 40-Year Careers with an Open Unresolved Malpractice Claim" (2013) 32 Health Affairs 111 at 116.
65   Pushing clients before they are psychologically ready to face trauma, for example: Gutheil et al, *supra* note 19 at 15. See also Feldthusen et al, *supra* note 38 at 93.
66   In a study of tort litigants, Lind and colleagues found that client perceptions of control was a key factor in their satisfaction or dissatisfaction with the litigation process. Lind et al, *supra* note 16 at 958. See also Winick, *supra* note 25 at 113, stressing that exercising a degree of control and self-determination is important to psychological well-being. Loss of control is exacerbated by the intrusive nature of litigation and lack of privacy: Strasburger, *supra* note 27 at 207.
67   Cohen & Vesper, *supra* note 21 at 6. As the case continues, the amount of time spent with attorneys has been identified as a specific type of litigation stress: Picou, *supra* note 24 at 1497.
68   Cohen & Vesper, *supra* note 21 at 9.
69   O'Connell, *supra* note 61 at 334.
70   Lawson & Fitzgerald, *supra* note 37 at 217.
71   Elston et al, *supra* note 18 at 1147; Fulcher, *supra* note 18 at 81; Vesper & Cohen, *supra* note 52 at 333.
72   Fulcher, *supra* note 18 at 80. Serious consequences can result from the sensitizing nature of the interview regime, which Fulcher calls "litigation-induced trauma sensitisation (LTS)" (at 82).
73   David Mendeloff, "Trauma and Vengeance: Assessing the Psychological and Emotional Effects of Post-Conflict Justice" (2009) 31 Hum Rts Q 592 at 613. See also Brandon Hamber, "The Need for a Survivor-Centered Approach to the Truth and Reconciliation Commission" (1996) 9 Community Mediation Update 5. Although some counsel defendants to "tell their story" on their own terms, in a safe setting accompanying litigation: N.A. Ryll, "Living through Litigation: Malpractice Stress Syndrome" (2015) 34:1 J Radiology Nursing 35.
74   Dennis P. Stolle & Mark D. Stuaan, "Defending Depositions in High-Stakes Civil and Quasi-Criminal Litigation: An Application of Therapeutic Jurisprudence" (2003) 4 Western Criminology Review 134 at 134.
75   Strasburger, *supra* note 27 at 205.
76   Mendeloff, supra note 73 at 613.
77   Cohen & Vesper, *supra* note 21 at 13.
78   Strasburger, *supra* note 27 at 207.
79   We define organizations to include corporate/not-for-profit and governmental/non-governmental entities.

80 Michaela Keet, Heather Heavin, & Shawna Sparrow, "Indirect and Indivisible Organizational Costs: Making Informed Decisions about Litigation and Settlement" (2018) 20
Cardozo J Conflict Resolution 49.

81 The *New Oxford American Dictionary* defines opportunity cost as the loss of potential
gain from other alternatives when one alternative is chosen.

82 John Wade has suggested that various questions should be asked by an organization in order
to ascertain the costs of litigation to an organization: How far will I and my employees
be able to concentrate on new projects over the next X years of conflict? How many days
of work time will I and my employees lose over the next X years preparing for this dispute?
What pressures will X years of conflict put on our families? Wade, *supra* note 2.

83 Corporate Early Case Assessment Commission of the International Institute for Conflict
Prevention and Resolution, *Resources for Navigating Complex Business Disputes: Corporate
Early Case Assessment Toolkit* (New York: CPR, 2009) at 10 advocates that lawyers should
pay particular attention to the "business concerns" of the client, including short-term and
long-term economic goals, publicity and reputation, psychological concerns, relationships
(including confidentiality), and a host of others. This investigation will enable the lawyer
to define a successful resolution from the client's perspective. The focus here is on the
outcome (ideally, the terms of an agreement), but we argue that the same exploration can
and should occur with a discussion of process steps and their impact, and this deserves
equal consideration.

84 Intangible assets are distinguished from tangible physical and monetary assets: see the
International Accounting Standards Board's IAS 38 – *Intangible Assets,* whose definition
includes "an identifiable non-monetary asset without physical substance" and includes
the critical elements of identifiability, control (power to obtain benefits from the asset),
and future economic benefits (such as revenues or reduced costs): online: Deloitte <https://
www.iasplus.com/en/standards/ias/ias38>. See also Robert G. Eccles, Scott C. Newquist,
& Roland Schatz, "Reputation and Its Risks" (February 2007) 85:2 Harv Business Rev,
online: <https://hbr.org/2007/02/reputation-and-its-risks>.

85 See Sharon A. Israel & Brandon Baum, "Rethinking Litigation Strategy in a Down Economy: Can We End This Thing Quickly?" (July/August 2009) 15:4 IP Litigator 8 at 8.

86 Beyond legal fees and expenses, which are also the focus of software tools for risk assess-
ment, with some exceptions: Paul Prestia & Harrie Samaras, "Beyond Decision Trees:
Determining Aggregate Probabilities of Time, Cost, and Outcomes" (2010) 28:4 Alter-
natives to the High Cost of Litigation 1. Also, Michael Palmer's case valuation model,
"Which Is Better? The Deal or the Ordeal? An Examination of Some Challenges of Case
Valuation" (2010) 36:3 Vt BJ 1.

87 Laurie Shanks, "Whose Story Is It, Anyway? Guiding Students to Client-Centered Interviewing through Storytelling" (2008) 14:2 Clinical L Rev 509 at 510.

88 *Ibid* at 513.

89 Some psychologists suggest that a "family style" and degree of functionality will affect the
way the family, and ultimately the litigant, deals with the process: Vesper & Cohen, *supra*
note 52 at 333.

90 Psychologists and clinical social workers have established a precise methodology for assessing personal risk associated with future events, with a clinical interview and psycho-
metric testing. Certain claims should call for this kind of process. For example, sexual
abuse litigation also comes with heavy costs to participants. A study of victims indicated
that 84 percent experienced some negative consequences from litigation, and 18 percent
would not have chosen to litigate if presented with the same choice again: Feldthusen et
al, *supra* note 38 at 113.

91 Robbennolt & Sternlight, *supra* note 8 at 12.

92 *Ibid* at 13.

93 Cohen & Vesper, *supra* note 21 at 26.

94 See Robbennolt & Sternlight, *supra* note 8 at 157–61 for a discussion of how lawyers can build a foundation for effective communication. Active listening skills are linked with enhanced therapeutic benefits: Diesen & Koch, *supra* note 14 at 24. The most effective exploration of psychological factors requires a balance of open and closed questions – Donald E. Wiger & Debra K. Huntley, *Essentials of Interviewing* (New York: John Wiley and Sons, 2002) at 46 – and "attending skills" – Rita Sommers-Flanagan & John Sommers-Flanagan, *Clinical Interviewing*, 2nd ed (New York: John Wiley and Sons, 1999) at 87.

95 See Chris Guthrie, "Be Curious" (2009) 25 Negotiation J 401.

96 Although Tremblay employs the concept to make room for cultural difference, it can also be applicable here, where the intangible impacts of litigation may be quite personal: Paul Tremblay, "Interviewing and Counseling across Cultures: Heuristics and Biases" (2003) 9 Clinical L Rev 373 at 373.

97 Lind et al, *supra* note 16 at 961; Diesen & Koch, *supra* note 14 at 24; Winick, *supra* note 25 at 115; Feldthusen et al, *supra* note 38 at 83. Clients feel part of the process when the lawyer conveys genuineness and empathy: Diesen & Koch, *supra* note 14 at 24.

98 Robbennolt & Sternlight, *supra* note 8 at 99. Diesen and Koch suggest that litigation stress can be reduced when lawyers provide a clearer dissemination of information to claimants about the litigation process: Diesen & Koch, *supra* note 14 at 23.

99 Robbennolt & Sternlight, *supra* note 8, see discussion at 166–69.

100 Tools exist in popular literature to help clients identify goals and weigh priorities. See, for example, mind maps: "How to Do a Mind Map for Goal Setting," online: Achieve-Goal-Setting-Success.com <http://www.achieve-goal-setting-success.com/mind-map-for-goal-setting.html>. See also J.S. Hammond, R.L. Keeney, & H. Raiffa, *Smart Choices: A Practical Guide to Making Better Decisions* (Cambridge, MA: Harvard Business School Press, 1999).

101 Seamone, *supra* note 25 at 196; Fulcher, *supra* note 18 at 83; Diesen & Koch, *supra* note 14 at 23.

102 See Law Society of Upper Canada, "Sample Long Form Litigation Cost Estimate Template" and "Sample Short Form Litigation Cost Estimate," online: Law Society of Upper Canada <http://www.lsuc.on.ca>; Law Society of British Columbia, "General Litigation Procedure" checklist," online: Law Society of British Columbia <https://www.lawsociety.bc.ca/Website/media/Shared/docs/practice/checklists/E-2.pdf>; Ontario Bar Association, "Discovery Best Practices: General Guidelines for the Discovery Process in Ontario," online: Ontario Bar Association <http://www.oba.org/en/pdf_newsletter/DTFGeneralDiscoverybest.pdf>; Paula Hannaford-Agor & Nicole L. Waters, "Estimating the Cost of Litigation" (National Center for State Courts, Court Statistics Project, Caseload Highlights, January 2013), online: <http://www.courtstatistics.org>. For information about billing rates and litigation costs in Canada, see Michael McKiernan, "The Going Rate: The 2015 Canadian Legal Fees Survey," *Canadian Lawyer* (June 2015) at 33–37, online: <http://www.canadianlawyermag.com/images/stories/pdfs/Surveys/2015/CL_June_15_GoingRate.pdf>.

103 See Douglas W. Hubbard, *How to Measure Anything: Finding the Value of "Intangibles" in Business*, 3rd ed (Hoboken, NJ: John Wiley and Sons, 2014) at 295. See Joachim Weimann, Andreas Knabe, & Ronnie Schob, *Measuring Happiness: The Economics of Well-Being* (Cambridge, MA: MIT Press, 2015); Pedro Conceição & Romina Bandura, "Measuring Subjective Well-Being: A Summary Review of the Literature" (2008) United Nations Development Programme Working Paper, online: Russia Longitudinal Monitoring Survey – Higher School of Economics <http://www.cpc.unc.edu/projects/rlms-hse/

publications/924>; Paul Dolan, Richard Layard, & Robert Metcalfe, "Measuring Subjective Wellbeing for Public Policy: Recommendations on Measures" (March 2011) Centre
for Economic Performance, London School of Economics, Special Paper No 23, online:
London School of Economics <http://cep.lse.ac.uk/pubs/download/special/cepsp23.
pdf>; Richard Layard, "Measuring Subjective Well-Being" (January 2010) 327 Science 534.

104 The premise for Hubbard's book is that anything is measurable, including "intangibles," but
that, as with any hard problems, one must start with asking the right questions to get at
how people have framed their problems. Hubbard, *supra* note 103.

105 *Ibid* at 292. This method has been used to value avoiding the loss of endangered species,
and improvements to public health and the environment.

106 The Honourable George W. Adams, *Mediating Justice: Legal Dispute Resolutions*, 2nd ed
(Toronto: CCH Canadian, 2011) at 158.

107 For example, Gordon Johnson provides examples of how civil process steps can be used
in strategic ways to employ limited client resources for maximum benefit, including offers
to settle, summary trials and interim rulings, and involving corporate clients in brief
preparation and responses to discoveries: Gordon R. Johnson, *Litigation for Solicitors:
Managing Litigation Costs* (Vancouver: Continuing Legal Education Society of British
Columbia, November 2012).

108 Kiser, *supra* note 1 at 234.

109 Nancy Chausow Shafer, "Dispute Resolution Processes in Limited Finance Cases: Step-
ping Up to Client-Centred Decision Making" (Fall 2013) 36:2 Family Advocate 39; Jennifer
A. Brandt, "Preparing a Client for Settlement" (Winter 2015) 37:3 Family Advocate 16.

110 Martin Gramatikov and colleagues suggest a broader focus on "paths to justice," which
means "a commonly applied process which users address in order to cope with their legal
problem," which "begins when a person takes a step to resolve [that problem] through
external norms or intervention" and ends with "a final decision by a neutral, joint agreement of the parties, or ... because one of the parties quits": Martin Gramatikov, Maurits
Barendrecht, & Jin Ho Verdonschot, "Measuring the Costs and Quality of Paths to Justice:
Contours of a Methodology (2011) 3 Hague J Rule L 349 at 358–59.

111 Strasburger, *supra* note 27 at 204.

15

Regulating Contingency Fees
A Consumer Welfare Perspective

Noel Semple

GOOD, BAD, AND UGLY: all three adjectives may seem to describe contingency fee arrangements for legal services. The good is that contingency arrangements facilitate access to justice, respond to widespread concerns about the affordability of legal fees, and help align law firms' incentives with the interests of their clients.[1] The bad is that they encourage law firms to "screen out" potential clients, and perhaps to settle some cases prematurely.[2] As for the ugly, contingency arrangements have generated extraordinary and perhaps exploitative profits for law firms in some cases, notably in Canada's residential schools litigation.[3] There is also evidence of questionable firm practices surrounding the drafting and interpretation of contingent retainer contracts with inexperienced and often vulnerable clients.[4]

How can we preserve and extend what is good about contingency fees while minimizing the bad and the ugly? In order to identify the best regulatory tools for this challenging task, this chapter proposes a consumer welfare analysis.[5] The consumers of contingency fee legal services are the individual clients and the members of classes represented by law firms compensated in this way. These consumers, like other consumers, have interests in (1) quality, (2) price, (3) fairness, and (4) choice. I will analyze these four sets of consumer interests, all of which are affected by the regulation of contingency fees, and evaluate various regulatory approaches to contingency fees against the consumer welfare criterion. I argue that "heavy-hand" interventions, such as fee caps and retrospective price review, can do as much harm as good for consumers. "Light-touch" alternatives, such as disclosure and standardized contracts and fostering the "invisible hand" of the market, should be considered seriously by regulators interested in maximizing consumer welfare.

Damages-Based Contingency Fee Regimes

A legal fee regime, according to Herbert Kritzer in Chapter 13, involves (1) a method for computing fees, (2) a party to pay the fees, and (3) a method for regulating fees.[6] A fee computation method is "contingent" if the amount payable depends in some way on the degree of success achieved in the matter.[7] Contingency-billed legal services for plaintiffs in civil litigation (including class actions) are the focus of this chapter.

Contingency fee arrangements typically include a "no-win, no-fee" term, whereby the client will pay no legal fee unless and until money is recovered for the client through settlement or judgment. If money *is* recovered, under a damages-based contingency fee, the firm is entitled to a percentage of the recovery.[8] The firm's percentage may be flat, for example, 15 percent or 33 percent of the amount recovered. The percentage may also vary depending on the stage at which the litigation is resolved, the amount recovered, or both. In addition to the firm's compensation, several other important questions arise between client and firm in a contingency retainer:

- *Disbursements* are payments for goods or services made by a law firm in order to advance a client's case. The client might bear full financial responsibility for all disbursements, or responsibility for disbursements, like the legal fee, could be contingent on the outcome of the case. The firm might absorb these costs if little or nothing is recovered for the client.
- *Tax* is assessed on disbursements and fees.[9] Liability for tax must also be assigned between lawyer and client under the various outcome scenarios.
- If the retainer is *terminated* before the lawsuit is concluded, the contingency rate cannot be applied. What, if any, fee is the law firm to be receive in this case? Does the fee depend on the circumstances of the termination?
- In Canada and the United Kingdom, *cost awards* are made by courts after litigation in order to partially compensate successful litigants for their legal fees.[10] Cost awards give rise to three issues in a civil litigation contingency retainer:

  - If a court makes a cost award in favour of a plaintiff, how is that amount divided between firm and client?
  - If a plaintiff releases a defendant from all liability in exchange for a settlement payment, should some portion of that payment be characterized as "for costs," and therefore allocated between firm and client in a different manner than the portion "for damages"?
  - If the suit is unsuccessful and the plaintiff must *pay* costs, how should this debt be allocated between firm and client?[11]

Regulation of Contingency Fees

There is consensus that legal fees, including contingency fees, must be regulated in some way. Consumers of plaintiff-side legal services are typically legally inexperienced "one-shotters," while their law firms are knowledgeable "repeat players."[12] Because of this information asymmetry,[13] in an unregulated market consumers would be vulnerable to exploitation.[14] In class actions, there is another source of market failure necessitating regulation of contingency fee arrangements: because the stakes for individual class members are often small, there is insufficient motivation for them to negotiate retainers with law firms or monitor firms' performance.[15]

There are multiple regulators of contingency fees. Like other aspects of legal practice, they are governed by self-regulatory organizations – law societies in Canada and bar associations in the United States. Codes of conduct promulgated by these organizations generally contain rules applicable to contingency fees specifically, in addition to rules applicable to all legal fee arrangements.[16] Legislatures also regulate contingency arrangements, imposing formal requirements and sometimes substantive rules such as fee caps.[17] Finally, courts and tribunals may regulate contingency fee agreements pursuant to inherent jurisdiction or statutory powers.[18]

Consumer Welfare

It is a truism that regulators of legal services should advance not the interests of legal practitioners but rather the public interest.[19] The premise of this chapter is that, with regard to contingency fee regulation, the consumer interest is the most important aspect of the public interest. In other words, contingency fee regulation succeeds to the extent that it improves the welfare of contingency fee consumers,[20] including both individual tort plaintiffs and class members in class actions. While consumer *protection* focuses on saving consumers from "bad deals" in the market,[21] a consumer *welfare* approach also tries to foster the market's ability to generate *good* deals for consumers. The welfare of legal services consumers is served by (1) low and affordable *prices*, (2) high-*quality* legal services, (3) *fairness* in retainer contracts, and (4) broad and informed *choice* in the market for legal services.

Price

Lower prices mean greater consumer welfare, if all else is equal. Contingency-billed legal services are seldom cheap. In American personal injury actions, contingency fees generally amount to 30–33 percent of recoveries.[22] Allan Hutchinson found fourteen reported Ontario personal injury cases from the period 2010–16 in which the contingency fee was specified; the firm's total recovery in these cases ranged from 8 percent of the plaintiff's damages to 40 percent.[23] A Law Society of Upper Canada Working Group reported a typical range of 25–35 percent for Ontario personal injury retainers.[24] These fees can cut deeply into plaintiffs' compensation for their injuries. In *Batalla v St Michael's Hospital,* for example, the retainer contract would have produced a fee of over $1.4 million for a lawyer who spent 155 hours working on the case – over $9,000 for each hour of work. In *Batalla,* the plaintiff was a severely injured child who would require lifelong care.[25]

Likewise, in class actions, every dollar retained by counsel is a dollar unavailable for distribution to the consumers (class members). Several Canadian class actions have produced fees amounting to tens of millions of dollars for the firms involved.[26] Benjamin Alarie and Peter Flynn reviewed Canadian class actions and found that judges approved class counsel fees averaging 22 percent of the settlement amount.[27] Among forty-five recent Quebec class actions studied by Catherine Piché, there were six in which legal fees for the class exceeded the amount actually distributed to class members.[28] The extraordinary contingency fees generated by residential schools cases have been the subject of especially widespread comment.[29] Lower fees increase the likelihood that a class action will produce real access to justice at proportionate cost.[30]

A second aspect of the price interest is that consumers should pay lower contingency percentages in cases with higher expected recoveries, lower labour requirements, and/or less risk for their law firms. Such consumers place fewer requirements on their law firms, so in a well-functioning market they should not have to pay as much. In fact, however, evidence suggests that contingency fee prices are "sticky" – firms often charge "strong and simple" cases the same percentages that they charge weaker and more onerous ones.[31]

Quality
Quality is the second major interest of consumers. Regulators of contingency fees must attend to the effect of regulation on the quality of legal services received by plaintiffs. The quality of a legal service depends in large part on its effectiveness in accomplishing consumers' legal goals and protecting their interests.[32] Obtaining as large a net monetary recovery as possible, as soon as possible, is the most important goal in most personal injury matters and class actions. There is some evidence that contingency-billing lawyers obtain higher-quality results for their clients than other lawyers do in comparable cases, perhaps because contingency billing creates a relatively strong incentive for the firm to maximize recovery.[33]

What makes a legal service more or less effective in accomplishing the consumer's legal goals? First is the talent and industry of the lawyers and other people who provide the service on behalf of the firm. Profit motive is one way to attract talent to plaintiff-side tort and class action practice,[34] and one way to compensate lawyers for the risks that contingency practice involves. Consumer welfare will suffer if regulators suppress fees to the extent that talented lawyers leave contingency-billed tort practice in favour of other work.

Second, legal service quality depends on the *investments* that firms make in the cases. To an economist, each case that a firm accepts on a contingency basis is "an investment of the lawyer's time and resources in the hopes of a return ... [made] under conditions of uncertainty."[35] The hours of labour allocated to the case will not be directly compensated by the client as they would in a time-based retainer,[36] so the firm's financial payoff from each additional hour is uncertain. If the firm will completely or partially absorb its disbursements in the event of a poor case outcome, disbursements are also investments made by the firm under conditions of uncertainty.[37]

Maximizing the client's recovery may require significant investments of labour and disbursements by the firm. These investments generally improve the evidence and advocacy, which in turn produces higher settlement offers and larger damage awards. When the law firm is unwilling or unable to make the necessary investments – and especially when the defendants *know* this – plaintiffs' recoveries suffer.[38]

Contingency fees incentivize the firm to choose the labour and disbursement investments that are most likely to increase the plaintiff's recovery. There is some evidence that the number of hours a firm will dedicate to a contingency-billed case is, in fact, proportionate to the perceived monetary value of the case.[39] Contingency fee regulation should seek to avoid deterring firms' labour and disbursement investments in their clients' cases.

Fairness and Predictability

Fairness and predictability constitute a third important aspect of consumer welfare in this context.[40] A tort lawsuit is a joint venture between consumer(s) and law firm. It involves multiple possible outcomes, potential sources of income, and potential sources of financial obligation. The respective obligations of client and firm under all of the different outcome scenarios should be as substantively fair as possible, and also as predictable as possible, to the consumer(s). The fiduciary nature of the lawyer-client relationship,[41] along with the information asymmetry that characterizes most contingency fee retainer negotiations,[42] reinforces the importance of fairness as a goal for regulators.[43]

Recent Canadian decisions offer examples of the unpleasant surprises to consumers that regulators should try to prevent.[44] One contract allowed a firm to unilaterally choose the portion of an "all-in" settlement that constituted "costs" as opposed to "damages," and then retain 100 percent of the "costs" portion for itself.[45] Another required the client to pay all disbursements, taxes, and adverse cost awards, even in the event that nothing was recovered for the client in the litigation.[46] Disbursements are usually paid entirely by the client, and most clients probably expect that disbursements are incurred by the firm for the exclusive benefit of the client. However, disbursements may include items that enrich the firm[47] or protect the firm from risks associated with litigation.[48]

Choice

Broad and informed *choice* is the fourth major interest of consumers. Choice has three aspects in the context of contingency fees. First, regulators should try to maximize the number of consumers who are able to choose contingency-billed legal services. Most tort plaintiffs, given the option, prefer contingency fee arrangements over time-based fees or self-representation.[49] Contingency offers both *price certainty* (the fee is guaranteed to be proportionate to the recovery and to be nil if there is no recovery) and *deferred payment* (the fee need not be paid until the point at which money is recovered, when the client is in a relatively good position to pay).[50] Personal injury firms as well as class action firms already act as gatekeepers and "screen out" most would-be consumers of their services.[51] Regulators should aim for as high an acceptance rate as possible.

Second, regulators should help consumers compare contingency-billing firms in order to make intelligent and informed choices among them. At present, it is difficult for a consumer to compare firms in terms of price and almost impossible to do so in terms of quality.[52] Finally, some consumers would value the ability to choose, or at least express preferences among, different terms in contingency fee arrangements. For example, a consumer who is relatively risk-averse might be willing to pay a higher contingency fee in exchange for the firm's acceptance of the risk associated with adverse cost awards. Tort plaintiff consumers are typically legally inexperienced, however, and the number willing and able to express preferences among potential terms is probably small.[53]

Options for Regulating Contingency Fees

Consumers of contingency fee services have interests in price, quality, fairness, and choice. As Michael Trebilcock has suggested, regulators should seek to maximize the *net* welfare of consumers, which means taking all of these into account.[54] This section will evaluate regulatory tools against the consumer welfare criterion.

"Heavy-Hand" Regulation: Fee Caps and Retrospective Price Review

Fee Caps

A fee cap restricts the amount that a law firm may charge for a contingency legal service. Approximately sixteen US states and three Canadian provinces cap contingency fees, as do England and Wales.[55] Caps, like contingency fees themselves, may be "flat," or they may "slope," based on the amount recovered or the stage to which the litigation progresses.[56]

A fee cap clearly serves the price interests of those consumers who would otherwise pay fees above the cap. A critically injured tort plaintiff who receives $5 million in damages would save $900,000 if her firm's contingency fee were capped at 15 percent of damages instead of being 33 percent of damages. This could make a significant difference in the plaintiff's long-term financial security.

Fee caps do not advance the price interests of those who would otherwise have paid less than the cap percentage.[57] In fact, some evidence suggests that a cap can *increase* prices that would otherwise have been lower, by serving as a "focal point" for collusion among firms.[58] In other words, capping fees at 25 percent could cause firms to experience more temptation and perhaps pressure from their peers to avoid charging any consumer *less* than 25 percent.

Contingency fee caps may also damage consumers' quality interests. Because legal fees in most other practice areas are not capped by regulators, a cap could cause a "brain drain" from contingency-billed niches into other niches, to the detriment of contingency fee consumers. Perhaps more importantly, reducing a firm's compensation in a case reduces the anticipated payoff of the firm's labour and disbursement investments in that case. This may, in turn, discourage the firm from making some such investments.

Turning to choice interests, caps also compromise consumers' interest in having firms accept as many cases as possible on a contingency basis.[59] Most obviously, if a firm would be willing to accept a certain case only for a contingency fee of 30 percent or more but regulators cap the rate at 25 percent, the firm will presumably screen out the case and the consumer will lose the option of retaining that firm.[60] Consumers whose cases are legally tenuous, involve modest damages, or are likely to require large firm investments are likely to be screened out by *all* contingency-billing firms if the cap is low enough. Empirical evidence from the United States suggests that introducing a cap also reduces the number of cases that a firm will accept for prices *under* the cap amount. This is perhaps because, in the absence of a cap, these less profitable cases can be cross-subsidized by profits from the higher-fee cases.[61]

More sophisticated fee caps mitigate these problems somewhat. First, if a cap permits upward-sloping fees, then the retainer contract can protect the firm from some of the labour requirement risk associated with cases and induce it to accept more such cases.[62] However, no statutory cap can eliminate the litigation risk associated with a claim – the risk that the case will produce no recovery or a very low recovery.[63] Caps necessarily, therefore, disincentivize firms from taking on "difficult" or legally tenuous cases, which is contrary to the choice interests of plaintiffs and class members with claims of this nature.[64]

Retrospective Price Review

Retrospective review by a court or tribunal is another "heavy-hand" tool for regulating contingency fees. In this context, courts may scrutinize the "reasonableness" of the price at the conclusion of the litigation. The amount of the fee will be assessed relative to factors such as the time expended by the firm, the complexity of the case, the results achieved for the client or class, and the court's impression of the risk associated with the case.[65] The court will reduce any fee that it determines to be "unreasonable," whether or not there was any unfairness in the retainer contract or negotiations.[66]

For consumers, retrospective price review does have advantages over fee caps. The process is available to protect the price interests of any consumer who can get his or her case before the reviewer, not just those who would have paid more than the maximum. Retrospective price review is meant to take into account case complexity and time spent by the firm in assessing a fee. Therefore, it should be less likely than a fee cap to discourage firms from accepting and investing in cases. The more such investments a firm makes, the higher the fee it should be able to justify on retrospective review.

However, retrospective price review also creates risk for law firms and therefore discourages them from accepting and investing in contingency cases. In order to pick a "reasonable" fee that compensates the firm for the risk it assumed, the judge is supposed to evaluate the level of risk that appeared at the outset of the case. It seems doubtful that any judge can perform this speculative task with much accuracy. Hindsight is 20/20, and after the defendant has agreed to settle for a significant amount, it is hard for anyone to take seriously the possibility that the defendant might have paid little or nothing.

Moreover, evaluating the degree of success achieved by the firm requires the judge to compare the actual settlement to a hypothetical adjudicated outcome. Again, it is hard to put much faith in such judicial conclusions. The settlement reflects the best estimate of the case's value from the point of view of the parties themselves. In the absence of a trial, the parties are much better informed than the judge is regarding the case's prospects.

For a firm considering whether to accept a contingency case, or considering how much to invest in a case it has already accepted, retrospective price review changes the risk/reward calculus.[67] If the case goes well, the court may intervene to curtail the fee (and compel the firm to spend time defending the fee). If the case goes poorly, the loss will of course be entirely borne by the firm. Imposing this "fee haircut risk" is likely to hurt consumers' quality interests by reducing the level of investments in cases. It also hurts consumers' choice interests by reducing the willingness of firms to accept contingency cases.

Retrospective review has further problems if it is not automatic but rather must be triggered by a consumer complaint. In this case, obtaining any benefit from this regulatory tool requires a consumer to do difficult things: (1) undergo the expense and inconvenience of triggering the process, and (2) confront one's former law firm in an adversarial process.[68] Complaint-triggered retrospective review may also suffer from a "squeaky-wheel" problem that can undermine the price interests of consumers who do *not* complain. If firms cannot predict what retainer terms will lead to fee haircuts after retrospective price review, then they cannot change their normal behaviour in order to minimize the risk. Instead, they may increase the "rack rate" that they charge all clients, and then offer discounts to settle fee complaints, whether merited or not.[69] In this scenario, complaisant clients who do not complain effectively pay for the unmerited discounts the firm will use to grease the "squeaky wheels" who do complain.

"Light-Touch" Regulation

Fee caps and retrospective price review undermine some consumer interests even as they advance others. The alternative regulatory tools considered in this section may be more unequivocally beneficial for consumers.

Disclosure Requirements and Retrospective Fairness Review

Retainer contracts can be made more predictable and more fair if firms are required to disclose certain matters to clients.[70] Regulators may require information to be provided to the client either orally or in writing as part of the contract itself.[71] The common requirements that contingency fee retainers be in writing and provided to the client increase the predictability of the outcome to the client and reduce the scope for unpleasant surprises.[72] A similar effect is produced by a requirement that the contract include a hypothetical calculation of the fee under a possible outcome scenario.[73]

Retrospective *fairness* review focuses not on price but rather on firms' compliance with disclosure requirements, the manner in which the contract was negotiated, and the client's comprehension of the terms.[74] Especially if the process is low-cost for firms and clients, retrospective fairness review can protect consumers' fairness interests without undermining the market's ability to serve their other interests. Provided that the criteria for disclosure and fairness are clear to firms *ex ante,* this process can improve their treatment of all consumers.

Prospective "Safe-Harbour" Review

If regulators determine that price must also be reviewed, they should consider using prospective rather than retrospective review. Firms could be allowed or even required to submit retainer contracts for review at the outset rather than at the conclusion of a matter.[75] Prospective review would constitute a "safe harbour" for firms if the process were to immunize the contract from retrospective price review. This would protect firms from the unpredictable fee haircut risk described above, and perhaps make contingency fee arrangements attractive to them in more cases.

The reasonableness of a proposed contingency rate in a certain case would depend on the case's apparent profile of risks, rewards, and necessary investments for the firm.[76] Of course, assessing these factors *ex ante* is an inexact science for either a firm or a regulator. Thus, I will argue below that robust competition is the most reliable way to arrive at welfare-maximizing prices.

Disclosure to the Regulator

Mandatory disclosure of contracts and fees to the regulator is another relatively light touch tool, endorsed by both Michael Trebilcock and Allan Hutchinson.[77] As Trebilcock explains, this would enable the regulator to provide consumers with information about prevailing prices, thereby mitigating the information asymmetry they experience in shopping for representation.[78] Some Canadian provinces already require contingency fee contracts to be filed with courts.[79]

Contractual Coverage Requirements

A slightly more interventionist approach requires each contract to explicitly address certain questions while leaving it to the parties to determine the actual answers to those questions. For example, the American Bar Association's model rule says that a contingency retainer contract must state how disbursements are to be dealt with and whether their repayment by the client is contingent on the outcome.[80] Such terms impinge very little on freedom of contract, and they respect the consumer's choice interest in a custom-made retainer contract.[81] However, given that most contingency clients are inexperienced, these rules probably have little effect on fairness and predictability. In most cases, the firm probably answers these questions in the manner it sees fit and then obtains the client's signature on its standard retainer contract.

Regulatory Standardization of Contracts

Standardization goes further: it requires questions to be answered in a particular way by the contract. The province of New Brunswick has standard contracts for all contingency legal services,[82] which parties may vary only through application to court.[83] Drafting a mandatory standard contingency retainer contract is a complex balancing act involving competing incentives, interactions with civil litigation dynamics, and trade-offs among the various consumer interests considered above. However, regulator-drafted standard contracts seem, on balance, to be favourable for consumer interests in fairness, price, and choice.[84]

Fairness and predictability are fostered by this approach. It is problematic to allow firms to include clauses that transfer risks and costs to clients who are usually inexperienced and sometimes traumatized. This is especially true given the complexity of the contracts and the fiduciary obligation of lawyer to client. As Trevor Farrow has shown with regard to the Canada's residential schools cases, an excessively "entrepreneurial" approach to drafting and interpreting retainer contracts is impossible to reconcile with legal professionalism.[85]

A regulator that has written the only permissible contract can assure itself that the contract addresses all of the many details and possibilities involved in a contingency tort case in a fair way.[86] The contract could include a list of permissible office disbursements (e.g., printing), including maximum rates for each.[87] Standardized contracts also make it easier for regulators and others to inform the public about how those contracts work.

Mandatory standard contracts can also advance consumers' interests in lower prices, by fostering price competition and comparability.[88] The heterogeneity of retainer contracts offered by different firms makes it more difficult for consumers to engage in comparison shopping.[89] If the contracts are required to be otherwise identical, a consumer can receive a "single, clear signal of price" from each contract in the comparison.[90]

Although standardization impinges on consumers' choice interests, realistically freedom of contract is of limited value to most consumers of contingency fee legal services.[91] To the extent that tort plaintiff retainer contracts are not standardized by regulators, they will generally not be freely negotiated compromises between equally matched parties, but rather contracts of adhesion written by law firms.

Regulatory contract standardization is a matter of degree, the level of which can be chosen to compromise between the various interests at stake.[92] "Light" regulatory standardization, found in most common law jurisdictions today, merely prescribes or limits a number of terms in a contingency fee contract.[93] At the other end of the spectrum, complete standardization mandates a single contract and leaves only the price term to the parties. An intermediate standardization would leave a handful of variables open in addition to price or let the parties select one out of three or four possible contracts.

"Invisible-Hand" Regulation: Towards the Consumer's Paradise

To advance consumer welfare, regulators should try to help the "invisible hand" of the competitive market deliver its benefits to consumers. In a consumer's paradise, each consumer or class of consumers would be able to easily shop their case to every firm that might be willing to accept it on a contingency basis. Each firm would have the opportunity to bid for each case by identifying the contingency fee for which it would be willing to accept that case. Consumers would also be able to easily ascertain the quality characteristics of the bidders before making an informed decision. Regulators would not need to rely on heavy-handed interventions such as fee caps and retrospective price review. A contingency contract giving a law firm as much as 60 percent or even 90 percent of the recovery might be unproblematic. If no other firm is willing to accept it for any lower percentage, then such a contract might give the consumer the best access to justice available. The consumer would be better off than under the status quo, where contingency fees over 50 percent are unlikely to survive fee caps and/or judicial retrospective review, and therefore no contingency fee services whatsoever are offered to consumers with such cases. The need for retrospective price review would also be reduced or even eliminated in the consumer's paradise. A transparent price that is set in a highly competitive market is unlikely to require this regulatory intervention.

The consumer's paradise will never entirely exist on earth. The market for tort plaintiff legal services can probably never be as transparent and competitive as (for example) the market for food is. Nevertheless, the potential of competitive markets to assist contingency fee consumers should not be overlooked. Already today, "beauty contests" are reportedly held for some critically injured people. In this process, personal injury firms compete to be retained by claimants and their families. In choosing among them, the consumers sometimes have sophisticated and experienced advice, for example, from hospital staff.

Regulators can help our earth better imitate the consumers' paradise. Standardizing contracts would encourage beauty contests and other healthy competition by making it easier for consumers to shop their cases and compare the prices offered by bidders. Eliminating unnecessary restrictions on firms' access to capital would improve their ability to bear the risk that comes with contingency cases, and thereby offer consumers better-quality service at lower prices.[94] Three other options to assist the invisible hand should also be considered.

Providing Price and Quality Information to Consumers

Firms can be required to post price (and perhaps even quality) information on their websites. Regulators can gather data on firms' price and quality attributes and make the data available to consumers.[95] They could do so on a public website designed to facilitate informed consumption decisions about legal services.[96] They could then require all law firm advertising to prominently display the URL for this website.

Brokerage and Sale of Claim

Brokerage is one way to foster welfare-enhancing competition. Tort claimants could provide evidence about their claims to a brokerage operated or overseen by the regulator. Law firms would be able to log in to a secure website, review the data, and then bid for the cases by specifying the rates they would charge for them.

Sale of claim is a more radical variant, and one that is currently illegal. A brokerage would arrange for the consumer to sell his or her claim to a law firm outright for a predetermined sum. The brokerage would hold the firm's payment for the case in escrow, pending the client's participation in the lawsuit as a witness.[97]

Expert Advisers and Agents for Consumers

Expert advisers and agents might help tort plaintiffs overcome the stark information asymmetry they experience when seeking out and negotiating with law firms. A regulator could organize independent legal advice for seriously injured people who are trying to organize beauty contests or seeking help in comparing firms. This service could be priced at a flat rate, to be deducted from the eventual recovery.

Class action consumers of legal services would also benefit from expert agents. At present, the representative plaintiff is meant to protect class members' interests in negotiating with and monitoring class counsel. The problem is that representative plaintiffs are often legally inexperienced individuals who lack the motive and ability to perform these functions.[98] Class action firms often devise the cases and then select representative plaintiffs, which makes the expectation of negotiation and oversight even less realistic.[99] In short, it is hard to believe that most representative plaintiffs drive hard bargains with their firms.

The price and quality interests of these consumers might be better served if they had experienced and sophisticated agents to represent them in selecting, negotiating with, and monitoring class counsel. Class action legislation could be amended to provide that an independent expert party will be the agent for the class in retaining counsel. Although not actually part of the claimant class, such an official might be more likely to protect their interests in securing the best possible representation at the lowest possible price. Standard contracts (and their deleterious effects on consumers' choice interests) might be dispensed with if the agent for the class could effectively negotiate contractual terms on their behalf. In determining how to instruct counsel on matters such as settlement, this official could consult with class members using pre-established protocols.[100]

Conclusion

Contingency fees are an important piece of the access to justice puzzle. In this chapter, I have argued that contingency fees should be regulated so as to maximize the interests of consumers: low price, high quality, fairness, and choice. "Heavy-hand" interventions such as fee caps and retrospective price review are currently regulatory mainstays. They are unlikely to completely disappear, and they can be improved. For example, retrospective fee review might be made less arbitrary if regulators had better information about firms' case portfolios,[101] or if they used guideline formulas based on factors such as time spent and amount recovered in a case.[102]

However, heavy hand interventions can suppress welfare-enhancing market transactions and deter firms from accepting and investing in cases. Their use can be curtailed, even if it cannot be completely abandoned. "Light-touch" alternatives, including disclosure and standardized contracts, should be preferred where possible. Ultimately, a fair, transparent, and competitive market for contingency fee legal services would produce the broadest and deepest benefits for tort plaintiffs. Regulators should do what they can to help the "invisible hand" work for consumers.

Notes

1   Trevor C.W. Farrow et al, *Everyday Legal Problems and the Cost of Justice in Canada: Overview Report* (Toronto: Canadian Forum on Civil Justice, 2016) at 14, online: Canadian Forum on Civil Justice <http://www.cfcj-fcjc.org/sites/default/files//Everyday%20 Legal%20Problems%20and%20the%20Cost%20of%20Justice%20in%20Canada%20 -%20Overview%20Report.pdf> [*Everyday Legal Problems*]; Allan C. Hutchinson, "A Study of the Costs of Legal Services in Personal Injury Litigation in Ontario: Final Report" (2017) at 4–5, online: <https://www.scribd.com/document/336923555/Hutchinson-Report>; Law Society of Upper Canada Advertising and Fee Arrangements Issues Working Group [LSUC Working Group], *Fifth Report* (Toronto: Law Society of Upper Canada, 2017) at paras 161–62, 173–79.
2   Nora Freeman Engstrom, "Run-of-the-Mill Justice" (2009) 22 Geo J Legal Ethics 1485.
3   Trevor C.W. Farrow, "Residential Schools Litigation and the Legal Profession" (2014) 64 UTLJ 596 at 610–11 ["Residential Schools Litigation"].
4   Hutchinson, *supra* note 1.
5   Michael Trebilcock, "Regulating the Market for Legal Services" (2008) 45 Alta L Rev 215 ["Regulating the Market"].
6   Herbert Kritzer, "Legal Fee Regimes and the Cost of Civil Justice," this volume ["Legal Fee Regimes"].

7 *Solicitors Act,* RSO 1990, c S.15, s 28.1(2).

8 An alternative is the "lodestar" contingency fee, which entitles the firm to its docketed time multiplied by a "success fee" factor.

9 Richard Moorhead, "Filthy Lucre: Lawyers' Fees and Lawyers' Ethics – What Is Wrong with Informed Consent?" (2011) 31 L.S. 345 at 362; Canada Revenue Agency, "Lawyers' Disbursements," online: Canada Revenue Agency <https://www.canada.ca/en/revenue-agency/services/forms-publications/publications/p-209r/lawyers-disbursements.html>.

10 Erik S. Knutsen, "The Cost of Costs: The Unfortunate Deterrence of Everyday Civil Litigation in Canada" (2011) 36 Queen's LJ 113.

11 Regarding "adverse" cost awards and the necessity of dealing with them in fee regimes, see Kritzer, "Legal Fee Regimes," *supra* note 6.

12 Marc Galanter, "Why the 'Haves' Come Out Ahead: Speculations on the Limits of Legal Change" (1974) 9 Law & Soc'y Rev 59, online: <http://jan.ucc.nau.edu/~phelps/Galanter%201974.pdf>.

13 Malcolm Mercer, "Access to Justice and Market Failure," online: (1 November 2016) Slaw <http://www.slaw.ca/2016/11/01/access-to-justice-and-market-failure/> ["Access to Justice"].

14 The Honorable Charles Kocoras, "Contingent Fees – A Judge's Perch" (1998) 47 DePaul L Rev 421; Moorhead, *supra* note 9.

15 Jasminka Kalajdzic, *Access to Justice for the Masses? A Critical Analysis of Class Actions in Ontario* (LLM Thesis, University of Toronto Faculty of Law, 2009), online: <https://tspace.library.utoronto.ca/bitstream/1807/18780/6/Kalajdzic_Jasminka_200911_LLM_Thesis.pdf> at 160 [*Access to Justice for the Masses?*].

16 See Hutchinson, *supra* note 1, app 4 for a useful summary of Canadian rules.

17 David A. Hyman, Bernard Black, & Charles Silver, "The Economics of Plaintiff-Side Personal Injury Practice" (2015) 2015 U Ill L Rev 1563 at 1572–74.

18 On inherent jurisdiction, see *Rosquist v Soo Line Railroad,* 692 F.2d 1107 (7th Cir 1982), online: Casetext <https://casetext.com/case/rosquist-v-soo-line-rr> at 1107, 1111. On statutory powers, see Herbert M. Kritzer, "Fee Regimes and the Cost of Civil Justice" (2009) 28 CJQ 344. See also the text accompanying notes 65–69 below.

19 E.g., Adam Dodek & Emily Alderson, "Risk Regulation for the Legal Profession" (2017) 55 Alta L Rev 623; Amy Salyzyn, "From Colleague to Cop to Coach: Contemporary Regulation of Lawyer Competence" (2017) 95 Can Bar Rev 489, s IV(e).

20 Trebilcock, "Regulating the Market," *supra* note 5.

21 Gillian K. Hadfield, Robert Howse, & Michael J. Trebilcock, "Information-Based Principles for Rethinking Consumer Protection Policy" (1998) 21 J Consumer Policy 131.

22 Hyman, Black, & Silver, *supra* note 17 at 1581; Herbert M. Kritzer, *Risks, Reputations, and Rewards: Contingency Fee Legal Practice in the United States* (Stanford, CA: Stanford University Press, 2004) at 39 [*Risks, Reputations*]; Lester Brickman, *Lawyer Barons: What Their Contingency Fees Really Cost America* (New York: Cambridge University Press, 2011) at 6.

23 Hutchinson, *supra* note 1 at 17.

24 LSUC Working Group, *supra* note 1 at para 193.

25 *Batalla v St. Michael's Hospital,* 2016 ONSC 1513 (CanLII), online: <http://canlii.ca/t/gnq6b>.

26 Adam M. Dodek, "Canadian Legal Ethics: Ready for the Twenty-First Century at Last" (2008) 46 Osgoode Hall LJ 1 at 13.

27 Benjamin Alarie & Peter Flynn, "Accumulating Wisdom: An Updated Empirical Examination of Class Counsel's Fees in Ontario Class Actions" (2014) 9 Can Class Action Rev 355 at 371, online: SSRN <https://ssrn.com/abstract=2363798>.

28 Catherine Piché, "The Value of Class Actions," this volume.

29 Farrow, "Residential Schools Litigation," *supra* note 3 at 610–11.

30 Minimization of costs and proportionality are among the attributes of "optimal class actions," as defined by Piché, *supra* note 28, s III.B.

31 Brickman, *supra* note 22 at 180; Noel Semple, *Legal Services Regulation at the Crossroads: Justitia's Legions* (Cheltenham, UK: Edward Elgar, 2015) at 279 [*Justitia's Legions*].

32 Legal service quality also depends on the client experience of working with the firm, and other factors: Noel Semple, "Measuring Legal Service Value" (2019) 52:3 UBC L Rev 943, online: SSRN <https://ssrn.com/abstract=3144771> ["Measuring Legal Service Value"].

33 See Herbert Kritzer, *Legal Advocacy: Lawyers and Nonlawyers at Work* (Ann Arbor: University of Michigan Press, 1998) at 146–47.

34 Moorhead, *supra* note 9 at 349.

35 Kritzer, *Risks, Reputations, supra* note 22 at 11. Regarding the potential and limitations of the economic analysis of civil justice issues, see Michael Trebilcock, "Prices, Costs, and Access to Justice," this volume ["Prices, Costs"].

36 Hutchinson, *supra* note 1 at 5.

37 Hyman, Black, & Silver, *supra* note 17 at 1584.

38 Nora Freeman Engstrom, "Sunlight and Settlement Mills" (2011) 86 NYU L Rev 805 at 838–41 ["Sunlight and Settlement Mills"]; Noel Semple, *Accessibility, Quality, and Profitability for Personal Plight Law Firms: Hitting the Sweet Spot* (Ottawa: Canadian Bar Association, 2017), s 6.1.1, notes 651–53 and accompanying text, online: Canadian Bar Association <http://www.cba.org/PersonalPlight> [*Accessibility, Quality*].

39 See Herbert Kritzer, *The Justice Broker: Lawyers and Ordinary Litigation* (New York: Oxford University Press, 1990) at 117.

40 "Transparency" to consumers is a similar concept, identified as a regulatory goal in Ontario: LSUC Working Group, *supra* note 1 at para 180ff.

41 *Mide-Wilson v Hungerford Tomyn Lawrenson and Nichols,* 2013 BCCA 559 at para 92 (CanLII), online: <http://canlii.ca/t/g2gds>.

42 See notes 12 and 14 above, and accompanying text.

43 For empirical evidence that UK consumers do not understand their contingency fee arrangements very well, see Moorhead, *supra* note 9 at 364.

44 See Hutchinson, *supra* note 1 for a comprehensive account of fairness issues in the personal injury context.

45 *Hodge v Neinstein,* 2017 ONCA 494, online: Ontario Courts <http://www.ontariocourts.ca/decisions/2017/2017ONCA0494.htm>.

46 *Edwards v Camp Kennebec (Frontenac) (1979) Inc,* 2016 ONSC 2501 (CanLII), online: <http://canlii.ca/t/gpfzs>. After-the-event (ATE) insurance is available to cover the risk of adverse costs awards: Kritzer, "Legal Fee Regimes," *supra* note 6.

47 E.g., photocopying and printing charges set above the cost recovery level: Semple, *Justitia's Legions, supra* note 31 at 272–73. See Hutchinson, *supra* note 1 at 15 for other examples.

48 E.g., interest on litigation loans made to the firm: Nora Freeman Engstrom, "Lawyer Lending: Costs and Consequences" (2014) 63 DePaul L Rev 377 at 380, s 7.5.

49 Eyal Zamir & Ilana Ritov, "Revisiting the Debate over Attorneys' Contingent Fees: A Behavioral Analysis" (2010) 39 J Legal Stud 245; Trebilcock, "Prices, Costs," *supra* note 35, "Prices and Costs" section; Semple, *Accessibility, Quality, supra* note 38, s 3.5.

50 Semple, *Accessibility, Quality, supra* note 38.

51 On personal injury firms, see Kritzer, *Risks, Reputations, supra* note 22, c 3; Hyman, Black, & Silver, *supra* note 17 at 1586. On class action firms, see Kalajdzic, *Access to Justice for the Masses? supra* note 15 at 21.

52 Engstrom, "Sunlight and Settlement Mills," *supra* note 38 at 812; Noel Semple, "Personal Plight: Mending the Market," online: (7 August 2017) Slaw <http://www.slaw.ca/2017/08/11/Personal-Plight-Mending-the-Market>.

53 Moorhead, *supra* note 9 at 368.

54 Trebilcock, "Regulating the Market," *supra* note 5 at 217.

55 New Brunswick has the lowest cap among the Canadian provinces, at 25 percent. Ontario caps fees at 50 percent: *Contingency Fee Agreements*, O Reg 194/04, s 7, online: Government of Ontario <https://www.ontario.ca/laws/regulation/040195>.

56 For a chart showing caps in sixteen states, see Hyman, Black, & Silver, *supra* note 17 at 1574.

57 See note 31 and accompanying text above.

58 Christopher R. Knittel & Victor Stango, "Price Ceilings as Focal Points for Tacit Collusion: Evidence from Credit Cards" (2003) 93 American Economic Rev 1703.

59 Hyman, Black, & Silver, *supra* note 17 at 1568.

60 Moorhead, *supra* note 9 at 369.

61 Hyman, Black, & Silver, *supra* note 17 at 1593. For an explanation of how contingency-billing firms assemble "portfolios" of cases with different risk and reward profiles, see Kritzer, *Risks, Reputations, supra* note 22.

62 Regarding labour requirement risk, see Semple, *Accessibility, Quality, supra* note 38, s 2.2.

63 Michael J. Trebilcock, "The Case for Contingent Fees: The Ontario Legal Profession Re-thinks Its Positions" (1989) 15 Can Bus LJ 360 at 365 ["Case for Contingent Fees"].

64 Malcolm Mercer, "Contingent Fees, Portfolio Risk and Competition – Calls for Reform," online: (5 July 2017) Slaw <http://www.slaw.ca/2017/07/05/contingent-fees-portfolio-risk-and-competition-calls-for-reform/> ["Contingent Fees"]. Regarding the role of compensation in encouraging class action firms to accept difficult cases, see Kalajdzic, *Access to Justice for the Masses? supra* note 15 at 150.

65 *Raphael Partners v Lam*, 2002 CanLII 45078 (ONCA) at paras 50–58, online: <http://canlii.ca/t/1cnns> [*Raphael Partners*].

66 However, many settlement approval hearings in class actions are very cursory: Piché, *supra* note 28, s IV(A)(i).

67 Semple, *Accessibility, Quality, supra* note 38 at 58.

68 Moorhead, *supra* note 9 at 368–69; LSUC Working Group, *supra* note 1.

69 Semple, *Justitia's Legions, supra* note 31 at 267.

70 For a legal-economic analysis of disclosure requirements, see Leone Niglia, "Standard Form Contracts in Europe and North America: One Hundred Years of Unfair Terms?" in Charles E.F. Rickett & Thomas G.W. Telfer, eds, *International Perspectives on Consumers' Access to Justice* (New York: Cambridge University Press, 2003) at 113–14.

71 For example, in Ontario the contract must state that "that the client and the solicitor have discussed options for retaining the solicitor other than by way of a contingency fee agreement": *Contingency Fee Agreements, supra* note 55, s 2(3)(i).

72 Hutchinson, *supra* note 1, app 4.

73 *Contingency Fee Agreements, supra* note 5, s 2(6).

74 *Raphael Partners, supra* note 65 at para 37.

75 Some jurisdictions already require prospective review for contingency contracts that are exceptional in some way, e.g., with a fee above the presumptive cap (*Legal Profession Act (British Columbia)*, SBC 1998, c 9, ss 66(6), 66(7)) or entitling the firm to some or all of the plaintiff's costs (*Contingency Fee Agreements, supra* note 55).

76 Kritzer's concept of "expected effective hourly rate" could be helpful in this regard. This is the amount that the firm expects to receive per hour of its work, based on a weighted average of the possible outcomes and a weighted average of the possibly necessary labour and disbursement investments. Kritzer, *Risks, Reputations, supra* note 22.

77 Hutchinson, *supra* note 1 at 22. To protect confidentiality and privilege, information could be disclosed to the regulator without divulging the client's identity.

78 Trebilcock, "Case for Contingent Fees," *supra* note 63 at 366–67.

79 Hutchinson, *supra* note 1, app 4.

80 American Bar Association, "Model Rules of Professional Conduct, Rule 1.5: Fees," online: American Bar Association <http://www.americanbar.org/groups/professional_responsibility/publications/model_rules_of_professional_conduct/rule_1_5_fees.html>.

81 See also the text accompanying notes 49–53 above.

82 Law Society of New Brunswick, "Form 1: Contingent Fee Agreement," online: Law Society of New Brunswick <http://lawsociety-barreau.nb.ca/uploads/forms/Form_1_Contingent_Fee_Agreement.pdf>.

83 Law Society of New Brunswick, "Contingent Fee Rules under Section 83 of the Law Society Act, 1996" (1 January 1997), s 3(1), online: Law Society of New Brunswick <http://lawsociety-barreau.nb.ca/uploads/forms/Contingent_Fee_Rules_-_Règles_sur_les_honoraires_conditionnels.pdf>.

84 A Law Society of Upper Canada working group proposed that Ontario adopt a mandatory standard contingency fee contracts: LSUC Working Group, *supra* note 1 at paras 186–90.

85 Farrow, "Residential Schools Litigation," *supra* note 3 at 611–12.

86 Compliance will probably be higher than it is under Ontario's status quo regulatory framework, which is widely disregarded by firms: Kenyon Wallace and Michele Henry, "Double-Dipping Lawyers Take Big Slice of Injury Settlements," *Toronto Star*, 28 January 2017, online: <https://www.thestar.com/news/investigations/2017/01/28/double-dipping-lawyers-taking-big-slice-of-injury-settlements.html>. If regulation requires terms to be included but lets firms draft the contracts themselves, then the regulatory requirement may be misunderstood or ignored by the firm. This is impossible, or at least less likely, if the entire contract is specified by regulation. See LSUC Working Group, *supra* note 1 at 189.

87 Semple, *Justitia's Legions,* supra note 31 at 272. This would apply to all retainers, including contingency-based ones.

88 Hutchinson, *supra* note 1 at 22.

89 Noel Semple, "Mystery Shopping: Demand-Side Phenomena in Markets for Personal Plight Legal Services" (2018) 27 Int'l J Legal Profession 181, online: Taylor & Francis <https://www.tandfonline.com/doi/full/10.1080/09695958.2018.1490292>.

90 Moorhead, *supra* note 9 at 370, and Niglia, *supra* note 70 at 113: "[A] search for price is less expensive than a search for other terms." Michael Trebilcock notes that "standardising the format and content of contractual offerings, while leaving a few key terms for tailored negotiation may facilitate the consumer search-and-selection process": M.J. Trebilcock, "Rethinking Consumer Protection Policy" in Rickett & Telfer, *supra* note 70 ["Rethinking"].

91 See the text accompanying notes 49–53 above.

92 Trebilcock, "Rethinking," *supra* note 90 at 77.

93 Hutchinson, *supra* note 1, app 4.

94 Semple, *Accessibility, Quality, supra* note 38 at 7.5.

95 Defining and measuring law firm quality is still a challenge: Semple, "Measuring Legal Service Value," *supra* note 32; Mercer, "Access to Justice," *supra* note 13.

96 See, for example, Legal Choices, online: <http://www.legalchoices.org.uk> (operated by legal services regulators of England and Wales), and Law Society Referral Service, online: <http://www.findlegalhelp.ca> (operated by the Law Society of Ontario).

97 Semple, *Accessibility, Quality, supra* note 38 at 3.3.5.

98 Jasminka Kalajdzic, "How Much Is Too Much? Contingency Fees in Class Actions" (2014) 10 Class Action 615, online: SSRN <https://ssrn.com/abstract=2518646>; Charles Silver, "Representative Lawsuits and Class Actions" in B. Bouckaert & G. De Geest, eds, *International Encyclopedia of Law and Economics* (Cheltenham, UK: Edward Elgar, 1999) at 215; Alarie and Flynn, *supra* note 27 at 362.

99 A particularly striking example was the case of *Cassano v Toronto-Dominion Bank,* 2009 CanLII 35732 (ONSC), online: <http://canlii.ca/t/24grf>, where the representative plaintiff was the spouse of the lawyer who was co-counsel for the class.

100 One concern that would have to be addressed is the potential for "pay to play." In the United States, there is evidence that class counsel donations to political campaigns lead to the favouring of donor firms by officials in negotiating class action retainers: Stephen J. Choi, Drew T. Johnson-Skinner, and A.C. Pritchard, "The Price of Pay to Play in Securities Class Actions" (2011) 8 J Empirical Leg Studies 650, online: University of Michigan Law School <http://repository.law.umich.edu/cgi/viewcontent.cgi?article=2576&context=articles>.

101 Mercer, "Contingent Fees," *supra* note 64.

102 Alarie and Flynn, *supra* note 27.

Contributors

Carolyn Carter, BA (UOIT), MA (York), is a PhD student at Osgoode Hall Law School, York University. Prior to this, she worked at the Institute for Social Research at York University, and Community Legal Education Ontario as a senior researcher for the Evolving Legal Services Research Project. She completed her MA in socio-legal studies at York University, where her major research paper focused on the legal consciousness of people in Ontario experiencing family legal problems. She graduated with an honour's distinction at the University of Ontario Institute of Technology, earning a BA in legal studies. She is a paralegal and a member of the Law Society of Ontario. Her current doctoral research focuses on the lived experiences of Black Women navigating Ontario's Family Justice System. This involves two major streams of investigation. First, she sketches a map of the legal consciousness of low- and modest-income Black Women who lose full or temporary custody of their children through Ontario Children's Aid Society (CAS) involvement. Her second stream examines the effectiveness of public legal education and information in helping low- and modest-income Black Women gain meaningful access to justice to address their family legal problems.

The Honourable **Thomas A. Cromwell**, CC, BMus (Queen's), LLB (Queen's), ARCT Diploma (Royal Conservatory of Music), BCL (Oxford), LLD (Queen's, Dalhousie, Moncton, Law Society of Upper Canada), was appointed to the Supreme Court of Canada in December 2008, following a previous appointment to the Nova Scotia Court of Appeal in 1997. He has held a host of positions, including professor of law at Dalhousie University, vice-chair of the Nova Scotia Labour Relations Board and Construction Industry Panel, president of the Continuing Legal Education Society of Nova Scotia, president of the Canadian Association of Law Teachers, president of the Canadian Institute for the Administration of Justice, chair of the board of the Canadian Forum on Civil Justice, research director for the Canadian Bar Association's Court Reform

Task Force, chair of the Canadian Bar Association's Interim Organizational Committee for the National Organization on Civil Justice Reform, and founding chair of the National Action Committee on Access to Justice in Civil and Family Matters. Justice Cromwell retired from the Supreme Court of Canada in September 2016. He is currently senior counsel at Borden Ladner Gervais. In 2017 he was voted one of Canada's most influential lawyers, and in 2018 he was made a Companion of the Order of Canada.

Ab Currie, PhD (Toronto), is a senior research fellow at the Canadian Forum on Civil Justice. A sociologist and demographer, he previously served as the chief research adviser and the principal researcher for the Legal Aid and Access to Justice Office of the federal Department of Justice. He has carried out extensive research on unmet needs for legal aid and on the incidence and patterns of justiciable problems. He has been a leading scholar of access to justice research for over twenty-five years and has authored more than fifty reports, articles, and book chapters on a range of access to justice topics.

Matthew Dylag, BA (Toronto), LLB (Queen's), LLM (Osgoode), PhD candidate (Osgoode), is a graduate student member of the Costs of Justice research alliance and is active in access to justice research. His doctoral dissertation examines the unmet legal needs of Canadians and has been awarded the Joseph-Armand Bombardier CGS research grant. His other research interests include legal ethics and technology's impact on law and justice. Through his work with the Costs of Justice national survey data, he has quickly become a leading voice in the specific area of legal needs research in Canada. Prior to entering academia, Matthew was a civil litigator whose practice focused on debtor-creditor law and judgment enforcement.

Trevor C.W. Farrow, AB (Princeton), BA/MA (Oxford), LLB (Dalhousie), LLM (Harvard), PhD (Alberta), is a professor at Osgoode Hall Law School at York University. He served as associate dean from 2014 to 2016 and associate dean (academic) from 2018 to 2019. He is the chair of the Canadian Forum on Civil Justice and was the founding academic director of the Winkler Institute for Dispute Resolution. Professor Farrow's teaching and research focus on the administration of civil justice, including legal process, legal and judicial ethics, access to justice, advocacy, and globalization. He is an award-winning teacher and is published widely in Canada and internationally.

Heather Heavin, BSc, LLB, LLM, is the associate dean, Graduate Studies and Research, at the University of Saskatchewan College of Law. She graduated from the University of Saskatchewan with a Bachelor of Science (Hons.) in 1992 and Bachelor of Laws *(magna cum laude)* in 1996. After clerking for Chief Justice Edward D. Bayda of the Saskatchewan Court of Appeal, she practised with the firm of MacPherson Leslie and Tyerman in their Regina office. She completed her Master of Law degree at Harvard University in 2003 and has been on the faculty at the University of Saskatchewan since that time. Heather is an award-winning teacher and is engaged in teaching and research in the areas of international trade law, business law and dispute resolution, contract law, and oil and gas law.

Lesley A. Jacobs, BA, MA (Western Ontario), DPhil, (Oxford), LLM Special Student (Harvard Law School), FRSC, is vice-president, research and innovation, at Ontario Tech University. Previously, he was the York Research Chair in Human Rights and Access to Justice at York University, teaching in political science and the Law & Society program as well as in the graduate program in law at Osgoode Hall Law School. He is the former executive director and now senior research fellow at the Canadian Forum on Civil Justice. He also serves as a senior fellow at the Institute for International Economic Law at the Georgetown University Law Center. He has also held a range of visiting appointments, including at the European University Institute, University of California at Berkeley, Harvard Law School, the University of British Columbia, Wolfson College, Oxford University, Emory University, Waseda Law School, and the Law Commission of Canada. He is the author of numerous books and government reports on human rights, equality of opportunity, racial profiling, privacy, and international trade. He was appointed a fellow of the Royal Society of Canada (FRSC), the highest recognition for a Canadian scholar, for his influential international contributions to data science on access to justice, equality of opportunity, and human rights.

Devon Kapoor, BA (Jt. Hons., McGill), completed his JD/MBA at Osgoode Hall Law School and the Schulich School of Business. While at Osgoode, Devon served as a senior contributor for TheCourt.ca, a research assistant to former dean Lorne Sossin and Professor Signa Daum Shanks, and the senior style editor for the *Osgoode Hall Law Journal.* He received a number of subject-matter and other academic awards, including the Harry R. Rose Criminal Law Prize, a J.S.D. Tory Research and Writing Award, and the Bronze Medal for third-overall standing. He completed his articles as a judicial law clerk at the Court of Appeal for Ontario, where he worked for Chief Justice George R. Strathy and Justice Michael H. Tulloch. He is currently serving as a judicial law clerk to the Honourable Justice Michael J. Moldaver of the Supreme Court of Canada.

Michaela Keet, BA, LLB, LLM, is a professor at the University of Saskatchewan College of Law. She has been involved in curriculum development in the dispute resolution area at every level in the college's program. Her teaching and research have focused on negotiation, mediation, and the integration of dispute resolution programs into court systems – as well as their evaluation. She is the author of numerous journal articles on topics including collaborative law, lawyers' roles in mediation, and judicial settlement conferencing. Along with Heather Heavin, she is a joint author of a recent book on litigation risk assessment, published by the American Bar Association

Jennifer Koshan, BSc (Calgary), LLB (Calgary), LLM (UBC), is a professor in the Faculty of Law at the University of Calgary. She has served as graduate program director and as associate dean (research) for Calgary's Faculty of Law and is a co-founder and co-editor of the faculty's blog, ABlawg.ca. Her research and teaching interests are in the areas of constitutional law, equality and human rights, state responses to interpersonal violence, feminist legal theory, and public interest advocacy. She is the principal investigator on the Domestic Violence and Access to Justice Within and Across Multiple Legal Systems project (2016–22), funded by the Social Sciences and Humanities Research Council of Canada.

Herbert M. Kritzer holds the Marvin J. Sonosky Chair of Law and Public Policy at the University of Minnesota Law School. Previously he taught at the University of Wisconsin–Madison and William Mitchell College of Law. His recent research has focused on the empirical study of the legal profession, civil justice, and judicial selection. He is the author or co-author of ten books, editor or co-editor of three others, and the author or co-author of almost 150 journal articles and book chapters. His recent books include *Justices on the Ballot* (2015), *Lawyers at Work* (2015), *When Lawyers Screw Up* (2018), and *Judicial Selection in the States: Politics and the Struggle for Reform* (2020); *Advanced Introduction to Empirical Legal Research* is expected to be published in 2021 or 2022.

Moktar Lamari, DEA, MA, PhD, is among the 100 most-quoted scientists in the world in the area of knowledge transfer and knowledge management. He is a full professor at the École nationale d'administration publique (School of Public Administration) at the Université du Québec. From 2010 to 2015 he served as head of the Centre de recherche et d'expertise en évaluation. His research has explored a range of topics, including the impact of web 2.0 and digital tools on knowledge transfer and knowledge absorptive capacity. Dr. Lamari has also won numerous awards, including the Louis Brownlow Award in 2003 for the best article published by *Public Administration Review;* the Elsevier Award in 2002 for the best article published by the international journal *Technological Forecasting and Social Change;* and the 2014 award for Outstanding World Research Leader, delivered by the International Multidisciplinary Research and the University of the Philippines Open University.

Marylène Leduc obtained her BA in international studies from Bishop's University and her MA in public affairs from Laval University. Her research focuses on the evaluation of programs and on the rights of marginalized groups, including women, children, and Indigenous Peoples. She has varied work experiences, including with the United Nations in Cameroon, at the federal government, at the Centre de recherche et d'expertise en évaluation at the École nationale d'administration publique (School of Public Administration), in international cooperation organizations in Montreal, and in programs in Senegal that focus on women's empowerment. Her involvement in this research involving access to justice when she was a student contributed to several reflections for the beginning of her career.

M. Jerry McHale, QC, held the Lam Chair in Law and Public Policy at the University of Victoria till 2017, teaching in the areas of public policy, legislation, dispute resolution, and access to justice. From 2001 to 2011, he served as an assistant deputy minister with the BC Ministry of Attorney General, where he was responsible for civil, criminal, and family law policy and legislation, as well as for legal aid, family law programs, dispute resolution, and justice reform. From 1996 to 2001, he was the director of the ministry's Dispute Resolution Office, responsible for developing mediation programs and expanding the use of alternative dispute resolution processes in the courts and in government. From 1980 to 1991, he worked as a barrister, solicitor, and mediator in the private sector. He chaired the BC Family Justice Reform Working Group, which published *A New Justice System for Families and Children* in 2005, and the Family Working Group of the National Action Committee, which published *Meaningful Change for Family Justice: Beyond Wise Words* in 2013.

Lisa Moore is the director of research and operations at the Canadian Forum on Civil Justice. She obtained her BA in English literature and Spanish from Williams College, a graduate degree in business management with a concentration in marketing from McGill University, and a degree in French from McGill University. Lisa has worked in a number of Canadian and international non-profit positions, including with the United Nations at Global Action on Aging, and she currently serves as a board member for one of the largest international relief and development organizations in the world. She has authored numerous articles, reports, and other publications on access to justice.

Janet Mosher, BMusA (Western Ontario), LLB (Queen's), LLM (Toronto), is an associate professor at Osgoode Hall Law School at York University. She has served two terms as the academic director of Osgoode's Intensive Program in Poverty Law at Parkdale Community Legal Services and is currently the co-director of the Feminist Advocacy: Ending Violence Against Women clinical program. Her research and teaching interests are in the areas of gender-based violence and legal interventions, access to justice for marginalized populations, welfare policy, poverty law, homelessness, legal aid, and clinical legal education. She is a co-investigator on the Domestic Violence and Access to Justice Within and Across Multiple Legal Systems project (2016–22), funded by the Social Sciences and Humanities Research Council of Canada.

Pierre Noreau has been a professor at the Université de Montréal's Centre de recherche en droit public since 1998. A political scientist and jurist by training, he is particularly interested in the sociology of law. His empirical research focuses on the functioning and evolution of the judicial system, non-contentious conflict resolution, access to justice and political mobilization of the law, ethnocultural diversity from the perspectives of legal pluralism, and the study of institutionalization processes regulating social relationships. He is a jurist with a doctoral degree from the Institut d'études politiques in Paris. Pierre Noreau is the principal investigator of the Accès au droit et accès à la justice interdisciplinary research consortium (adaj.ca). He is currently the president of the Institut Québécois de réforme du droit et de la justice.

Mitchell Perlmutter, BA (Hons.) (York), JD (Osgoode Hall), is an immigration lawyer at Desloges Law Group PC. While in law school, he worked as a research assistant at the Canadian Forum on Civil Justice, where he spearheaded projects, published articles, and performed research aimed at promoting access to justice. Prior to attending Osgoode Hall Law School, he worked as a court reporter for the Attorney General of Ontario, where he rendered on-site reports for Ontario and Superior Court of Justice hearings. As an Osgoode Hall student, he showed a keen interest in promoting access to justice through his extracurricular activities, including working as a Dean's Scribe and participating in the Parkdale Legal Services program.

Catherine Piché, LLB (Dalhousie), LLL (Ottawa), LLM (New York University), DCL (McGill), is a professor of law at the University of Montreal. She specializes in civil proof and procedure, complex litigation, comparative law, and private international law. Her thesis at McGill University focused on fairness in class action settlements and was published by Carswell in 2011. Prior to joining the faculty at the University of Montreal, Professor Piché was a law clerk for the Appeal Division of the Federal Court of Appeal of Canada. She is a member of the Quebec Bar (Barreau du Québec), the New York Bar, and the Massachusetts Bar, and practised commercial litigation for national law firms in New York City and Montreal for more than six years. She is particularly interested in class actions and complex litigation cases, and has written numerous articles on both procedural law and civil proof and procedure.

Noel Semple, JD (Toronto), LLM (York), PhD (York), is associate professor of law at the University of Windsor. He teaches and writes in the fields of civil dispute resolution, legal ethics and professionalism, and family law. His doctoral focus was the custody and access arrangements made for children following the breakdown of their parents' relationships, and his dissertation critically analyzed the litigation and settlement mechanisms used to resolve these disputes, and their costs and benefits for the children involved. His work has appeared in the *International Journal of the Legal Profession, Osgoode Hall Law Journal, Canadian Journal of Women and the Law,* and *Family Court Review,* among others. Professor Semple was editor-in-chief of the *Windsor Yearbook of Access to Justice* between 2017 and 2019. He has taught Legal Process at the University of Toronto Faculty of Law, and Children and the Law at the University of Western Ontario Faculty of Law.

The Honourable Justice **Lorne Sossin**, BA (McGill), MA (Exeter), PhD (Toronto), LLB (York), LLM, JSD (Columbia), is a judge of the Ontario Superior Court of Justice. Prior to this, he was a professor of law and the dean of Osgoode Hall Law School at York University, former associate dean of the University of Toronto, and the inaugural director of the Centre for the Legal Profession. He was also a faculty member at Osgoode Hall Law School and the Department of Political Science at York University. His former teaching interests spanned administrative and constitutional law, the regulation of professions, civil litigation, public policy, and the judicial process. Justice Sossin was a law clerk to former Chief Justice of Canada Antonio Lamer, a former associate in law at Columbia Law School, and a former litigation lawyer with the firm of Borden & Elliot.

Michael Trebilcock, LLB (Canterbury), LLM (Adelaide), is a professor of law at the University of Toronto. He specializes in law and economics, international trade law, competition law, economic and social regulation, and contract law and theory. He was a fellow in law and economics at the University of Chicago Law School, a visiting professor of law at Yale Law School, a global law professor at New York University Law School, and a visiting professor at Harvard Law School. In 1987, he was elected a fellow of the Royal Society of Canada. Professor Trebilcock has received honorary doctorates in law from McGill University and the Law Society of Ontario and was awarded the Canada Council Molson Prize in the Humanities and Social Sciences. He has published on many subjects and won awards for his work, including the Donner Prize in 2014 for his book, *Dealing with Losers: The Political Economy of Policy Transitions.*

Wanda Wiegers, LLB (Saskatchewan), BA (Saskatchewan), LLM (Toronto), is a professor at the University of Saskatchewan College of Law. She practised law in a number of different settings, including private practice, legal aid, and the Saskatchewan Human Rights Commission, before obtaining her Master of Law degree and joining the College of Law as a faculty member. Her research and teaching interests are in the areas of economic analysis of law, feminist and critical legal theory, family law, children and the law, domestic violence, autonomous motherhood, women and the welfare state, child welfare reform, economic inequality, and poverty law. She is a co-investigator on the Domestic Violence and Access to Justice Within and Across Multiple Legal Systems project (2016–22), funded by the Social Sciences and Humanities Research Council of Canada.

David Wiseman, BEc (Monash), LLB Hons. (Monash), LLM (Toronto), SJD (Toronto), is an associate professor at the University of Ottawa Faculty of Law – Common Law Section. He is joint coordinator of the JD program's Social Justice Option and coordinator of Access to Justice Initiatives. He is the academic supervisor for the Access to Justice Lab experiential learning course. His principal areas of research and activity are access to justice, social and economic human rights, and the institutional competence of courts in Charter litigation. Professor Wiseman has published a number of articles on access to justice issues in the regulation of the legal profession and is currently undertaking research, in collaboration with Julie Mathews (executive director of Community Legal Education Ontario), on advancing access to justice by supporting and enabling non-legal community workers to provide community justice help.

Index

Trebilcock, Michael: about, 25; consumer welfare, 309; legal services costs and gap, xiii–xiv; "light-touch" regulation, 313, 321n90; research overview, 15
Trudeau, Prime Minister Justin, 137–38
Truth and Reconciliation Commission (TRC): Calls to Action, 137–38, 139, 142n24; creation of, 131; survivor revictimization, 134–35, 144n70. See also residential school survivors' claims
Tyler, Tom, 9

Ukraine rule of law, 27
United Kingdom: access to justice, 4, 6, 277–83; "after-the-event" (ATE) insurance, 269, 277–79, 283n3; alternative business structures (ABSs), 33, 78–79, 82; before-the-event (BTE) insurance, 275, 282; civil justice legislation, 277–80; conditional-fee arrangements (CFA), 277–79, 281–83, 285n36; fee shifting, 268–69, 283n3; judges per capita, 49; judicial independence perceptions, 64–65(f); justice system efficiency, 59(f); lawyers and uplift fee, 277–78, 279, 281–82; legal aid, 101, 277, 284n26; legal fee regulations, 271; legal needs, 5; litigation costs review, 279; loser-pay system, 280, 285n40; percentage-fee lawyers, 281; personal injury law firms, 281–82; proceedings length, 54(f)–55(f), 56; public access to laws and legal data, 51–52(f); "qualified one-way cost shifting" (QOCS), 269, 280, 285n37; recoverable costs, 279–82, 285nn37–39, 285n41, 286n50; third-party litigation funding companies, 269
United Nations (UN), 4
United Nations Human Development Report 2015, 59
United States: access to justice gaps, 4, 6; class action retainers, 322n100; contingency fee regulations, 271; fee caps, 310; fee shifting system, 274–75; "great society," 253, 264n26; judicial appointments, 30; law firms survey, 252, 264n22; law schools, 31; lawyer incentives, 276; legal aid funding, 101; legal culture change resistance, 259; legal fees review, 271–

72; legal needs study, 5, 94; legal services providers, 34; litigation funding companies, 269; mandatory family law information, 194; medical-legal partnerships (MLPs), 80; "multi-district litigation" (MDL), 273; no-win, no-pay lawyers, 278–79; paralegal services analysis, 174, 189n5; percentage-fee lawyers, 284n27; personal injury claims, 306; social innovation programs, 232; "vanishing trial," 29
United States Supreme Court, 7
University Health Network financing platform, 79
University of Montreal (Class Action Compensation Project), 205–22, 223n2
University of Victoria, 138
University of Windsor, 237
US Comprehensive Legal Needs study, 94

victims: barriers to justice, 159–60, 160–64; "blame-the-victim," 133; domestic violence, 153–54, 159–64, 168n45, 169n48; residential school survivors, 133–35, 144n70; terminology, 164n1
vulnerable populations: community lawyering, 187; empowerment, 233; legal problems likelihood, 228, 242n9, 242n11; psychological impact, 289; self-represented, 117. See also residential school survivors' claims

Wade, John, 301n82
Wagner, Chief Justice Richard (SCC), 138, 139
Wiegers, Wanda, 15
Wilde, Oscar (quips), 25, 37
Winkler, Warren K., 266n54
Winkler Institute for Dispute Resolution programs, 235–36
Wiseman, David, 15–16, 76
women: access to justice barriers and domestic violence, 150–51, 159–63, 166nn16–17; immigrant domestic violence victims, 153–54, 160–63, 168n45, 169n48; Indigenous, 137; parolees employment program, 239; violence as coercive control, 164n1
Woolley, Alice, 296n5